The
GARDEN TO
KITCHEN EXPERT

Judith Wills & Dr. D. G. Hessayon

Published by Expert Books
a division of Transworld Publishers

Copyright © Judith Wills & Dr. D. G. Hessayon 2011

TRANSWORLD PUBLISHERS
61–63 Uxbridge Road
London W5 5SA
a division of the Random House Group Ltd

Contents

MIX
Pulp from responsible sources
FSC
www.fsc.org
FSC® C023561

The Random House Group Ltd supports the Forest Stewardship Council (FSC), the leading international forest-certification organization. All our titles that are printed on Greenpeace-approved FSC-certified paper carry the FSC logo. Our paper procurement policy can be found at www.rbooks.co.uk/environment

Printed and bound by Butler Tanner and Dennis Ltd, Frome & London

ISBN 978 0 903505 92 5

CHAPTER 1

GETTING STARTED

This book is written for the kitchen gardener – the person who likes to grow their own vegetables, herbs and fruit. After a downturn in home-grown food in the decades after World War II, recent years have seen a renewed surge of interest in growing for the kitchen. Sales of vegetable seeds now account for nearly two-thirds of all seed sales and flower borders are being dug up to accommodate vegetables in even the smallest garden. Figures from the Allotments Regeneration Initiative show that there is an average waiting list of 59 people for every one of the 330,000 allotments in the UK, with more than a third waiting over a year for a plot.

There are three Expert books to show you how to start growing your own produce – where and what to grow, how to look after your plants and how to deal with pests and diseases: *The Vegetable & Herb Expert*, *The Fruit Expert* and *The Greenhouse Expert*. This book is a companion to all three. Kitchen gardening is not just about growing the produce but about making best use of it – dealing with inevitable gluts with imagination, and storing leftovers so that you have food throughout the year. And, of course, providing the freshest and tastiest food for yourself and your family – food everyone really wants to eat.

USING THIS BOOK

The Garden to Kitchen Expert sets out in two main chapters (Vegetables and Fruit) how to prepare, cook and serve the food that you grow in the garden. Each chapter lists plants alphabetically. Information on the preparation of each vegetable or fruit is grouped according to the table below:

NO COOKING REQUIRED: The vegetable or fruit is eaten raw, either in its natural state or blanched (page 248) etc.
   It is served on its own or as a basic part of the dish with other ingredients. These ingredients may require cooking as instructed.

BASIC COOKING: The vegetable or fruit is cooked.
   It is prepared on its own or as a basic part of the dish with one or more of these ingredients:

oil	flour	garlic
butter	sugar	vinegar
milk	seasoning	lemon juice
eggs	spices/herbs	stock

RECIPE: The vegetable or fruit is cooked.
   It is used as a basic part of the dish in which there are one or more ingredients not listed above.

NOT JUST VEGETABLES AND FRUIT

It is not only vegetables and fruit that have a place in our kitchens. Herb seeds and plants are selling faster than ever before and the herb garden – or windowbox – helps provide flavour and interest in the kitchen. There are also uses for the leaves, flowers, seeds, roots etc. from some other plants in the garden – chapters on Ornamentals and Weeds show you how to make use of these non-food plants.

NOT JUST GARDEN PRODUCE

No gardeners grow all the produce described in this book. We all pick and choose according to space, time and other factors, so some produce needs to be bought from shops or markets. All the recipes are equally suitable for bought items, but try to buy the freshest you can – avoid produce showing any signs of wilting or discoloration. Make sure 'best before' dates fit in with when you plan to use the items.

NOT JUST RECIPES

In Chapter 2 there are general notes on some aspects of bringing in and using vegetables and fruit in the kitchen – choosing varieties, harvesting, storing and preserving. This is followed by chapters with detailed information on preparing each individual fruit or vegetable for the table. Chapter 8 provides information and recipes for making jams, pickles and preserves, and finally there is a Cook's Miscellany in Chapter 9. Here you will find notes on equipment, a glossary defining cooking terms used in this book and finally often-used basic 'toolbox' recipes.

ABBREVIATIONS

tsp = teaspoon
tbsp = tablespoon
g = gram
kg = kilogram
oz = ounce
lb = imperial pound

ml = millilitre
fl. oz = fluid ounce
cm = centimetre
in. = inch
C = centigrade

MEASUREMENTS

All measures are given as metric with imperial in brackets. Spoon measures are UK level spoons.

See page 243 for a full metric/imperial conversion chart and how to convert measures for US readers.

A NOTE ON OILS

For simplicity, most recipes specify all-purpose vegetable oil (which is usually a blend of several oils) or olive oil, but you can use other oils if you prefer.

Vegetable oil is highly refined, inexpensive and good for general use and for deep-frying and all high-temperature frying.

Olive oil is good when a strong taste is required – e.g. salad dressings, dips – and for Mediterranean-style dishes. Choose extra-virgin olive oil for dressings – buy light olive oil for cooking.

Groundnut (peanut) oil is excellent in Asian dishes such as curries and stir-fries. It has a high 'smoke point' which means you can cook with it at high temperatures, and is the traditional oil for such cuisine.

Rapeseed oil is a good substitute for vegetable oil or light olive oil, again with a high smoke point.

Speciality oils such as walnut oil or pumpkin seed oil are expensive and have a low smoke point. They are best used in small quantities in dishes that require no cooking.

BASICS

CHOOSING VARIETIES

Catalogues and seed racks offer a bewildering array of varieties. The choices we make can determine just how large the crop will be and also the success of the recipe. Useful guidelines are as follows:

CHOOSE FOR A LONG HARVESTING PERIOD

Try to choose varieties which will prolong the supply and avoid a glut. Catalogues list early, mid-season and late varieties of many plants and there is an ever-increasing number of varieties on sale with a prolonged harvesting period.

Where appropriate, it is best to sow 'little and often' to give continuous supplies. This is particularly important for types of vegetable or fruit that do not store or freeze well – for example, lettuce or strawberries.

CHOOSE FOR CULINARY VALUE

Sometimes the variety of fruit or vegetable you choose does not matter. However, in other cases the variety you sow or plant can make a substantial difference to the final taste, texture and overall success of the dish. With fruit there are wide differences in flavour. Vegetable varieties generally have a narrower range of flavours. In many cases the high-flavour types give less-than-average yields. Notable examples of how the variety can affect results are:

Onions Onions can be powerfully strong, sweet and/or mild and these characteristics will have a bearing on the flavour of a dish and on whether or not you can use the onions raw in a salad. Red onions are attractive and moderately hot, but their colour can spoil the appearance of a pale dish.

Potatoes Some types are better for mashing, others for roasting and others for serving plain boiled. New potatoes do not roast well but are ideal for steaming/boiling. Not all maincrops are good for boiling/mashing/roasting – most are either 'waxy' (best for boiling) or 'floury' (good for mashing and roasting).

Other roots Grow a selection of varieties that will give you roots for picking young (e.g. carrots, beets) and others that will stand in the ground well and then store well.

Squash and pumpkin There are dozens of different sizes and colours of flesh, and tastes from nutty through sweet to savoury. Check the notes for each variety carefully. Orange-fleshed pumpkins like Crown Prince are suitable for pumpkin pie as well as for roasting, soups and many savoury dishes, so are ideal all-rounders. Small summer squashes are good for baking whole or stuffing, but won't keep.

Tomatoes Small cherry tomatoes tend to be sweetest and are easy and convenient for using raw in salads, or stirred into pasta. Large and beefsteak tomatoes may have less flavour but can be baked whole or halved and stuffed. Plum tomatoes have thick fleshy walls and are ideal for de-seeding and cooking.

Apples Apples can range from distinctly tart to very sweet. The basic choice is between cooking and dessert apples. Generally cookers are used in recipes, dessert apples are best as a snack and for salads.

CHOOSE FOR KEEPING QUALITY

Varieties of some vegetables and fruit differ quite markedly in their storage life. Notable examples are:

Garlic 'Softneck' varieties store better than 'hardneck' types (which have a thinner skin and larger cloves).

Onions Varieties with thin necks tend to store better.

Pumpkins and squashes Those with thick skins store better than thin-skinned varieties.

Apples Cookers usually keep better than dessert apples.

Pears Hard pears such as Conference store better than the juicier, softer varieties.

HARVESTING

Harvesting at the right time is crucial for getting the best from your produce. A daily walk around the kitchen garden or allotment – certainly in summer months – is a necessity, as some items (especially asparagus, salad leaves, radishes, peas, soft fruits, sprouting broccoli and tomatoes) grow fast and can quickly spoil, go to flower, or over-ripen. Harvest with care.

It is all too easy to stab through your best roots with a fork when harvesting potatoes, for example. Use two hands when picking berries and currants, one to hold the cane, the other to pick the fruit. Use a small knife or simply twist the fruit when cutting courgettes. Damaging plants encourages disease and causes waste. Never harvest in haste – take your time.

VEGETABLES

Timing
Be guided by the harvesting notes in *The Vegetable & Herb Expert*. It is extremely important for you to choose the right time to take the crop from the garden and into the kitchen. Harvesting too early results in a reduced yield and may give you produce which cannot be used – see below. It is only natural to aim for the highest yield you can get, but waiting too late can be just as serious. Picking at the right time, therefore, is very important.

Picking early
Early harvesting gives you small vegetables which look attractive on the plate but flavour may be reduced. However, baby carrots, beets and leeks are noted for their sweetness.

Apart from yield loss there are other dangers to early picking. For example, immature corn cobs do not ripen and green rhubarb stalks do not redden.

Picking late
Picking vegetables after the recommended stage can result in all sorts of problems. Some may toughen or become stringy (e.g. runner beans, rhubarb). Vegetable fruits such as courgettes, pumpkins and squash lose flavour the larger they become, and can also become coarse-textured. Leafy vegetables may run to seed (e.g. broccoli) and some of the sugars will convert into starches which results in loss of sweetness (e.g. peas, broad beans).

FRUIT

Picking early
For many fruits and fruiting vegetables (e.g tomatoes, apples, plums, pears) it is better to pick slightly under-ripe rather than over-ripe, as produce will continue to ripen in the kitchen or on a windowsill. Remember that fruits growing on the upper, south side of a tree will ripen more quickly than those on the north side and lower branches.

Soft berries are also best picked just before full ripeness as they over-ripen and spoil quickly.

For preserving, especially jam-making, under-ripe fruit is preferable as pectin content diminishes with ripening and there may be little in over-ripe fruits.

Picking late
Once fully coloured, blackcurrants will stay on the cane for a week or two without spoiling. Pick a few from each little bunch and leave the others to grow on for a week or more – they will get much bigger and juicier. Red currants and white currants need picking as soon as they are ripe – pick with care, as they are very delicate. Gooseberries will happily stay on the bush for a week or two once ripe.

However, one word of caution – if you leave ripe fruits unprotected, they will soon be spotted and eaten by the birds!

When to pick
If possible it is best to harvest your fruits – especially soft fruits – on a dry, sunny day, as they will keep better. Don't harvest berries in the rain as it will be impossible to dry them without damaging them and the moisture will encourage early moulding in storage. For early-season produce, pick in the afternoon so that the sun has dried out any early-morning dew on the fruits.

For more detailed advice on harvesting see *The Fruit Expert* and *The Vegetable & Herb Expert*.

STORING

Not many decades ago vegetable and fruit growers had either to consume much of their fresh produce before it spoilt, or resort to bottling, drying or making preserves. While these preservation methods are effective and are still used today, most of us are lucky enough to have both a fridge and a freezer at our disposal, which makes almost any fruit or vegetable something you can keep and use throughout most or all of the year.

Some of the produce we grow can be stored for long periods in nothing more than a wooden box in a cool, dry place. If you have a glut you can't use, check with a neighbour to see if they have a glut of something you can exchange.

SHORT-TERM STORAGE

Fresh vegetables should ideally be stored in a plastic bag or well wrapped in cling film in the salad crisper of a fridge. Otherwise, store them in a cool larder or other cool, dark place, ideally kept at a temperature below 16°C. This is essential for lettuces and salad leaves, celery and radishes, all of which turn to mush if frozen – nor are they suitable for bottling, preserving or drying. Lettuces will last longer if you dig them up with taproot intact and either put the root into water or put the whole lettuce in a large plastic bag in the fridge.

All ripe fresh fruits for eating should be stored in a suitable bag or container in the fridge. They will rapidly lose moisture and vitamin C if left in a fruit bowl in the light and heat of a kitchen.

FREEZING

While many vegetables (particularly loose-leaf green vegetables like spinach, sprouting broccoli, asparagus, peas and beans), soft fruits (particularly strawberries) and tomatoes are best eaten or used fresh, most will also freeze – either raw or cooked in some way. Ensure produce is very fresh and not over-ripe. For larger items, make sure to prepare and cut, if necessary, into the size you are likely to need when defrosted.

Freezing methods:

Freeze as they are Washed, dried, peeled (if necessary), chopped (if necessary) raw vegetables can be frozen in bags or containers as they are, although they may deteriorate more quickly than blanched items. Suitable for peas, broad beans, French and runner beans, broccoli, cauliflower, small tight Brussels sprouts, chopped cabbage, carrots, kale, courgettes, parsnips, rhubarb, sweet corn kernels, sweet and chilli peppers.

Some herbs freeze well in bags, such as chopped curly parsley, bay leaves and sage.

Peeled, cored or stoned and sliced apples, pears, quinces, plums, peaches and apricots can be dipped into water with lemon juice to stop them turning brown, then drained and bagged to freeze. Currants can be de-stalked then put in containers and frozen, and raspberries without stalks can be frozen in the same way.

Blanch and freeze Blanching breaks down the enzymes that can hasten deterioration in the freezer, so it is worth doing if you have more produce than you can use within 2–3 months.

All vegetables for freezing can be blanched by boiling rapidly in unsalted water for 1–2 minutes (depending on size), then drained, cooled and bagged or boxed – either in single-portion or family-portion sizes. Blanching is not suitable for fruits.

USING FROZEN VEGETABLES

If a vegetable has lost some texture in the freezer and cannot be used whole, purée as a side dish or use in soups, sauces, casseroles and stews. When using blanched frozen items, reduce cooking time accordingly.

Open-freeze Place prepared (blanched or unblanched) produce individually on open trays, freeze, then bag or box. This prevents damage to individual items and makes it easier to remove the amount of produce you want without having to defrost more than you need. This method is suitable for raw berry fruits, particularly raspberries and other soft or delicate items, which tend to compress when frozen together (but see strawberries, below). Gooseberries can be topped, tailed and frozen, but they will lose texture so use in sauces, crumbles, pies and cooked recipes. Melon balls can be open-frozen to use in fruit salads and sorbets.

Prepare or cook and freeze Some produce won't freeze well raw but will freeze with some preparation or cooking. Tomatoes: turn these into a basic tomato sauce (page 156) and then freeze the sauce; or simply peel (page 154), chop, put into bags or containers and freeze – when defrosted they will be suitable for flavouring soups, stews, sauces etc. Spinach: cook as normal, then squeeze out excess moisture, bag and freeze. Strawberries: purée with icing sugar for a sauce, or make a coulis (page 220), then freeze in containers. Cooking apples: will freeze raw but also good to freeze as apple sauce (page 173), or part-cook in a pan with a little sugar and water then freeze – they can be used in a crumble.

LONG-TERM STORAGE

All maincrop root vegetables, onions, garlic, some members of the pumpkin family and some tree fruits are suitable for storing in autumn and winter months in cool (but frost-free), dark, dry conditions. Choose perfect specimens or they may spoil or rot and contaminate nearby produce. Ideally, items for long-store should be picked, dug up or cut after several days of dry weather. Clean most of the soil from them, then dry with towels or kitchen paper if necessary.

Layer roots in sand or dry soil in sturdy boxes so that they don't touch each other and are not exposed to light.

Store apples in sturdy boxes, individually wrapped in oiled paper or newspaper and not touching. Pears are best stored in slatted trays between layers of newspaper. Ensure they do not touch. Store quinces in trays in a cool, dark place and keep them well away from other produce as their aroma is very strong.

Pumpkins and squashes with thick skins will keep on a shelf in a cool room for several weeks or months.

Onions and garlic can be strung up by the neck and tied to a rafter or similar in a frost-free shed or cool larder, or can be stored in special onion sacks.

DRYING

Many vegetables and fruits can be successfully dried in a domestic oven or by other means and will store for up to several months in airtight containers. Check frequently – light and heat will cause deterioration and insufficient drying will cause spoilage.

Drying methods:

In the pod Peas and beans can be dried in the pod (on the growing plant) until black, then shelled.

Oven drying Podded peas and beans, quartered tomatoes, peppers, aubergines and sliced onions can be dried on a baking tray in a cool oven (120°C/gas mark ½) for 4–6 hours, turning once or twice during the process.

Brush apple, pear, peach and other firm fruit slices with lemon juice and dry the same way. They are ready when they look dried and hard but still have a little 'give' when pressed with your fingers. Cool thoroughly before packing.

Herbs such as parsley, oregano and dill can also be dried in the oven (2–3 hours).

Hanging Dry chilli peppers and woody herbs such as rosemary, thyme and sage branches by tying them into small bundles and stringing them up in a dry, warm place for several days – the time necessary depends on conditions. Store them in containers in a cool, dark place. Remove herb leaves from stalks before storage.

BOTTLING AND MAKING PRESERVES

A wide range of vegetables and fruit can be bottled, including carrots, peas, cherries, figs, peaches, pears, and plums – but they do lose some texture. Alternatively, many can be used to make jams, jellies, pickles and chutneys. For details on preserving, see Chapter 8.

Some herbs are best preserved in oil – see Chapter 4 for details.

COOKING

For most produce you will have a choice of several basic cooking methods. Each method has points to recommend it, either for general use or for just a particular type or group of vegetable or fruit.

RAW While most of us think only of fruits, salad leaves, radish and tomatoes as suitable for consumption without cooking, most vegetables can be eaten raw – notable exceptions being potatoes and pumpkin. For eating raw, produce should be very fresh. For larger vegetables, it should be thinly sliced or grated. Small tender items such as peas can be eaten whole.

BOILING The first method of choice for most people for cooking vegetables: boiling is easy, low-cost, fairly quick, and clean. However, boiling vegetables does need to be carefully timed to avoid over-cooking. Use the minimum amount of cooking water (although roots are best completely covered) – this can be kept afterwards for use in stocks or soups.

Hard fruits such as apples and pears can also be boiled or, better, simmered, until tender.

STEAMING Place vegetables in a steamer, metal colander or sieve over a pan of boiling water, cover and cook until tender. Steaming retains flavour better than boiling. While it is still possible to over-cook steamed vegetables, under-cooking is more common. Time carefully and test vegetables with a sharp knife before removing from the steam.

MICROWAVING Any vegetable or fruit that can be boiled or steamed can also be cooked – with 2 tbsp water – in a covered bowl in the microwave oven, adding salt or sugar to taste. Microwaving, like steaming, retains very good levels of nutrients.

FRYING Frying in oil adds calories but also adds flavour and variety. Choose from **deep-frying** (good for root-vegetable chips, battered vegetables and fruits) – an electric fryer makes this process safer; **shallow-frying/sautéing** in a frying pan (good for onions, mushrooms and peppers); or **stir-frying** in a wok or frying pan, using minimal oil (good for thin slices of carrot, onion, pepper and broccoli).

GRILLING Brush vegetables with oil as required and grill/griddle under or over medium-high or high heat, turning halfway through. Most vegetables will be ready within 5–10 minutes, depending mainly on their thickness and distance from the heat source. Suitable vegetables include peppers, tomatoes, courgettes, onions and asparagus. Root vegetables, legumes and leaves are generally not suitable for grilling.

Fruits suitable for grilling (brushed with oil or melted butter) include halved plums, peaches, apricots, figs and pears.

ROASTING Many vegetables are suitable for roasting in fat in the oven. Roast potatoes are familiar to us, but all roots can be roasted. Parsnips are particularly good and so are onions and shallots. Vegetables from the Mediterranean area such as aubergines, peppers, fennel, garlic, tomatoes; slices of pumpkin, squash, marrow and courgette; chunks of corn on the cob, and even asparagus, cauliflower and broccoli can all be roasted successfully.

Fruits that can be roasted (with oil or butter and perhaps sprinkled with a little sugar or honey) include prepared halved or quartered apples, pears, apricots, figs, peaches, plums.

BAKING Baking is oven-cooking without the fat used for roasting. Root vegetables can be baked whole – maincrop potatoes should be pricked or they may explode, but other roots, including beetroots and turnips, should be baked without pricking. Other vegetables suitable for baking whole are sweet peppers, aubergines, tomatoes, onions, summer squash and courgettes. Hollow vegetables such as peppers and tomatoes – or those that can be hollowed out – can be stuffed before baking.

Baking should be done in a hot to very hot oven, and can take 30–60 minutes, depending on the vegetable used.

BRAISING Braising is a cross between gentle sautéing and boiling or stewing. Suitable vegetables include cabbage, carrots, fennel, leeks, onions, chicory and peas. Prepare as necessary, then put in a heavy, lidded pan with fat and a little stock or water and flavourings of choice. Cover and cook on low heat until tender (up to 2 hours).

Fruits such as apples, pears, figs and plums can also be braised in a little water or juice with sugar or butter and flavourings.

STEWING/CASSEROLING Traditionally, a stew is cooked on the hob and a casserole is put in the oven.

Usually, onion, leek or celery is sautéed in a little fat before other vegetables, such as roots, tomatoes, peas and beans, together with liquid and flavourings, are added to the pan. The stew/casserole is cooked at low heat for 1–2 hours until everything is tender. This cooking method is useful for advance preparation and is a good way of tenderizing older vegetables.

CHAPTER 3

VEGETABLES

There are hundreds of vegetable varieties, and looking at what is available in catalogues and stores is enjoyable. But deciding what to grow can be a problem.

For people with a good-sized plot, tried and tested, long-time favourites such as runner beans, carrots, beetroot, new potatoes, onions and lettuce may be good starting points. Other vegetables, such as kohl rabi, salsify and chard, may be less popular in our gardens and plots but are wonderful additions to the kitchen and deserve to be more widely grown and used.

A good tip is to write a list of the vegetables you actually like to eat and use most often in your own kitchen, then check in *The Vegetable & Herb Expert* to find out which would be most suitable for your plot size and soil, skill levels and time available. Some varieties need more care (e.g. protection from frosts and pests, pinching out, regular watering), while others are easier. The area in which you live may also dictate what you choose – for example, sweet corn is not reliable in northern parts of the UK. And do try out something new every year – you just might love it!

TIPS FOR STORING VEGETABLES

Detailed information for each specific vegetable is given in the pages that follow.

- Store vegetables as far from fruits as possible.
- Don't store potatoes or carrots with apples: the gas these fruits release can cause potatoes to sprout and carrots to become bitter.
- Avoid keeping cabbage and turnips alongside celery, pears and apples, as cabbage and turnips will transfer their odours to this produce.
- Don't store potatoes with onions: when close together they produce gases that spoil both.
- Don't store potatoes in the fridge: they will become too sweet.
- Store cabbage, kale, swede and turnips in a frost-free shed rather than in the house, as they give off strong odours.

VEGETABLES IN SEASON

This chart shows the period during which each vegetable can be picked, from the start of the season for early varieties to the end of the season for later varieties.

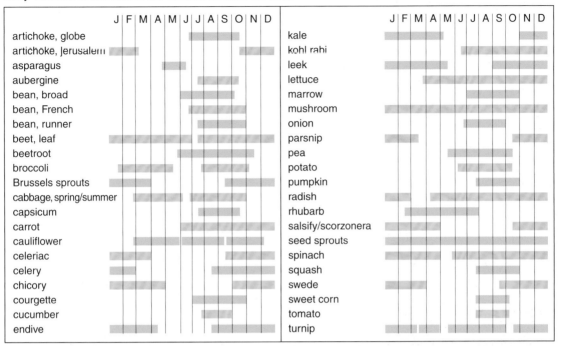

TIPS FOR PREPARING VEGETABLES

Cleaning vegetables

- Firm vegetables (roots, onions etc): brush off dry dirt and remove long roots. Scrub off stubborn dirt in cold water using a brush reserved for this purpose; if vegetables are to be peeled this is not necessary. Do not soak. Rinse under cold running water.

- Leaves and delicate vegetables: drop into salted water to kill insects and slugs.

- Cabbages and lettuces: remove roots and tough stalks.

- Vegetables that have had no contact with the earth or pesticides, or grow in a protective sheath, are unlikely to need cleaning.

To peel or not to peel?

The skin of almost all produce is edible, either raw or cooked. Remove peel if skin is old and tough or damaged, or simply unpleasant (e.g. onion, garlic, old beetroot, pumpkin).

For recipes in this book, assume onions and garlic should be peeled unless otherwise stated. Potatoes can be peeled or left unpeeled (but for mash, peeled is best). For tomatoes, the skin is left on unless otherwise stated.

Whole, cut, sliced or diced?

- The smaller a vegetable is cut, the quicker it will cook.

- Do not cut or chop vegetables until just before cooking.

- Do not leave prepared vegetables soaking in water.

TIPS FOR USING VEGETABLES

- The simplest way to use vegetables is to cook them as necessary then serve them as a side dish with meat, fish or poultry.

- If serving vegetables without meat as a meal in themselves (e.g. in a spinach lasagne, a root vegetable curry, a leek and potato soup), try to add a high-protein element – e.g. lentils, chick peas, broad beans or cheese.

- Try to serve vegetables from each group (roots, cooking leaves, vegetable fruits, peas, beans and salad leaves) regularly, rather than just from one group. This will ensure you provide variety and all the nutrients that vegetables contain.

- Most of us add salt to the water when boiling vegetables – a pinch tends to bring out the flavour, but it isn't necessary.

- Shorten cooking time (and preserve more vitamins) by putting vegetables into boiling water rather than cold.

ARTICHOKE, GLOBE

Globe artichokes are the edible immature flower heads of a tall, thistle-like perennial plant. They have been cultivated in the Mediterranean area and much loved by the Italians for centuries. In the UK the small range of varieties available to grow from seed includes the common Green Globe, which has an excellent flavour, and several purple types. The French Camus from Brittany has a large and tasty heart. Harvest from mid-June if you want to cook the baby heads whole. Bigger whole heads with firmly packed scales can be trimmed, then cooked and used in many ways – in salads, pasta dishes, casseroles, soups, dips or stuffed. Once the scales of the flower head begin to open and the purple flower starts to emerge, the artichoke will be tough.

The taste is smooth, delicately nutty and unique. It marries particularly well with lemon, and lemony sauces, egg and cheese, but can lift a wide range of dishes from the ordinary to the luxurious.

STORING

Globe artichokes are best harvested and eaten the same day, but will keep for a few days in a plastic bag in the fridge. If still on their stalks, put them in water, like flowers, in a cool place. Cooked whole artichokes can be brushed with lemon juice to prevent discolouration and kept in the fridge in a bag for a day.

NO COOKING REQUIRED

Very small whole baby artichokes no wider than 4 cm (1¾ in.) can be eaten raw dressed with olive oil or melted butter and lemon. They are a delicacy in Italy, but the vegetable is usually cooked.

BASIC COOKING

BOILED MATURE ARTICHOKES

Slice off the top third of scales with a breadknife, cut off the stem to make a flat base and pull off the tough outer leaves. Boil in water with 1–2 tsp lemon juice for 25–40 minutes until a pulled scale comes away easily. Drain upside down in a colander. Eat hot or cold, serve with melted butter, olive oil, mayonnaise or Hollandaise sauce.

To eat, pull each scale from the artichoke and suck the tender base of the leaf, discarding the remainder. Near the centre the scales will become small and purple-tipped – pull out these and the hairy choke (the unformed flower) and discard. The remaining disc-shaped base (the fond) is delicious and tender.

BOILED BABY ARTICHOKES

Boil whole baby artichoke heads in water with 1–2 tsp lemon juice for 15–20 minutes or until tender. Drain and serve whole with French dressing (page 250) or melted butter, lemon juice and black pepper. They can also be halved and shallow-fried in olive oil, grilled or used in a recipe.

BOILED ARTICHOKE HEARTS

Remove outer leaves from large artichokes until you reach paler green ones. Cut heart in half lengthwise and remove central hairy choke. Cut in half again and boil quarters in water with lemon juice for 15–20 minutes, or until tender when pierced with a knife. Drain.

GRILLED ARTICHOKE HEARTS

Brush boiled artichoke heart quarters with olive oil, season and grill under medium heat, turning regularly, until golden.

ROAST ARTICHOKE HEARTS

Brush boiled artichoke heart quarters with olive oil, season and roast at 180°C/gas mark 4 for 15–20 minutes until lightly golden, turning halfway through.

GLOBE ARTICHOKE RECIPES

ARTICHOKE SOUP

An extremely smooth soup with a delicate flavour –
one of the best summer soups.

Serves 3–4

6 artichokes	500 ml (17 fl. oz) chicken
1 large onion	or vegetable stock
75 g (3 oz) butter	salt, black pepper
4 tbsp dry white wine	3 tbsp double cream

- Prepare artichokes using method for boiled artichokes – only fonds are used. Thinly slice and drop into water with lemon juice.
- Sweat chopped onion in half the butter for 5 minutes, then drain artichoke pieces, pat dry on kitchen paper and add to pan for a further 5 minutes. Don't allow vegetables to colour.
- Add wine. Cook over medium heat for 2 minutes, add stock and seasoning. Simmer for 10 minutes.
- Tip pan contents into a blender and blend until smooth. Reheat gently, turn heat off and add remaining butter in small knobs, whisk in, then whisk in cream.

STUFFED ARTICHOKES

For an even more luxurious dish, top the stuffed artichokes with spoonfuls of Hollandaise sauce before serving.

Serves 2 as main course, 4 as starter

4 artichokes
400 g (14 oz) mushrooms
3 cloves garlic
4 tbsp olive oil
25 g (1 oz) butter
1 tbsp fresh thyme leaves
salt, black pepper
25 g (1 oz) grated Parmesan
50 g (2 oz) stale breadcrumbs
juice of ½ lemon

- Prepare artichokes using method for boiled artichokes.
- Open up the centres and remove the purple-tipped leaves, then the hairy choke, using a teaspoon.
- Stir-fry finely chopped mushrooms and garlic in butter and half the oil, with thyme and seasoning, over medium-high heat for 3 minutes. Stir in cheese and breadcrumbs. Remove from heat, cool slightly, then stuff artichoke centres with the mixture.
- Sit them in an oiled roasting tin, drizzle with remaining oil and bake at 180°C/gas mark 4 for 15 minutes. Drizzle with lemon juice and a little more oil to serve.

ARTICHOKE AND EGG SALAD

You can use any crisp salad leaves for this recipe if you don't have Little Gems to hand.

Serves 4

4 artichokes	4 slices lean back bacon
250 g (9 oz) waxy	2 Little Gem lettuces
potatoes	6 tbsp French dressing
3 eggs	(page 250)

- Prepare artichokes using method for grilled artichoke hearts. Boil potatoes and, if large, cut into chunks.
- Hard-boil, peel and quarter eggs. Grill or dry-fry bacon and crumble.
- Arrange quartered lettuces in a serving bowl and top with artichokes, potatoes, eggs and bacon. Drizzle dressing over the salad.

ARTICHOKE, LEMON AND PARMESAN PASTA

Artichokes are very widely used in Italy and make an interesting addition to pasta.

Serves 4

6 artichokes	2 tbsp chopped fresh
300 g (11 oz) spaghetti	basil + extra whole
juice of 1 lemon	leaves
25 g (1 oz) grated	4 tbsp olive oil
Parmesan	2 tbsp toasted pine nuts

- Prepare artichokes using method for grilled artichoke hearts. Cook spaghetti, drain and keep warm.
- Mix remaining ingredients in a large bowl. Toss with pasta and serve garnished with basil leaves.

ARTICHOKE, JERUSALEM

These knobbly tubers are sadly neglected in the kitchen but deserve a comeback, as they are tasty, versatile and make a welcome change from potatoes. They are the Marmite of the root vegetable world – people seem either to love or hate them. In fact they are not related to artichokes at all and neither do they come from Jerusalem! They are members of the sunflower family, said to originate from South America, and were brought to France in the 17th century.

Their flavour is nutty and sweet with a hint of water chestnut and truffles. They are good sautéed as well as roasted, mashed or thinly sliced and used in Chinese recipes and salads, and they make a connoisseur's velvety soup. They are also very good for you despite their reputation for causing flatulence!

STORING

Jerusalem artichokes don't store as long as most tubers, but they will keep in a plastic bag in the fridge for 2 weeks or more, or in a paper bag in a cool, dry, dark cupboard. To help prolong their life, it is best just to remove most dirt with kitchen paper or your hands, and leave washing until you are ready to use them.

NO COOKING REQUIRED

Very thinly sliced, peeled raw artichokes can be added to a salad with, for example, radishes and crisp lettuce or endive, or they can be grated into a coleslaw.

BASIC COOKING

Jerusalem artichokes are almost always peeled – use a small vegetable knife with a pointed end, or a standard vegetable peeler to make the job easier. If you have sown the Fuseau variety – which is smoother, larger and less knobbly than the standard – you will have an easier time preparing them. Once peeled (and sliced if required), put the tubers in a bowl of water with 1–2 tsp lemon juice to prevent browning. For roasting or sautéing, you can, if you prefer, thoroughly scrub newly dug artichokes with a firm brush under running water until much of the skin is removed.

BOILED JERUSALEM ARTICHOKES

Cook in lightly salted boiling water with 1 tsp vinegar for 15 minutes, or until tender when pierced with a knife. Be careful not to over-cook.

MASHED JERUSALEM ARTICHOKES

Boil, then add a 10 g (¼ oz) knob of butter for every 100 g (3½ oz) artichokes. Season and mash thoroughly.

ROAST JERUSALEM ARTICHOKES

Dry artichokes and keep smaller ones whole; halve larger ones crosswise. Toss in olive oil, season well and roast on a baking tray at 190°C/gas mark 5 for 40 minutes, or until golden and tender.

SAUTÉED JERUSALEM ARTICHOKES

Parboil artichokes until almost tender – approx. 10 minutes – then cut crosswise into 0.5 cm (¼ in.) slices and dry thoroughly on kitchen paper. Sauté in a thin layer of vegetable oil over medium-high heat, turning once or twice, until cooked through and golden: approx. 8 minutes.

ARTICHOKE PATTIES

Mash artichokes as above and, when cool enough to handle, form them into small patties. Dust with flour and sauté.

JERUSALEM ARTICHOKE RECIPES

CREAM OF JERUSALEM ARTICHOKE SOUP

Add crispy plain or garlic croutons before serving.

Serves 4

900 g (2 lb) Jerusalem artichokes	1.2 litres (2 pints) chicken stock
1–2 tsp lemon juice	salt, black pepper
100 g (3½ oz) butter	100 ml (3½ fl. oz) double cream
2 onions	2 tbsp fresh chopped parsley
1 stalk celery	
2 cloves garlic	

- Peel and slice artichokes, dropping them into water with lemon juice.
- Melt most of the butter in a large saucepan and fry chopped onions, celery and garlic over low heat for approx. 8 minutes to soften but not colour.
- Add drained artichokes and stock. Simmer for 20 minutes, or until artichokes are completely tender. Remove from the heat, cool for a few minutes, then blend in a blender.
- Return to the pan, reheat gently and whisk in seasoning, cream, parsley and remaining butter. Reheat gently before serving.

WARM SCALLOP, BACON AND JERUSALEM ARTICHOKE SALAD

A great combination for a starter or a light lunch.

Serves 4

4 large Jerusalem artichokes	1 tsp butter
juice of 1 lemon	16 shelled fresh scallops
3 tbsp olive oil	2 tbsp fresh chopped parsley
4 slices lean back bacon	black pepper

- Peel and trim each artichoke into a neat oblong. Cut off either end to form a barrel shape. Parboil in water with 1–2 tsp lemon juice until almost tender – approx. 10 minutes – then cut each crosswise into 4 thick slices. Sauté in a non-stick pan in half the oil over medium-high heat, turning once or twice, for approx. 8 minutes, or until golden. Turn out on to kitchen paper and keep warm.
- Cut bacon into thin strips and add to pan. Cook until crisp, then remove. Add a dash of the oil and the butter to the pan, heat to sizzling, then cook scallops over high heat for 1½ minutes each side – more or less, depending on thickness.
- Arrange artichoke slices on serving plates, top each with a scallop, then scatter parsley and crumbled bacon over and season. Drizzle on remaining olive oil and lemon juice.

CHICKEN AND JERUSALEM ARTICHOKE PASTIES

The artichokes lend a wonderful richness to the thick sauce in these pasties. If you prefer, you can make traditional envelope-style pasty shapes to encase the filling. You can also use all-butter puff pastry.

Serves 4

1 onion	4 tbsp small tender peas (fresh or frozen)
2 garlic cloves	200 ml (7 fl. oz) white sauce (page 251)
25 g (1 oz) butter	
400 g (14 oz) Jerusalem artichokes	salt, black pepper
2 skinless chicken breast fillets	500 g (1¼ lb) shortcrust pastry (page 251)
1 tsp flour	1 egg
100 ml (3½ fl. oz) chicken stock	

- Sweat finely chopped onion and garlic in butter over medium heat for 8 minutes to soften but not colour.
- Cut artichokes and chicken into 1 cm (½ in.) cubes and add to pan with flour. Stir for a minute. Add stock and peas, then simmer for 10 minutes, uncovered, until there are just 2 tbsp or so of sauce in the pan. Leave to cool for a few minutes.
- Stir in white sauce until thoroughly combined. Season and set aside to cool.
- Preheat the oven to 200°C/gas mark 6 and roll out the pastry into a 30 cm x 30 cm (12 in. x 12 in.) square on a dry, floured surface. Using a sharp knife, trim edges to neaten and cut into 4 squares.
- Put quarter of the filling on to each square (do not overfill) and brush edges with beaten egg. Bring each corner up to the centre and press all edges firmly together. Brush outside of pasties with more egg and place on a baking tray. Bake for 15–20 minutes, or until pasties are golden. Allow to cool slightly before serving.

ASPARAGUS

Asparagus has a short but prolific season, from late April to the middle of June in the UK. The thick male spears make a wonderful starter or lunch served with melted butter, Hollandaise sauce or French dressing for dipping, or can be used as a side dish. While they are best eaten when the shoots are no more than 15 cm (6 in.) long, older shoots – even those where the tightly budded tips have become looser – can be harvested, chopped and used to make soups or to flavour casseroles or sauces. You can also use the thin 'sprue' asparagus – which will always appear in the asparagus bed in varying amounts – for similar purposes.

STORING

Fresh asparagus is best used on the day you cut it, but it will keep in a plastic bag in the fridge for a day or two. You can also freeze firm spears – blanched for a minute first – but the texture will deteriorate so these are best used in recipes such as soups or tarts.

NO COOKING REQUIRED

Young tender spears of asparagus can be eaten raw. Thinly slice them into a salad, or use them as crudités with a mayonnaise dip or a lemon and olive oil mix.

BASIC COOKING

Rinse the spears in cold water then trim the stalks to make them an even length. If the ends of the stalks are tough and 'woody', peel them with a sharp knife or simply break them off – the stalk should break at the point of woodiness. Asparagus can be steamed, grilled or roasted. It is ready to serve when the stalks can be pierced easily with a sharp knife.

STEAMED ASPARAGUS

Traditionally, asparagus is cooked in a tall, narrow asparagus steamer, but spears can also be set upright in a saucepan with a little water in the base so that the lower stalks boil while the more delicate tips steam. It helps to tie the spears into a bundle with string. Spears will take 3–7 minutes to cook, depending on the thickness of their stalks. Drain and pat dry on kitchen paper.

Asparagus goes very well with eggs, bacon, fresh and smoked salmon, shellfish and tangy cheese. Its strong flavour means it is also complemented by cream and butter.

Don't waste the water the asparagus has steamed in – it contains vitamins and minerals, and adds flavour to stocks, stews, sauces and soups.

GRILLED ASPARAGUS

Blanch any thick spears for 2 minutes, drain and pat dry. Coat all spears with olive oil, season and lay on a grill pan, griddle or barbecue tray. Grill under or over high heat for 2 minutes each side.

ROAST ASPARAGUS

Prepare spears as for grilling, then arrange in one layer on a baking tray. Cook at 200°C/gas mark 6 for 10–12 minutes, turning once.

ASPARAGUS RECIPES

ASPARAGUS TART

You could serve this tart as a starter before a light main course, or eat and enjoy it for lunch.

Serves 4

500 g (1¼ lb) shortcrust pastry (page 251)   **1 tbsp vegetable oil**   **50 g (2 oz) grated Parmesan**
400 g (14 oz) asparagus   **4 eggs**   **75 g (3 oz) grated Gruyère**
1 onion   **250 ml (8 fl. oz) double cream**   **salt, black pepper**

- Line a 24 cm (9½ in.) round, non-stick tart tin with the pastry and bake blind at 200°C/gas mark 6 for 15 minutes.
- Steam asparagus until just tender; dry thoroughly. Sweat chopped onion in oil over low heat for 8 minutes to soften but not colour.
- Combine remaining ingredients in a bowl, reserving a quarter of the Parmesan.
- Scatter cooked onion over base of tart, pour on the filling and lay the spears evenly on top. Sprinkle remaining cheese over. Bake for 25 minutes, or until filling is just set. Leave to cool for a few minutes before serving.

ASPARAGUS, POACHED EGG AND PARMESAN

Try this sprinkled with a pinch of Hungarian paprika for a tasty twist.

Serves 4

800 g (1¾ lb) asparagus
4 eggs
4 tbsp French dressing (page 250)
65 g (2½ oz) Parmesan in a piece

- Steam asparagus and drain well. Poach eggs until whites are thoroughly cooked but yolks are still runny.
- Divide spears between warm serving plates and top each with an egg. Drizzle the dressing over and shave large slivers of Parmesan over the top.

PASTA PRIMAVERA

Primavera is the Italian word for 'springtime' and this classic, fresh-tasting pasta dish zings with flavours from the spring vegetable garden. Traditionally this is made with whole baby vegetables but you can use whatever you have.

Serves 4

75 g (3 oz) soft butter
1½ tbsp each fresh chopped parsley, mint and chives
200 g (7 oz) carrots
200 g (7 oz) courgettes
400 g (14 oz) tagliatelle
250 g (9 oz) small asparagus spears
250 g (9 oz) peas
3 tbsp olive oil
1 lemon
salt, black pepper

- Beat butter with herbs and set aside. Chop carrots and courgettes into 2.5 cm (1 in.) chunks.
- Cook pasta in a large pan of salted water.
- Bring another pan of water to the boil, add carrots and cook for 2 minutes, then add asparagus and courgettes and cook for a further 2 minutes. Add peas and cook for a further 2–3 minutes or until everything is tender but still with a bit of bite.
- Drain pasta and vegetables well. Toss the pasta in its pan with the oil, half the herb butter and the lemon juice and grated zest. Toss vegetables with remaining herb butter and seasoning.
- Serve the pasta topped with the vegetables.

ASPARAGUS SOUP

There are many recipes for asparagus soup, some including garlic, bacon and other ingredients, but this classic version is hard to beat. It can also be served cold.

Serves 4

750 g (1 lb 10 oz) asparagus
1 onion
40 g (1½ oz) butter
1 tbsp flour
1 litre (1¾ pints) chicken stock
100 ml (3 ½ fl. oz) double cream
salt, black pepper

- Cut asparagus into 2.5 cm (1 in.) pieces.
- Sweat finely chopped onion in the butter in a large, lidded pan over low heat for 8 minutes to soften but not colour. Stir in asparagus, put the lid on and sweat for 15 minutes, stirring once or twice.
- Sprinkle on flour and stir for a minute. Pour in stock, 50 ml (2 fl. oz) at a time. Bring to a simmer and cook, covered, for 20 minutes.
- Allow to cool a little, then blend in a blender. Return to pan, add cream and seasoning, stir well and reheat gently.

ASPARAGUS AND CRAB LINGUINE

If you want to cook something really easy but truly impressive and tasty for guests, then this should be one of your first choices. Asparagus and crab taste wonderful together.

Serves 4

300 g (11 oz) linguine   **5 tbsp olive oil**
400 g (14 oz) asparagus   **200 g (7 oz) crab meat**
1 red chilli   **salt, black pepper**
3 cloves garlic   **2 tbsp fresh chopped**
8 spring onions   **parsley**
12 cherry tomatoes

- Cook pasta in a large pan of salted water. Blanch asparagus, drain and dry.
- De-seed and chop the chilli, chop garlic and spring onions and halve tomatoes. Heat 2 tbsp of the oil in a large frying pan and stir-fry asparagus for 2 minutes over medium-high heat, stirring now and then.
- Add garlic, onions and chilli to the pan, stir for a further 2 minutes, then stir in the crab meat, tomatoes and seasoning for 30 seconds to warm through. Remove from heat.
- Serve pasta topped with the crab and vegetable mixture, garnished with parsley.

ASPARAGUS RISOTTO

Making a risotto isn't quick – but it is relaxing. Allow about 45 minutes to make this dish and invite friends to chat with you in the kitchen while you stir.

Serves 4

500 g (1¼ lb) asparagus
1 onion
75 g (3 oz) butter
300 g (11 oz) risotto rice
1 glass dry white wine
750 ml (1¼ pints) hot vegetable stock
65 g (2½ oz) grated Parmesan
black pepper

- Steam asparagus and drain, reserving 100 ml (3½ fl. oz) liquid. Cut into 3 cm (1½ in.) pieces.
- Sweat finely chopped onion in 50 g (2 oz) of the butter over low heat for 8 minutes to soften but not colour.
- Add rice and stir for 2 minutes. Add wine and stir again until bubbling.
- Add asparagus cooking liquid to the stock. Stir a large ladle (about 75 ml/2½ fl. oz) of the stock into the risotto and continue stirring until stock has been absorbed by rice. Repeat until all stock is used up or rice is cooked through and creamy.
- Add remaining butter, asparagus, half the cheese and the seasoning. Stir and serve in warm bowls, sprinkled with remaining cheese.

ASPARAGUS FRITTATA

The cold frittata – an Italian omelette – makes a great picnic or lunchbox addition. Cut into squares, it can also be a perfect canapé.

Serves 3–6

450 g (1 lb) asparagus	**2 tbsp fresh chopped**
6 large eggs	**chives**
50 g (2 oz) grated	**1 tbsp olive oil**
Parmesan	**1 tbsp butter**
salt, black pepper	

- Steam asparagus, drain and dry thoroughly. Cut into 2.5 cm (1 in.) pieces.
- Beat eggs with most of the cheese, the seasoning and chives, then stir in the asparagus.
- Preheat the grill. Heat oil and butter in a 25 cm (10 in.) frying pan. Pour in the mixture and cook over medium heat for 3 minutes. Turn heat to low and cook for a further 5 minutes until underside is golden. Put pan under grill for 1–2 minutes to cook and brown the top. Sprinkle remaining cheese on top, cut into wedges and serve warm or cold.

ASPARAGUS WITH PARMA HAM AND MOZZARELLA

If you feel like making something both easy and elegant, this really fits the bill and is good for a light lunch or starter. Use buffalo Mozzarella if you can – it is more tender and succulent than the kind made from cow's milk.

Serves 4

16 asparagus spears
125 g (4 oz) ball buffalo Mozzarella
12 slices Parma ham
4 tbsp olive oil
1 tbsp white wine vinegar
8 tomatoes

- Blanch asparagus, refresh under cold water and dry thoroughly.
- Cut Mozzarella into 8 pieces. Put 2 pieces on top of 2 asparagus spears, then place 2 more spears on top of that. Tightly wrap 3 Parma ham slices round the stuffed asparagus, leaving green tips showing. Repeat to make 4 parcels.
- Heat 1 tbsp of the oil in a pan. Fry the parcels over medium-high heat for 5 minutes, carefully turning once with a fish slice, until the ham is crisp and golden and the Mozzarella melted.
- Combine remaining oil, vinegar, chopped tomatoes and 1tbsp of their juice. Serve each parcel with dressing drizzled over.

AUBERGINE (Eggplant)

For us the aubergine is an occasional vegetable which we are most likely to find in Mediterranean dishes such as moussaka, or in ratatouille – the vegetable stew of Provence. In many of the warm countries of the world, however, it is an important vegetable.

Aubergines are available in a range of colours and sizes, from round to narrowly oval and from white to near black. In this country you are only likely to find seeds of the dark purple, truncheon-shaped ones that are suitable for greenhouse rather than outdoor cultivation. To us they are aubergines – in the United States they call them eggplants.

The aubergine's taste is bland, but the flesh readily absorbs oil and also the flavour of any other ingredients that are present. Because of the oil-absorbing problem many cooks prefer roasting and char-grilling aubergine to frying, and its flavour take-up makes it a good ingredient for casseroles, kebabs and stir-fries.

STORING

Handle with care. Aubergines can be kept in the refrigerator for up to 2 weeks. For long-term storage they can be frozen, although the texture will deteriorate. Chop and blanch for 1 minute, bag and freeze. Use for stews and casseroles.

NO COOKING REQUIRED

Raw aubergine is not part of our national diet – there are much better vegetables for the crudités bowl. Despite our rejection, it is used in some Mediterranean dishes. For an aubergine salad, slice 1 large aubergine thinly and blanch in boiling salted water for about 5 minutes. Combine 2 tsp lemon juice or vinegar with 1 tbsp olive oil and 100 ml (3½ fl. oz) Greek yogurt. Season, then mix dressing with the aubergine.

BASIC COOKING

Wipe the skin, top and tail, and either slice, halve or cut into cubes – there is no need to remove the skin, although some cooks prefer to do so. There are several basic methods of preparation – in each case the dish is ready to serve when you can push a fork through the flesh without any pressure.

SAUTÉED AUBERGINES

One of the simplest cooking methods. Lightly coat aubergine slices with flour and fry in olive oil for 2–3 minutes until golden brown.

ROAST AUBERGINES

Cut the aubergines in half and score the flesh with a sharp knife. Place in a roasting tin with the cut surfaces uppermost and drizzle oil over. Bake for 30 minutes at 200°C/gas mark 6.

AUBERGINE FRITTERS

Dip flour-coated slices into seasoned beaten egg. Fry for approx. 5 minutes on each side or until golden brown.

In early times aubergines were thought to cause insanity. Hence their Italian name – melanzana ('mad apple').

AUBERGINE RECIPES

IMAM BAYILDI (The Priest Fainted)

The imam fainted with delight when he first tasted this extremely popular Middle Eastern dish, or so the story goes.

Serves 4

2 aubergines	6 cloves garlic	fresh chopped parsley
6 tbsp olive oil	4 tomatoes	100 ml (3½ fl. oz) water
2 onions	salt, black pepper	

- Strip lengths of skin from aubergines, cut them in half lengthwise and fry in oil. Place in an ovenproof dish, sliced sides up.

- Fry chopped onions and garlic over medium-low heat to soften and tinge gold. Add peeled, chopped tomatoes, season and fry for a further 5 minutes. Mix in parsley and remove from heat.

- Split centre of aubergine halves and stuff with the mixture. Add water, cover and bake for 1 hour at 180°C/gas mark 4. Allow to cool and serve cold.

MELANZANE PARMIGIANA

A simple version of a great Italian favourite.

Serves 3

1 large aubergine	**3 tbsp grated Parmesan**
4 tbsp olive oil	**225 g (8 oz) sliced**
200 ml (7 fl. oz) passata	**Mozzarella**
(page 153)	

- Peel aubergine and cut into thin slices. Fry in oil until golden brown and drain well on kitchen paper. Place a layer of aubergines in an ovenproof dish, cover with passata, sprinkle with Parmesan and cover with a layer of Mozzarella slices.
- Repeat until all the aubergine is used, ending with Mozzarella.
- Bake for 15 minutes at 200°C/gas mark 6.

RATATOUILLE

This easy vegetable stew is a tasty accompaniment to roast lamb, beef or chicken – or top with poached eggs for supper.

Serves 4–6

2 aubergines	**6 tbsp olive oil**
2 courgettes	**4 tomatoes**
2 red onions	**salt, black pepper**
2 red or yellow peppers	**2 tbsp fresh basil**
3 cloves garlic	**leaves**

- Cut aubergines and courgettes into slices about 1 cm (1/2 in.) thick.
- Heat 3 tbsp oil in a large, lidded saucepan. Sweat sliced onions and roughly chopped peppers over low heat for 5 minutes to soften but not colour. Add aubergine and courgette to pan with remaining oil and chopped garlic. Stir-fry for 5 minutes.
- Peel tomatoes, chop and stir into pan. Add 50 ml (2 fl. oz) water and season well. Turn heat down low, cover and simmer for 30 minutes, stirring 2–3 times.
- Stir in basil leaves before serving.

Salting, like peeling, is an optional extra. The age-old practice of sprinkling aubergines with salt for about 15 minutes and then washing before use is no longer essential, as modern varieties are not bitter. However, some chefs do recommend salting before frying aubergines.

BABA GANOUSH (Poor Man's Caviar)

This smoky aubergine purée, widely eaten in eastern Mediterranean countries, is good with flatbread or as a side dish with lamb chops. Tahini (sesame-seed paste) is a classic Baba Ganoush ingredient, but omit for a milder flavour.

Serves 4–6

2 large aubergines
2 cloves garlic
2 tbsp light tahini
2 tbsp thick natural yogurt
juice of 1 lemon
1/2 tsp ground cumin
salt, black pepper

- Roast aubergines, leave to cool, then halve and scoop out flesh.
- Crush garlic and add to aubergine flesh with the rest of the ingredients. Blend until smooth.

Aubergine goes especially well with lemon, tomatoes, lamb, mint, cumin, chicken and natural yogurt.

STUFFED AUBERGINES

Aubergine halves are ideal for stuffing – meat and rice is a typical combination.

Serves 4

2 large aubergines
1 onion
3 large tomatoes
2 tbsp olive oil
200 g (7 oz) lean minced beef
200 g (7 oz) cooked long-grain rice
1 tbsp fresh chopped mixed herbs
salt, black pepper

- Halve aubergines lengthwise. Scoop out most of the flesh, leaving about 1 cm (1/2 in.) intact.
- Finely chop the scooped-out aubergine flesh, onion and tomatoes. Fry in oil over medium heat for 5 minutes.
- Add mince to pan and stir to brown, then mix in rice, herbs and seasoning.
- Put aubergine shells in an oiled baking dish, pile stuffing mixture into each shell, sprinkle 125 ml (4 fl. oz) water round the bases, cover with foil and bake at 180°C/gas mark 4 for 30 minutes.

MOUSSAKA

Rich and comforting, lamb moussaka is one of Greece's most famous dishes.

Serves 4

1 large onion	1 tbsp tomato purée
2 cloves garlic	½ lamb stock cube in
4 tbsp olive oil	75 ml (2½ fl. oz)
500 g (1¼ lb) minced lamb	hot water
	2 large aubergines
4 tomatoes	salt, black pepper
1 tsp ground cinnamon	400 ml (14 fl. oz) white sauce (page 251)
1 tbsp fresh or 1 tsp dried oregano	3 tbsp grated Parmesan
	2 eggs

- Fry finely chopped onion and crushed garlic in half the oil over medium-low heat for 10 minutes to soften and tinge gold. Push onion to one side and add mince. Cook for a few minutes to brown. Add peeled, chopped tomatoes, cinnamon, oregano, tomato purée and stock, stir and simmer for 20 minutes.
- Cut aubergines lengthwise into 0.5 cm (¼ in.) slices. Brush both sides with remaining oil. Season and bake on a rack in a roasting tin at 190°C/gas mark 5 for 20 minutes. Set aside but leave heat on.
- Make white sauce and stir in cheese. Cool for a few minutes, then beat in eggs and season to taste. As an alternative you can make a quick topping by beating together 400 ml (14 fl. oz) Greek yogurt, 1 egg and 3 tbsp grated Parmesan.
- Place half the aubergine slices in a large, flat, ovenproof dish and cover with meat mixture. Top with remaining aubergine and pour on white sauce. Bake for 30 minutes – the surface should be brown and bubbling.

GRILLED AUBERGINE TOASTS

Delicious as a light lunch or starter.

Serves 4

2 aubergines
5 tbsp olive oil + extra for brushing
juice of ½ lemon
1 tbsp fresh chopped mint leaves
salt, black pepper
4 thick slices crusty bread

- Cut aubergines lengthwise into 0.5 cm (¼ in.) slices. Brush each slice on both sides with a little olive oil. Arrange on grill pan in a single layer and cook under high heat until slices start to brown – approx. 3 minutes. Turn and repeat.
- Combine olive oil, lemon juice, mint and seasoning to make a dressing. Arrange aubergines in a shallow dish, pour dressing over and leave for 30 minutes to marinate.
- Toast bread and top each slice with a quarter of the aubergine mixture.

AUBERGINE CURRY (Brinjal Bhaji)

Aubergines may have Indian origins – they take up the flavours and aromas of spices very well.

Serves 4 as a side dish, 2 as a main course with rice or naan bread

1 onion	1 tbsp medium curry paste
4 tbsp vegetable oil	juice of ¼ lemon
2 aubergines	4 tbsp thick natural yogurt
4 tomatoes	2 tbsp fresh coriander leaves
2 cloves garlic	

- Fry chopped onion in 1 tbsp of the oil over medium-low heat to soften and tinge gold. Remove to a warm plate.
- Cut aubergines into bite-sized chunks and fry in 2 batches, adding 1 tbsp oil with each batch, until golden and soft. Remove to a warm plate.
- Peel tomatoes and quarter them, chop garlic and fry with curry paste in remaining oil for 1 minute. Return onions and aubergine to pan with lemon juice and 2 tbsp water. Cook for 5 minutes.
- To serve, drizzle yogurt over and top with coriander leaves.

Meaty fried aubergine chunks make a great alternative to beef or chicken in a Thai-style curry with coconut milk.

BEAN, BROAD

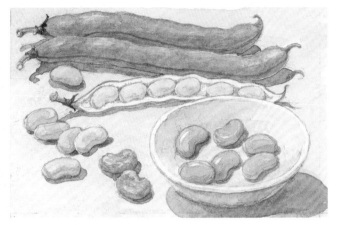

Broad beans are a member of the pea family and have been an important part of Mediterranean cuisine for at least 4,000 years. Fresh broad beans have a fairly short summer season, but choosing early and later types and sowing in autumn can prolong the picking time. The beans have a distinctive flavour, with young ones being smooth and sweet and older ones more floury and nutty.

Young, thin pods can be eaten whole, but larger pods need to be shelled before cooking the beans. Old beans may need to have their skins slipped off.

STORING

Picked whole pods can be stored in a fridge or cool place for a day or two if necessary, though they are best podded and the beans eaten as soon as possible. Don't pod the beans until needed as they will turn brown. Beans freeze well – blanch them for a minute, drain and put into bags, allow to cool, then freeze.

Broad beans can also be dried for use in winter. Either leave them on the plants in their pods until the pods are black, by which time the seeds inside should be dry, or harvest the whole mature pods and hang them in a dry place. Store in an airtight container.

NO COOKING REQUIRED

Tender young beans can be podded and their skins slipped off, then eaten raw in a salad. In Italy raw beans are often eaten at the end of a meal with shavings of Pecorino cheese.

BASIC COOKING

BOILED/STEAMED BROAD BEANS

Small tender pods – boil or steam whole without salt for 7 minutes. Drain, season and serve.

Larger pods – break open the pods with your fingers, remove the beans and boil or steam for 3–5 minutes, depending on size. Drain, season and serve.

Old beans – boil or steam. Peel away the skin around each bean and eat the tender, bright green beans.

BOILED DRIED BROAD BEANS

Soak in cold water overnight; drain. Boil in unsalted water for 75 minutes or until tender; drain.

BROAD BEAN MASH

After podding, boil or steam the beans. Remove skins, then mash beans with butter or olive oil and seasoning.

BROAD BEANS IN PARSLEY SAUCE

Boil or steam 450 g (1 lb) broad beans and stir into 400 ml (14 fl. oz) white sauce (page 251). Add 5 tbsp fresh chopped parsley and cook, stirring, over medium heat. Serve with gammon, carrots and new potatoes.

Broad beans were not always cultivated as a vegetable – they are closely related to a plant grown as a cattle food!

BROAD BEAN RECIPES

BROAD BEAN RISOTTO

You can serve this with grilled or baked chicken breast – or even add chopped cooked chicken to the risotto with the beans.

Serves 4

300 g (11 oz) broad beans	300 g (11 oz) risotto rice	juice of ½ lemon
1 onion	750 ml (1¼ pints) hot vegetable stock	50 g (2 oz) grated Parmesan
4 tbsp olive oil	2 tbsp fresh chopped parsley	
3 cloves garlic	1 tbsp fresh chopped mint	

- Boil or steam beans.
- Sweat finely chopped onion in the oil in a large pan over low heat for 5 minutes to soften but not colour, adding chopped garlic for the last minute.
- Stir in rice until coated with oil. Stir a large ladle (about 75 ml/ 2½ fl. oz) of the hot stock into the risotto and continue stirring until stock has been absorbed by rice. Repeat until all stock is used up or rice is cooked through and creamy.
- Stir in beans, parsley, mint, lemon juice and half the cheese. Serve sprinkled with remaining cheese.

BROAD BEANS, PEAS AND MINT

Serendipity – broad beans and peas are often ready for picking at the same time and they go extremely well together as a side dish. This is very good with gammon steaks or chicken.

Serves 4

300 g (11 oz) broad beans
150 g (5 oz) fresh peas
40 g (1½ oz) butter
4 tbsp fresh chopped mint
salt, black pepper

- Boil or steam beans and peas.
- Melt butter with mint and stir over low heat for 1 minute. Pour over vegetables and season.

BROAD BEAN AND HAM SALAD

A delightful, easily assembled salad. Any type of air-dried ham will do, but Serrano – a salt-cured ham from Spain – is intensely flavoured and really complements the sweet broad beans.

Serves 4

500 g (1¼ lb) broad beans
100 g (3½ oz) Serrano ham
4 tbsp olive oil
1 tbsp sherry vinegar
1 tsp Dijon mustard
2 tbsp fresh chopped mint

- Boil or steam beans and slip from their skins.
- Tear ham into bite-sized pieces and arrange on serving plates with beans scattered over.
- Combine oil, vinegar, mustard and mint. Drizzle over plates to serve.

GREEK BROAD BEAN DIP

A delicious way to use up a glut of fresh broad beans and it can be frozen in lidded containers. Serve with fingers of pitta.

Serves 4

500 g (1¼ lb) broad beans
4 cloves garlic
100 ml (3½ fl. oz) Greek yogurt
juice of 1 lemon
salt, black pepper

- Boil or steam beans, then skin and mash.
- Crush garlic and combine all ingredients in a bowl. Chill to serve.

In Egypt, the eastern Mediterranean and North Africa, broad beans are known as fava beans and are used fresh, or often dried, in stews and soups, or to make salads, spreads and purées.

BROAD BEAN AND FETA SALAD

A great starter for vegetarians, or a light lunch for all. You can use soft goat's cheese or buffalo Mozzarella instead of the feta if you have that to hand instead.

Serves 4

500 g (1¼ lb) broad beans
10 spring onions
5 tbsp olive oil
juice of ½ lemon
salt, black pepper
200 g (7 oz) feta cheese
25 g (1 oz) rocket leaves
4 slices crusty bread

- Boil or steam beans; drain. Chop spring onions and gently stir into the beans.
- Combine olive oil, lemon juice and seasoning and stir into beans while still warm.
- Before serving, stir in the crumbled cheese and sprinkle rocket over. Heat bread in the oven.

BROAD BEANS WITH EGG AND ANCHOVIES

If you have a can of anchovies in the cupboard, before you say 'No' – give this a go. It really works.

Serves 4

400 g (14 oz) cooked broad beans
2 hard-boiled eggs
45 g (1½ oz) can anchovies
2 tbsp fresh chopped chives
3 tbsp olive oil
juice of 1 lemon
salt, black pepper

- Put cold beans in a serving bowl. Chop eggs and scatter over beans.
- Drain and chop anchovies and add to bowl with the chives.
- Drizzle olive oil and lemon juice over and season.

SAUTÉED BROAD BEANS, POTATOES AND BACON

This is a wonderful combination of flavours. The dish can be a lunch or a supper – or for something even heartier, serve it as a side dish for roast chicken. If you have no summer savory, use parsley instead.

Serves 4

6 slices lean back bacon
4 tbsp olive oil
400 g (14 oz) cooked potatoes
400 g (14 oz) cooked broad beans
juice of 1 lemon
4 tbsp fresh chopped summer savory
4 tbsp fresh chopped mint
salt, black pepper

- Cut bacon into strips and fry in a large pan in 1 tbsp of the oil until golden; remove with a slotted spoon.
- Roughly chop potatoes, add another tbsp oil to the pan and fry for 4 minutes, turning once or twice, until lightly crisped and golden.
- Add remaining oil, beans, lemon juice, herbs, seasoning and bacon to the pan and stir gently for a minute to heat beans through. Serve hot or cold.

BROAD BEAN AND BROWN RICE SALAD

Broad beans and almonds go very well together and the nutty-flavoured brown basmati rice enhances their flavour.

Serves 4

200 g (7 oz) brown basmati rice
300 g (11 oz) cooked broad beans
40 g (1½ oz) flaked toasted almonds
12 cherry tomatoes
5 tbsp olive oil
1 tbsp balsamic vinegar
salt, black pepper
2 tbsp fresh chopped mint

- Cook rice, allow to cool a little, then stir in beans, almonds and halved tomatoes.
- Combine oil, vinegar, seasoning and half the mint. Pour over the salad and stir.
- Serve with the remaining mint sprinkled over.

Summer savory is a traditional partner for broad beans.

FAVA FALAFEL

Falafel patties are normally made with chick peas but they are lovely made with dried broad beans too. These can make part of a buffet and are good cold. Or serve them stuffed into pittas with salad.

Serves 4–6

450 g (1 lb) dried broad beans
1 onion
3 cloves garlic
5 tbsp fresh chopped parsley
2 tbsp fresh chopped coriander leaves
1 tsp sweet paprika
salt, black pepper
flour for dusting
3 tbsp vegetable oil
lemon wedges

- Soak beans overnight. Drain and remove skins. Put in a blender and blend for a few seconds.
- Finely chop onion and garlic and add to the blender with the herbs and seasoning. Blend to a thick, fairly dry paste. Add 1 tbsp water if necessary to help the paste form.
- Remove mixture from blender and form 16 round patties. Dust in flour.
- Heat oil in pan and fry patties over medium heat, turning a few times, until golden on both sides. Drain on kitchen paper. Serve with lemon wedges.

BEAN, FRENCH

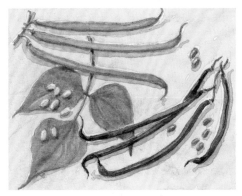

Also known as fine beans, dwarf beans or green beans (*haricots verts*), French beans in fact come in a range of colours, including purple, yellow and cream. They have traditionally been regarded as more of a delicacy than runner beans, as they were rare and expensive until the 20th century. French beans, like runner beans, were first cultivated for their seeds and it wasn't until the 1700s that the whole pods were eaten.

The beans can be harvested throughout summer when young and tender – if a bean snaps easily it is fresh. Late-season beans which aren't picked young can be podded and the seeds treated as **flageolets** (fresh green beans cooked like peas), or the pods can be left on the plant to dry and produce **haricot beans**.

STORING

Store in a plastic bag in the fridge for up to a week. French beans are ideal for freezing – trim, blanch, bag and freeze soon after picking.

Beans for drying (haricot beans) should be left on the plant in the ground until they have turned straw coloured, then picked and hung indoors to dry. When the shells start to split, remove the beans, lay them on paper in a warm place to dry out completely, then store in an airtight container.

VARIETIES

FLAT POD

The beans are fairly flat and wide and can easily become stringy if not picked early. The Prince and Hunter are two of the best varieties.

PENCIL POD

Round, stringless pods, including the 'fine' bean types. Tendergreen is one of the best.

COLOURED VARIETIES

Yellow and cream beans hold their colour when cooked. Try the flavoursome Kinghorn Wax.

NO COOKING REQUIRED

Very young and tender beans can be eaten raw, but in the UK French beans are usually cooked to serve. The young podded flageolets can also be eaten raw as you would eat small fresh peas.

BASIC COOKING

There should be no need to string French beans. Top and tail, and leave whole or cut into pieces as required.

BOILED/STEAMED FRENCH BEANS

Steam or boil in lightly salted water for 4–7 minutes, depending on thickness.

BOILED HARICOT BEANS

Soak for 6 hours, drain, add to fresh water and boil for 45 minutes or until tender.

STIR-FRIED FRENCH BEANS

Halve the beans and stir-fry in vegetable oil over high heat for 3 minutes until lightly golden and tender but still with a little bite. Season.

FRENCH BEAN MASH

Drop the flageolets into boiling water and simmer for 2–3 minutes until tender. Mash with olive oil or butter as desired.

FRENCH BEAN RECIPES

FRENCH BEANS AND ALMONDS

Almonds and French beans are a perfect match. Try serving with roast chicken.

Serves 4

400 g (14 oz) French beans   **juice of ½ lemon**
2 tbsp olive oil   **salt, black pepper**
75 g (3 oz) flaked almonds

- Boil beans until just tender; drain thoroughly.
- Heat oil in a pan, add almonds and stir-fry over medium heat for 1–2 minutes until golden (take care not to burn). Add beans, lemon juice and seasoning and stir to coat. Serve.

ITALIAN THREE BEAN SALAD

You could use this as a starter, part of a buffet or as a light lunch with some crusty bread.

Serves 4

4 rashers smoked   **300 g (11 oz) cooked**
  back bacon   **French beans**
4 tbsp natural yogurt   **200 g (7 oz) cooked**
3 tbsp olive oil   **red kidney beans**
2 tbsp sherry vinegar   **200 g (7 oz) cooked**
2 tsp Dijon mustard   **broad beans**
salt, black pepper

- Grill bacon until golden and crisp, then crumble.
- Combine yogurt, oil, vinegar, mustard and seasoning. Mix in beans. Top with bacon to serve.

CHINESE STIR-FRIED FRENCH BEANS

You can add thin slices of chicken, turkey or pork fillet to this dish with the onion to turn it into a complete meal. Noodles make a good accompaniment.

Serves 4

2 tbsp vegetable oil   **2 tbsp soy sauce**
8 spring onions   **50 g (2 oz) raw**
400 g (14 oz) French beans   **cashew nuts**
3 cloves garlic   **black pepper**
1 red chilli

- Heat oil in a large frying pan and stir-fry chopped spring onions over medium-low heat for 1 minute to soften and tinge gold. Add halved beans and continue to stir for 2 more minutes. Add chopped garlic and chilli and stir for another minute.
- Add soy sauce, nuts and pepper and stir for a further minute.

SALADE NIÇOISE

You can either add small chunks of cooked, cooled new potatoes to this delicious French salad, or serve it with hunks of bread.

Serves 4

4 fresh tuna steaks
1 Cos lettuce
4 tomatoes
6 large spring onions
150 g (5 oz) cooked French beans
1 clove garlic
4 tbsp French dressing (see page 250)
45 g (1½ oz) can anchovies
12 stoned black olives
4 hard-boiled eggs

- Dry-fry or grill the tuna on high heat for 1½ minutes each side.
- Prepare lettuce then remove outer leaves individually and arrange in a salad bowl. Cut hearts into quarters and add to bowl. Quarter tomatoes, halve spring onions lengthwise and arrange over lettuce with the beans. Cut tuna steaks into 4 pieces each and add to bowl.
- Combine the well-crushed garlic with the dressing and pour over salad. Decorate with drained anchovies, halved olives and quartered eggs.

In the USA, French beans are called string beans, though they should be stringless if picked early.

BEAN, RUNNER

Runner beans are more popular in Great Britain than anywhere else in the world – allotments and vegetable gardens would not be the same without the vibrant red (or sometimes pink or white) flowers of these relatively easy-to-grow plants. While most of the runner beans we grow are cooked simply and served as a side vegetable (ideal with any Sunday roast), they can be cooked in other ways and added to curries, casseroles and minestrone-type soups.

Dozens of varieties are available – choose one to suit your own kitchen and storing needs. Stringless beans save time in preparation, and varieties that freeze well may also be important: in a good year there will be a glut around late August.

STORING

Store in a plastic bag in the fridge for up to a week. To freeze, trim young pods and either slice or cut into chunks, blanch, bag and freeze.

Beans for drying should be left on the plant in the ground until pods have turned straw coloured, then picked and hung indoors to dry. When the shells start to split, remove the beans, lay them on paper in a warm place to dry out completely, then store in an airtight container.

VARIETIES

STRINGLESS

Polestar is one of the best stringless varieties, with a long harvesting season and high yield.

NON-STRINGLESS

Scarlet Emperor is often grown as it is a reliable cropper and has a reasonable flavour. Sunset is an early variety and freezes well.

NO COOKING REQUIRED

Runner beans are best served cooked. The dried beans must be cooked because they contain toxins which are destroyed by fast boiling.

BASIC COOKING

Cut off tops and tails and pull off stringy edges. Cut into thin slices or diagonal chunks. Chunks take longer to cook but are less likely to break up when stir-frying. Discard beans that don't slice easily: they will be tough.

BOILED/STEAMED RUNNER BEANS

Boil or steam in lightly salted water for 4–7 minutes, depending on age and tenderness.

BOILED PODDED RUNNER BEANS

Drop the podded beans into boiling water and simmer for 3–4 minutes until tender.

STIR-FRIED RUNNER BEANS

Cut beans into 1 cm (½ in.) diagonal slices. Stir-fry in vegetable oil over high heat for 3–4 minutes until tinged gold and tender but still with a little bite. Season.

BOILED DRIED RUNNER BEANS

Soak overnight, drain, add fresh water, fast-boil for 10 minutes, then boil for 1 hour or until tender.

RUNNER BEAN RECIPES

BRAISED RUNNER BEANS

Great with roast chicken or lamb chops or even with a meaty fish like swordfish or monkfish.

Serves 4

1 onion	500 g (1¼ lb) runner beans
3 tbsp olive oil	4 large tomatoes
1 clove garlic	salt, black pepper

- Sweat thinly sliced onion in half the oil over low heat to soften but not colour, adding chopped garlic for the last minute.
- Cut beans into thick slices and stir-fry in remaining oil for 3 minutes. Add peeled tomatoes with a little water. Season, stir, bring to a simmer and cook for 15–20 minutes or until beans are tender.

Runner beans are perfect companions for roast beef, almonds and spices.

SUMMER VEGETABLE SOUP

You can vary what you use in this soup, substituting similar amounts and types of vegetable. It is supposed to be more like a broth than a thick soup. Red pesto is not essential but adds depth.

Serves 4

1 large onion
2 tbsp olive oil
2 carrots
2 stalks celery
150 g (5 oz) runner beans
1 courgette
1 litre (1¾ pints) vegetable stock
100 g (3½ oz) pasta shapes
100 g (3½ oz) flageolet beans, fresh or
 canned
salt, black pepper
2 tbsp red pesto (page 58)

- Sweat chopped onion in the oil over low heat for 5 minutes to soften but not colour. Add chopped carrots and celery and stir for a minute, then add chopped beans and courgette with the stock, pasta and flageolets.
- Bring to a simmer and put the lid on. Cook for 20 minutes, or until all the vegetables are tender. Add seasoning. Serve, spooning a little pesto into each bowl and stirring lightly.

SPICED RUNNER BEANS

Try this with pan-fried tuna steaks or chicken breasts.

Serves 4

400 g (14 oz) runner beans	½ tsp cayenne pepper
5 spring onions	1 tsp ground cumin
3 tbsp vegetable oil	1 tsp ground coriander
2 cloves garlic	juice of ½ lemon
salt, black pepper	

- Cut beans into thick chunks, slice spring onions diagonally and stir-fry in the oil over high heat for 2 minutes. Add chopped garlic, seasoning and spices, turn heat down to medium and stir for a further 3 minutes. Add lemon juice, stir for a minute and serve.

RUNNER BEAN AND SWEET POTATO CURRY

If you are making an Indian meal for friends, try this as a vegetable side dish. It also makes a light supper with some naan bread.

Serves 4

1 tbsp vegetable oil	1 tsp each ground coriander,
2 hot red chillies	turmeric and garam masala
4 cloves garlic	1 sweet potato
2.5 cm (1 in.) piece	300 g (11 oz) runner beans
fresh ginger	200 ml (7 fl. oz) coconut milk
½ tsp fennel seeds	

- Heat oil over medium heat and add the chopped chillies, garlic and ginger, the fennel seeds and ground spices. Stir-fry for a minute to soften and release the aromas.
- Add diced sweet potato and runner beans, stir and cook for a minute, then add the coconut milk. Stir, put lid on, turn down heat to low and cook for 15 minutes.
- Remove lid and cook for a further 10 minutes. Check vegetables are tender before serving.

BEET, LEAF

Leaf beet (sometimes inaccurately called 'perpetual spinach') and its relative Swiss chard are both easier to grow and hardier than spinach but are just as useful in the kitchen and equally delicious. Even better, you can harvest crops most of the year round.

Leaf beet looks and tastes like spinach, but it is stronger and the leaves are coarser and less inclined to disappear when cooked. The standard Swiss chard has bright green leaves with thick white veins and an edible white, fleshy stalk. Ruby chard has deep green leaves and thin red stalks, while other chard varieties have green leaves and thick stalks which can be red, orange, yellow or white. The various types are often mixed and sold as 'rainbow chard' – a prized talking point at the dinner table. You can also use the young leaves of standard beetroot as a vegetable.

All the leaf beets can be easily prepared and used as side vegetables or in a wide variety of dishes, including soups, stir-fries, curries, tarts and pies, and baby leaves can be used in salads. Leaf beet is also a good spinach substitute in vegetable lasagne.

STORING

Harvested leaves are best eaten within 24 hours of picking, preferably earlier. The 'perpetual spinach' in particular won't keep for long but if you must, put it in the crisper of the fridge in a large plastic bag with airholes in it. Chards and beet tops will last a little longer. Don't wash leaves before storing them.

Leaf beets can be frozen to use when you don't need a good texture. Cook, drain, cool, then bag to freeze.

NO COOKING REQUIRED

All the baby beet leaves can be eaten raw, as part of a salad or simply dressed on their own. Chard stalks can also be sliced and eaten raw, perhaps as crudités.

BASIC COOKING

Like spinach, leaf beet leaves will shrink when you steam them, so allow one large saucepan full for 4 small–medium portions.

BOILED LEAF BEET

Wash the leaves in cold water. Discard any over-large leaf beet stems; remove chard stems and stir-fry separately (see right). Leave small leaves whole, chop large leaves. Add to a large saucepan with the water that clings to the leaves plus 1 tbsp extra. Cook over high heat, stirring with a long-handled spoon until the leaves have softened and reduced considerably in bulk. Drain off any excess liquid and season to serve. You can also add a knob of butter and some nutmeg.

PURÉED LEAF BEET

Stir-steam the leaves, then drain thoroughly and squeeze dry. Add to a blender with 10 g (¼ oz) butter and a pinch of ground nutmeg per 100 g (3½ oz) leaf beet. Blend to a purée and taste for seasoning.

> Swiss chard doesn't come from Switzerland – it is native to the Mediterranean area, but is now grown worldwide. However, the 19th-century botanist who named it was Swiss.

STIR-FRIED LEAF BEET

Leaves: use small leaves or slice larger ones. Wipe to clean if necessary. Heat sesame oil in a wok or large pan and stir-fry over high heat for 1–2 minutes. Add sesame seeds or chopped garlic for extra flavour.

Stalks: stalks of chard can be used as a vegetable in their own right. Remove from the leaves then slice and stir-fry over high heat for 2–3 minutes until golden and lightly crisped.

LEAF BEET RECIPES

BUTTER-BRAISED SWISS CHARD

This is quite rich, so serve with a simple grilled or baked meat or fish.

Serves 4

2 kg (4½ lb) Swiss chard	75 g (3 oz) grated Parmesan
75 g (3 oz) butter	salt, black pepper

- Stir-steam the chard. Drain well and return to pan. Add butter, half the cheese and the black pepper and stir for a minute over low heat. Add remaining cheese, check seasoning and serve.

RAINBOW CHARD GRATIN

A good supper dish served with a salad of butterhead lettuce and some baked tomatoes on the vine.

Serves 4

800 g (1¾ lb) rainbow chard stalks
knob butter
400 ml (14 fl. oz) white sauce (page 251)
50 ml (2 fl. oz) milk
75 g (3 oz) Cheddar
40 g (1½ oz) stale breadcrumbs

- Stir-fry whole chard stalks in butter over medium heat for 3 minutes or until just soft. Arrange in the base of a shallow ovenproof dish.
- Thin the white sauce with milk, stir in thoroughly and pour over the chard.
- Top with grated cheese mixed with breadcrumbs. Bake at 200°C/gas mark 6 for 20–25 minutes, or until top is golden and bubbling.

RUBY CHARD WITH CHICK PEAS AND GARLIC

This gutsy side dish makes a great partner to roast lamb or can be topped with poached eggs for supper.

Serves 4

6 shallots	150 ml (¼ pint) vegetable stock
8 cloves garlic	
2 tbsp olive oil	400 g (14 oz) can cooked chick peas
1 kg (2¼ lb) ruby chard	salt, black pepper

- Stir-fry finely chopped shallots and garlic in the oil in a large frying pan over medium heat for 3 minutes to soften and tinge gold.
- Chop larger ruby chard leaves and stalks. Add half to the pan, stirring until volume is reduced – approx. 2 minutes. Add remaining chard and stir again.
- Pour stock over, add drained chick peas and simmer for 5 minutes.
- Drain thoroughly. Drizzle a little olive oil over, season and serve.

LEAF BEET AND RICOTTA LASAGNE

Serve with garlic bread and salad.

Serves 4

8 lasagne sheets*
1 kg (2¼ lb) leaf beet
½ tsp ground nutmeg
500 g (1¼ lb) Ricotta
salt, black pepper
400 ml (14 fl. oz) tomato sauce (page 156)
400 ml (14 fl. oz) white sauce (page 251)
75 g (3 oz) grated Parmesan

* **Note** Don't use the 'no pre-cooking' type, as this recipe does not contain enough liquid.

- Preheat oven to 190°C/gas mark 5. Boil lasagne sheets until cooked, then drain all but 1 tbsp water from the sheets.
- Stir-steam the leaf beet, drain very well, season and add nutmeg. Stir in the Ricotta and keep warm. Heat the tomato and white sauces.
- Layer up the lasagne in a square, greased, ovenproof dish as follows: a layer of pasta, half the tomato sauce, all the beet/Ricotta filling, the rest of the tomato sauce, the rest of the pasta, all the white sauce. Sprinkle over the cheese to finish. Bake for 20 minutes.

BEETROOT

Soft, sweet purple slices doused in vinegar and added to a cold meat or cheese salad is for many people the classic image of how to use this root vegetable. But beetroot lends itself well to a variety of cooking methods and recipes and combines easily with many flavours. It is not always purple, either – red, gold and even striped varieties are available as seed.

STORING

In season from late summer to late autumn, beets will keep for months in a cool, dry, frost-free room or shed. Washed, dried and trimmed, kept in bags with airholes, they will store in the larder or fridge for weeks.

Cooked beetroot keeps in the fridge in a lidded container for a few days. Beetroot loses texture if frozen but can be pickled (page 242).

NO COOKING REQUIRED

Beets can be trimmed, peeled, washed and dried, then grated raw into salads. For a beetroot slaw, peel and grate 2 beetroots. Combine 100 ml (3½ fl. oz) crème fraîche with 2 tsp white wine vinegar and 1 tbsp drained capers. Season, then mix this dressing with the beetroot. If liked, replace half the beetroot with grated carrot.

BASIC COOKING

Trim off the leaves leaving 5 cm (2 in.) of stalk on the beets. Leave the thin base root on. Wash in cold water and cook without peeling. Once the beetroot is cooked, the skin will rub away.

BOILED BEETROOT

Take care not to damage the skin – if it is pierced, the beetroot will 'bleed' its juice into the water throughout boiling and lose colour, nutrients and flavour. Boil in lightly salted water for 45 minutes–2 hours, depending on size. Drain and rub away skin, using fingers.

BEETROOT IN VINEGAR

Slice boiled beets into discs and layer in a dish. Pour over vinegar of choice: malt is traditional but balsamic vinegar brings out the sweetness of beets best of all.

PURÉED BEETROOT

Boil, skin, roughly chop then mash with a 10 g (¼ oz) knob of butter for each beetroot. Season to taste.

ROAST BEETROOT

Clean small whole or medium quartered beets, rub with oil and place in a roasting tin. Season well, sprinkle with thyme leaves or cumin seeds, and roast, turning halfway through and adding a dash more oil, at 190°C/gas mark 5 for 30–45 minutes, or until tender and a little charred at the edges.

BAKED BEETROOT

Wrap small–medium beets loosely in foil, place on a baking tray and cook at 180°C/gas mark 4 for 30–60 minutes, depending on size. Cool slightly and rub away skin with fingers. Serve with roast meats or fish. Unpeeled larger beets can be eaten like baked potatoes: cut the top off and add a spoonful of sour cream mixed with a little horseradish sauce.

BEETROOT CRISPS

Peel medium beets and slice as thinly as possible using a mandoline. Dry with kitchen paper. Fill one-third of a deep-fat fryer with rapeseed or safflower oil and heat to 180°C, or until a cube of bread dropped in turns golden in 30 seconds. Add beets in small batches. Fry for 1–2 minutes, depending on thickness, remove from oil, drain on kitchen paper, season and serve. Crisps will keep in an airtight container but will lose some of their crispness.

In Roman times beetroot was said to be an aphrodisiac. It was also used to help calm fever and as an aid to kidney function.

BEETROOT RECIPES

BORSCHT

The classic beetroot soup from Eastern Europe has dozens of variations, but most contain potato, vinegar and sour cream. Traditionally the soup wasn't liquidized in a blender – but it does improve it.

Serves 4

2 tbsp vegetable oil
1 onion
1 stalk celery
3 medium-large beetroots

2 floury potatoes
2 tbsp red wine vinegar
1.2 litres (2 pints) vegetable stock
2 tsp sugar

salt, black pepper
4 tbsp sour cream
1 tbsp fresh chopped dill

- Heat oil in a large pan and stir-fry the chopped onion and celery over low heat for 3 minutes to soften but not colour. Peel and chop the beetroots and potatoes.

- Add beetroot, potato and vinegar to pan, then bring to a bubble for half a minute. Add stock, bring to the boil, reduce heat and simmer, stirring occasionally, for 40 minutes. Add sugar. Cool a little, then liquidize the soup in a blender.

- Return to pan to reheat and season to taste. Garnish with sour cream and dill to serve.

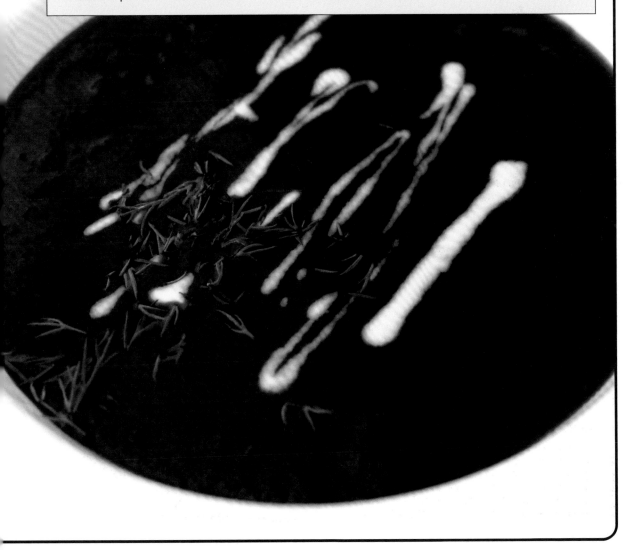

ROAST BEETROOT DIP

You can use this like any dip – with breadsticks or crudités as a starter, snack or part of a buffet.

Serves 4–6

3 beetroots
200 ml (7 fl. oz) Greek yogurt
1 tbsp lemon juice
½ tsp ground cumin
½ tsp ground sweet paprika
salt, black pepper

- Roast beetroots, skin and put into a blender.
- Add remaining ingredients and blend until you have a just-about-smooth purée. Put in a bowl, cover and chill.

BEETROOT AND GOAT'S CHEESE SALAD

Good served with crusty bread. You can also try this recipe using slices of warm grilled Haloumi cheese instead of the soft goat's cheese.

Serves 4

8 small beetroots
1 tsp cumin seeds
1 tbsp olive oil
salt, black pepper
200 g (7 oz) soft goat's cheese
4 tbsp honey and mustard dressing (page 250)

- Roast beetroots with cumin, oil and seasoning.
- While still warm, halve beetroots and put 4 halves on each serving plate, scatter small chunks of the cheese over and drizzle dressing on top.

TANGY HOT BEETROOT

This is really delicious as a hot side dish with gammon or roast beef – in fact, with any cooked meat. And it is very good with fish too.

Serves 4

1 tbsp butter	½ tsp mixed spice
1 tbsp vinegar	1 tsp soy sauce
2 tsp sugar	salt, black pepper
¼ tsp cayenne pepper	2–3 boiled beetroots
¼ tsp mustard powder	

- Melt butter over medium heat, stir in vinegar, sugar, spices, soy sauce and seasoning. Cook for a minute.
- Cut beetroots into small chunks and add to the pan. Simmer with the lid on for 2 minutes to warm through.

BEETROOT AND CREAM SAUCE

Here's a superb easy sauce for roast lamb or pork – or chops. If you don't have any fresh horseradish, use a strong ready-made horseradish sauce.

Serves 4

3 beetroots (about 400 g/14 oz in all)
100 ml (3½ fl. oz) crème fraîche
1 tbsp freshly grated horseradish
salt

- Boil beetroots and remove skins. Allow to cool a little, then cut into 1 cm (½ in.) chunks and put in a bowl.
- Stir crème fraîche, horseradish and salt together and combine with the beetroot to make a vivid pink sauce. Serve at room temperature.

HONEY-ROAST MIXED ROOTS

An easy recipe for a Sunday roast – the honey and vinegar really bring out the flavour of the sweet roots. If you use this season's garlic (rather than long-stored garlic) the flesh in the cloves will be soft and delicious.

Serves 4–6

3 beetroots
4 thick carrots
3 medium–large parsnips
whole garlic bulb
2 tsp fresh chopped rosemary
4 tbsp olive oil
2 tbsp cider vinegar
salt, black pepper
1 tbsp runny honey

- Cut beetroots into quarters, peel carrots and parsnips and halve lengthwise. Divide garlic into cloves, keeping skins on.
- Put all vegetables and garlic into a roasting tin. Toss with the oil, vinegar and seasoning. Roast at 200°C/gas mark 6 for 25 minutes, then stir and drizzle the honey over. Return to oven for a further 20–25 minutes or until tender.
- Slip soft garlic flesh from skins and stir into any pan juices to serve.

Beetroots can be juiced to make a nutritious and low-cost alternative to orange or tomato juice. Beetroot juice is said to boost stamina and ability to exercise.

SMOKED MACKEREL, BEETROOT AND POTATO SALAD

This is a salad that takes a while to put together but is very much worth it for the end result.

Serves 4

2 beetroots
2 tbsp balsamic vinegar
2 tbsp olive oil
salt, black pepper
300 g (11 oz) new potatoes
2 tbsp vegetable oil
8 spring onions
1 tbsp fresh chopped parsley
200 ml (7 fl. oz) extra-thick cream
2 tbsp freshly grated horseradish
4 smoked mackerel fillets
rocket leaves

- Put the quartered beetroots in a roasting dish, drizzle with the vinegar and olive oil and season well. Cut potatoes into small chunks and put in another roasting dish with vegetable oil and seasoning.
- Roast everything until crisp and tender, adding chopped onions to potato pan for last 10 minutes of cooking and combining well.
- Mix cream and horseradish together. Combine beetroot with potato and stir in parsley. Slice mackerel fillets and arrange on plates with vegetables. Garnish with rocket leaves.

BEETROOT, ORANGE AND WALNUT SALAD

An excellent winter salad to serve with cheese or chicken.

Serves 4

3 beetroots
1 orange
4 tbsp olive oil
1 tbsp balsamic vinegar
salt, black pepper
65 g (2½ oz) walnut pieces
25 g (1 oz) rocket leaves
1 tbsp fresh chopped chives

- Boil or roast beetroot and slice. Peel and segment the orange, remove white pith and cut each segment in two – as you do this, reserve all the juice and squeeze any remaining juice from the peel. Arrange beetroot slices and orange pieces on a serving platter.
- Combine oil, vinegar, seasoning and all the reserved orange juice and drizzle over the salad. Scatter on the walnut pieces, rocket and chives to serve.

Food manufacturers use beetroot extracts called betanins as natural red colourants – for example, in jams, sauces and ice cream.

BEETROOT AND MINT SALSA

This makes a delicious accompaniment for grilled meats or fish, or you can use it as part of your salad platter instead of basic beetroot in vinegar.

Serves 4–6

2 beetroots
8 spring onions
1 lime
2 tbsp fresh finely chopped mint
salt, black pepper

- Boil beetroots and rub off skins. Allow to cool a little, then cut into 1 cm (½ in.) cubes and put in a bowl.
- Add chopped spring onions, lime juice and finely grated zest, mint and seasoning. Stir, cover and leave for 1 hour for the flavours to combine. Serve at room temperature.

BROCCOLI

Broccoli features in many traditional Italian dishes – the vegetable originated in Italy and has been used there in recipes since the 1500s. The large-headed green florets are more correctly called calabrese and are in season in autumn. The true broccoli – usually purple, but it can be white – is what we call sprouting broccoli and is picked in spring.

While broccoli may look a little like cauliflower, and white sprouting broccoli is a good substitute for it, broccoli is closer in taste to asparagus, and tender sprouting broccoli tips can be used in many asparagus recipes.

STORING

Store in the fridge in a plastic bag with airholes for 1–2 days (sprouting type), 2–4 days (calabrese). Calabrese can also be frozen: blanch, arrange on trays and open-freeze before putting the frozen florets in bags or lidded containers.

NO COOKING REQUIRED

Tender broccoli can be eaten raw – the 'Tenderstem' varieties of sprouting broccoli are particularly suitable.

BASIC COOKING

Heads or florets turning yellow or brown are too old to eat. Don't over-cook or under-cook broccoli – under-cooked it is tasteless and joyless and can be hard to chew; over-cooked it turns into an unpleasant-smelling and -tasting mush. For most recipes it is best divided into small florets before cooking. Remove tough lower stalks. Don't soak in water before cooking to avoid leaching vitamins.

BOILED/STEAMED BROCCOLI

Steam for 3–5 minutes (check after 3 by piercing a stem with a sharp knife) or place florets in 2 cm (¾ in.) lightly salted boiling water in a pan and simmer for 3–5 minutes. If using in a recipe, refresh in cold water to retain colour and stop cooking; otherwise drain and serve immediately, as broccoli soon loses heat.

The word 'broccoli' comes from the Italian word *brocco*, which means branch or arm.

Broccoli is a perfect partner for chilli, anchovies, almonds, garlic, cream, peppers and cheese.

PURÉED BROCCOLI

Put boiled broccoli into a blender with 10 g (¼ oz) butter and a pinch of ground nutmeg for every 100 g (3½ oz) broccoli and purée for a few seconds; season to taste. Good with fish.

STIR-FRIED BROCCOLI

Use very small florets or cut larger ones into thin slices. Heat vegetable oil in a pan or wok and stir-fry the florets over high heat for 2–3 minutes.

BROCCOLI RECIPES

BROCCOLI SOUFFLÉ

Broccoli is the best green vegetable to add to a cheese soufflé – it makes it delicious. For a supper party you can spoon the mixture into individual soufflé dishes, reducing cooking time by 10 minutes.

Serves 4

15 g (½ oz) butter
1 tbsp grated Parmesan
500 g (1¼ lb) broccoli
400 ml (14 fl. oz) white sauce (see page 251)

100 g (3½ oz) mature Cheddar
½ tsp ground nutmeg
½ tsp mustard powder
salt, black pepper

4 eggs
1 egg white

- Grease a 1.7 litre (3 pint) soufflé dish with butter and dust the inside with Parmesan. Preheat oven to 190°C/gas mark 5.

- Steam broccoli, drain and mash or blend until smooth. Heat white sauce through and stir in 75 g (3 oz) of the grated Cheddar, the broccoli, nutmeg, mustard and seasoning. Mix well.

- Cool a little, then separate the eggs and beat the yolks into the sauce. Whisk the 5 egg whites in a clean, dry, non-greasy bowl until they are stiff, then fold gently into the broccoli mixture, taking care not to over-mix.

- Spoon mixture into soufflé dish and sprinkle remaining Cheddar over the top. Place on a baking tray and bake for 35 minutes until risen and golden brown on top. Serve immediately.

PASTA WITH BROCCOLI, ANCHOVIES AND CHILLIES

An unusual way to serve broccoli – and pasta – but it really works well and is full of flavour.

Serves 4

400 g (14 oz) spaghetti
1 head broccoli
3 tbsp olive oil
salt, black pepper
40 g (1½ oz) can anchovies
4 cloves garlic
1 large red chilli
½ lemon
50 g (2 oz) breadcrumbs
50 g (2 oz) piece Parmesan

- Cook pasta, steaming broccoli over it until just tender. Drain, then toss pasta and broccoli with 1 tbsp of the oil and the seasoning. Keep warm.
- Drain and finely chop the anchovies, chop garlic and chilli and stir-fry all in 1 tbsp oil for 1–2 minutes. Remove with a slotted spoon and stir into the pasta with the broccoli and lemon juice and zest.
- Stir breadcrumbs in the remaining oil in a pan over high heat until golden. Sprinkle over pasta with shaved cheese.

BROCCOLI AND STILTON SOUP

This hearty soup is really easy to make and ideal for an autumn supper. If you don't have any full-fat milk, use skimmed or semi-skimmed and add 2 tbsp cream.

Serves 4

1 onion
2 tbsp olive oil
40 g (1½ oz) butter
1 potato
1 litre (1¾ pints) vegetable stock
1 large head broccoli
200 ml (7 fl. oz) full-fat milk
200 g (7 oz) Stilton

- Sweat chopped onion in oil and butter over low heat for 5 minutes to soften but not colour. Peel and cut potato into small cubes and add to pan with stock. Simmer for 10 minutes.
- Cut broccoli into small florets and add to pan with milk. Simmer for a further 5 minutes.
- Allow to cool slightly, then put into a blender for a few seconds and blend to a rough purée. Add crumbled cheese, reheat until all cheese is melted, stir well and serve.

BROCCOLI, WALNUT AND BLUE CHEESE PASTA

Dolcelatte is a lovely, soft blue Italian cheese to use in this easy supper dish, but you could also try St-Agur or blue Brie.

Serves 4

400 g (14 oz) rigatoni
400 g (14 oz) broccoli
2 tbsp olive oil
175 g (6 oz) soft blue cheese
65 g (2½ oz) walnut pieces
juice of ½ lemon

- Cook pasta, steaming broccoli over it until just tender. Drain, then toss pasta and broccoli in the oil.
- Stir the cheese into the warm pasta. When it has melted, serve with walnuts scattered over and lemon juice squeezed over.

BROCCOLI AND TOMATO GRATIN

This is a complete supper, but you could add strips of ham or cooked chicken to make it even more substantial.

Serves 4

600 g (1 lb 6 oz) broccoli
12 cherry tomatoes
400 ml (14 fl. oz) white sauce (page 251)
1 tsp Dijon mustard
100 g (3½ oz) Cheddar
25 g (1 oz) breadcrumbs

- Steam broccoli in large florets, drain and arrange in a shallow ovenproof dish with heads all facing upwards. Halve cherry tomatoes and arrange around the broccoli.
- Warm white sauce through, add mustard and three-quarters of the grated cheese and stir until cheese is thoroughly melted. Pour over the broccoli, making sure tops are covered.
- Mix remaining cheese with the breadcrumbs and sprinkle on top. Grill under medium-high heat for 5 minutes or until golden, or bake at 190°C/gas mark 5 for 20–25 minutes.

Broccoli can also be braised in wine, and try making fritters by dipping broccoli heads into batter and deep-frying them.

SPROUTING BROCCOLI PASTRIES WITH HOLLANDAISE AND PARMA HAM

A delicious, indulgent way to serve broccoli. It makes a lovely starter before a light main course. Hollandaise sauce can be bought ready-made in supermarkets.

Serves 4 as a starter

250 g (9 oz) puff pastry
1 tsp vegetable oil
100 g (3½ oz) Parma ham
500 g (1¼ lb) sprouting broccoli
175 ml (6 fl. oz) Hollandaise sauce
pinch smoked paprika

- Preheat oven to 220°C/gas mark 7. Roll out pastry into a thin square; trim edges, cut into 8 oblongs and chill for 30 minutes. Place on a baking tray and bake for 10–15 minutes until golden brown. Remove and keep warm.

- Brush a frying pan with the oil and fry the ham over high heat for 1–2 minutes to crisp lightly. Cut into small pieces.

- Steam broccoli until just tender. Arrange stalks on serving plates with puff pastries and warmed Hollandaise, scattering ham and paprika on top.

SPROUTING BROCCOLI WITH SPICY PEANUT DRESSING

This could be a starter or light lunch – or add cooked noodles for a main meal.

Serves 4

600 g (1 lb 6 oz) sprouting broccoli
100 g (3½ oz) baby corn cobs
1 head pak choi
4 tbsp crunchy peanut butter
juice of 1 lime
2 tbsp soy sauce
½ tsp sugar
½ tsp ground ginger

- Steam broccoli and corn cobs, then refresh under cold water and drain. Arrange on serving plates with sliced pak choi leaves.

- In a saucepan combine the remaining ingredients with 4 tbsp hot water until you have a sauce. Pour over the vegetables and serve.

BROCCOLI, LENTIL AND SWEET POTATO SALAD

It takes time to prepare this salad, but it is delicious and well worth the effort.

Serves 4

1 large sweet potato
1 tbsp vegetable oil
150 g (5 oz) Puy lentils
200 g (7 oz) brown rice
300 g (11 oz) broccoli
1 beef tomato
2 tbsp fresh coriander leaves
2 tbsp fresh chopped mint leaves
½ tsp Tabasco
3 tbsp soy sauce
2 tbsp balsamic vinegar
2 tbsp sesame oil
3 tbsp groundnut oil
1 tbsp finely chopped stem ginger + 2 tsp syrup

- Peel and cut sweet potato into 2.5 cm (1 in.) cubes and roast at 190°C/gas mark 5 in 1 tbsp oil for 30–40 minutes until soft and golden. Boil lentils in unsalted water for 30 minutes or until cooked; drain. Simmer rice in 500 ml (17 fl. oz) salted water for 25 minutes or until cooked; drain.

- Divide broccoli into small florets and steam. Chop tomato into small cubes.

- Combine vegetables, lentils, rice and herbs.

- Blend together the remaining ingredients, then stir into the salad.

SPROUTING BROCCOLI, RED PEPPER AND ALMOND STIR-FRY

This colourful stir-fry makes part of a mixed Chinese meal. You could add beef, pork or chicken pieces to the pan with the broccoli for a complete meal served with noodles or rice.

Serves 4

500 g (1¼ lb) sprouting broccoli
2 red peppers
2 tbsp vegetable oil
1 hot red chilli
2.5 cm (1 in.) piece fresh ginger
3 cloves garlic
2 tbsp soy sauce
2 tbsp sesame oil
1 tbsp sweet chilli dipping sauce (page 60)
100 g (3½ oz) toasted flaked almonds
1 tbsp sesame seeds

- Cut broccoli spears in two halfway down the stem, then divide the lower stems in half lengthwise. Thinly slice peppers. Stir-fry broccoli and peppers in the vegetable oil over high heat for 3 minutes or until coloured and just tender.
- Add finely chopped chilli, ginger and garlic, stir for a further minute, then add remaining ingredients and stir for 1 minute more. Sprinkle with sesame seeds to serve.

BROCCOLI AND LEMON SOUP

This is much less rich than the broccoli and Stilton soup, but if you want to add a touch of luxury, swirl some cream into the bowls to serve.

Serves 4

1 large onion
2 tbsp vegetable oil
3 cloves garlic
600 g (1 lb 6 oz) broccoli
1 large floury potato
1 litre (1¾ pints) vegetable stock
salt, black pepper
juice of ½ lemon

- Sweat chopped onion in the oil over low heat, stirring from time to time to soften but not colour, add chopped garlic and fry for a further minute.
- Add broccoli, peeled and diced potato, stock and seasoning. Stir and simmer for 15 minutes or until potatoes are tender.
- Cool a little, then blend in a blender. Reheat, check seasoning and stir in lemon juice to serve.

BROCCOLI AND CHICKEN SUPREME

An easy recipe that always turns out well. It shouldn't need extra salt as the butter, bacon and stock are salty. Serve on rice or with mashed potatoes.

Serves 4

300 g (11 oz) broccoli
1 onion
4 cloves garlic
1 tbsp vegetable oil
15 g (½ oz) butter
4 rashers lean back bacon
4 skinless chicken breast fillets
100 ml (3½ fl. oz) strong chicken stock
400 ml (14 fl. oz) double cream
black pepper

- Steam small broccoli florets until just tender. Fry finely chopped onion and garlic in the oil and butter over medium-low heat to soften and tinge gold; remove from pan with a slotted spoon.
- Cut bacon into strips and fry until golden. Remove from pan. Cut chicken into strips and fry (adding a little extra butter/oil if necessary) for 3–4 minutes until cooked through but not too browned.
- Return onion, garlic and bacon to pan with the broccoli, stock, cream and pepper; stir. Simmer for a minute or two, check seasoning and add a little salt if necessary.

TERIYAKI SALMON AND BROCCOLI STIR-FRY

The strong taste and texture of salmon is a good match for broccoli in this very easy and quick recipe (discounting marinade time). You can use any type of broccoli that you have. Serve with noodles or rice.

Serves 4

500 g (1¼ lb) thick salmon fillet
3 tbsp teriyaki marinade
2 tbsp sesame oil
300 g (11 oz) broccoli
200 g (7 oz) black bean sauce
2 tsp ground ginger

- Cut salmon fillet into 20 pieces and arrange in one layer in a non-metallic dish. Spoon the marinade over, cover and leave for 30 minutes.
- Heat the oil in a wok or frying pan, add sliced broccoli and salmon, then stir-fry over high heat for 1 minute, turning gently to prevent salmon breaking up too much.
- Add some of the marinade, the black bean sauce, ginger and 2 tbsp hot water. Simmer for 2–3 minutes until broccoli is tender.

BROCCOLI AND PEPPER QUICHE

Use whatever colour peppers you have to hand, although red ones makes the quiche look very colourful. Try a similar recipe using 150 g (5 oz) cooked corn kernels instead of peppers.

Serves 6

500 g (1¼ lb) shortcrust pastry (page 251)
1 large onion
1 red pepper
1 green pepper
2 tbsp vegetable oil
500 g (1¼ lb) broccoli
4 large eggs
350 ml (12 fl. oz) milk
2 tsp Dijon mustard
salt, black pepper
100 g (3½ oz) Cheddar

- Oil a deep, 24 cm (9½ in.) flan tin. Roll out the pastry and lay over the tin, pressing in gently. Bake blind at 200°C/gas mark 6 for 15 minutes.
- Sweat sliced onion and peppers in oil over low heat to soften but not colour. Blanch small broccoli florets for 2 minutes; drain. Whisk together eggs, milk, mustard and seasoning.
- Arrange vegetables in pastry case and sprinkle with half the grated cheese. Pour egg mixture over and sprinkle with remaining cheese. Bake for 40 minutes at 180°C/gas mark 4 until the eggs are set but not too solid and the top is golden. Allow to cool a little before serving.

BROCCOLI, CHICKEN AND PASTA BAKE

This is an all-in-one meal that will prove very popular with adults and children alike – a good way to get kids to eat their broccoli.

Serves 4

300 g (11 oz) pasta shapes	**1 clove garlic**
250 g (9 oz) broccoli	**2 tbsp sun-dried tomato paste**
4 skinless chicken breast fillets	**100 g (3 ½ oz) cream cheese**
2 tbsp olive oil	**300 ml (½ pint) single cream**
8 spring onions	**salt, black pepper**
	12 cherry tomatoes
	100 g (3½ oz) Cheddar

- Cook pasta until just tender, steaming broccoli over it for 3 minutes. Drain.
- Cut chicken into bite-sized pieces. Fry in oil over medium-high heat for approx. 4 minutes until cooked through and golden. Add chopped spring onions and garlic for the last 2 minutes. Add tomato paste, cream cheese and cream, season, stir and bring to a simmer.
- In a large bowl, combine pasta with broccoli, chicken, sauce and halved tomatoes until all pasta is thoroughly coated. Tip into a shallow, ovenproof dish and sprinkle grated cheese on top. Bake at 190°C/gas mark 5 for 20 minutes until golden on top.

VEGETABLE FILO FAMILY PIE

The filo pastry turns this vegetable pie into something even more special.

Serves 4

100 g (3½ oz) yellow dried split peas	**50 g (2 oz) Cheddar**
1 potato	**3 tbsp vegetable stock**
4 carrots	**400 ml (14 fl. oz) white sauce (page 251)**
2 leeks	**salt, black pepper**
100 g (3½ oz) peas	**15 g (½ oz) butter**
300 g (11 oz) broccoli	**1 tbsp oil**
1 tsp mustard powder	**6 sheets filo pastry**

- Boil split peas for 30 minutes or until tender; drain. Cut potato, carrots and leeks into bite-sized pieces. Boil potato in salted water for 3 minutes, then add carrots, leeks and peas and cook for a further 5 minutes until tender.
- Steam broccoli until just tender.
- Stir mustard, grated cheese and stock into warmed white sauce.
- Arrange all vegetables in a deep, square, ovenproof dish, season and pour the sauce over. Preheat oven to 190°C/gas mark 5.
- Melt butter with oil in a pan and brush over filo sheets, top sides only, then arrange pastry over vegetables. Bake for 25 minutes.

BRUSSELS SPROUTS

According to hearsay, the name of this member of the cabbage family is misleading as sprouts were first imported into Belgium from Italy by the Roman legions. The first sprout recipes in Brussels date from the 16th century. Nowadays it would seem that more people enjoy growing sprouts than eating them – they topped one poll as the UK's most hated vegetable. But properly prepared and not over-boiled, they can be delicious and they are a useful fresh green vegetable in the winter months. Their strong flavour is tempered, improved and made more acceptable to many by cooking them with oil and/or butter or goose/duck fat rather than drowning them in water.

STORING

Freshly picked sprouts will keep in a plastic bag with airholes in the fridge for several days. They also freeze well – choose small, tight-headed sprouts, pick off any loose outer leaves, blanch for 1½ minutes, drain and freeze in bags or containers.

NO COOKING REQUIRED

Finely slice raw sprouts and add to winter salad with raw cabbage, onion and carrot plus a tasty mayonnaise or walnut oil dressing.

BASIC COOKING

Sprouts should not be too large and should have tight heads with a sheen on the leaves and no sign of yellowing. There is no need to put a cross in the base before cooking as has long been recommended. Trim them by peeling off damaged outer leaves and trim the base if necessary.

Sprouts are one of the few vegetables that don't marry well with olive oil. Use groundnut (peanut) oil or a light seed oil to cook them.

SAUTÉED SPROUTS

Blanch sprouts for 2 minutes or until about half cooked. Drain and slice. Heat 10 g (¼ oz) butter in a pan for every 100 g (3½ oz) sprouts and fry over medium-high heat, stirring from time to time, until lightly golden.

ROAST SPROUTS

Put prepared sprouts in a bowl with 1 tbsp oil for every 150 g (5 oz) sprouts, adding plenty of salt and black pepper and a pinch of nutmeg. Combine everything well, then roast at 190°C/gas mark 5 for 30 minutes or until sprouts are dark gold and tender when pierced with a knife.

BOILED SPROUTS

Put in boiling, lightly salted water and cook for 4–6 minutes, depending on size. Test with a sharp knife to see if they are done. Do not over-cook or they will become unappetizing with an unpleasant smell and changed flavour. Drain and toss with butter and black pepper.

STEAMED SPROUTS

Steam on top of a pan of boiling water for 4–6 minutes, depending on size.

Sprouts make perfect partners for butter, bacon, chestnuts, cream, almonds and garlic.

BRUSSELS SPROUT RECIPES

BRUSSELS SPROUTS WITH CHESTNUTS

This is the classic Christmas lunch combination. If you're not having bacon rolls, you can add crispy strips of lean back bacon to the finished dish. For added luxury, stir a little cream into the pan before serving. If you don't have your own store of sweet chestnuts, they can be found ready-cooked in vacuum packs in the supermarket.

Serves 4

350 g (12 oz) Brussels sprouts   200 g (7 oz) cooked chestnuts
50 g (2 oz) butter   black pepper

- Boil or steam sprouts until two-thirds cooked; drain.
- Fry in the butter over medium heat for 4–5 minutes until golden.
- Add the halved chestnuts and heat through for a minute. Grind black pepper over to serve.

BRUSSELS SPROUT PURÉE

The cream in this dish mellows the strong flavour of the sprouts. Excellent with game or chicken.

Serves 4

600 g (1 lb 6 oz) Brussels sprouts
40 g (1½ oz) butter
salt, black pepper
100 ml (3½ fl. oz) double cream

- Boil or steam sprouts until barely tender; drain.
- Put in a blender with butter, seasoning and cream. Blend to a purée.

BRUSSELS SPROUTS WITH BACON

Try this more-ish side dish with roast chicken or turkey – children will love it.

Serves 4

350 g (12 oz) Brussels sprouts
salt, black pepper
25 g (1 oz) butter
4 rashers smoked streaky bacon
4 shallots
2 cloves garlic
1 tbsp oil

- Quarter the sprouts, season and fry in the butter over medium-low heat until cooked through.
- Cut bacon into strips and add to pan with finely chopped shallots and garlic, and the oil. Turn heat up to medium-high and stir-fry until bacon strips and sprouts are golden.

WINTER MASH

Parsnips and sprouts are a lovely combination – the sweetness of the roots counters the strength of the sprouts.

Serves 4

2 parsnips
3 floury potatoes
250 g (9 oz) Brussels sprouts
75 ml (2½ fl. oz) milk
25 ml (1 fl. oz) cream
3 tsp wholegrain mustard
salt, black pepper

- Peel and chop parsnips and potatoes into 2.5 cm (1 in.) chunks. Boil for 7 minutes, then add shredded sprouts to the pan and boil for a further 2 minutes or until vegetables are tender.
- Drain and mash the vegetables with the remaining ingredients.

SPROUT AND POTATO PATTIES

The classic way to use up leftover vegetables. If you have cold boiled potatoes rather than leftover mash, simply roughly mash them – any small lumps will add texture to the patties.

Serves 4

40 g (1½ oz) butter
1 tbsp vegetable oil
200 g (7 oz) Brussels sprouts
1 onion
400 g (14 oz) mashed potato
salt, black pepper
¼ tsp ground nutmeg
1 tbsp flour

- Melt half the butter in a frying pan with half the oil. Boil or steam sprouts until just tender then shred and add to pan. Stir-fry for 1–2 minutes over medium-high heat until tinged gold. Remove with a slotted spoon.
- Turn heat down to medium-low. Add finely chopped onion and sweat until softened but not coloured.
- Mix sprouts and onions in a bowl with mashed potato, seasoning and nutmeg. Sprinkle flour on to a plate. Form mixture into 8 patties and dip each into flour.
- Fry the patties in remaining butter and oil until golden brown on both sides.

MIDWINTER SOUP

This is a great soup for using up all those bits of vegetables you've got hanging around. Ideal for a cold winter's day.

Serves 4

1 onion	**1 tbsp curry paste**
2 stalks celery	**1.2 litres (2 pints)**
2 tbsp vegetable oil	**vegetable stock**
2 potatoes	**250 g (9 oz) Brussels sprouts**
1 parsnip	**4 tbsp cream**

- Sweat chopped onion and celery in oil over low heat to soften but not colour. Add peeled and diced potatoes and parsnip, frying for a further 1–2 minutes over medium heat.
- Stir in curry paste and cook for a minute, then pour in stock and stir well. Bring to the boil, lower heat, cover and simmer for 20 minutes, adding chopped Brussels sprouts for the last 10 minutes.
- Cool a little, put in a blender and blend until smooth. Reheat and add salt if necessary. Serve with cream on top.

SUPREME GRATIN OF BRUSSELS SPROUTS

Something very special – try it instead of traditional sprouts with Christmas lunch or with cold cuts on Boxing Day. It is also hearty enough to make a delicious supper for two on its own, and it is even good cold, if there is any left.

Serves 4

800 g (1¾ lb) Brussels sprouts
3 cloves garlic
40 g (1½ oz) butter
250 ml (8 fl. oz) double cream
½ tsp ground nutmeg
salt, black pepper
50 g (2 oz) breadcrumbs
50 g (2 oz) grated Parmesan

- Boil or steam sprouts until two-thirds cooked. Drain and slice each into three.
- Fry sprouts and finely chopped garlic in butter over medium heat until tinged gold. Stir in cream, nutmeg and seasoning, and bubble for a minute.
- Transfer to a shallow ovenproof dish and top with the breadcrumbs mixed with the cheese. Bake at 190°C/gas mark 5 for 20 minutes.

SPICY STIR-FRIED SPROUTS

When you've tried sprouts all the traditional ways and still have more, give this modern take a try. It is very good with grilled or roast chicken. Do use crusty bread and not the ready-sliced variety.

Serves 4

2 slices white bread	1 hot red chilli
800 g (1¾ lb) Brussels sprouts	1 tbsp groundnut oil
	1 tbsp sesame oil
3 cloves garlic	

- Chop bread into 0.5 cm (¼ in.) cubes, put in one layer on a baking tray and bake at 190°C/gas mark 5 for 10 minutes or until dry and golden.
- Boil or steam sprouts until just tender.
- Stir-fry finely chopped garlic and chilli in the oils over medium heat for a minute. Add sprouts, stir for a minute and serve scattered with toasted bread.

Sprouts have been cultivated for hundreds of years in the Channel Islands, where the dry canes of the sprout plant were used to make walking sticks.

VEGETABLE BHAJIS

Perfect for an Indian supper or as a starter with some mango chutney on the side. Find chick pea (gram) flour in the speciality section of the supermarket, or in delis or ethnic shops.

Makes 12

2 onions
1 large leek
250 g (9 oz) Brussels sprouts
½ tsp each ground cumin, ground coriander, chilli powder and turmeric
salt, black pepper
150 ml (¼ pint) vegetable stock
250 g (9 oz) chick pea flour + extra for dusting
vegetable oil for frying

- Finely slice onions, leek and sprouts and put in a bowl. Combine spices and seasoning and add to bowl with stock. Combine well, using hands.
- Sprinkle flour over and combine again, using hands. Form into 12 slightly flattened cakes and sprinkle with a little more flour.
- Heat at least 2.5 cm (1 in.) oil in a frying pan or deep-fat fryer until the oil will crisp a cube of bread in 30 seconds. Add bhajis in 2 batches, allowing oil to reheat between batches. Fry for 6 minutes or until crisp and golden. Drain on kitchen paper.

CABBAGE

The cabbage is a member of the brassica family and is the most well-known and widely grown of the cruciferous vegetables. Sprouts and cauliflower are among many others: the lesser known and lesser grown mizuna, rocket, mustard and tatsoi are all cruciferous vegetables too.

Throughout most of the year cabbage is one of the most common sights in the vegetable patch and comes in a variety of shapes, colours and sizes – yet it is rarely used to its full potential in the kitchen. Boiled cabbage has a poor reputation because of the smell it can produce, but if it is properly treated this needn't be the case. Cabbage is in fact versatile and useful and, depending on type, can be used in a much wider range of recipes than is often appreciated – from stir-fries to soups, braises and mashes.

STORING

Don't cut cabbage before storing. Clean if absolutely necessary and remove outer yellow or diseased leaves and root. All leaf vegetables should be stored in a cool, dark place (the fridge is ideal) to prevent wilting and loss of vitamin C. Store in a plastic bag with airholes. Length of storage time will depend on variety: spring greens types keep for a few days, while firm drumhead white and red cabbages and Chinese cabbage (but not pak choi) will keep for at least 2 and up to 4 weeks.

Firm cabbage leaves can be chopped and frozen in lidded containers or bags and will be fine for use in soups, stews or casseroles. Red and white cabbages can also be pickled in vinegar for long-term storage or can be included in chutneys.

VARIETIES

SPRING CABBAGES
Includes spring greens and collard greens. Tender tasty greens ideal for steaming, or for soups or any cooked chopped cabbage recipe.

SUMMER CABBAGES
With a firm heart, ball-shaped or conical, they can vary from light to dark green.

WINTER CABBAGES
Usually have large, firm, tight ball/drumheads. Hardy, providing valuable leaf greens for the kitchen during winter. The white cabbage is widely used for winter salads.

SAVOY CABBAGES
Can be harvested from early autumn through to early spring. Crinkly, strongly flavoured leaves and pale hearts. Ideal for braising in wedges or shredded in soups and stir-fries.

RED CABBAGES
Much less common in the kitchen than the green/white types, which is a pity as they can be used in many ways. Firm, tight ballheads will keep for weeks. Ideal braised or in winter salads.

CHINESE CABBAGES
Look unlike any other cabbage. Cylindrical in shape, with large stalks dominating each leaf. Similar to a Cos lettuce in colour and appearance. Ideal for stir-fries.

Pak choi is a more delicate, smaller, tender Chinese cabbage.

NO COOKING REQUIRED

Most cabbages can be eaten raw if finely shredded. White, red and Chinese varieties are particularly suitable.

CLASSIC COLESLAW

There are dozens of different mayonnaise slaw recipes, but the basic version here is as nice as any. Ideal with ham, chicken or cheese.

Serves 4–6

½ white cabbage
2 carrots
1 small onion
50 g (2 oz) sultanas
150 ml (¼ pint) mayonnaise
2 tbsp natural yogurt
juice of ¼ lemon
1 tsp caster sugar
salt, black pepper

- Shred cabbage, peel and grate carrots and onion. Combine vegetables and sultanas.
- Mix together remaining ingredients and combine thoroughly with the vegetables.

Traditionally a bay leaf or a whole chilli pepper is put into the pan to diminish the strong odours given off by over-cooked cabbage.

SPICED SAVOY AND RED CABBAGE COLESLAW

Try this slaw with grilled lamb chops or sausages. If you have no rice vinegar, use sherry or white wine vinegar instead. The salad improves if kept in the fridge overnight.

Serves 4–6

¼ Savoy cabbage
¼ red cabbage
2 tbsp sesame oil
2 tbsp soy sauce
2 tbsp rice vinegar
2 tsp caster sugar
2.5 cm (1 in.) piece fresh ginger
1 hot red chilli
50 g (2 oz) chopped roasted peanuts

- Remove all stalk from cabbages, slice leaves very thinly and put into a large bowl.
- Whisk or shake together oil, soy sauce, vinegar and sugar. Peel and very finely chop ginger, de-seed and chop chilli and add to the dressing. Combine well, then mix thoroughly with the cabbage. Cover and let stand for half an hour, stirring once or twice.
- Sprinkle with nuts before serving.

BASIC COOKING

Cabbages from the garden need to be thoroughly checked for caterpillars, snails, droppings and damage. Discard tough outer leaves or cut away the inedible parts and discard all but the top 2–3 cm (1 in.) of the root stalk. Wash in plenty of cold water but don't soak for long.

Either shred or cut into wedges, depending on preference and recipe, and cook in the minimum amount of water. Some cabbages, particularly the tight-packed drumhead type, have a hard central 'core' which you may prefer to remove, although it is perfectly edible.

BOILED CABBAGE

Divide tender (usually pale, central) leaves and tougher (usually darker, outer) leaves and shred or chop each type. Put the tougher leaves in 2.5–5 cm (1–2 in.) boiling, lightly salted water. Bring back to the boil and cook for 2–3 minutes, then add the tender leaves to the pan without stirring. Continue boiling until just tender. Spring greens and Chinese cabbage cook faster than winter and drumhead types. Allow 15 minutes for wedges. Serve with butter and black pepper.

STEAMED CABBAGE

Shred or thinly chop and put in a steamer over boiling water. Steam for 3–4 minutes until just tender, then season. Wedges can be steamed but will take up to 15 minutes – less if you remove the central core.

STIR-FRIED CABBAGE

Stir shredded cabbage in a little nut or seed oil in a wok or large pan over medium-high heat for 2–3 minutes until tender. Season, adding whole cumin or caraway seeds or chopped garlic if liked.

BRAISED CABBAGE (1)

Cut cabbage hearts into thick wedges: 4–6 to an average head. Arrange in a casserole dish or saucepan in one layer, pour vegetable stock over to come halfway up the wedges and simmer for 20 minutes or until tender. The remaining stock can be thickened with a little cream before serving.

BRAISED CABBAGE (2)

Shred cabbage leaves. In a heavy-based, lidded frying pan melt 10 g (¼ oz) butter for every 100 g (3½ oz) cabbage and add cabbage to pan, stirring well to coat all the leaves; season. Stir for a minute over medium heat then add 2 tbsp vegetable stock and 1 tbsp lemon juice. Stir again, put lid on, turn heat down and cook gently for 3 minutes.

CABBAGE RECIPES

BRAISED RED CABBAGE WITH APPLE

This is a lovely, sweet-and-sour side dish for pork, lamb or game.

Serves 4–6

1 red cabbage	50 g (2 oz) butter	1 tbsp brown sugar	¼ tsp ground nutmeg
1 large onion	1 cooking apple	2 tbsp wine vinegar	salt, black pepper

- Sweat thinly sliced cabbage and onion in butter in a large pan over low heat to soften but not colour.
- Peel, core and finely chop apple and stir into cabbage with sugar, vinegar, nutmeg and seasoning. Add 2 tbsp water. Bring to a gentle simmer over low heat.
- Cover with a well-fitting lid and simmer for 1 hour, stirring 3–4 times and adding 1–2 tbsp more water if the braise looks dry. Check seasoning before serving.

TRADITIONAL STUFFED CABBAGE

A recipe that has fallen out of fashion in recent years but should have a revival. Any type of minced meat can be used for the filling.

Serves 4

12 large Savoy cabbage leaves
1 tbsp olive oil
350 g (12 oz) lean minced beef
1 onion
150 g (5 oz) cooked long-grain rice
2 tsp dried mixed herbs
1 tbsp tomato purée
salt, black pepper
600 ml (1 pint) vegetable stock
400 ml (14 fl. oz) tomato sauce (page 156)

- Remove tough central stalk from cabbage leaves, then blanch for 2 minutes and refresh under cold water. Pat dry with kitchen paper.
- Stir-fry meat in oil over medium-high heat until brown. Add grated onion, rice, herbs, tomato purée and seasoning with 150 ml (¼ pint) of the stock. Stir well, bring to a simmer and cook for 5 minutes or until most of the stock has been absorbed.
- Place 1 tbsp meat mixture in the centre of each cabbage leaf and roll up, tucking in the ends to make a package.
- Put rolls in a casserole of suitable size so they fit snugly side by side. Bring the remaining stock to the boil and pour over rolls to half cover.
- Put on lid and cook at 180°C/gas mark 4 for 45 minutes, then remove stuffed leaves with a slotted spoon, drizzle a little of the stock over and serve with hot tomato sauce.

BUBBLE AND SQUEAK

Legend has it that this tasty way to use up any leftover cabbage and mash derived its name because the vegetables are first boiled – hence 'bubble' – and then fried, during which a squeaking noise can be heard coming from the pan.

Serves 4

250 g (9 oz) cooked cabbage
350 g (12 oz) mashed potato
salt, black pepper
25 g (1 oz) butter
1 tbsp vegetable oil

- Chop cabbage, combine with mash and season.
- Heat butter and oil in a frying pan and, when hot, add the mash to the pan, spreading it evenly across like a cake. Fry over medium heat until underside is golden, then, using two spatulas, flip over to brown the other side.

DOLMADES

In Greece and Turkey vine leaves are used for this popular dish, which makes a good starter or part of a *meze* – a Greek selection of small savoury dishes. Using cabbage leaves works just as well.

Serves 4 as a starter

20 cabbage leaves
4 shallots
2 cloves garlic
1 tbsp olive oil
150 g (5 oz) long-grain rice
50 g (2 oz) sultanas
50 g (2 oz) toasted pine nuts
juice of 1 lemon
salt, black pepper
175 ml (6 fl. oz) vegetable stock
12 spring onions
1 tbsp each fresh chopped mint, oregano and parsley
300 ml (½ pint) tzatziki (page 80)

- Remove tough central stalk from cabbage leaves, then blanch for 2 minutes and refresh under cold water. Pat dry with kitchen paper.
- Sweat finely chopped shallots and garlic in oil over low heat until soft but not coloured. Add rice, sultanas, pine nuts and lemon juice and fry for 1 minute. Season, then add stock. Cover and simmer for 15 minutes.
- Cool, then add chopped spring onions and herbs, stirring in well. Put 2 heaped tsp of the rice mixture in the centre of each cabbage leaf and roll into a tight parcel, tucking ends under.
- Place snugly side by side in a steamer over boiling water and steam for 5 minutes.
- Serve warm or cold, with tzatziki.

CABBAGE SOUP

The kind of soup we all crave on a cold winter's day – and it is quick to make.

Serves 4

50 g (2 oz) butter
150 g (5 oz) potatoes
2 onions
1.2 litres (2 pints) chicken stock
100 ml (3½ fl. oz) milk
1–2 heads spring greens
  (about 300 g/11 oz prepared weight)
salt, black pepper

- Sweat peeled chopped potatoes and onions in butter over low heat in a lidded pan to soften but not colour.
- Add stock and milk and simmer for 10 minutes. Add shredded greens and cook for 5 minutes.
- Cool a little, then purée in a blender. Reheat and season.

MINESTRONE SOUP

A big bowlful of this hearty soup is a meal in itself if served with crusty bread. For a starter, this recipe will make 8 small bowls.

Serves 4–8

1 onion
100 g (3½ oz) smoked streaky bacon
3 cloves garlic
2 carrots
2 stalks celery
2 tbsp olive oil
½ Savoy cabbage
400 g (14 oz) can borlotti beans
400 g (14 oz) can chopped tomatoes
1 tbsp tomato purée
1.2 litres (2 pints) vegetable stock
salt, black pepper
4–8 tbsp basil pesto (page 161)
4–8 tbsp grated Parmesan

- Fry chopped onion, bacon, garlic, carrots and celery in oil over medium heat, stirring occasionally, until vegetables are soft but not coloured and bacon is cooked.
- Add shredded cabbage, drained rinsed beans, tomatoes, tomato purée and stock. Stir well, bring to a simmer and cook for 20 minutes.
- Taste before seasoning. Serve, garnishing each bowl with pesto and cheese.

CABBAGE AND LENTIL CASSEROLE

This dish is a good one-pot rustic winter supper but is also nice served with brown rice or pasta. Use Puy lentils if you can, as they have a full taste and smooth texture.

Serves 4

6 rashers lean back bacon
1 tbsp vegetable oil
1 onion
250 g (9 oz) lentils
1 green cabbage
2 carrots
200 g (7 oz) can chopped tomatoes
2 tsp tomato purée
600 ml (1 pint) vegetable stock
salt, black pepper

- Chop bacon and fry in oil over medium-high heat for 2 minutes until golden. Add chopped onion and stir for a further 3 minutes, then stir in lentils and sliced cabbage.
- Cut carrots into chunks and add to pan with tomatoes, tomato purée, stock and seasoning. Stir everything well, bring to a simmer, turn heat down, put lid on and cook for 40 minutes. Check seasoning and serve.

STIR-FRIED CABBAGE WITH CASHEWS

Try this as a side dish with any meat, or as part of a Chinese meal.

Serves 4

100 g (3½ oz) cashew nuts
1 tbsp groundnut oil
1 tbsp sesame oil
225 g (8 oz) white or green cabbage
1 large carrot
2 cloves garlic
2 tbsp soy sauce
juice of 1 lime
black pepper

- Stir-fry cashews in groundnut oil until golden, remove with a slotted spoon and drain on kitchen paper.
- Add sesame oil to pan and stir-fry thinly sliced cabbage and carrot over high heat for 2 minutes.
- Add finely chopped garlic, soy sauce, lime juice and pepper and stir for a further minute or until vegetables are just tender. Stir in nuts to serve.

To prevent red cabbage losing its colour when chopped and cooked, add an acid such as vinegar or lemon juice.

SAVOY CABBAGE WITH PASTA AND MOZZARELLA

When using olive oil to drizzle over food or for salads it is best to choose a good-quality extra-virgin oil – in this case, a peppery Italian one. For cooking, basic olive oil is fine. Smoked streaky bacon can be used in place of pancetta.

Serves 4

150 g (5 oz) pancetta
2 tbsp olive oil
1 clove garlic
2 tsp fresh thyme leaves
1 Savoy cabbage
400 g (14 oz) farfalle
1 tbsp extra-virgin olive oil
salt, black pepper
40 g (1½ oz) grated Parmesan
200 g (7 oz) Mozzarella
50 g (2 oz) toasted pine nuts

- Fry small pieces of pancetta in half the oil over medium-high heat until golden. Add chopped garlic and thyme and stir.
- Add thinly sliced cabbage and remaining oil, stir, turn heat down to medium and cook for 5 minutes, stirring regularly.
- Cook and drain pasta. Stir in extra-virgin olive oil and seasoning, then the cheeses and cabbage mixture. Sprinkle with pine nuts to serve.

SAUTÉED SAVOY CABBAGE WITH ONION

A really nice side dish with game or beef.

Serves 4–6

1 large onion
50 g (2 oz) butter
2 cloves garlic
1 bay leaf
1 glass white wine
salt, black pepper
1 Savoy cabbage

- Sweat thinly sliced onion in a large pan with half the butter over low heat to soften but not colour, adding finely chopped garlic and bay leaf for last minute.
- Add wine and seasoning, bring to bubble over high heat and cook for a minute. Add shredded cabbage and remaining butter, stirring to coat well. Turn heat down to medium-low and cook with lid on for 3–4 minutes until cabbage is soft. Remove bay leaf, check seasoning and serve.

RED CABBAGE, CIDER AND SAUSAGE CASSEROLE

Three ingredients that really were made to go together make this low-cost supper a winner.

Serves 4

8 large pork Cumberland sausages
1 tbsp vegetable oil
1 small red cabbage
1 onion
25 g (1 oz) butter
100 ml (3½ fl. oz) cider
1 tbsp soft brown sugar
1 large cooking apple
25 g (1 oz) sultanas
150 ml (¼ pint) chicken stock
salt, black pepper

- Fry sausages in oil in a flameproof casserole over high heat, turning until browned on all sides. Turn heat down to medium, add thinly sliced cabbage and onion to casserole with butter and fry for 5 minutes to soften slightly.
- Mix cider and sugar and pour into casserole. Peel and finely chop apple and add to casserole with sultanas, stock and seasoning; stir.
- Cook with lid on at 180°C/gas mark 4 for an hour, stirring once or twice. Check seasoning.

CHINESE CABBAGE AND PORK STIR-FRY

This dish is good served with egg-thread noodles.

Serves 4

400 g (14 oz) pork tenderloin
2 tbsp soy sauce
2 tbsp groundnut oil
8 spring onions
1 large carrot
300 g (11 oz) Chinese cabbage
1 tsp Chinese five-spice
2 tbsp plum sauce
100 ml (3½ fl. oz) vegetable stock

- Slice pork into 0.5 cm (¼ in.) slices and lay in a non-metallic dish, pour soy sauce over and marinate for 15–30 minutes.
- Heat half the oil in a large frying pan or wok and cook pork over high heat for a minute, then turn, add spring onions (halved lengthwise) and cook for a further minute or until pork is cooked through. Remove from pan.
- Add remaining oil to pan and stir-fry very thinly sliced carrot, chopped cabbage and five-spice over high heat for 3 minutes.
- Return pork and onions to pan. Stir in plum sauce, soy sauce from marinade and stock until bubbling. Serve.

CAPSICUM

Capsicums are related to tomatoes and are properly fruits rather than vegetables. The family includes sweet (or bell) peppers and chilli peppers, which are a common sight in the supermarket but not in the garden.

Sweet peppers are quite easily grown in the greenhouse or even outside in mild sunny years. They make handsome plants, the fruits changing from green through to red as they ripen. They can also be yellow, orange or purple and come in a huge variety of shapes: cylindrical, elongated cones, long and thin, or squat and round.

Chillies vary widely in 'heat', which is measured in Scoville units. While mild chillies may be only 2,000–3,000 units, very hot varieties can be 500,000 plus and should perhaps come with a warning! Green (unripe) chillies are often milder than red, which have been on the plant longer.

STORING

Freshly picked, whole, glossy-skinned sweet or chilli peppers will store well in a plastic bag with airholes in the fridge for 1–2 weeks. Both sweet peppers and chillies freeze well: de-seed and slice or chop, then freeze in bags. Chillies can be frozen whole.

Fresh chillies are ideal for drying: simply thread cotton through the stalks and hang in a warm, dry area to dry out naturally. Smaller ones can be dried in a basket on a shelf in the kitchen. Once dry, keep in an airtight jar.

You can grind dried chillies and turn them into cayenne pepper, which should be stored in an airtight opaque jar – glass jars allow light in and the pepper will deteriorate in colour and flavour.

NO COOKING REQUIRED

Sweet peppers can be sliced or chopped and eaten raw – green ones are less sweet and appetizing than the other colours – but all are better eaten with a little oil or oily dressing. It's inadvisable to try hot chilli peppers raw as they can burn the mouth and make you ill. Milder varieties can be eaten raw – e.g. finely sliced into salads.

SWEET PEPPER SALAD

To make a tangy, refreshing side salad, combine 1 chopped red pepper with a few sliced black olives and 4 drained anchovies. Toss in olive oil mixed with a little balsamic vinegar and seasoning. Good with hard-boiled eggs or cheese.

CHILLI AND TOMATO SALSA

Finely chop and combine 3 mild chillies, 1 onion and 2 peeled tomatoes with the juice of a lime and 2 tbsps fresh chopped coriander. Season with salt and leave for an hour for flavours to meld. Excellent with barbecued or grilled meat or fish.

BASIC COOKING

Slice off the stalk-end top and remove the seeds with a spoon and membranes with a knife. Chilli seeds are hotter than the flesh so can be used to increase heat in a recipe. Slice, dice or keep whole, depending on the recipe. Peppers are easily peeled after cooking – place in a plastic bag and wait 10 minutes before peeling.

STIR-FRIED SWEET PEPPERS

Thinly slice peppers. Stir-fry in oil over high heat until tender and tinged gold. Season.

GRILLED SWEET PEPPERS

Halve or quarter peppers lengthwise, brush with olive oil and place under a hot grill for about 10 minutes until skins begin to char and they are tender when pierced with a knife. Eat hot, or allow to cool and toss in an olive oil and balsamic vinegar dressing.

ROAST SWEET PEPPERS

Quarter and thickly slice peppers, toss in oil and seasoning and tip on to a baking tray. Roast at 190°C/gas mark 5 for 30 minutes, turning once or twice, until slightly charred at the edges and tender when pierced with a knife.

FRIED CHILLI PEPPERS

Fry mild, whole, de-seeded chillis with the stalks left on, such as Hungarian Hot Wax or Pimentos Padron, in vegetable oil for 4–5 minutes until soft and lightly coloured. Drain, cool, then season. Hold by the stalk to eat as an appetizer.

GRILLED CHILLI PEPPERS

De-seed, brush with oil and place under a hot grill until lightly charred. Eat as fried chillies (above), or stuff.

SWEET PEPPER RECIPES

MIXED PEPPERS BRUSCHETTA

A pretty lunchtime snack or a starter. If you cut up the bruschettas into small pieces they make a good warm canapé.

Serves 4

2 red and 2 yellow peppers	**1 tbsp balsamic vinegar**	**8 small slices crusty bread**
3 cloves garlic	**salt, black pepper**	**fresh basil leaves**
2 tbsp olive oil	**½ tsp sweet paprika**	

- Halve peppers and grill. Peel, slice and put into a small pan.
- Finely crush 2 garlic cloves and add to pan with half the oil, the vinegar, seasoning and paprika. Cook over medium-low heat for 3–4 minutes, stirring once or twice.
- Toast the bread, then brush with remaining oil and the whole peeled clove of garlic. Top with pepper mixture and garnish with basil. Serve immediately so the bread doesn't go soft.

SWEET PEPPER SALSA

Good as a dip or to accompany grilled chicken, steak or burgers.

Serves 4

2 red peppers
2 tbsp olive oil
2 tomatoes
1 small red onion
juice of 1 lime
2 tbsp fresh chopped coriander leaves

- Halve peppers, brush with a little oil and roast for 25 minutes. Remove skin, chop peppers and put into a serving dish.
- Peel, de-seed and chop tomatoes, finely chop onion and add to peppers.
- Combine remaining oil with lime juice and stir into peppers and tomato.
- Serve decorated with coriander.

ROMESCO SAUCE

This truly versatile, traditional Spanish red pepper and almond sauce is perfect with grilled fresh tuna or white fish, as a pasta sauce, stirred into a fish stew or as a dip. Thinned down with passata (page 153), it even becomes a hot or cold soup.

Serves 4

3 red peppers
2 medium-hot red chillies
2 tomatoes
5 tbsp olive oil
1 clove garlic
2 tbsp red wine vinegar
1 tbsp water
salt, black pepper
50 g (2 oz) ground almonds

- Halve peppers, chillies and tomatoes, toss with a little of the oil and roast for 15 minutes. Remove pepper and tomato skins. Crush garlic.
- Put all ingredients except ground almonds in the bowl of a blender and blend until smooth. Stir in almonds and blend for another few seconds. Reheat gently to serve, or serve cold.

Peppers are native to South America, dating back around 5,000 years. They were introduced into Europe in the Middle Ages by Spanish and Portuguese explorers.

RED PEPPER AND ALMOND PESTO

This will keep in the fridge in a lidded container for a week or two. It is an ideal sauce for a pasta supper and a good addition to vegetable soups; it also makes an excellent toast topping. For best flavour, use a block of Parmesan and grate it yourself.

Serves 4

3 red peppers
25 g (1 oz) blanched almonds
2 cloves garlic
25 g (1 oz) grated Parmesan
1 tbsp sun-dried tomato paste
salt, black pepper
2 tbsp olive oil

- Halve and roast peppers, then peel. Crush almonds using a pestle and mortar or food processor so that they retain some crunch.
- Put peppers, garlic, cheese, tomato paste, seasoning and oil into a blender and blend for 30–60 seconds to combine. Stir in almonds and blend for a further 2 seconds.

ROAST RED PEPPER AND COUSCOUS SALAD

For a meal in itself you could add some feta, Mozzarella or cooked chicken pieces. Otherwise this goes well with a barbecue or as part of a buffet.

Serves 4

200 g (7 oz) couscous
200 ml (7 fl. oz) vegetable stock
2 red peppers
2 small courgettes
3 tbsp olive oil
salt, black pepper
8 spring onions
1 tbsp white wine vinegar

- Put couscous into a heatproof bowl, pour in stock, stir and allow to stand until stock is absorbed. Fluff up with a fork.
- Chop peppers into small pieces. Top, tail and chop courgettes. Fry in oil in a large pan over medium-high heat, stirring frequently, for 10 minutes or until soft and the courgettes are golden brown. Season, then stir in chopped spring onions and vinegar.
- Combine vegetable mixture with couscous and leave to stand for a few minutes. Serve warm or cold.

RED PEPPER SOUP

If you are serving this for a supper party, top it with a few toasted croutons spread with some red pepper and almond pesto (page 58).

Serves 4

6 red peppers	4 large tomatoes
1 onion	2 tbsp tomato purée
1 clove garlic	1.2 litres (2 pints)
1 tbsp olive oil	vegetable stock
1 potato	salt, black pepper

- Halve peppers, grill and peel.
- Sweat chopped onion and garlic in the oil over low heat for 5 minutes until softened but not coloured. Add diced potato and fry for a further minute.
- Add peeled tomatoes, tomato purée, peppers, stock and seasoning. Bring to the boil, cover and simmer for 20 minutes. Cool a little.
- Blend in a blender until smooth. Reheat to serve.

CHICKEN-STUFFED BAKED PEPPERS

An excellent way to turn peppers into an uncomplicated but tasty main meal.

Serves 4

2 large red peppers
3 tbsp olive oil
15 g (½ oz) butter
1 small onion
2 skinless chicken breast fillets
2 cloves garlic
2 tbsp basil pesto (page 161)
1 tomato
salt, black pepper
50 g (2 oz) breadcrumbs
1 egg yolk

- Halve peppers lengthwise, cutting through the stalk, and brush skins with some of the oil. Place on an oiled baking tray, cut-side up.
- Melt butter with 1 tbsp of the oil and fry finely chopped onion over medium-low heat to soften and tinge gold. Push to edges, add finely chopped chicken and stir for 3 minutes over medium heat.
- Add well-crushed garlic, pesto, chopped tomato and seasoning. Stir for a minute, then stir in half the breadcrumbs and the egg yolk.
- Spoon mixture into each pepper half, top with remaining breadcrumbs and drizzle remaining oil over.
- Cover and bake at 190°C/gas mark 5 for 35 minutes.

BEEF FAJITAS WITH RED PEPPERS

A supper that will please all the family.

Serves 4

250 g (9 oz) lean beef steak
1 tsp ground paprika
1 onion
2 red peppers
3 tbsp vegetable oil
1–2 medium-hot chillies
salt, black pepper
4 flour tortillas
4 tbsp chilli and tomato salsa (page 56)
4 tbsp sour cream

- Cut beef into long thin strips and coat with paprika. Fry thinly sliced onion and peppers in 2 tbsp of the oil over medium-high heat for approx. 10 minutes, stirring regularly, to soften and tinge gold. Add finely chopped chillies for last 3 minutes; season well.
- Remove vegetables from pan, add remaining oil and stir-fry beef over high heat for 2 minutes or until golden.
- Warm tortillas: microwave for 30 seconds or put on a heatproof plate covered in foil and heat in the oven for 5 minutes. Divide beef and vegetables between tortillas and add salsa to each. Roll up, then serve with sour cream.

CHILLI PEPPER RECIPES

CHILLI CON CARNE

For more heat add extra chillies and/or some Tabasco. Serve with boiled rice, jacket potatoes or Mexican flatbreads, plus sour cream and green salad. Sliced avocado also complements this well.

Serves 4

1 onion	400 g (14 oz) can
3 cloves garlic	chopped tomatoes
1 green pepper	2 tbsp tomato purée
2 tbsp olive oil	1 tbsp Worcestershire
450 g (1 lb) lean	sauce
minced beef	225 ml (8 fl. oz) strong
3–4 hot red chillies	beef stock
1 tsp ground cumin	200 g (7 oz) cooked
1 tsp ground coriander	red kidney beans
salt, black pepper	4 tbsp fresh coriander
1 glass red wine	4 wedges lime

- Finely chop onion and garlic, cut pepper into bite-sized pieces and sweat in oil over low heat to soften but not colour – approx. 8 minutes.
- Increase heat, push vegetables to side and add mince to brown, breaking down any chunks. Stir in finely chopped chillies, spices and seasoning.
- Pour in wine, bring to bubble and stir. Mix in the tomatoes, tomato purée, Worcestershire sauce and stock. Bring to a simmer, cover with lid and cook over gentle heat for 1 hour, stirring occasionally, until mixture is rich and a deep red-brown colour.
- Add kidney beans and cook for 20 minutes, uncovered. Check seasoning and serve, garnished with coriander and lime.

CHEESE-STUFFED CHILLIES

These make ideal nibbles with drinks. The recipe uses whole chillies, but you could also halve them and open-stuff, which looks nice on a canapé plate. Use chillies large enough to stuff easily.

Serves 4–6

12 large red chillies	1 tsp fresh chopped oregano
2 spring onions	½ tsp fresh chopped thyme
100 g (3½ oz) cream	salt, black pepper
cheese	

- Fry chillies. Set aside.
- Combine very finely chopped spring onions with remaining ingredients and spoon mixture into chillies.
- Eat as they are, or return to oven or low grill for a minute to warm through.

PRAWNS WITH CHILLI, GARLIC AND PARSLEY

The best prawns to use are giant ones weighing about 25 g (1 oz) each, but you can use smaller ones. If your prawns are already cooked, just add them to the pan for the last minute of cooking.

Serves 4

20 prawns	juice of 1 lemon
50 g (2 oz) butter	4 tbsp fresh chopped
1 tbsp groundnut oil	parsley
3–4 medium-hot red	black pepper
chillies	4 lemon wedges
5 cloves garlic	

- Shell prawns, leaving tails on. Make an incision down the backs to remove the dark membrane. Pat dry.
- Heat butter and oil in a pan and fry finely chopped chillies and garlic over medium heat for 1 minute. Add prawns and stir-fry until nearly cooked through: 2–5 minutes, depending on size.
- Stir in lemon juice and parsley and continue cooking for approx. 2 minutes more until prawns are done. Serve garnished with black pepper and lemon wedges.

SWEET CHILLI SAUCE

A glut of chillies can be used to make quantities of this tangy sauce. Use it as a dip, serve with Thai fishcakes or add to stir-fries or grilled meats and fish. Hot chillies work best. The sauce will keep for several weeks in the fridge.

Makes 250 ml (8 fl. oz)

6–8 red chillies	1 cm (½ in.) piece fresh ginger
1 clove garlic	1 tbsp Thai fish sauce
125 ml (4 fl. oz) rice	pinch salt
wine vinegar	1 tbsp arrowroot
125 g (4 oz) caster sugar	

- Finely chop chillies. Crush then finely chop garlic.
- Heat vinegar and sugar in a saucepan with 100 ml (3½ fl. oz) water, stirring until sugar is dissolved. Stir in chillies, garlic, chopped ginger, fish sauce and salt. Bring to a simmer and cook for 5 minutes.
- Mix arrowroot with a little cold water and add to pan, stirring in thoroughly. Bring back to a simmer, then remove from heat. Check seasoning and add a little more salt if necessary. Cool before use.

MEXICAN MOLE

This traditional recipe contains chocolate alongside chillies – a common combination in Mexican cooking. Serve with rice or flatbreads.

Serves 4

2–3 tbsp vegetable oil
8 red chillies
6 tomatoes
50 g (2 oz) raisins
1 onion
3 cloves garlic
40 g (1½ oz) toasted flaked almonds
25 g (1 oz) toasted sesame seeds
1 tsp each ground coriander, ground
   cinnamon and black pepper
150 ml (¼ pint) chicken stock
50 g (2 oz) dark chocolate
8 chicken leg pieces

- Brush a pan with a little of the oil and stir roughly chopped chillies over medium heat for a minute to colour slightly. Soak raisins in enough warm water to cover.

- Add chillies to a blender with chopped onion and garlic, almonds, sesame seeds, spices, pepper and 2 tbsp of the stock. Blend to a paste.

- Melt chocolate in a bowl over simmering water and fry drained raisins in a little more of the oil over medium heat for 2 minutes. Remove and reserve.

- Add a little more oil to pan and fry chilli paste for a minute, then stir in remaining stock, the peeled, chopped tomatoes and the raisins. Simmer for 15 minutes, then add melted chocolate.

- Brown chicken in remaining oil in a flameproof casserole over high heat (you may have to do this in batches). Pour sauce over and bake at 180°C/gas mark 4 for 40 minutes.

SPAGHETTI WITH CHILLI AND GARLIC

You are unlikely to find a simpler cooked savoury recipe than this. If you can use new season's garlic, so much the better. Add anchovies or Parmesan to serve if liked, but it doesn't really need them.

Serves 4

400 g (14 oz) spaghetti
100 ml (3½ fl. oz) olive oil
4 cloves garlic

2 or more hot red chillies
2 tbsp fresh chopped
   flat-leaf parsley

- Cook spaghetti and drain.

- Heat oil in a large pan and add finely chopped garlic and chilli. Sweat over medium-low heat for 3–4 minutes until garlic is tinged gold. Remove pan from heat immediately.

- When spaghetti is ready, return garlic and chilli oil pan to heat, add spaghetti and parsley and toss for a minute.

CHILLI CRAB CAKES

These are nice served with green salad and a sweet chilli sauce (page 60) as a main course or starter. Use fresh or frozen crab meat. If using frozen, make sure the brown meat is not waterlogged – place in a colander over a bowl and allow to drain for at least 15 minutes.

Serves 4 as main course, 6 as starter

300 g (11 oz) white
   crab meat
100 g (3½ oz) brown
   crab meat
100 g (3½ oz) stale
   white bread
2 or more hot red chillies
8 large spring onions
salt, black pepper
juice of 1 lime

1 tbsp Thai green curry
   paste
4 tbsp fresh chopped
   coriander leaves
2 tbsp fresh chopped
   parsley
1 tbsp Thai fish sauce
2 eggs
1 tbsp flour
2 tbsp groundnut oil

- Combine crab meats in a large bowl. Use a food processor to make bread into crumbs and add half to crab meat. Add finely chopped chillies and chopped spring onions to the bowl, season and stir well.

- Add lime juice, curry paste, coriander, parsley and fish sauce and thoroughly combine.

- Beat eggs in a bowl and add a quarter to the chilli crab bowl, stirring until mixture starts to bind. If this doesn't happen, add a little more egg until it does. Set aside leftover egg.

- Using your hands, form mixture into 12 patties and put on plate. Dust with flour, cover lightly with clingfilm and chill for 30 minutes.

- Heat oil in a large frying pan and dip each cake into first the beaten egg and then the crumbs. Fry over medium-hot heat for 2 minutes each side until golden.

CARROT

Carrots are one of our most popular and versatile vegetables. They can be used raw or cooked, lend richness, flavour and colour to soups and stews, are an ideal side vegetable and can even be used in baking and for jam. You can start pulling up baby carrots in summer – successional sowing means you can harvest them until Christmas.

STORING

Don't wash, allow to dry after digging and remove dirt with a soft brush. Cut leaves 1 cm (½ in.) above crowns. Place between layers of sand or dry compost in boxes. Store in a dry shed. Inspect monthly – should keep until March.

Maincrop carrots will store for up to 2 weeks in plastic bags in the fridge – airholes in the bags will help. Baby carrots will keep for more like a week.

Freeze young carrots whole: wash, trim, blanch for 2–3 minutes and bag. Wash, peel, slice and blanch large ones for 3–4 minutes before freezing.

NO COOKING REQUIRED

Raw, tender carrots are an excellent ingredient in winter salads such as coleslaw, or simply grated and tossed with French dressing (page 250). Their crunchiness makes them an ideal crudité.

CARROT SLAW

Try this instead of a cabbage coleslaw with ham or cheese. You can omit apricots, or use 2 tbsp sultanas.

Serves 4

2–3 carrots	salt, black pepper
4 dried apricots	2 tsp sesame seeds
3 tbsp olive oil	1 tbsp sunflower seeds
juice of ½ orange	

- Grate carrots, finely chop apricots and combine.
- Mix oil with orange juice and seasoning. Stir seeds into dressing and pour over carrots, stirring well.

CARROT AND CORIANDER SALAD

The salad is improved if you use a mandoline to produce long, very thin, ribbon-like strips of carrot.

Serves 4

2–3 carrots	1 tsp coriander seeds
juice of 1 lemon	salt, black pepper
1 tbsp light olive oil	3 tbsp fresh coriander
1 tbsp sesame oil	leaves

- Grate carrots into a bowl. Combine lemon juice, oils, lightly crushed seeds and seasoning. Stir into carrots. Leave for 30 minutes. Stir in coriander leaves.

BASIC COOKING

Wash baby carrots and scrub with a brush if necessary. Leave the lower 2.5 cm (1 in.) of leaves on if you like. Older carrots should be washed, topped and tailed, peeled and cut up as required. Cooking time varies depending on age and size of pieces. Carrots are cooked when easily pierced with a sharp knife.

BOILED CARROTS

Put into hot, lightly salted water to barely cover, bring to the boil and simmer for 5–15 minutes. Drain and toss with butter or olive oil and black pepper.

STEAMED CARROTS

Put in a steamer over boiling water and steam for 15–25 minutes. Season and serve tossed in butter or olive oil.

ROAST CARROTS

Use baby carrots, or cut maincrop carrots into large, even chunks. Toss in olive or vegetable oil and seasoning – adding fresh herbs such as sage if you like. Roast at 190°C/gas mark 5 for 40 minutes. Roasting time can be reduced by 10–15 minutes if carrots are blanched for 3 minutes first.

STIR-FRIED CARROTS

Cut carrots into thin strips. Stir-fry for 3 minutes in 1 tbsp vegetable oil for every 250 g (9 oz) carrots. Season and add spices or herbs – crushed cumin seeds work well.

PURÉED CARROTS

Boil or steam carrots until very tender, drain and either mash thoroughly with 10 g (¼ oz) butter per 100 g (3½ oz) carrots and seasoning, or purée in a blender with butter, seasoning and a dash of cooking water.

CARROT RECIPES

HONEY-GLAZED BABY CARROTS

Vary this recipe by using orange juice instead of lemon. Omit the ginger if you prefer.

Serves 4

500 g (1¼ lb) baby carrots	**2 tbsp runny honey**	**1 cm (½ in.) piece fresh ginger**
2 tbsp vegetable oil	**juice of ½ lemon**	**salt, black pepper**

- Boil carrots until tender; drain.
- Heat oil in a pan over medium heat, add honey and stir for a minute to combine. Add lemon juice and finely chopped ginger, season and stir again for a minute.
- Add carrots to pan, stir to coat and warm through for 2 minutes. Serve with extra black pepper ground over.

Carrots go well with cumin, coriander, nutmeg, sugar, butter, vinegar, oranges and peas.

CARROT AND SWEDE MASH

This sweet, colourful root mash can be used as a change from potato mash and goes well with most beef and lamb dishes.

Serves 4

4 carrots
1 small swede
15 g (½ oz) butter
1 tbsp vegetable oil
⅓ tsp ground nutmeg
salt, black pepper

- Peel and dice carrots and swede, then boil in the same pan until tender – approx. 15 minutes. Drain, reserving 1 tbsp of the cooking water.
- Add remaining ingredients to pan and mash thoroughly.

ROOT VEGETABLE GRATIN

This makes a nice supper on its own – or, for hungry people, serve it as an accompaniment to meat or even grilled fish.

Serves 4–6

4 carrots
3 parsnips
1 large potato
2 large leeks
150 g (5 oz) Cheddar
2 cloves garlic
3 tbsp fresh chopped chives
½ tsp ground nutmeg
salt, black pepper
1 egg
300 ml (½ pint) milk
300 ml (½ pint) cream
5 tbsp breadcrumbs

- Layer thinly sliced carrots, parsnips, potato and leeks in a shallow, ovenproof dish, sprinkling two-thirds of the grated cheese, the finely chopped garlic, chives, nutmeg and seasoning between the layers.
- In a mixing bowl, beat the egg and whisk in the milk, cream and more seasoning, then pour over vegetables to just cover.
- Sprinkle with breadcrumbs and remaining cheese and bake at 180°C/gas mark 4 for 45 minutes.

ROASTED CARAMELIZED CARROTS AND ONIONS

A delicious way to serve carrots with a Sunday roast.

Serves 4–6

5 carrots
4 red onions
2 tbsp olive oil
50 g (2 oz) butter
1 tbsp soft brown sugar
3 tbsp red wine
1 tbsp fresh thyme leaves
1 tbsp balsamic vinegar

- Cut carrots into 2.5 cm (1 in.) chunks and blanch for 2 minutes; drain and dry.
- Cut peeled onions into eighths. Toss carrots and onions with oil and melted butter in a roasting tin on the hob to coat well.
- Stir in sugar, wine and thyme, then bring to bubble. Add vinegar, stirring well. Cover with foil and roast at 170°C/gas mark 3½ for 40 minutes, or until vegetables are cooked, stirring once or twice.

CARROT AND ORANGE SOUP

A refreshing light soup which makes a good starter for a winter meal as it isn't too filling.

Serves 4

1 onion
1 leek
2 tbsp vegetable oil
5 carrots
½ tsp ground nutmeg
½ tsp ground coriander
1 litre (1¾ pints) vegetable stock
salt, black pepper
1 tsp sugar
1 large orange
salt, black pepper

- Sweat chopped onion and leek in oil over low heat to soften but not colour. Add chopped carrots, nutmeg and coriander, and stir for a minute.
- Add stock, seasoning and sugar. Grate zest from half the orange and add to pan. Bring to a simmer and cook for 30 minutes. Stir in orange juice.
- Cool a little, then blend in a blender until smooth. Reheat, checking seasoning.

75% of Britons say they eat carrots regularly: we crunch our way through more than 10 billion carrots each year.

CARROT AND CORIANDER SOUP

This is one of the best-known carrot soups, with a good, fresh taste. Swirl in some single cream before serving if you prefer a richer flavour.

Serves 4

1 tbsp vegetable oil	salt, black pepper
1 onion	4 tbsp fresh coriander
500 g (1¼ lb) carrots	leaves
1 tsp ground coriander	
1.2 litres (2 pints) vegetable stock	

- Sweat finely chopped onion in oil over low heat to soften but not colour. Add sliced carrots and ground coriander and stir for a minute.
- Pour in stock, season and bring to a simmer. Cook for 20 minutes or until vegetables are tender. Blend in a blender until smooth. Check seasoning, stir in coriander leaves and serve.

SWEET POTATO-TOPPED VEGETABLE PIE

Another recipe for the thrifty cook as it contains no meat but is packed with nutrients. The red and orange colours and the velvety topping make the pie mouthwatering.

Serves 4

1 large onion
1 tbsp olive oil
2 large carrots
400 ml (14 fl. oz) vegetable stock
200 g (7 oz) yellow dried split peas
400 g (14 oz) tomatoes
2 tsp dried mixed herbs
½ tsp ground cumin
salt, black pepper
3 sweet potatoes
25 g (1 oz) butter
75 g (3 oz) Cheddar

- In a lidded pan, sweat finely chopped onion in oil over medium-low heat for 5 minutes to soften but not colour.
- Add finely chopped carrots, stock, split peas, chopped tomatoes, herbs, cumin and seasoning. Bring to a simmer, put lid on and cook for 30 minutes or until split peas are well cooked. The mixture should not be too sloppy as it needs to support a potato topping. If it is, cook for a little longer with the lid off.
- Meanwhile, peel and chop sweet potatoes and boil for 15 minutes or until tender. Drain and mash with butter and seasoning. Pile vegetable mixture into a pie dish, smooth mash over, then sprinkle on grated cheese. Bake at 190°C/gas mark 5 for 20 minutes.

CARROT LATKES

Latkes are small potato pancakes traditional to Jewish cuisine. Try the carrot version for something different. They are usually made with matzo meal, which you can buy in specialist shops, but you can use fine white breadcrumbs or half breadcrumbs, half plain flour instead.

Serves 4–6

450 g (1 lb) carrots
2 shallots
2 eggs
salt, black pepper
75 g (3 oz) matzo meal
vegetable oil for frying
4–6 tbsp sour cream

- Grate carrots and shallots. Drain in sieve/kitchen paper to dry. Beat eggs in a bowl with seasoning. Add the vegetables and matzo meal, stir well and leave to stand for 10 minutes. Stir again to make a firm dropping consistency, adding a little more matzo if necessary.
- Drop spoonfuls of the mixture into shallow, very hot oil in a large, deep frying pan and fry until both sides are golden brown – approx. 3 minutes. Remove with a slotted spoon on to kitchen paper to drain. Serve with sour cream.

VEGETABLE BOLOGNESE SAUCE

A good and quick alternative to meat bolognese sauce. It does have a rich 'meaty' flavour and so is a great way of getting children to enjoy their vegetables.

Serves 4

1 onion	400 g (14 oz) chopped tomatoes
1 clove garlic	1 vegetable stock cube
1 tbsp olive oil	1 tbsp Worcestershire sauce
3 carrots	1 tbsp sun-dried tomato paste
1 courgette	2 tbsp fresh chopped parsley
4 mushrooms	salt, black pepper
150 g (5 oz) brown lentils	

- Sweat very finely chopped onion and garlic in half the oil over low heat to soften but not colour. Add finely chopped carrots, courgette and mushrooms with the remaining oil and stir for a minute. Add the remaining ingredients, stir well and add enough water to cover.
- Bring to a simmer, cover and cook for 1 hour, checking every 15 minutes and adding a little more water if the mixture looks too dry (the lentils will absorb liquid). Check seasoning.

BEEF AND CARROT HOTPOT

To make a change, you could use neck of lamb or even shoulder of pork for this recipe instead of the beef.

Serves 4

500 g (1¼ lb) lean braising beef
2 tbsp oil
1 large onion
4 carrots
600 g (1 lb 6 oz) potato
1 beef stock cube
400 g (14 oz) can chopped tomatoes
400 g (14 oz) can cannellini beans
1 tbsp Worcestershire sauce
salt, black pepper
2 tbsp fresh chopped parsley

- Cut beef into small 1 cm (½ in.) cubes and fry in half the oil over high heat for 3 minutes to brown all sides. Remove from pan.
- Add chopped onion to pan with remaining oil and sweat over low heat to soften but not colour.
- Add carrots, cut into thick rounds, diced potato, crumbled stock cube, tomatoes, drained and rinsed beans, Worcestershire sauce and seasoning. Stir well and add water to just cover.
- Bring to a simmer, put lid on and cook for 1 hour or until meat is tender. Sprinkle with parsley to serve.

CARROT FRITTERS

This recipe is one very good way to get children eating up their carrots – but adults will love the fritters too. Serve with salad and a few chips.

Serves 4

600g (1 lb 6 oz) carrots	2 eggs
1 onion	50 ml (2 fl. oz) single cream
100 g (3½ oz) Cheddar	
1 tsp ground cumin	200 ml (7 fl. oz) milk
salt, black pepper	3 tbsp vegetable oil
3 tbsp flour	

- Coarsely grate carrots and onion and put into a bowl. Stir in grated cheese, cumin and seasoning.
- Put flour in another bowl and gradually beat in eggs, then cream and finally milk. Add more seasoning and combine well with carrot mixture.
- Put 8 large spoonfuls of mixture into a large frying pan and fry in oil over medium-high heat for approx. 3 minutes each side or until golden brown.

CARROT BREAD

A delicious, semi-sweet loaf that is good as an accompaniment to cheese, ham or chicken salad, or as part of a dinner-party bread basket.

Makes 1 x 1 kg loaf (16 slices)

400 g (14 oz) carrots	2 tsp salt
2 shallots	1 sachet easy-blend dried yeast
400 g (14 oz) strong white bread flour	125 ml (4 fl. oz) milk
150 g (5 oz) wholemeal flour	1 tbsp vegetable oil
	1 egg

- Finely grate half the carrots and the shallots. Dice remaining carrots and boil. Drain well and purée.
- Combine flours, salt and yeast. Combine milk with 125 ml (4 fl. oz) warm water and add carrot purée and oil. Stir well.
- Combine dry and wet mixtures to make a dough, then knead on a lightly floured surface for 10 minutes or until smooth. Place inside an oiled bowl and cover with a tea-towel. Leave in a warm place to double in volume – approx. 1 hour.
- Knock back dough on a floured surface, sprinkle grated carrot and shallot on the dough and knead for 2–3 minutes to combine. Shape into a round. Put on an oiled baking sheet, cover with a tea-towel and leave for a further 45 minutes to rise.
- Heat oven to 200°C/gas mark 6, brush top of loaf with beaten egg and bake for 30 minutes or until golden and the base of the loaf sounds hollow when tapped with your knuckles. Cool on a wire rack.

CARROT MUFFINS

This recipe makes little moist muffins ideal for lunchboxes or kids' tea parties, and they freeze very well too. Try to use a very light, flavourless oil. Walnuts make a pretty decoration.

Makes 24 x 100 g (3½ oz) muffins

300 g (11 oz) plain flour
150 g (5 oz) wholemeal flour
1 tbsp bicarbonate of soda
1 tbsp ground cinnamon
300 g (11 oz) caster sugar
300 ml (½ pint) vegetable oil
5 eggs
1 tbsp vanilla extract
150 g (5 oz) walnut pieces
150 g (5 oz) sultanas
300 g (11 oz) carrots
250 g (9 oz) can pineapple pieces
200 g (7 oz) cream cheese icing (page 250)

- Preheat oven to 180°C/gas mark 4. Sift first 5 ingredients into a bowl.

- Beat in oil, eggs and vanilla. Stir in walnuts, sultanas, grated carrot and drained pineapple.

- Divide mixture between muffin cases and bake for 10–15 minutes or until golden and a skewer inserted in the centre comes out clean. Cool for 30 minutes in their tins, then spoon a little cream cheese icing on top of each muffin.

CARROT CAKE

You will find several versions of carrot cake. If liked, you can add either 100 g (3½ oz) sultanas or walnut pieces to this basic mixture when you add the carrot. Ice with cream cheese icing (page 250).

Makes 12–15 slices

175 g (6 oz) soft brown sugar
175 ml (6 fl. oz) vegetable oil
3 eggs
3 carrots
juice of ½ orange
175 g (6 oz) self-raising flour
1 tsp bicarbonate of soda
1 tsp ground cinnamon
⅓ tsp ground nutmeg

- Grease and line an 18 cm (7 in.) square or 20 cm (8 in.) round cake tin with lightly greased baking parchment.

- Beat together sugar, oil and eggs. Grate carrot and stir into mixture with orange juice.

- In another bowl, combine flour, bicarbonate of soda and spices, then sift into the carrot bowl and combine. Pour into tin and bake at 180°C/gas mark 4 for 40 minutes or until cake feels firm yet springy when middle is pressed.

- Cool for 10 minutes, turn out on to a wire rack and cool further.

CARROT WINE

There are many different recipes for carrot wine – sometimes called carrot whisky. This is a simple one.

Makes 6 x 75 cl (1¼ pint) bottles

2 kg (4½ lb) carrots	juice of 2 lemons
50 g (2 oz) piece fresh ginger	juice of 2 oranges
	1 pack wine yeast
1 cinnamon stick	4.5 litres (8 pints) water
2 kg (4½ lb) sugar	

- Grate carrots and ginger and put into a very large pan with the cinnamon stick. Pour water over, then boil for approx. 20 minutes. Strain through muslin into a clean bucket.

- Add sugar and juices while still hot and stir until sugar has dissolved. Allow to cool to blood temperature, then add yeast.

- Allow to ferment for 24 hours, then transfer to a demijohn and leave until fermentation stops – 2–3 weeks. Add a campden tablet and allow yeast to settle. When clear, filter into bottles and leave for a year to mature.

CAULIFLOWER

Cauliflowers are members of the cabbage family (brassicas). The large, tightly packed flower heads are usually creamy white, but you can grow purple varieties. The green types are normally classed with calabrese (broccoli).

New varieties mean you can harvest cauliflower for much of the year, and it is useful for late winter and very early spring when there are few green vegetables around. While the familiar ways of cooking this surprisingly delicate vegetable are plain boiled or in a cheese sauce, it lends itself to a variety of excellent recipes. Like cabbage, overcooked cauliflower can impart unpleasant sulphur aromas, so it is best lightly cooked. The green leaves near the head are edible.

STORING

Cauliflowers are quick to deteriorate. Heads that are uniformly pale cream are in good condition – brown mottling, yellow leaves or limpness mean the vegetable is past its best. Store in a plastic bag with airholes in the fridge for up to a week.

Florets freeze very well: blanch for 2 minutes, drain, cool, then freeze in bags. To save space you can also purée it before you freeze (see below).

NO COOKING REQUIRED

Fresh small florets can be eaten raw – perhaps as a crudité – or tossed in a French dressing (page 250) with garlic and shredded carrot as a side salad.

BASIC COOKING

BOILED CAULIFLOWER

Put florets in lightly salted boiling water to come halfway up the florets and boil for 5–7 minutes, depending on size. Drain.

STEAMED CAULIFLOWER

Put florets in a steamer over a pan of boiling water and steam for 8–15 minutes, depending on size.

STIR-FRIED CAULIFLOWER

Slice florets lengthwise into 1 cm (½ in.) pieces. Stir-fry in 1 tbsp vegetable or olive oil per 200 g (7 oz) cauliflower over high heat until golden and tender with a little bite. Season.

ROAST CAULIFLOWER

Blanch medium–large florets for 3 minutes, drain and dry on kitchen paper. Toss in a bowl with 1 tbsp vegetable oil per 200 g (7 oz) cauliflower and 15 g (½ oz) melted butter. Season. You can add 1 tsp curry powder or well-crushed coriander seeds. Roast at 190°C/gas mark 5 for 20 minutes or until browned and tender.

SPICED CAULIFLOWER

Stir-fry 1 tsp each ground cumin, turmeric, chilli and coriander in 2 tbsp vegetable oil over medium heat for 30 seconds. Add small cauliflower florets and fry for 2 minutes. Add 25 g (1 oz) butter and 100 ml (3½ fl.oz) vegetable stock and simmer, uncovered, for 7 minutes.

PURÉED CAULIFLOWER

Chop a head of cauliflower into small florets and put in a pan with vegetable stock or water to just cover and 15 g (½ oz) butter. Season, cover and bring to a simmer, then remove lid and cook for 5 minutes or until tender and all but 2 tbsp of liquid has evaporated. Add 15 g (½ oz) butter to pan and stir until it is melted. Transfer pan contents to a liquidizer and blend until smooth. Check seasoning and serve.

CAULIFLOWER RECIPES

CAULIFLOWER CHEESE

There is little to beat this long-time favourite as an accompaniment to roast beef or gammon, or as a supper on its own. It's crucial not to over-boil the cauliflower or it will lose shape or break up in the final cooking stages. Add some breadcrumbs to the cheese topping if you like a bit more crunch, but it isn't traditional.

Serves 4

1 large head cauliflower	150 g (5 oz) Cheddar
salt	400 ml (14 fl. oz) white
½ tsp English mustard powder	sauce (page 251)

- Divide cauliflower into medium–large florets and boil in salted water until nearly tender.

- Drain immediately and refresh under cold running water. Drain again and dry pieces on kitchen paper, then arrange, flower heads up, in an ovenproof dish.

- Stir mustard and two-thirds of the grated cheese into warmed white sauce to melt. Pour evenly over cauliflower to cover all the tops. Sprinkle remaining cheese over and bake at 190°C/gas mark 5 for 25 minutes or until top is golden and bubbling.

CREAM OF CAULIFLOWER SOUP

For a vegetable which, some say, has a strong flavour, this is a particularly delicate and smooth soup that could convert any cauliflower-hater. For a dinner party or special supper, crumble crisp bacon on top to serve.

Serves 4

1 onion	200 ml (7 fl. oz) milk
25 g (1 oz) butter	½ tsp freshly
1 head cauliflower	ground nutmeg
1 floury potato	1 bay leaf
(approx. 200 g/7 oz)	100 ml (3½ fl. oz)
salt, black pepper	single cream
900 ml (1½ pints)	
vegetable stock	

- Sweat finely chopped onion in butter over low heat for 5 minutes to soften but not colour. Divide cauliflower into small florets, peel and dice potato and stir into pan with seasoning. Cook for 2 minutes, stirring – make sure nothing browns.
- Pour in stock, turn heat up, bring to a simmer, then add milk, nutmeg and bay leaf. Bring back to a simmer, stir, turn heat down low and cook for 20 minutes or until vegetables are tender.
- Cool a little, remove bay leaf and blend in a blender until smooth. Return to pan, stir in cream and reheat gently. Check seasoning.

CAULIFLOWER, GARLIC AND SAFFRON

When you've had enough of cauliflower plain, boiled or in cheese sauce, this unusual combination is well worth trying. Great with grilled chicken or roast lamb.

Serves 4

1 tsp saffron threads	3 tbsp olive oil
75 g (3 oz) raisins	2 cloves garlic
1 cauliflower	25 g (1 oz) toasted pine nuts
1 onion	salt, black pepper

- Stir saffron into 3 tbsp boiling water in a small dish and set aside. Soak raisins in enough hot water to cover. Divide cauliflower into medium florets, blanch for 3 minutes, drain and dry.
- Sweat finely chopped onion over low heat in 2 tbsp of the oil to soften. Turn heat up and stir for a minute to brown very lightly, then remove onion from pan with a slotted spoon.
- Add cauliflower to pan and stir over medium-high heat for 2–3 minutes to colour lightly, adding finely chopped garlic for last minute. Return onion to pan with saffron water, pine nuts, drained raisins and seasoning. Stir well, turn heat down and simmer for 2 minutes or until most of the liquid has gone.

CAULIFLOWER, SQUASH AND GREEN BEAN CURRY

Try serving this with natural yogurt and mango chutney. For a hotter curry, leave the chilli seeds in.

Serves 4

1 small onion	1 small head cauliflower
4 cloves garlic	1 small butternut squash
5 cm (2 in.) piece	100 g (3½ oz) French beans
fresh ginger	2 tomatoes
2 hot chillies	juice of ½ lemon
2 tsp ground cumin	200 ml (7 fl. oz) vegetable
1 tsp ground turmeric	stock
½ tsp chilli powder	salt, black pepper
2 tbsp vegetable oil	

- Roughly chop onion, garlic, ginger and chillies, then add to a blender with spices and 1 tbsp of the oil. Blend to a paste. Divide cauliflower into medium–large florets. Peel, de-seed and chop squash into 2.5 cm (1 in.) chunks and halve beans.
- Fry paste for a minute in remaining oil in a large, lidded pan over medium heat to release aromas. Add chopped tomatoes, lemon juice, stock and seasoning. Stir, add vegetables and bring to a simmer. Put lid on. Reduce heat and cook for 20 minutes. Remove lid, stir and cook for a further 10 minutes or until you have a thick sauce.

CRISPY VEGETABLE PIE

Using sliced potatoes for a pie topping is a pretty alternative to pastry and also very easy to do.

Serves 4

1 head cauliflower	salt, black pepper
100 g (3½ oz) broccoli	1 tsp mustard powder
1 carrot	150 g (5 oz) Cheddar
2 baking potatoes	400 ml (14 fl. oz) white
100 g (3½ oz) peas	sauce (page 251)

- Cut cauliflower and broccoli into small–medium florets. Dice carrot into 1 cm (½ in.) pieces. Peel potatoes, cut into 0.5 cm (¼ in.) rounds and boil in a large pan of salted water for 5 minutes, steaming all other vegetables over the potatoes. All vegetables should be just tender.
- Drain potatoes and reserve one third. Arrange the remaining potatoes and all the other vegetables in an ovenproof dish. Season.
- Stir mustard and two-thirds of the grated cheese into warmed white sauce, then pour over the vegetables. Stir so sauce reaches base of dish. Lay remaining potato slices on top, slightly overlapping.
- Sprinkle on remaining cheese and bake at 200°C/ gas mark 6 for 20 minutes or until top is golden.

CAULIFLOWER FRITTERS

Frying alters the flavour of cauliflower, so try this dish if your family doesn't enjoy the boiled version.

Serves 4

1 small head cauliflower
1 egg
125 g (4 oz) plain flour
pinch salt
vegetable oil for frying
100 g (3½ oz) mayonnaise
2 tsp mild curry paste
squeeze of lemon juice

- Blanch small cauliflower florets for 3–4 minutes until barely tender. Refresh under cold running water and dry on kitchen paper.
- Beat egg with 100 ml (3½ fl. oz) cold water, then stir in flour and salt and combine until smooth.
- Pour oil either into a deep-fat fryer to come halfway up, or into a large, deep frying pan to come 2 cm (¾ in.) up the side. Heat to 180°C or until a cube of bread dropped in turns golden in 30 seconds.
- Dip florets into batter and lower into the hot oil with a long-handled spoon, in batches if need be. Fry for 3 minutes or until crisp and golden. Remove using a slotted spoon and drain on kitchen paper.
- Thoroughly combine mayonnaise, curry paste and lemon juice and serve with the fritters.

CAULIFLOWER PILAFF

An easy, one-pot, meat-free, curry-type supper. Meat-lovers could always stir in some chopped leftover roast lamb towards the end of cooking.

Serves 4

1 head cauliflower	400 g (14 oz) can
1 onion	chopped tomatoes
2 tbsp vegetable oil	400 g (14 oz) can
2 tbsp balti curry paste	brown or green lentils
200 g (7 oz) basmati rice	900 ml (1½ pints)
75 g (3 oz) peas	vegetable stock

- Cut cauliflower into small–medium florets and blanch for 2 minutes; drain.
- Sweat finely chopped onion in oil in a lidded pan over low heat to soften but not colour. Increase heat to medium, add cauliflower and stir for a minute to colour lightly. Add curry paste and stir again to release aromas. Add rice and stir to coat.
- Add peas, chopped tomatoes, lentils and most of the stock, stirring everything well. Bring to a simmer, put lid on and cook for 25 minutes, stirring occasionally. Towards the end of cooking add remaining stock if pan looks dry. When rice is tender most of the stock should have been absorbed but the pilaff should still be moist.

CAULIFLOWER WITH PASTA, NUTS AND CHEESE

Pasta and cauliflower sound an unlikely combination, but they blend very well. If you happen to have a purple cauliflower, use that. Fontina is a tasty Italian cheese but you can use Taleggio or goat's cheese.

Serves 4

300 g (11 oz) penne	juice of ½ lemon
5 tbsp olive oil	50 g (2 oz) toasted
1 head cauliflower	flaked almonds
12 spring onions	75 g (3 oz) Fontina
4 cloves garlic	4 tbsp grated Parmesan
salt, black pepper	2 tbsp fresh chopped parsley

- Cook pasta, drain, toss in 1 tbsp oil and keep warm.
- Cut cauliflower into small florets, blanch for 2 minutes, drain and dry.
- Fry cauliflower in 2 tbsp of the oil in a large pan over medium-high heat for 4 minutes, season well and add chopped spring onions and finely chopped garlic. Fry over medium heat for a minute. Add lemon juice and nuts.
- Stir cauliflower mixture into hot pasta with Fontina cut into small pieces. Drizzle remaining oil over and sprinkle with Parmesan and parsley.

CELERIAC

Celeriac – sometimes called turnip-rooted celery – is a type of celery that produces a large, round, knobbly root to harvest from October to early spring. It has a thick skin and a creamy-white flesh with a flavour that is similar to, though milder than, celery. Celeriac makes a very useful addition to the winter kitchen as it can be boiled, mashed (on its own or with other roots such as potato, carrot or swede), braised or used in soups and stews. Roast celeriac chips make an interesting change from potato oven chips.

STORING

In most areas in normal winters you can leave celeriac in the ground – covered with soil or straw – until you want to lift it. Alternatively, lift in late autumn, twist off tops, cut off roots and store in boxes filled with compost or layered with newspaper. Store in a cool, dry outhouse. In the home, roots will keep for 2 weeks or so in a cool, dark, dry larder or in the fridge in a plastic bag with airholes. To freeze, peel, chop, blanch for 3 minutes and freeze in heavy-duty plastic bags.

NO COOKING REQUIRED

Grate the peeled root and use in winter salads.

CELERIAC REMOULADE

Combine 1 tbsp drained capers with 1 tbsp creamed horseradish sauce, 2 tbsp mayonnaise and 1 tbsp Dijon mustard. Peel and shred ½ celeriac and mix thoroughly with this dressing. Serve as an accompaniment to bacon or cold chicken, or stuffed in Parma ham.

BASIC COOKING

Scrub thoroughly to clean, then peel and cut into slices or chunks as required. Unless using immediately, put into water, adding 1 tbsp lemon juice to avoid the pieces turning brown.

BOILED CELERIAC

Boil in salted water to cover for 5–10 minutes, depending on chunk size; drain.

MASHED CELERIAC

Boil, drain thoroughly, then season and mash with 15 g (½ oz) butter for every 250 g (9 oz) celeriac.

Celery salt (a delicious seasoning for hard-boiled eggs) is in fact made from celeriac.

ROAST CELERIAC

Cut into chunks approx. 1 cm (½ in.) thick and 5 cm (2 in.) long. Toss in olive oil, arrange in a single layer in a roasting tin and season. Roast at 190°C/gas mark 5 for 40 minutes or until tender and golden, turning once.

Perfect partners for celeriac include roast lamb, chicken, thyme, chilli, garlic and cheese.

CELERIAC JULIENNES

Cut peeled celeriac into strips approx. 5 cm (2 in.) long and 0.5 cm (¼ in.) square. Blanch or steam for 2 minutes, refresh under cold running water and dry. Add to a frying pan with 15 g (½ oz) butter for every 250 g (9 oz) celeriac, a pinch of sugar and seasoning. Sweat over low heat for 10–15 minutes until tender. Serve with chopped parsley.

CELERIAC RECIPES

CREAM OF CELERIAC SOUP

The slight nuttiness of celeriac gives this simple yet fine winter soup a lovely taste.

Serves 4

1 celeriac	salt, black pepper
1 potato	4 tbsp single cream
1 large leek	2 tbsp fresh chopped chives
25 g (1 oz) butter	
1 litre (1¾ pints) vegetable stock	

- Peel celeriac and potato. Discard green section of leek. Chop all the vegetables and sweat in butter in a lidded pan for 5 minutes.
- Add stock and seasoning, bring to a simmer and cook for 25 minutes. Cool a little, then blend in a blender until smooth. Return to pan and reheat, adjusting seasoning to taste and stirring in cream.
- Serve garnished with chives.

PAN-BRAISED CELERIAC WITH ONIONS AND HERBS

An accompaniment to almost any roast, grilled or pan-fried meat, especially lamb, chicken or pork.

Serves 4

1 celeriac	1 tsp fresh chopped
1 small onion	rosemary
3 tbsp olive oil	salt, black pepper
2 cloves garlic	100 ml (3½ fl. oz)
1 tbsp fresh thyme leaves	vegetable stock
1 tbsp fresh chopped parsley	

- Peel celeriac and chop into 1 cm (½ in.) cubes. Fry with finely chopped onion in oil in a large, lidded pan over medium heat to soften and brown, stirring occasionally.
- Add chopped garlic, herbs and seasoning and stir for a minute.
- Add stock, turn heat down, put lid on and simmer for 20 minutes or until celeriac and onion are tender and there is still some liquid left.

CELERIAC AND POTATO GRATIN

An easy dish to make when you're cooking a roast or casserole. For a richer dish, substitute 50 ml (2 fl. oz) of the milk with cream.

Serves 4–6

75 g (3 oz) butter
3 floury potatoes
1 celeriac
½ tsp ground nutmeg
1 large clove garlic
salt, black pepper
250 ml (8 fl. oz) vegetable stock
200 ml (7 fl. oz) milk
2 tbsp grated Parmesan

- Grease a shallow baking dish with some of the butter. Peel potatoes and celeriac and cut into thin slices (no more than the thickness of a coin). Layer into the dish alternately, dotting with remaining butter and adding nutmeg, chopped garlic and seasoning as you go.
- Combine stock with milk and gently pour over the vegetables, then top with cheese. Bake at 200°C/gas mark 6 for 1 hour until golden and vegetables are tender when pierced with a sharp knife.

LAMB CHOP CASSEROLE WITH CELERIAC

An oven-cooked dish that makes a tasty change from grilled lamb chops. Good served with kale or spring greens.

Serves 4

8 lamb loin chops	1 tsp paprika
2 tbsp olive oil	1 tbsp fresh thyme leaves
1 onion	salt, black pepper
½ celeriac	200 ml (7 fl. oz) lamb stock
2 cloves garlic	

- Brown chops in a little of the oil in a flameproof casserole over high heat; remove and set aside. Slice onion and chop peeled celeriac into 1 cm (½ in.) cubes and fry in remaining oil over medium heat to soften and brown on all sides.
- Add chopped garlic, paprika, thyme and seasoning and stir for a minute. Return chops to casserole and pour stock over. Put on lid and cook at 170°C/gas mark 3½ for 1 hour or until everything is tender.

CELERY

With several new, easier-to-grow varieties of celery now available, more and more of us are bringing this distinctive vegetable into our kitchens. Celeries range from the classic, almost-white varieties, which need more care in the kitchen garden and have a fine flavour, through to the green-stalked, less-demanding kind and then to speciality red- and pink-stalked types. All are versatile and add plenty of flavour to many dishes both hot and cold, including soups, casseroles and salads. In general, the larger the stems, the tougher they are.

STORING

Trim roots, then put whole celery head into a plastic bag and store in the fridge for a week or more. It will go limp if not protected from the air. Celery can be chopped, blanched, bagged and frozen and will be fine for use in soups and casseroles.

NO COOKING REQUIRED

Celery is most often used raw in the UK and it is the classic accompaniment to the cheese board. Fresh, tender, crispy stalks make ideal party snacks cut into short lengths and filled with cream cheese. Chopped celery can be used in several salads – the flavour goes well with chicken, walnuts, grapes and apples, as well as cheese and many other salad items. For eating raw, use tender, crisp young stalks from the centre of the head with no 'string' – the membrane that appears on tougher outer stalks. Unblemished younger celery leaves can be left on the stalk to eat, or removed and used in any green salad or as a tasty garnish.

Dip celery leaves into a tempura batter and deep-fry until crisp. Use as a garnish for soups, grilled poultry or fish.

CRUDITÉS WITH BLUE CHEESE DIP

A classic party favourite and so easy to prepare. The soft blue cheeses Dolcelatte or St-Agur are both suitable. Combine cream, mayonnaise and pepper. Stir in cheese and chill for an hour. Top and tail carrots; cut carrot and celery into batons. Put the dip in a serving dish on a large plate and surround with the vegetables.

CELERY, GOAT'S CHEESE AND GRAPE SALAD

Arrange Cos lettuce leaves and chopped hearts on each of 4 plates. Dice 4–6 stalks celery and halve 100 g (3½ oz) red seedless grapes. Scatter over lettuce, then drizzle with French dressing (page 250). Grill four 75 g (3 oz) slices soft goat's cheese, with rind, for 3 minutes until cheese begins to bubble and turn gold. Remove immediately from heat and place in the centre of each plate. Drizzle with a little balsamic vinegar and top with walnut pieces and celery leaves. Serve with crusty bread.

CELERY, CARROT AND LENTIL SALAD

Cut 5 stalks celery and 2 carrots into small, bite-sized chunks. Halve and finely slice a small red onion. Toss vegetables and 150 g (5 oz) warm, cooked Puy lentils in 5 tbsp French dressing (page 250), then stir in 2 tbsp fresh chopped parsley. Goes well with strong cheese or ham, or makes a good addition to a party buffet.

WALDORF SALAD

This was invented at the New York Waldorf-Astoria Hotel in 1896. This version is close to the original but walnuts have been added. You can make a lighter version using half mayonnaise, half natural yogurt. Use crisp, slightly tart apples – Granny Smith or Cox are ideal.

Serves 4–6

3 apples	**5 stalks celery**	**75 g (3 oz) walnut pieces**
1 tbsp lemon juice	**75 ml (2½ fl. oz) mayonnaise**	**a few celery leaves**

- Core apples and chop into approx.1 cm (½ in.) pieces. Put in a serving bowl and sprinkle with lemon juice.

- Chop celery and combine all ingredients. Garnish with celery leaves.

BASIC COOKING

Slice off roots and tough base and trim off top of head to neaten and remove any damage. Discard tough or blemished outer stalks, or clean and use for making stock. Single stalks can be removed from the head by hand or with a knife. Scrub under running water to clean, moving up and down the stalk. Remove membrane from larger stalks if necessary, using a vegetable peeler or knife.

Celery hearts may need little cleaning. Halve or quarter them as the recipe requires.

BRAISED CELERY

Halve stalks crosswise and blanch for 5 minutes. Put in one layer in a buttered, lidded frying pan. Season, add 4–5 tbsp water, bring to a simmer, put lid on and braise for 45 minutes, or until tender when pierced.

STIR-FRIED CELERY

Slice stalks into thin batons approx. 5 cm (2 in.) long and fry in oil over high heat, stirring for 3–4 minutes or until just tender. Season.

> Celery seeds taste similar to fennel seeds and can be used as a seasoning.

CELERY RECIPES

CELERY À LA MILANAISE

A classic, rich recipe which goes well with firm, baked white fish or a roast game bird.

Serves 4

8–10 stalks celery	50 g (2 oz) butter
200 ml (7 fl. oz) vegetable stock	75 g (3 oz) grated Parmesan

- Quarter each celery stalk by halving lengthwise then cutting across. Add to saucepan with stock and simmer for 8 minutes; drain.
- Arrange half the celery in a small, shallow, ovenproof dish, greased with a little butter. Sprinkle with half the cheese.
- Add remaining celery and cheese, then melt remaining butter and pour over. Bake uncovered at 220°C/gas mark 7 for 10 minutes or until browned and tender.

TRADITIONAL BRAISED CELERY

Flavoursome braised celery is the essence of winter – a warming side dish for any meat, poultry or game.

Serves 4

2 celery hearts	15 g (½ oz) butter
1 large onion	300 ml (½ pint) chicken stock
2 carrots	salt, black pepper

- Cut each heart into four, lengthwise, and simmer in a little boiling salted water for 7 minutes; drain.
- Arrange sliced onion and carrot in a buttered flameproof casserole. Lay celery on top and pour stock over. Season to taste. Bring to a simmer, transfer to the oven and cook uncovered at 170°C/gas mark 3½ for 1 hour or until celery is tender and there is just a little liquid left in the casserole.
- Serve the celery hearts with the liquid poured over. Discard the remaining vegetables.

CREAM OF CELERY SOUP

A great way to use up a glut of celery – and a soup that is popular even with people who say they don't like the vegetable.

Serves 4

1 large onion
1 head celery
25 g (1 oz) butter
450 ml (¾ pint) vegetable stock
300 ml (½ pint) milk
1 bay leaf
salt, black pepper
2 tbsp single cream
2 tbsp fresh chopped celery leaves

- Chop onion and celery and sweat in butter in a large saucepan over low heat to soften but not colour.
- Add stock, milk and bay leaf, then season to taste. Bring to the boil, cover and simmer gently for 25 minutes.
- Cool a little, remove bay leaf, then blend in a blender. Return to pan, reheat and season to taste. Stir in cream and serve garnished with celery leaves.

> The white trench varieties of celery have the best flavour but they are not as easy to grow and tend to be more stringy than self-blanching varieties.

BAKED CELERY WITH BUTTERCRUNCH TOPPING

Baking celery reduces its strong flavour, making this dish with its delicious crunchy topping popular with children as well as adults. Serve it as a light supper or as a side dish. You can use celery stalks – approx. 700 g (1 lb 9 oz) – instead of the hearts.

Serves 4

2 large or 4 small celery hearts
1 small onion
1 bay leaf
200 ml (7 fl. oz) vegetable stock
50 g (2 oz) butter
1 tbsp flour
100 ml (3½ fl. oz) milk
salt, black pepper
50 g (2 oz) breadcrumbs
50 g (2 oz) mixed chopped nuts

- Cut celery hearts into 1 cm (½ in.) slices and put into a pan with sliced onion, bay leaf and stock. Bring to a simmer and cook for 20 minutes or until tender when pierced with a sharp knife.

- Drain celery, reserving cooking liquid and discarding onion and bay leaf. Arrange celery in a shallow, ovenproof dish greased with 10 g (¼ oz) of the butter.

- Melt 15 g (½ oz) of the butter in a saucepan over medium heat, add flour and stir to combine. Cook for a minute, stirring. Gradually stir in the reserved celery liquid mixed with the milk, until you have a smooth sauce. Season to taste and pour over celery.

- Melt remaining butter and stir in breadcrumbs to coat thoroughly, then stir until golden. Stir in nuts and scatter mixture over celery. Bake at 180°C/gas mark 4 for 20 minutes until top is golden and sauce bubbling.

> You can make a garnish of celery curls for fish or chicken by immersing thin strips of celery into ice-cold water for an hour or two.

BREASTS OF CHICKEN CASSEROLE WITH CELERY HEARTS

You could use pheasant or guinea fowl instead of chicken for this creamy, easy casserole, which brings out the best in both the bird and the celery. Good with steamed carrots and mashed potato.

Serves 4

1 onion
4 stalks celery
2 tbsp vegetable oil
15 g (½ oz) butter
1 celery heart
4 chicken breast fillets, skin on
salt, black pepper
300 ml (½ pint) chicken stock
1 tbsp flour
50 ml (2 fl. oz) single cream

- Finely chop onion and celery stalks and put into a flameproof casserole with half the oil and 1 tsp of the butter. Sweat over low heat to soften but not colour. Remove from pan.

- Quarter celery heart and add to pan with remaining oil. Stir over medium heat for 3–4 minutes to soften and tinge gold, then remove from pan.

- Turn heat to medium-high and brown chicken breasts in the pan, one or two at a time.

- Turn heat down and return everything to pan, then season and add stock. Bring to a simmer, put lid on and cook gently for 40 minutes.

- Make a roux by heating remaining butter in a saucepan over medium heat. Add flour and stir to combine. Cook for a minute, stirring. Remove chicken breasts and celery from casserole on to warm plates.

- Gradually pour liquid out of casserole dish into the roux, stirring until you have a smooth sauce. Add a little hot water if the sauce is not of pouring consistency. Cook for 2–3 minutes, then return to casserole and stir well to combine.

- Stir in cream. Serve with the chicken and celery.

CHICORY

The classic chicory (known as Belgian endive or *witloof* on the Continent) has smooth, tightly packed crisp leaves and forms flame-shaped, smallish heads (or 'chicon') with a refreshing, slightly bitter taste; the greener the leaves, the more bitter they will be. The vegetable is forced and blanched and ready for use in the early winter months. You can also grow red chicory – radicchio – and non-forcing types, which are useful for mid- and late-winter recipes.

STORING

Keep in a black plastic bag in the fridge to avoid exposure to light, which would increase bitterness. Use heads as soon as possible, but they will keep for several days – longer for non-forcing varieties.

NO COOKING REQUIRED

Chicory is usually eaten raw in the UK. Leaves can be separated and dressed with French dressing (page 250), or can form part of a mixed salad. Both white and red chicories work well in salads with fruit, eggs or cheese.

CHICORY AND ORANGE SALAD

An easy, festive salad with turkey, chicken or ham.

Serves 4

2 oranges	pinch caster sugar
1 tbsp dried cranberries	salt, black pepper
2 tbsp olive oil	2 heads chicory
1 tsp Dijon mustard	bunch watercress

- Peel and segment oranges, removing all white pith. Squeeze juice from one quarter into a bowl and reserve remainder. Finely chop cranberries, stir into orange juice and leave for at least 20 minutes.
- Add oil, mustard, sugar and seasoning to juice bowl and combine thoroughly.
- Put chicory leaves, remaining orange segments and watercress in bowls. Spoon dressing over.

RADICCHIO AND FIG SALAD

Try this simple salad – it makes a good starter.

Serves 4

1 head radicchio	6 tbsp honey and mustard
4 handfuls rocket	dressing (page 250)
4 fresh figs	

- Arrange radicchio leaves and rocket on 4 plates.
- Quarter figs and add to the plates. Spoon dressing over.

CHICORY, APPLE AND BRIE SALAD

An excellent salad lunch, or use it to fill a baguette.

Serves 4

2 rashers back bacon	2–3 handfuls lamb's
3 tbsp olive oil	lettuce
1 tbsp balsamic vinegar	200 g (7 oz) ripe Brie
salt, black pepper	2 small red dessert
1–2 heads chicory	apples

- Grill bacon and crumble. Combine oil, vinegar and seasoning.
- Arrange chicory leaves, lettuce and small slices of Brie on 4 serving plates. Core and thinly slice apples and add to plates.
- Spoon dressing over and scatter bacon on top.

REFRESHER SALAD

A salad to refresh your palate after a rich main course.

Serves 4

1 head chicory	1 firm but ripe pear
1 head radicchio	25 g (1 oz) walnut pieces
8 radishes	4 tbsp French dressing
3 stalks celery	(page 250)

- Arrange chicory and radicchio leaves on 4 plates. Add thinly sliced radishes and celery.
- Peel, core and slice pear and add to salads, Sprinkle with walnuts, then spoon dressing over.

BASIC COOKING

Trim away any damaged leaves and rinse quickly, if necessary, under cold running water – don't soak, as this can increase bitterness. Removing a cone shape from the base of each head with a small sharp knife may help to reduce the bitter taste.

BRAISED CHICORY

Lay whole chicory heads snugly together in a lidded, flameproof casserole or frying pan with 10 g (¼ oz) butter and a squeeze of lemon juice for each chicory. Season, add a little water or stock to cover the base of the pan, bring to a simmer, put the lid on and cook over medium-low heat for 30–40 minutes or until heads are tender when pierced with a sharp knife.

GRILLED CHICORY

Braise chicory heads, drain, then grill or barbecue until lightly charred.

SAUTÉED CHICORY

Cut chicory lengthwise into quarters. Heat 1 tbsp olive oil for each chicory in a shallow pan over medium heat and soften chopped garlic (1 clove per chicory) for 2 minutes. Add chicory and cook for 3 minutes. Turn, put lid on pan and cook for a further 3 minutes, then season with salt and pepper or drizzle with French dressing (page 250). Use for warm salads or as a simple side dish.

BAKED CHICORY

Cut chicory lengthwise into quarters and arrange in an oiled, ovenproof dish in one layer. Drizzle with 1 tbsp olive oil for each chicory, pour round a little water or stock and season well. Bake at 180°C/gas mark 4 with lid on, or covered with foil, for 30 minutes, then remove lid or foil, baste and cook for a further 10 minutes to brown lightly.

CHICORY RECIPES

CHICORY GRATIN

The slight bitterness of chicory is well tempered by the addition of a creamy cheese – and caramelizing it also sweetens the flavour so this easy dish will be enjoyed by all the family. Try it with grilled gammon or chicken.

Serves 4

4 heads chicory
4 tbsp olive oil
4 cloves garlic
salt, black pepper
200 g (7 oz) soft mild goat's cheese

● Sauté sliced chicory in oil with garlic and seasoning.
● Thinly slice cheese and layer it over chicory in the pan, then put pan, handle outwards, under a hot grill until cheese is melted and golden. Serve immediately.

CHICORY AND HAM MORNAY

This is a supper in itself, but you could add a green salad, or some grilled or baked tomatoes, and crusty bread. Gruyère is traditional for Mornay, but Cheddar will work as well.

Serves 4

4 heads chicory
200 g (7 oz) ham
1 egg yolk
100 g (3½ oz) Gruyère
400 ml (14 fl. oz) white sauce (page 251)

● Braise chicory heads and arrange in a shallow, greased, ovenproof dish. Cut ham into bite-sized pieces and scatter around the chicory.
● Beat egg yolk and two-thirds of the grated cheese into warmed white sauce and spoon evenly over the chicory. Sprinkle remaining cheese over and bake at 190°C/gas mark 5 until the top is bubbling and flecked brown.

Instead of braising chicory in water, try adding dry cider or apple juice – an ideal accompaniment to gammon or duck.

CUCUMBER

A member of the gourd family, the cooling cucumber is a traditional part of the British summer, conjuring up pictures of tea on the lawn and salad days. Fruits grown outdoors tend to have more flavour and can be less 'watery' than those from the greenhouse, but all make a welcome addition to a range of recipes and dishes. Cucumber is most commonly eaten raw, but it can be cooked. Gherkins are small cucumbers used for pickling.

STORING

Wrap in cling film and keep in the fridge for about a week. Don't freeze – the high water content turns cucumber almost to mush, although you can freeze cucumber soup.

NO COOKING REQUIRED

Peel and thinly slice for cucumber sandwiches. Slice for cucumber salad and sprinkle with French dressing (page 250), or simply with a little vinegar to accompany fish. Add to leaves and tomatoes for a mixed salad.

Thick batons can be used for crudités with a dip. Or cut into chunks, halve, de-seed and fill the centre with cream cheese or tuna mayonnaise for a canapé.

For most raw uses, peeling is optional as the skin of modern cucumbers is rarely tough or bitter, particularly that of greenhouse varieties.

Cucumber is an important contributor to many cold dishes, such as gazpacho (page 81) and yogurt relishes (below).

CUCUMBER, APPLE AND CELERY JUICE

Chop a cucumber, a stalk of celery and 2 cored dessert apples and put into a juicer with the juice of a lime. Juice, then serve with ice cubes.

CUCUMBER RAITA

This yogurt relish is one of the many variations of the traditional north Indian dish served as a curry accompaniment. Variations include the addition of mint, chopped green chilli or onion.

Makes 300 ml (½ pint)

⅓ cucumber	½ tsp crushed cumin seeds
250 ml (8 fl. oz) natural yogurt	2 tbsp fresh coriander leaves salt, black pepper

- Peel, de-seed and finely chop cucumber and combine with remaining ingredients. Allow to stand for an hour, then serve immediately.

TZATZIKI

The classic Greek side dish for grilled lamb and meat kebabs, also often used as a dip. Tzatziki packs a powerful garlicky punch, cooled by the smooth Greek yogurt and plenty of cucumber. Mint is an optional addition. Keeps for a few days, covered, in the fridge. Also available ready-made in supermarkets.

Makes 300 ml (½ pint)

½ cucumber	250 ml (8 fl. oz) Greek yogurt
2 tsp salt	salt, black pepper
2 cloves garlic	dash of white wine vinegar
1 tbsp olive oil	

- Peel, de-seed and finely chop cucumber, toss with salt and set aside in a strainer for 1–2 hours, then put into a clean tea towel and press out excess liquid.

- Beat together cucumber, well-crushed garlic, oil, yogurt and seasoning to taste until thoroughly combined. Stir in vinegar. Serve chilled.

GAZPACHO

Everyone returns from visiting Spain keen to try this 'no-cook' soup recipe at home – it couldn't be easier. In summer it is best chilled, but it can also be served hot in winter.

Serves 4

50 g (2 oz) stale bread	2 cloves garlic
1 large cucumber	2 tbsp sherry vinegar
6 tomatoes	2 tbsp olive oil
2 green peppers	salt, black pepper
1 onion	

- Break bread into small pieces. Peel cucumber and tomatoes and de-seed peppers. Chop all vegetables and garlic (reserving a quarter of the cucumber). Combine in a large bowl with the bread and remaining ingredients.

- Purée in a blender until smooth, adding water until you have a soup consistency (you may need to do this in two or more batches).

- Put into a serving bowl, chill for 1–2 hours, then check seasoning. Serve topped with the reserved chopped cucumber and one or more garnishes, such as chopped red pepper, chopped onion, garlic croutons, chopped black olives or ground Spanish paprika.

BASIC COOKING

BRAISED CUCUMBER

Cut a cucumber into 0.5 cm (¼ in.) slices and simmer in a lidded frying pan with 40 g (1½ oz) butter, seasoning and 3 tbsp water for 30 minutes.

CUCUMBER RECIPES

CHILLED CUCUMBER SOUP

This packs more flavour than you might think and is one of the best chilled soups for summer.

Serves 4

3 cucumbers	500 ml (17 fl. oz) chicken stock
25 g (1 oz) butter	200 ml (7 fl. oz) crème fraîche
1 tbsp flour	2 tbsp fresh chopped mint
salt, black pepper	

- Peel, halve and de-seed cucumbers, then roughly chop. Blanch for 30 seconds.

- Melt butter in a large pan, add cucumber and fry over medium-low heat for a minute. Stir in flour and seasoning and cook for 3 minutes.

- Gradually add warm stock, stirring until you have a smooth mixture. Add half the crème fraîche and simmer for 15 minutes.

- Allow to cool a little, then blend in a blender. Cover and chill. Check seasoning before serving with remaining crème fraîche stirred lightly in and garnished with mint.

STUFFED CUCUMBERS

Cucumbers hold their shape well when baked with a simple stuffing. This recipe makes a nice, easy supper.

Serves 4

2 cucumbers	1 tsp dried mixed herbs
400 g (14 oz) sausage meat	1 tbsp fresh chopped parsley + extra to garnish
6 spring onions	salt, black pepper
1 tomato	

- Halve cucumbers lengthwise, then cut each half crosswise to make 8 pieces in all. De-seed and blanch for 3 minutes, then place in a greased, ovenproof dish.

- Combine sausage meat, finely chopped spring onions, peeled and chopped tomato, herbs and seasoning. Fill the cucumber hollows with the sausage meat mixture.

- Bake at 190°C/gas mark 5 for 30–40 minutes or until golden. Serve sprinkled with parsley.

ENDIVE

This vegetable has a much more distinctive taste than lettuce and can be slightly or very bitter – the darker the leaves, the stronger-tasting they usually are. There are two main types. The **curly-leaved** (**frisée**) varieties are sown in spring for their finely divided leaves to be used in summer and autumn. The **broad-leaved** (**escarole**) varieties are generally hardy – under cloches they will survive the winter to provide lettuce-shaped leaves in the new year. The edges are often frilled.

Bitterness can be minimized by blanching – tie up mature heads or cover with a large pot, although you can also pick immature leaves to provide a cut-and-come-again, mild-flavoured vegetable. Several self-blanching varieties are now available.

STORING

Discard damaged or dark green outer leaves, trim off root and store in a plastic bag in the fridge for a few days.

NO COOKING REQUIRED

All types of endive make an excellent addition to a main-course salad or side salad – it is part of the classic Provençal mesclun salad, which also contains flowers, herbs and wild leaves. Strong flavours, such as liver, bacon, watercress and cheese, go well with endive. A simple salad can be made with endive leaves, orange segments and a French dressing (page 250).

Good varieties of curly-leaved endive include Frisée Frenzy, Fin de Louvier and Moss Curled.

FRISÉE SALAD WITH BACON AND CHICKEN LIVERS

For this classic French endive salad, divide 1 head frisée between 4 serving bowls. Chop 200 g (7 oz) chicken livers into bite-sized pieces, season and fry in 1 tbsp olive oil for 3 minutes until tinged gold and just cooked through – don't over-cook or the liver will turn rubbery. Fry 8 slices streaky bacon and 2 thinly sliced shallots in a further tbsp oil. Stir liver, crumbled bacon, and shallots into frisée. Combine 6 tbsp French dressing (page 250) with 2 tsp Dijon mustard, stir through salad and top with garlic croutons to serve. Omit livers for a lighter salad.

ENDIVE, AVOCADO AND TOMATO SALAD

Tear leaves from 1 head endive into bite-sized pieces, put in a salad bowl with 2 peeled, thinly sliced avocados and 12 halved cherry tomatoes, then toss with a French dressing (page 250). Makes a good accompaniment for cold roast beef, or serve it with 100 g (3½ oz) Parma ham fried in 1 tbsp olive oil and crumbled over.

Good varieties of broad-leaved endive include Batavian Green, Broad Leaf, Endive Blond Full Heart, Escarole Alaska, Natacha and Pancalieri.

ENDIVE SALAD WITH MUSHROOMS AND HAZELNUTS

Use speciality mushrooms like oysters or shiitake, or any well-flavoured, open-gilled type. To toast hazelnuts, roast for 10 minutes at 170°C/gas mark 3½.

Serves 4

25 g (1 oz) packet dried wild mushrooms	1 tbsp hazelnut oil
400 g (14 oz) fresh mushrooms	1 tbsp balsamic vinegar
2 cloves garlic	salt, black pepper
6 tbsp olive oil	1 tsp Dijon mustard
1 head curly-leaved endive	100 g (3½ oz) toasted hazelnuts

- Soak dried mushrooms in hot water for 20 minutes.
- Slice fresh mushrooms; drain and dry wild mushrooms. Stir-fry with chopped garlic in 2 tbsp olive oil over medium heat for 3 minutes, or until fresh mushrooms are golden but still firm.
- Arrange torn endive in serving bowls and spoon mushroom mixture on top. Combine remaining olive oil, hazelnut oil, vinegar, seasoning and mustard. Stir into mushrooms and scatter with nuts to serve.

ENDIVE WITH JERUSALEM ARTICHOKES

The nutty, creamy taste of the artichokes combines with the slightly bitter escarole leaves to make a perfect winter starter salad or light lunch.

Serves 4

8 Jerusalem artichokes	50 g (2 oz) watercress
1 tbsp lemon juice	50 g (2 oz) lamb's lettuce
2 tbsp olive oil	100 g ((3½ oz) walnut pieces
1 tsp fresh thyme leaves	French dressing (page 250)
1 tbsp fresh chopped parsley	
1 head broad-leaved endive	

- Peel artichokes, dropping them into cold water with a squeeze of lemon juice as you go. Cut into 0.5 cm (¼ in.) rounds and blanch for 4 minutes.
- Sauté drained artichoke slices in olive oil over medium-high heat for 3–4 minutes each side, or until golden and tender. Add herbs for last minute.
- Tear endive leaves lightly and arrange all salad leaves on plates. Top with artichokes and walnuts. Drizzle dressing over. Eat while still warm.

BASIC COOKING

Wash leaves if necessary and remove discoloured portions and tough outer leaves. For a less bitter taste, keep only central or pale leaves.

BRAISED ENDIVE

Cut leaves from stem and base of the head and fry in 2 tbsp olive oil over medium heat for 3 minutes. Add 3 tbsp hot water or stock, seasoning and 1 tbsp lemon juice, cover and braise on low heat for 20 minutes.

STIR-FRIED ENDIVE

Cut leaves into 3–4 cm (1½–1¾ in.) pieces, heat oil in a wok or large frying pan and stir-fry over high heat for 2–3 minutes until wilted and just turning golden.

ENDIVE RECIPES

STIR-FRIED ENDIVE WITH LEMON

This warm, lemony salad with its crunchy bread topping makes a nice accompaniment to fish or chicken.

Serves 4

2 slices slightly stale bread	salt, black pepper
5 tbsp olive oil	1 head curly-leaved endive
½ lemon	1 tsp runny honey

- Chop bread into very small pieces and stir-fry over high heat in 1 tbsp of the oil until golden. Put into a bowl and stir in 1 tsp grated lemon zest and seasoning.
- Tear endive and stir-fry in 2 tbsp of the oil in a large pan over medium heat for a minute, or until just wilted.
- Combine 1 tbsp lemon juice with remaining oil, honey and seasoning. Toss into endive and top with bread.

KALE

Kale – sometimes known as borecole or collard greens – is a brassica grown for its strong-tasting, nutritious leaves. While there are several varieties, the most common are dark green with curly leaves that look rather like parsley. Kale is an underrated vegetable, its unpopularity most probably due to the wrong choice of variety, and the use of old and wilted leaves. These can be too strongly flavoured and bitter for the kitchen, but tender young leaves are tasty and have many uses for the imaginative cook – as a side vegetable, in soups and many recipe dishes.

Kale is in season from autumn to spring, is improved with some frost and marries well with other strong flavours. Most kales can be harvested like sprouting broccoli – top leaves first, then new shoots from the sides.

STORING

Choose kale leaves when they're still small and young – avoid yellowing leaves. Use as soon as you can after picking. Kale can be kept in a plastic bag in the fridge for up to 3 days, but longer storing increases bitterness. It can also be chopped and frozen in bags.

Good varieties of curly-leaved kale include the eye-catching Nero di Toscana and Cavolo Nero, which has an excellent peppery flavour and can be used as a substitute for Savoy cabbage. Redbor has pretty red leaves and is ideal for cut-and-come-again.

The variety of kale known as Jersey Walking Stick is so called because the 2 metre (6 ft 6 in.) tall hard stems of the plant can be cut and dried to use as walking sticks.

NO COOKING REQUIRED

Very young, tender kale can be eaten raw, sliced into a mixed-leaf salad or on its own, topped with a lemony dressing.

BASIC COOKING

Trim off all stringy stalks, wash leaves and thinly slice or prepare as required for the recipe.

BOILED KALE

Chop or thinly slice leaves. Add boiling water to come halfway up leaves. Season, simmer for 2–3 minutes until just tender; drain. Serve with a knob of butter.

STEAMED KALE

Add chopped or thinly sliced leaves to a steamer over boiling water and steam for 2–3 minutes until just tender. Season and add butter to taste.

STIR-FRIED KALE

Shred tender young leaves and flash-fry for a minute in a little butter or oil; season to taste. Slice and blanch older, larger leaves for 30 seconds before draining and stir-frying.

KALE RECIPES

KALE WITH SPRING ONIONS AND CHILLI

This is a fantastic midwinter stir-fry. Eat it as a side dish or toss in some sliced cooked chicken to make a quick supper.

Serves 4

800 g (1¾ lb) kale
12 spring onions
4 cloves garlic
2 red chillies
2.5 cm (1 in.) piece fresh ginger
3 tbsp vegetable oil
salt, black pepper
1 tbsp sesame oil

- Prepare kale for stir-frying, blanching any older leaves, and fry with chopped spring onions, garlic, chillies and ginger in vegetable oil over high heat until kale is wilted and tender: approx. 3 minutes.
- Season to taste and drizzle sesame oil over.

RIBOLLITA

A classic Italian soup that makes a hearty main meal and is easy to prepare. Use Cavolo Nero if you have it, but any type of kale will do.

Serves 4

400 g (14 oz) can cannellini beans
3 tbsp olive oil
3 stalks celery
3 carrots
1 onion
3 cloves garlic
300 g (11 oz) kale
400 g (14 oz) can chopped tomatoes
3 tbsp fresh chopped parsley
salt, black pepper
4 thick slices ciabatta bread

- Drain beans, roughly mash and set aside.
- Heat 2 tbsp of the oil in a large saucepan over medium heat and fry chopped celery, carrots, onion and garlic over medium-low heat for 10 minutes or until softened and tinged gold.
- Add thinly sliced kale, tomatoes and three-quarters of the parsley with enough boiling water to cover. Season, stir, turn heat to low and simmer for 30 minutes.
- Stir mashed beans into pan with a little boiling water to thin soup if needed. Reheat, checking seasoning.
- Drizzle bread with remaining olive oil and toast until golden. Arrange on top of the soup. Serve garnished with remaining parsley.

KALE AND CHORIZO SOUP

Try this quick, tasty soup with crusty bread.

Serves 4

2 onions	4 potatoes
3 tbsp olive oil	1.2 litres (2 pints)
4 cloves garlic	chicken stock
100 g (3½ oz)	salt, black pepper
chorizo	300 g (11 oz) kale

- Sweat finely chopped onions in oil in a large pan over low heat to soften but not colour.
- Add chopped garlic, diced chorizo and potatoes, and cook for a further 5 minutes. Pour in the stock, season and bring to the boil. Cook for 10 minutes or until potatoes are tender.
- Use a masher to squash the potatoes into the soup. Bring back to the boil. Add finely shredded kale and cook for 5 minutes. Stir and serve.

KALE WITH PASTA, TOMATOES AND MOZZARELLA

A quick, satisfying dish. The strong flavours of kale, chilli and anchovy are softened with creamy cheese.

Serves 4

400 g (14 oz) spaghetti	5 plum tomatoes
3 tbsp olive oil	salt, black pepper
5 cloves garlic	300 g (11 oz) kale
6 canned anchovies	1 ball Mozzarella
2 chillies	

- Cook spaghetti, drain, toss with 1 tbsp of the oil and keep warm.
- Fry chopped garlic, anchovies and chillies in remaining oil over medium heat for 1 minute. Add chopped tomatoes and seasoning. Stir for 5 minutes.
- Blanch shredded kale, add to pan and cook for a further 3 minutes. Break Mozzarella into small balls and stir into the pan, then remove from heat and combine sauce with pasta to serve.

KOHL RABI

Kohl rabi is the member of the brassica family which is not grown for its leaves, flower buds or green stems. It is a 'root' vegetable, although the edible globe is really the swollen stem base. It is thought to have originated in northern Europe in the 16th century and the highest consumption today is in Germany. The flavour is mild and slightly sweet. Versatile and easy to cook, it is good for mashing with other roots such as parsnip or carrot. It also has the ability to absorb the flavour of other ingredients, making it ideal for adding to soups, stews and stir-fries. Big globes can be woody – harvest when they are no bigger than a large apple. The cropping season lasts from July to November.

STORING

Store in a cool, dark place, such as a larder or fridge, in a plastic bag with a few airholes.

NO COOKING REQUIRED

Young, tender kohl rabi can be cut into juliennes or very thinly sliced and eaten raw. It is good in a winter salad with other roots, such as beetroot, and with firm fruit, such as apple or pear, dressed with a mustardy mayonnaise. Or use as a crudité with dips.

KOHL RABI SLAW

Grate 2 kohl rabi and thinly slice 10 radishes. Toss with 5 tbsp French dressing (page 250) and 2 tbsp fresh chopped parsley, then chill for 30 minutes. Serve with cheese, ham or smoked mackerel.

BASIC COOKING

Cut off the thin stalks that grow from the top of the globe and scrub it. There should be no need to peel. The young green leaves can be eaten – prepare and cook as for spinach.

BOILED KOHL RABI

Chop into chunks and boil in lightly salted water for up to 10 minutes, until just soft. Drain and add butter if liked.

MASHED KOHL RABI

Boil, drain, then mash with butter and/or cream and seasoning.

FRIED KOHL RABI

Thinly slice the globes, then fry over medium heat in 10 g (¼ oz) butter or 2 tsp vegetable oil for each globe, turning occasionally, until tender and lightly golden: approx. 10 minutes. Season.

'Kohl rabi' comes from German and literally means 'cabbage turnip'.

ROAST KOHL RABI

Cut globes into bite-sized chunks, add to a roasting tin with 1 tbsp vegetable oil and seasoning. Roast at 190°C/gas mark 5 for 30 minutes, turning halfway through, or until tender and lightly golden.

KOHL RABI RECIPES

KOHL RABI, FETA AND PEAR SALAD

A delicious autumn lunch salad which also makes a welcome addition to a party buffet or can be used as a starter.

Serves 4

2 kohl rabi	2 pears
5 tbsp olive oil	100 g (3½ oz) crisp
salt, black pepper	salad leaves
2 tsp maple syrup	100 g (3½ oz) feta cheese
2 tbsp balsamic vinegar	4 stoned dates

- Roast kohl rabi in 2 tbsp of the oil with seasoning. Combine remaining oil with syrup and vinegar, and season.
- When kohl rabi is cooked, peel and slice pears and arrange on plates with salad leaves.
- Top with the kohl rabi, crumbled cheese and dressing. Sprinkle with finely chopped dates.

BRAISED KOHL RABI WITH PARMESAN

A simple dish to accompany any grilled or roast meat, game or poultry.

Serves 4

2 kohl rabi	200 ml (7 fl. oz) vegetable stock
20 g (¾ oz) butter	salt, black pepper
1 clove garlic	2 tbsp grated Parmesan

- Fry the sliced globes in butter, adding chopped garlic for last minute.
- Add stock, bring to the boil, turn down heat and simmer with lid on for 15 minutes, or until kohl rabi is tender. Season and sprinkle with Parmesan.

KOHL RABI WITH CARROTS AND HONEY BUTTER

Try this with roast chicken or pork for Sunday lunch.

Serves 4

2 kohl rabi	juice of ½ lemon
2 carrots	2 tbsp honey
250 ml (8 fl. oz)	50 g (2 oz) butter
chicken stock	salt, black pepper
2 tbsp fresh chopped parsley	

- Cut kohl rabi and carrots into batons and simmer in stock, uncovered, in a wide pan for 10 minutes, or until tender and stock is reduced and thickened.
- Add parsley, lemon juice, honey, butter and seasoning, and stir for a minute.

KOHL RABI GRATIN

Try this gratin as an alternative to potatoes Dauphinoise – it's perfect with roast lamb.

Serves 4

3 kohl rabi	3 cloves garlic
300 ml (½ pint) cream	salt, black pepper
300 ml (½ pint) milk	25 g (1 oz) butter

- Thinly slice kohl rabi. Combine cream, milk, crushed garlic and seasoning.
- Layer kohl rabi in a buttered, shallow, ovenproof dish, seasoning each layer and adding some of the cream mixture as you go. Depending on size of kohl rabi, you may have some cream mixture left over – it wants to reach just to the top layer of vegetables. Dot top with any remaining butter.
- Cover with foil and bake at 200°C/gas mark 6 for 45 minutes, or until the kohl rabi is tender when pierced with a sharp knife. Remove foil for last 10 minutes of cooking.

LEEK

Leeks, the national emblem of Wales, are one of the most useful vegetables in the kitchen. A member of the onion family, they can be used in almost any recipe to replace mild onions, and are especially good in casseroles and soups or as an accompanying vegetable for fish and lamb. Try cooked leeks stirred into a white or cheese sauce. They can be added to mashed potato, potato rosti, or used in stuffings. But leeks are also happy in a starring role – great cooked and served cold in a vinaigrette, turned into tarts, omelettes, gratins and pies, or used in pasta and rice dishes.

STORING

Leeks will stand over winter in the garden until needed. Or lift, trim off roots and tops, and store in a plastic bag in the fridge for a few days – don't wash until needed for cooking. For use in casseroles and soups they can be cleaned, chopped, bagged and frozen as they are, or blanched or gently fried for 2 minutes, drained and dried before freezing to keep for up to a year.

NO COOKING REQUIRED

Thinly sliced or finely chopped tender young leeks can be added to a winter salad.

BASIC COOKING

Garden leeks can hold a lot of earth/grit inside their tightly packed leaves and need thorough washing. Trim off the root and the tough, dark green tops (which can be used for stock) and wash under running water. If whole leeks are required, open out the leaves with your fingers and wash. Slit down the centre of the plant a few centimetres to help open the leaves.

BOILED LEEKS

Cut into rounds, then boil in lightly salted water to barely cover for 5 minutes. Boil baby and small leeks whole: approx. 8 minutes. Don't over-boil or they will turn slimy. Drain thoroughly and return to a dry pan over very low heat to dry out for a minute or two.

STEAMED LEEKS

Cut into rounds and steam over boiling water for 5 minutes; season. Steam whole baby leeks for 8 minutes.

GRILLED LEEKS

Boil or steam whole baby or small leeks until just cooked. Brush with oil and grill for 1–2 minutes each side until streaked with brown.

FRIED LEEKS

Fry chopped or whole small leeks in vegetable oil or butter over medium heat, stirring occasionally until tender and turning golden: approx. 8 minutes. Season. For adding to a casserole or soup, sweat over low heat to soften but not colour.

STIR-FRIED LEEKS

Fry in oil, stirring over high heat until just tender and turning golden: approx. 3 minutes.

The Romans brought leeks to Britain. They believed the vegetable improved voice clarity.

BRAISED LEEKS

Add small whole or chopped leeks to a lidded frying pan with a knob of butter and stock to cover. Cook gently with lid on for 15–25 minutes, or until tender.

ROAST LEEKS

Add small whole or large chunks of leek to a roasting tin, then toss with olive oil and seasoning, coating well. Roast at 190°C/gas mark 5, turning once or twice, for 30 minutes, or until tender and golden.

LEEK RECIPES

LEEKS IN VINAIGRETTE

Try this classic dish as a starter – it's full of flavour and looks pretty. An alternative topping is chopped sun-dried tomatoes and crispy crumbled bacon. You can also use grilled leeks.

Serves 4

12 small leeks
4 tbsp French dressing (page 250)
2 hard-boiled eggs
2 tbsp fresh chopped chives

- Steam leeks, dry thoroughly and leave to cool.
- Arrange leeks side by side on serving plates. Pour dressing over, then sprinkle with finely chopped egg and chives.

COCK-A-LEEKIE

A warming leek and chicken broth from Scotland, which traditionally includes prunes.

Serves 4–6

3 chicken leg portions
25 g (1 oz) butter
4–6 leeks (approx. 500 g/1¼ lb
  trimmed weight)
1.5 litres (2½ pints) chicken stock
25 g (1 oz) rice
bouquet garni
salt, black pepper
8 stoned prunes
2 tbsp fresh chopped parsley

- Separate chicken thighs from drumsticks and fry in butter in a large pan over medium-high heat to brown on all sides.
- Turn heat down to medium-low, then add chopped leeks and fry for 5 minutes.
- Add stock, rice and bouquet garni. Cover and simmer for 1 hour.
- Season and add chopped prunes. Cover and simmer for a further 30 minutes.
- Remove chicken pieces from pan and strip the meat from the bones. Discard bones and return meat to pan to reheat. Skim soup if necessary and serve sprinkled with parsley.

LEEK FLAN

This traditional recipe uses a simple cheese sauce enriched with an egg, so it is moist and tender inside.

Serves 6

40 g (1½ oz) butter
350 g (12 oz) shortcrust pastry (page 251)
4 leeks
1 egg
400 ml (14 fl. oz) white sauce (page 251)
50 g (2 oz) Cheddar

- Grease a 25 cm (10 in.) flan tin with some of the butter. Line it with rolled-out pastry and bake blind.
- Fry chopped leeks in remaining butter over low heat for 8 minutes. Strain and reserve any juices.
- Beat egg into cool white sauce with the pan juices, then stir in the leeks. Fill the pastry case with the mixture, smooth out and sprinkle grated cheese on top. Bake at 190°C/gas mark 5 for 25 minutes, or until the pastry is brown and the top golden.

LEEK AND CHEESE SOUFFLÉ

A light but tasty soufflé with a green salad is a perfect winter supper and not that difficult to cook – it just needs eating as soon as it's out of the oven. You will need a 15 cm (6 in.), 1.2 litre (2 pint) soufflé dish.

Serves 2

1 large leek	**300 ml (½ pint) milk**
75 g (3 oz) butter	**4 eggs**
4 tbsp breadcrumbs	**100 g (3½ oz) mature**
40 g (1½ oz) plain flour	**Cheddar**
½ tsp mustard powder	**salt, black pepper**
pinch cayenne pepper	

- Sweat finely chopped leek in 10 g (¼ oz) of the butter until soft, then blend to a purée in a blender.
- Preheat the oven to 200°C/gas mark 6 with a baking sheet inside. Melt 15 g (½ oz) of the butter and use to brush the inside of a soufflé dish, then sprinkle breadcrumbs over the buttered bottom and sides.
- Melt remaining butter in a pan, stir in flour, mustard and cayenne, and cook for a minute. Gradually add milk, stirring until mixture simmers, thickens and is completely smooth. Remove from the heat.
- Separate eggs. Beat yolks and stir into the slightly cooled sauce with the leek mixture, finely grated cheese and seasoning until smooth and creamy.
- In a clean, dry, non-greasy bowl, whisk egg whites until stiff but not dry. Add to sauce, gently folding in a spoonful at a time.
- Spoon mixture into soufflé dish and bake for 25–30 minutes until golden and well risen. Serve immediately.

SMOKED HADDOCK AND LEEK CHOWDER

Another traditional way to use leeks is in a chowder – a creamy, chunky soup containing bacon, potatoes and a variety of other ingredients.

Serves 4

450 g (1 lb) smoked haddock fillet
500 ml (17 fl. oz) milk
1 bay leaf
black pepper
100 g (3½ oz) streaky bacon
1 tbsp olive oil
3 medium leeks
2 stalks celery
2 potatoes
100 g (3 ½ oz) sweet corn kernels
500 ml (17 fl. oz) fish stock
100 ml (3½ fl. oz) cream
2 tbsp fresh chopped parsley

- Simmer fish in a pan with milk, bay leaf and pepper for 3–4 minutes until barely cooked. Remove fish with a slotted spatula and reserve liquid. Remove skin from fish and flake flesh.

- Fry diced bacon in oil in a large pan over medium-high heat until starting to brown. Add chopped leeks, celery, potatoes and corn, and stir for a minute. Pour in stock and reserved milk, bring to a simmer, then turn heat down and cook for 20 minutes.

- Add the flaked haddock and cream, simmer for a further 2 minutes, then serve sprinkled with parsley.

WELSH RAREBIT WITH LEEKS

A tasty variation of a classic recipe which makes a good change from cheese on toast.

Serves 4

2 leeks	100 ml (3½ fl. oz) milk
50 g (2 oz) butter	50 ml (2 fl. oz) dry cider
1 tbsp flour	125 g (4 oz) Cheddar
1 tsp mustard powder	4 thick slices crusty
salt, black pepper	bread

- Fry finely chopped leeks in melted butter over medium heat until tender and just starting to turn golden: approx. 6 minutes.

- Stir in flour, mustard powder and seasoning. Gradually stir in milk and cider, then bring to simmering point to make a thick sauce. Stir in 100 g (3½ oz) of the grated cheese to melt.

- Toast the bread, spoon on rarebit mixture, then sprinkle with remaining cheese. Brown under the grill until bubbling and serve immediately.

LEEK AND GOAT'S CHEESE PUFF

The quickest-ever leek and pastry dish – but very tasty and impressive to look at.

Serves 4

3 leeks
25 g (1 oz) butter
50 ml (2 fl. oz) double cream
salt, black pepper
210 g (7½ oz) sheet ready-rolled puff pastry
1 egg
300 g (11 oz) goat's cheese log

- Slice leeks into 1 cm (½ in.) rounds and fry in melted butter over medium heat until tender and just starting to turn golden: approx. 6 minutes. Stir in cream and seasoning and leave to cool a little.

- Lay pastry on a lightly oiled baking sheet and, using a sharp knife, score round the edge approx. 1 cm (½ in.) in – don't cut through to the bottom. Brush the outer edges of the pastry with a little beaten egg, then stir the remaining egg into the cooled leek mixture.

- Spoon leeks evenly on to pastry inside the scored line. Slice cheese into 0.5 cm (¼ in.) rounds and arrange on top of the leeks. Bake at 200°C/gas mark 6 for 25 minutes until pastry and cheese are golden.

LEEK AND BACON QUICHE

All the family enjoy quiche, hot or cold, and this one makes a good addition to the lunchbox.

Serves 4

350 g (12 oz) shortcrust pastry (page 251)
25 g (1 oz) butter
3 leeks
2 tbsp olive oil
175 g (6 oz) streaky bacon
200 ml (7 fl. oz) double cream
4 eggs
125 g (4 oz) Cheddar
2 tbsp fresh chopped parsley

- Grease a 25 cm (10 in.) flan tin with some of the butter, line with the rolled-out pastry and bake blind.

- Heat remaining butter in a frying pan and fry chopped leeks over medium heat until softened and just turning golden: approx. 6 minutes.

- Grill or dry-fry bacon until crisp; crumble.

- Beat together cream and eggs, then stir in leeks, bacon, grated cheese and parsley. Pour carefully into the pastry case and bake at 190°C/gas mark 5 for 25 minutes, or until golden and set.

LETTUCE

One of the most popular of all garden vegetables in the UK and across much of the world, lettuces come in dozens of different shapes, sizes, textures and flavours, and are extremely useful in the kitchen. Careful breeding has also ensured that we can have lettuces all year long even without a greenhouse. While they are mostly used raw in salads, they are a useful vegetable for cooking too and there are several traditional recipes which include the leaves.

STORING

Whole heads, lifted with the root, can be stored in a plastic bag in the fridge and will keep, unwashed, for a week or more. Check for slugs. Bagged individual leaves stored in the fridge should keep for 2–3 days. You can also keep whole lettuce with the root immersed in water in a flower vase in a cool place in the house. Not suitable for freezing.

NO COOKING REQUIRED

Lettuce can be used in hundreds of different ways. Creating salads is their basic role, mixed with ingredients such as other vegetables, cheese, eggs, ham, cold meats, fish or pulses. Lettuce can also be used as a garnish, as an accompaniment for warm items or as a wrap. A white-bread sandwich of lettuce with a little mayonnaise is a delight.

   Leaves left out can wilt quickly and cut edges turn brown, so prepare lettuce just before serving. Don't add salad dressing until the last minute as this will also cause the leaves to darken and wilt. If only a portion of the lettuce is required, use outer leaves first, rather than slicing in half. The leftover inner section will remain in good condition for longer.

SIMPLE LEAF SIDE SALAD

A leafy salad is an ideal foil for numerous savoury dishes, from rich lasagnes or other pasta dishes to grills, burgers, cold meats, omelettes, quiches, fish cakes and many more. You can vary the leaves according to what you have, but try to include different flavours, textures and colours.

Serves 4

1 crisp green lettuce
100 g (3½ oz) red lettuce leaves
100 g (3½ oz) watercress
4 tbsp French dressing (page 250)

- Tear outer leaves from lettuce and cut heart into small wedges. Trim watercress of any overlarge stalks.
- Put leaves in a salad bowl with French dressing to coat thoroughly.

OLD-FASHIONED LETTUCE SALAD

Fans of bottled salad cream will enjoy this retro salad. Home-made salad cream is almost as enjoyable as ready-made!

Serves 4

100 ml (3½ fl. oz) single cream   salt, black pepper
1 tsp caster sugar   1 Butterhead lettuce
50 ml (2 fl. oz) white wine vinegar   4 spring onions

- Combine cream, sugar, vinegar and seasoning.
- Tear outer leaves from lettuce and cut heart into small wedges. Put into a salad bowl with chopped spring onions and toss with the dressing to serve.

Lamb's lettuce (corn salad) is not a true lettuce but a member of the valerian family of plants.

CAESAR SALAD

Named after its inventor, Caesar Cardini, this is a popular salad across the Western world. It makes an excellent starter and may also be served tossed with cooked chicken for lunch. Some recipes include the addition of a raw or coddled egg, and/or anchovies, but the original version is described below.

Serves 4

3 cloves garlic
100 ml (3½ fl. oz) olive oil
juice of ½ lemon
2 tbsp finely grated Parmesan

1 tsp mustard powder
1 tsp Worcestershire sauce
black pepper
2 large slices white bread

1 Cos lettuce
75 g (3 oz) piece Parmesan

- Peel and crush two of the garlic cloves and add to a blender with 5 tbsp of the oil, lemon juice, grated cheese, mustard, Worcestershire sauce and pepper. Blend until smooth.
- Rub bread all over with the whole peeled garlic clove, then brush with remaining oil and toast until golden and crisp. Tear into pieces.
- Toss lettuce leaves with dressing, tearing larger leaves as necessary, and arrange in a bowl. Shave Parmesan into large thin slices and add to salad with bread pieces.

PRAWN COCKTAIL

A 1970s classic which is still very popular today. For a change, add slices of ripe avocado on top.

Serves 4

200 ml (7 fl. oz) mayonnaise	dash Tabasco sauce
2 tbsp tomato ketchup	250 g (9 oz) cooked
1 lemon	peeled prawns
pinch cayenne pepper	½ Iceberg lettuce

- In a large bowl, combine mayonnaise, ketchup, juice of a quarter of the lemon, cayenne pepper and Tabasco. Remove 2 tbsp and reserve. Stir in prawns, reserving 4.
- Shred lettuce and divide equally among 4 serving glasses. Arrange prawn mix on top and finish with the reserved sauce and prawns. Sprinkle each salad with a little more cayenne pepper and garnish with a lemon wedge.

GREEK SALAD

One of the very best classic salads, combining crisp lettuce with the sweet, full flavour of perfectly ripe tomatoes, salty feta and olives.

Serves 4

½ Cos lettuce	16 stoned black olives
4 tomatoes	1 tsp fresh chopped
⅓ cucumber	oregano leaves
1 red onion	3 tbsp olive oil
1 sweet pepper	juice of ½ lemon
200 g (7 oz) feta cheese	

- Tear lettuce and arrange in salad bowls with roughly chopped tomatoes, diced cucumber, thinly sliced onion and pepper.
- Scatter crumbled feta, halved olives and oregano on top. Combine oil and lemon juice and sprinkle over.

EGG, BACON AND LETTUCE SALAD

Crisp lettuce with slightly runny egg and crumbly bacon is a sublime combination. Webb's Wonderful and Little Gem are ideal varieties.

Serves 4

4 eggs
2 thick slices crusty bread
2 tbsp olive oil
salt, black pepper
6 rashers smoked back bacon
1 small red onion
1 crisp lettuce
4 tbsp French dressing (page 250)

- Boil eggs for 5 minutes. Cool for 10 minutes.
- Cut bread into bite-sized pieces and combine with oil and seasoning. Fry over medium-high heat for 3 minutes, turning, until golden and crisp. Remove and reserve.
- Fry bacon slices until golden and turning crisp.
- Thinly slice onion and arrange lettuce leaves and quartered hearts in a serving bowl. Peel eggs and quarter – the centres should still be slightly runny. Crumble bacon over salad, toss with dressing then add eggs and croutons.

CHICKEN LETTUCE WRAPS

Children love the novelty of wraps made from lettuce rather than bread. Try any filling you would also use for tortilla. It's important to use large, pliable but strong leaves – Butterhead is ideal.

Serves 4

400 g (14 oz) skinless chicken breast fillet
1 tbsp vegetable oil
100 g (3½ oz) sweet corn kernels
1 avocado
1 lettuce heart
1 large tomato
3 tbsp chilli and tomato salsa (page 56)
salt, black pepper
4 large lettuce leaves
40 ml (1½ fl. oz) sour cream

- Cut chicken into thin strips and fry in oil over medium-high heat until golden and cooked: approx. 3 minutes. Boil sweet corn kernels and drain.
- Peel, stone and finely chop avocado and lightly mash, then mix with finely chopped lettuce heart and tomato, salsa and seasoning. Stir in chicken and corn.
- Place a quarter of the mixture in the centre of each lettuce leaf. Add a small spoonful of sour cream. Tuck lettuce ends over and roll up to serve.

BASIC COOKING

Remove outer tough, damaged or discoloured leaves and cut off stalk. Wash thoroughly under cold running water to remove dirt and debris – don't soak for more than a few minutes as this removes nutrients. Check carefully for slugs. Shake well to remove clinging water or for firmer leaves, pat dry on a tea-towel or kitchen paper.

SAUTÉED LETTUCE

Gently cook whole or sliced leaves in butter over low heat until wilted. Season.

The milky juice found in lettuce-leaf stalks is mildly sedative and, when eaten in the evening, is said to help insomniacs to sleep.

STIR-FRIED LETTUCE

Slice firm, crisp leaves and fry, stirring over high heat in a little oil until wilted. Season.

BRAISED LETTUCE

Put lettuces side by side in an ovenproof dish and pour vegetable stock over to come halfway up. Put lid on and cook at 190°C/gas mark 5 for 20 minutes, or until soft.

LETTUCE RECIPES

LETTUCE BRAISED IN WINE

Braising brings out a nice, mineral flavour in lettuce, which goes very well with game birds or roast chicken. Butterheads and Little Gem are both especially suitable.

Serves 4

50 g (2 oz) butter	8 spring onions
4 lettuces	2 tbsp white wine
salt, black pepper	1 tbsp fresh chopped chives

- Melt butter in a lidded pan over medium heat. Add lettuces, seasoning, sliced spring onions and wine. Bring to a simmer and turn lettuces over.
- Cover, reduce heat to very low and cook for 30 minutes, turning halfway through. Remove lid, turn up heat and reduce the liquid to serve. Sprinkle with chives.

LETTUCE SOUP

This is a favourite recipe in Wales, where lettuce soup – *cawl letysen* – has been eaten for centuries.

Serves 4

2 onions	1 litre (1¾ pints) vegetable stock
50 g (2 oz) butter	salt, black pepper
1 large potato	50 ml (2 fl. oz) cream
3 lettuces	

- Sweat chopped onions in butter over low heat to soften but not colour. Stir in diced potato. Cook for 2–3 minutes.
- Add chopped lettuce leaves and stock, bring to a simmer, cover and cook for 30 minutes.
- Allow to cool a little, then blend in a blender until smooth. Reheat, season and stir in cream.

LETTUCE, PEA AND MINT SOUP

Lighter than the previous soup, this makes a superb summer starter with a tangy, fresh but slightly sweet taste.

Serves 4

4 shallots
40 g (1½ oz) butter
1 lettuce
300 g (11 oz) peas
1 litre (1¾ pints) vegetable stock
3 tbsp fresh chopped mint
salt, black pepper

- Sweat chopped shallots in the butter in a large pan over low heat to soften but not colour. Chop lettuce and stir into pan to wilt: approx. 1 minute.
- Add peas, stock and mint. Bring to a simmer, cover and cook for 10 minutes. Allow to cool slightly, then blend in a blender, reheat and season to taste.

Wild lettuces were first eaten in the Mediterranean area and in the part of Asia that is now Iran and Iraq. Horticulturist John Evelyn introduced cultivated varieties to the UK in the 17th century.

MARROW AND COURGETTE

This group of fleshy-fruited vegetables is one of the easiest and most satisfying of the summer croppers to grow, the large green cylinder of the marrow being a familiar and traditional sight in allotments everywhere. **Marrows** are members of the gourd family, along with squash and cucumber; and **courgettes** (zucchini) are, basically, baby marrows. Indeed, stay away a day or two and the fast-growing courgette is well on its way to turning into a marrow! There are many recipes for this family, from 6 cm (2½ in.) babies to large fruits, and oversized courgettes can be used for marrow recipes. In general, the larger the fruit the greater its water content and so the less flavour it tends to have, so try to use marrows and courgettes when they are still of reasonable dimensions.

There are many different varieties of courgette and several of marrow. All are extremely useful in the kitchen, where they can be cooked in a variety of ways – stuffed, in soups, stews, curries, salads, roasts, bakes, stir-fries, grills, gratins, and even in fritters, pancakes and cakes. They blend well with many flavours – courgettes are particularly good in recipes from the Mediterranean area, where the vegetable is extremely popular.

While the most common courgette skin colour is dark green, they also come in other colours, from cream through palest green to yellow and gold. Specialist varieties may be knobbly, striped or round. Flavours don't vary a great deal, though the paler types are sweeter and a little more delicate.

Courgette flowers are regarded as a delicacy and can be stuffed and baked or fried.

STORING

Marrows harvested in late summer will store well in a cool, dark, dry, airy, frost-free place for several weeks, but earlier pickings will keep in the fridge for about a week. Put courgettes in a plastic bag in the fridge – they will last for up to a week.

Courgettes can also be chopped, blanched for 2 minutes, drained, bagged and frozen, after which they are best used in soups, stews and 'liquid' recipes. They will also keep in the freezer for up to 3 months unblanched and are then quite suitable for frying and roasting.

NO COOKING REQUIRED

Small marrows and courgettes can be eaten raw. Grate or very thinly slice, dress with olive oil, lemon juice and seasoning, leave to marinate, then eat as a side salad on their own or mixed with other raw, grated or thinly sliced vegetables such as carrot.

BASIC COOKING

Wash dirt from marrows and peel if necessary. If only part of the marrow is required for the recipe, cut off and peel only the amount you need – the rest will keep for a few days. Halve lengthwise and scoop out seeds and pith with a large spoon. (If marrow rings are required, cut the marrow into slices first, then remove central section of seeds and pith.) Slice or cut into chunks as recipe requires.

Wash courgettes, top and tail, then slice into thin or thick rounds, lengths, batons etc. as required. Don't peel unless recipe specifies, as the peel contains much of the flavour.

Some cookbooks suggest salting sliced courgettes and leaving in a colander to drain to remove bitterness. This is not really necessary for modern varieties, though it can help them to soak up less oil during frying.

STEAMED MARROW OR COURGETTES

Put sliced marrow or courgettes in a steamer over boiling water, cover and cook for 4–8 minutes, depending on thickness. Season.

BRAISED MARROW OR COURGETTES

Arrange fairly thick slices of marrow or courgette in a baking dish. Drizzle with oil or melted butter; season. Add 100 ml (3½ fl. oz) water or stock for every 500 g (1¼ lb) vegetable. Cover. Cook at 180°C/gas mark 4 for 45 minutes.

ROAST MARROW OR COURGETTES

Coat medium chunks of marrow or courgette thoroughly with oil, season, put in a roasting dish or tray in one layer and roast at 190°C/gas mark 5 for 40–45 minutes, turning halfway through, until tender and golden.

STIR-FRIED COURGETTES

Thinly slice courgette and stir-fry in oil for 2–4 minutes on high heat until softened and golden. Don't overcook or the slices will break up.

DEEP-FRIED COURGETTES

Cut courgettes into small batons, dust with flour, paprika and seasoning. Deep fry in small batches in hot vegetable oil until crisp: approx. 3 minutes. Season. Serve as chips.

GRILLED COURGETTES

Slice courgettes lengthwise into thickness of a pound coin. Brush with olive oil, season, arrange on grill rack and grill for 3–4 minutes until turning golden. Turn slices over and grill for a further 3 minutes until just tender. Serve hot or cold.

MARROW RECIPES

DEEP-FRIED MARROW

Good as a snack or with lamb chops or chicken.

Serves 4–6

1 marrow (approx. 1 kg/2¼ lb)	2 eggs
3 tbsp flour	50 g (2 oz) breadcrumbs
salt, black pepper	vegetable oil
	1 lemon

- Peel, de-seed and cut marrow into smallish chunks. Put seasoned flour in a shallow dish. Beat eggs and put in another dish, then the breadcrumbs in another, mixed with plenty of seasoning.
- Half fill a deep-frying saucepan with oil and heat to 180°C, or until a cube of bread dropped in turns golden in 30 seconds.
- Dip marrow pieces first in flour, then egg, then breadcrumbs to coat, and deep fry until golden: approx. 4 minutes. Drain on kitchen paper and serve garnished with lemon wedges

STUFFED MARROW

A traditional favourite, rather neglected in modern kitchens – which is a shame, as it is easy and warming. Some recipes bake the stuffed marrow with the two halves tied together, but this one is 'open-stuffed'. You can use pork mince instead of beef.

Serves 4

1 marrow (approx. 1.2 kg/2½ lb)	100 g (3½ oz) cooked rice
1 onion	2 tbsp fresh chopped parsley
4 tbsp vegetable oil	½ tsp ground cinnamon
350 g (12 oz) minced beef	salt, black pepper
100 g (3½ oz) mushrooms	50 ml (2 fl. oz) beef stock
2 tomatoes	75 g (3 oz) Cheddar

- Halve the marrow lengthwise, scoop out and discard seeds and pith. Evenly scoop out about a quarter of the flesh from each half.
- Fry finely chopped onion and chopped marrow flesh in half the oil over medium-low heat to soften and tinge gold. Remove from pan and put to one side. Increase heat to high, add minced beef and fry until lightly browned.
- Add finely chopped mushrooms and tomatoes with a little more oil if necessary, turn heat down to medium-low and cook for 2 minutes, stirring. Return onion mixture to pan with rice, parsley, cinnamon, seasoning and stock. Stir well and remove from heat.
- Place marrow halves in a roasting tin, brush with oil and fill both halves with the mixture. Drizzle any remaining oil over the top. Cover and bake at 180°C/gas mark 4 for 1 hour, then remove cover, sprinkle with grated cheese and bake for a further 20 minutes, or until marrow is tender.

ROAST MARROW WITH TOMATOES, HERBS AND SWEET PEPPERS

More-ish accompaniment for roast or grilled chicken, lamb or beef which would also go well with small, whole baked fish such as sea bass.

Serves 4

1 small marrow (approx. 750 g/1 lb 10 oz)	salt, black pepper
4 tbsp olive oil	1 tbsp fresh oregano
1 red pepper	2 tsp fresh thyme
1 yellow pepper	50 ml (2 fl. oz) passata (page 153)
4 tomatoes	

- Chop marrow into bite-sized pieces and toss in oil in a roasting dish with the sliced peppers, quartered tomatoes, seasoning and herbs.

- Roast at 190°C/gas mark 5 for 30 minutes, turning once. Combine passata with 50 ml (2 fl. oz) hot water and pour around the dish. Return to oven for a further 15 minutes, or until everything is tender and the marrow is coloured light gold.

MARROW SOUP

This is really nice served with garlic croutons.

Serves 4

1 marrow (approx. 1 kg/2¼ lb)	450 ml (¾ pint) vegetable stock
1 onion	pinch ground nutmeg
50 g (2 oz) butter	pinch cayenne pepper
½ tbsp flour	salt, black pepper
450 ml (¾ pint) milk	

- Peel, de-seed and chop marrow, then sweat with chopped onion in butter over low heat to soften but not colour.
- Stir in flour. Cook over medium heat for 2 minutes, then gradually stir in milk to form a thin sauce. Add remaining ingredients, stir well, bring to a simmer, put lid on and cook for 20 minutes.
- Cool a little, then blend in a blender. Return to the pan, reheat and check seasoning.

MARROW WITH CHEESY TOPPING

An easy way to turn marrow into an all-in-one supper or a side dish to liven up plain grilled meat.

Serves 2–3

1 small marrow (approx. 750 g/1 lb 10 oz)
65 g (2½ oz) butter
2 cloves garlic
salt, black pepper
100 g (3½ oz) Cheddar
2 tbsp fresh chopped parsley
50 g (2 oz) breadcrumbs

- Fry sliced marrow in half the butter in a shallow, flameproof casserole over medium-low heat for 5 minutes. Add finely chopped garlic, season and stir. Reduce heat to low and cook for a further 7–10 minutes until marrow is tender and tinged gold. Sprinkle half the grated cheese and half the parsley over and stir in lightly.
- Heat the grill. Mix breadcrumbs with remaining cheese and parsley; season. Melt remaining butter and stir in. Spoon the breadcrumb mixture over the top of the marrow.
- Put the dish under the grill (not too near the heat) for a few minutes until the top is golden.

If you're not sure whether a marrow needs peeling, press a fingernail lightly into the skin. If you don't see a small tear, the skin is probably too thick to become tender when cooked.

MARROW BAKED WITH ONIONS

Very good with the Sunday roast – especially pork or lamb.

Serves 4

1 marrow (approx. 1 kg/2¼ lb)
2 onions
2 cloves garlic
100 ml (3 ½ fl. oz) vegetable stock
salt, black pepper
2 tsp dried mixed herbs
25 g (1 oz) butter

- Peel, de-seed and slice marrow. Layer with the thinly sliced onion and chopped garlic in an ovenproof dish, sprinkling stock, seasoning and herbs in between each layer.
- Dot with butter, cover and bake at 180°C/gas mark 4 for 1¼ hours, or until tender.

MARROW AND LAMB BAKE

A meaty bake rich with Mediterranean flavours. You just need a simple side salad to go with it.

Serves 4

1 onion	salt, black pepper
4 tbsp olive oil	400 ml (14 fl. oz) white sauce (page 251)
2 cloves garlic	
1 marrow (approx. 1 kg/2¼ lb)	pinch ground nutmeg
	1 egg
400 g (14 oz) lamb mince	250 g (9 oz) Ricotta
400 ml (14 fl. oz) tomato sauce (page 156)	75 g (3 oz) grated Parmesan
1 tbsp fresh oregano	

- Sweat finely chopped onion in a large frying pan in half the oil over low heat to soften but not colour, adding chopped garlic for last minute. Remove with a slotted spatula.
- Slice marrow 0.5 cm (¼ in.) thick. Add remaining oil and fry over medium-high heat for a few minutes on each side to brown. Remove from pan with slotted spatula.
- Add mince to pan and fry for 3–4 minutes to brown, turning halfway. Return onion to pan, add tomato sauce, oregano and seasoning, and stir well.
- Spoon half the lamb mixture into a greased, oblong ovenproof dish, then layer half the marrow slices over, seasoning well. Repeat layers.
- Beat together the white sauce, nutmeg, egg, Ricotta and half the Parmesan, then spoon over top of dish and smooth. Sprinkle remaining cheese over and bake at 190°C/gas mark 5 for 30 minutes, or until bubbling and golden.

COURGETTE RECIPES

COURGETTE FRITTERS

Frying the courgettes like this gives them a mild, sweet and delicious flavour which children love, so this is an ideal kids' tea that mum and dad will enjoy too.

Serves 4

4 courgettes (approx. 800 g/1¾ lb)	1 tsp ground cumin
1 small onion	salt, black pepper
2 tbsp fresh chopped parsley	100 g (3½ oz) grated Parmesan
2 tbsp fresh chopped chives	200 g (7 oz) plain flour
3 eggs	100 ml (3½ fl. oz) vegetable oil
2 tsp paprika	juice of 1 lemon

- Grate courgettes and press in a clean tea-towel to remove moisture. Mix with finely chopped onion, parsley, chives, beaten eggs, paprika, cumin and seasoning.
- Stir in cheese and flour, then leave mixture to stand for 30 minutes.
- Heat oil in a large frying pan, then drop in large spoonfuls of the mixture and fry over medium heat, turning halfway, until golden on both sides: approx. 5 minutes. Remove with a slotted spoon and drain on kitchen paper. Serve sprinkled with lemon juice.

GRILLED COURGETTE, PINE NUT AND LEMON SALAD

Good served warm or cold, this salad can be a starter, side dish or part of a summer buffet. The dressing needs to be added to the courgettes while they are still warm.

Serves 4

50 g (2 oz) pine nuts	salt, black pepper
4 courgettes	1 lemon
6 tbsp olive oil	2 tbsp fresh chopped basil

- Put pine nuts in a dry, non-stick frying pan and toast until golden. Take care not to burn – once they begin to turn gold they need to be removed from the heat immediately.
- Slice courgettes thinly lengthwise and brush with 2–3 tbsp of the oil. Arrange on the rack of a grill pan and season. Grill for 2–3 minutes on each side until golden and just tender.
- Grate lemon zest. Combine remaining olive oil with lemon juice, seasoning and basil, then sprinkle dressing and pine nuts over the warm courgettes and finish with grated zest.

COURGETTE COUSCOUS WITH PISTACHIOS AND HERBS

Couscous makes a tasty salad, lifted by the addition of courgette and herbs. In summer it is good with roast lamb or chicken and green salad instead of the usual roast-lunch trimmings.

Serves 4

150 g (5 oz) couscous	50 g (2 oz) pistachios
300 ml (½ pint) vegetable stock	4 spring onions
1 tbsp fresh finely chopped mint	6 sun-dried tomatoes
1 tbsp fresh finely chopped basil	3 courgettes
	2 tbsp olive oil
	salt, black pepper

- Put couscous in a heatproof bowl. Heat stock to boiling and pour on. Stir and leave for 15 minutes. Fluff up with a fork.
- Add mint, basil, chopped nuts, spring onions and tomatoes and stir through.
- Chop courgettes into bite-sized pieces and stir-fry in oil over medium-high heat for 3–4 minutes until golden and just tender. Season well and stir into the couscous.

COURGETTE AND RED ONION PIZZA

A family favourite, full of flavour – but you can add pieces of cooked chicken or chorizo for extra protein if you like.

Serves 4

30 cm (12 in.) uncooked pizza base (page 251)	salt, black pepper
3 courgettes	2 tbsp fresh chopped basil
2 red onions	8 stoned black olives
3 tbsp olive oil	125 g (4 oz) ball Mozzarella
2 cloves garlic	50 g (2 oz) grated Parmesan
250 ml (8 fl. oz) tomato sauce (page 156)	

- Put pizza base on baking tray and preheat oven to 220°C/gas mark 7. Thinly slice courgettes into rounds, fry with the thinly sliced onions in oil over medium-high heat until just tender and golden. Add chopped garlic for last 2 minutes of cooking. Season well.
- Spread tomato sauce on pizza base, then top with the vegetable mixture and season. Add basil and sliced olives.
- Arrange thinly sliced Mozzarella on top, then sprinkle cheese over. Bake for 12 minutes, or until pizza edges and cheese are golden.

COURGETTE, PEPPER AND HALOUMI SKEWERS

An ideal barbecue recipe. Haloumi is a delicious, firm cheese from Cyprus made from a mixture of sheep's and goat's milk – it is widely available in supermarkets. If using wooden skewers, soak them in water for 30 minutes so that they don't burn on the grill or barbecue.

Serves 4

4 small courgettes
1 red pepper
1 yellow pepper
300 g (11 oz) Haloumi
6 tbsp olive oil
2 tbsp fresh chopped mint
2 tbsp fresh chopped parsley
2 tbsp drained capers
2 cloves garlic
salt, black pepper

- Cut courgettes, peppers and cheese into bite-sized pieces and thread on to skewers. Brush with 2 tbsp of the oil and grill for 5 minutes, turning halfway through, until the cheese is golden.
- Combine remaining oil with mint, parsley, finely chopped capers, garlic and seasoning.
- Drizzle dressing over each skewer. Serve hot.

COURGETTE CAKE

Use peeled courgettes or marrow for this recipe – the vegetable makes the cake really moist.

Makes 8 slices

100 g (3½ oz) sultanas	**1 dessert apple**
100 ml (3½ fl. oz) apple juice	**1 tsp salt**
225 g (8 oz) courgettes	**½ tsp ground**
225 g (8 oz) butter	**cinnamon**
225 g (8 oz) caster sugar	**225 g (8 oz)**
2 eggs	**self-raising flour**

- Soak sultanas in apple juice for approx. 15 minutes. Grate courgettes, then press them in a clean tea-towel to remove moisture.
- Cream together softened butter and sugar in a mixing bowl, then gradually beat in eggs. Stir in drained sultanas and courgettes. Peel and grate apple and add to mixture.
- Stir salt and cinnamon into flour and fold into the mixture. Spoon into a greased 1 kg (2¼ lb) loaf tin lined with lightly greased baking parchment and level off the top. Bake at 180°C/gas mark 4 for 50 minutes, or until golden and a skewer inserted in the centre comes out clean.
- Leave to cool in the tin for 15 minutes, then remove and peel off parchment, and finish cooling on a wire rack. Store in an airtight tin – it will keep for a week.

DEEP-FRIED COURGETTE FLOWERS

Female flowers have a small fruit behind them – male ones do not. Don't waste the large male flowers, they make an excellent crispy snack or canapé. If you use self-raising flour you will get a slightly lighter batter, but any flour will do.

Serves 2–4

125 g (4 oz) flour	**vegetable oil**
salt, black pepper	**8 courgette flowers**
25 g (1 oz) grated Parmesan	

- Combine flour and seasoning in a bowl. Gradually mix in up to 200 ml (7 fl. oz) cold water (you may need a little less) until you have a smooth batter. Stir in cheese.
- Put enough oil in a large saucepan to come no more than halfway up the sides and heat to 180°C, or until a cube of bread dropped in turns golden in 30 seconds.
- Dip each courgette flower in the batter, then drop in the oil. Fry for 2 minutes, or until golden. Drain on kitchen paper, sprinkle with salt and serve immediately.

MUSHROOM

If you are fortunate enough to grow mushrooms successfully you will appreciate the full flavour of the fungi harvested and eaten at their freshest. Button mushrooms appear first, becoming closed cap and then opening into flats, depending on how old the mushrooms are – they can double in size in just a day. Both the classic white-skinned mushrooms and the more recently popular brown-cap type (called chestnut when they are mid-sized and portabello when flat) may be grown at home.

Mushrooms are similar to onions and tomatoes in that they are an important addition to very many recipes, offering flavour, colour, aroma, texture and bulk to soups, stews, sauces and any number of other dishes. They are marvellous as companions to eggs for breakfast or brunch, in omelettes and quiches. But they are also suitable as the main, or only, ingredient – try a large baked or grilled flat mushroom in a bun instead of a beefburger, or fried mushrooms tossed with pasta, and don't forget the delight of well-seasoned fried or roast mushrooms on toast.

STORING

Once harvested, mushrooms are best eaten as fresh as possible, but if necessary put them in a paper bag in the fridge where they will keep for 2–3 days. They can also be sliced and frozen raw (or buttons frozen whole) and will then be suitable for adding to soups, casseroles and stews, or they can be lightly fried and then frozen.

DRIED MUSHROOMS

Dried mushrooms last for up to 2 years and can be used to enrich stews, sauces and many more dishes. There are three ways to dry them:

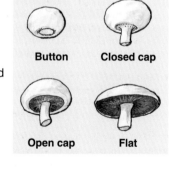

Button　　**Closed cap**

Open cap　　**Flat**

- String up (using needle and strong thread) above a stove or in a warm, dry, airy room for 2 weeks or until they feel thoroughly dry.
- Slice, arrange on a rack in a single layer and leave in the airing cupboard for several days until dry.
- Slice, arrange on a metal rack in a single layer and leave in a cool oven (140°C/gas mark 1) for 6–10 hours until dry.

Store in an airtight container and check regularly. Use dried direct into soups and stews, or rehydrate by soaking in hot water for 15–30 minutes.

NO COOKING REQUIRED

Thinly slice button mushrooms and eat raw in crisp salads, or toss with French dressing (page 250) on their own or with cooked prawns.

MUSHROOM DIP

Chop 2 stalks celery and 200 g (7 oz) mushrooms and put in a blender with 125 g (4 oz) Ricotta, 4 tbsp thick natural yogurt, a chopped clove garlic and 1 tbsp fresh chopped parsley. Season, then blend until fairly smooth. Cover and chill. Serve with crudités such as carrot, cucumber or radish. Keeps in the fridge for 2–3 days.

BASIC COOKING

Avoid washing, as water can spoil both flavour and appearance. Also avoid peeling. Simply use a clean, damp cloth to wipe off any clinging compost, then use whole or sliced as the recipe requires.

STEAMED MUSHROOMS

Put sliced or whole small mushrooms in a steamer over boiling water and steam for 4–10 minutes, or until tender. Season.

GRILLED MUSHROOMS

Brush flat mushrooms on each side with melted butter or vegetable oil, season and grill for 3 minutes on each side until golden, tender and cooked through.

FRIED MUSHROOMS

Slice or halve mushrooms, or use button mushrooms whole. Fry in 10 g (¼ oz) butter or 2 tsp vegetable oil for every 100 g (3½ oz) mushrooms over medium heat for 3–4 minutes until tender and darker in colour, stirring frequently. The mushrooms will soak up the fat quickly and seem dry, but if you keep stirring they will release their own juices. Season.

BAKED MUSHROOMS

Lay large mushrooms on an oiled baking tray, brush with melted butter or oil, season well and bake at 190°C/gas mark 5 for 15 minutes, or until tender. Or lay mushrooms on foil, top with butter or oil and seasoning, make a parcel and return to the oven for 15 minutes.

ROAST MUSHROOMS

Add whole, sliced or quartered mushrooms to a roasting tin and toss with 1 tbsp olive oil for every 150 g (5 oz) mushrooms. Season and roast at 190°C/gas mark 5, stirring once, for 15 minutes, or until tender.

MUSHROOM RECIPES

CREAM OF MUSHROOM SOUP

Add a dash of sherry or Madeira to turn this smooth soup into a true luxury.

Serves 4

50 g (2 oz) butter
2 shallots
450 g (1 lb) flat mushrooms
300 ml (½ pint) chicken stock
400 ml (14 fl. oz) white sauce (page 251)
salt, black pepper
100 ml (3½ fl. oz) single cream
2 tbsp fresh chopped chives

- Melt butter in a large pan, add sliced shallots and mushrooms and fry over medium-low heat for 5 minutes. Add stock, bring to a simmer, turn heat to low, cover and cook for 15 minutes.
- Allow to cool a little, then blend in a blender.
- Return mushroom mixture to pan and combine well with the white sauce. Bring to a simmer and add hot water to thin if necessary. Season and stir in cream. Sprinkle with chives to serve.

There is evidence that mushrooms have existed on earth for millions of years and were perhaps here even before the dinosaurs.

MUSHROOMS ON CIABATTA

Packed with flavour, this makes a great lunch. If you don't have any of your own dried mushrooms, they can be bought in small packs in most supermarkets. Use any leftover soaking liquid as stock for another dish.

Serves 2

25 g (1 oz) dried mushrooms
250 g (9 oz) closed-cap mushrooms
1 tbsp olive oil
25 g (1 oz) butter
2 cloves garlic
2 tsp balsamic vinegar
100 ml (3½ fl. oz) crème fraîche
2 tbsp fresh chopped parsley
salt, black pepper
2 slices ciabatta bread

- Put dried mushrooms into hot water to just cover, set aside for 15 minutes, then drain. Reserve soaking liquid.
- Quarter fresh mushrooms and stir-fry with drained mushrooms in oil and butter over high heat until golden and cooked through: approx. 3 minutes. Add finely chopped garlic and 1 tbsp of the soaking liquid halfway through.
- Stir in vinegar, crème fraîche, parsley and seasoning. Toast bread and pile the mushroom mixture on top.

MARINATED MUSHROOMS À LA GRECQUE

A classic recipe often served as part of a Greek *meze*, but it also makes a good starter on its own, served with crusty bread.

Serves 4

1 large onion
3 tbsp olive oil
2 cloves garlic
225 g (8 oz) button mushrooms
150 ml (¼ pint) dry white wine
4 plum tomatoes
salt, black pepper
3 tbsp fresh chopped parsley

- Fry finely chopped onion in oil over medium-low heat to soften and tinge gold. Add chopped garlic and whole mushrooms and sauté for a further minute.

- Add wine and peeled, chopped tomatoes; season well. Bring to a simmer and cook for 5 minutes until the sauce has thickened slightly.

- Cool to room temperature, then stir in parsley.

MUSHROOM PÂTÉ

Little could be easier to make than this pâté, which is great as a starter or a sandwich filling.

Serves 4

1 onion
50 g (2 oz) butter
1 tbsp oil
1 clove garlic
300 g (11 oz) open-cap mushrooms
25 g (1 oz) breadcrumbs
125 g (4 oz) cream cheese
pinch ground nutmeg
2 tsp lemon juice
salt and pepper

- Sweat finely chopped onion in half the butter and the oil over low heat to soften but not colour. Add chopped garlic and finely chopped mushrooms, cover and cook gently for 15 minutes.
- Remove lid, turn heat up to medium and cook off most of the moisture in the pan. Cool a little, add remaining butter and remaining ingredients.
- Blend in a blender until smooth. Cover and chill.

MUSHROOM SAUCE

Good for pasta, baked potato topping, steak, gratins or even on toast. Add a little Hungarian paprika and serve it as a mushroom stroganoff with rice. If you don't have any red wine or Marsala, use vegetable stock instead. Dark-gilled mushrooms make a better sauce, but you can use whatever you have.

Serves 4

25 g (1 oz) dried mushrooms
2 shallots
1 clove garlic
1 tbsp olive oil
300 g (11 oz) fresh mushrooms
100 ml (3½ fl. oz) red wine or Marsala

200 ml (7 fl. oz) passata (page 153)
1 tbsp tomato paste
1 tsp sugar
1 tbsp fresh oregano
salt, black pepper

- Put dried mushrooms into hot water to just cover and soak for 15 minutes; drain. Reserve liquid.
- Fry finely chopped shallots and garlic in oil over medium-low heat to soften and tinge gold.
- Add drained mushrooms and sliced fresh mushrooms. Cook over high heat for 3 minutes, stirring occasionally. Add wine and bring to a bubble. Stir in mushroom-soaking liquid, passata, tomato paste, sugar, oregano and seasoning. Bring to a simmer and cook for 20 minutes until the sauce is thick and rich.

STUFFED MUSHROOMS WITH TWO CHEESES

One of the nicest of starters, or it will serve two hungry people for lunch or supper. You can buy soft cheese ready-mixed with garlic and herbs at the supermarket.

Serves 2–4

4 large flat mushrooms
1 tbsp olive oil
4 rashers bacon
50 g (2 oz) butter
6 spring onions

50 g (2 oz) breadcrumbs
50 g (2 oz) Cheddar
150 g (5 oz) soft cheese with garlic and herbs

- De-stalk mushrooms and finely chop the stems. Brush outsides of mushrooms with oil and put on a baking tray, gills up.
- Fry chopped bacon in butter over medium-high heat until cooked. Add mushroom stems and chopped spring onions and cook for a minute.
- Remove from the heat, stir in breadcrumbs and grated cheese and set aside.
- Divide soft cheese between mushroom caps and top with the breadcrumb mixture. Bake at 190°C/ gas mark 5 for 15 minutes, or until golden.

MUSHROOMS IN A PASTRY PARCEL

If you want to offer guests something that looks and tastes impressive but is really easy to make, try this as your main course.

Serves 4

375 g (13 oz) ready-rolled puff pastry
4 large flat mushrooms
4 tbsp basil pesto
8 sun-dried tomatoes

150 g (5 oz) soft goat's cheese
salt, black pepper
a little milk
1 egg

- Cut pastry into four rectangles and put a mushroom in the centre of each.
- Top mushrooms with pesto sauce, finely chopped tomatoes, cheese and seasoning. Brush pastry edges with milk, bring together above the mushrooms and press firmly together to seal.
- Place on a baking tray, brush with beaten egg and bake at 220°C/gas mark 7 for 20 minutes.

Although wild mushrooms have been used both in medicine and as food for thousands of years, it is only since the 1600s, beginning in Europe, that they have been cultivated.

ONION

Onions have been cultivated for over 5,000 years, and no kitchen is complete without them. A high percentage of savoury recipes include this irreplaceable vegetable for its ability to add flavour, aroma and depth to dishes. There is also a large range of dishes in which the onion takes the centre stage – and who doesn't love a plate of golden fried onions as a side dish for sausages, liver, steak or bacon?

Today a wide range of varieties is available – from the mild, large onion to the hot, eye-watering strength of some of the mid-sized bulbs. Then there are shallots, the ever-popular red onions and, of course, spring onions.

STORING

Lift onions with a fork when two rain-free days are forecast to allow them to dry out, then bring into a warm, dry, place. Spread out on slats to dry thoroughly. Tie them up in the French 'rope' way – thread strong string through the dried stalks and hang in the cool, cutting off the onions as and when required. Alternatively store in a cool place in nets, or layer in a wooden box with newspaper – check weekly for rot. Thick-necked or soft onions will not store well – use within a few weeks or freeze. Firm, narrow-necked onions will keep for months if properly stored. Shallots should last 2–4 months.

Onions brought indoors may keep for only a few weeks. They are best not stored in the fridge.

To freeze, slice and blanch for 1 minute then drain and dry – peeled shallots and small onions can be left whole. Bag and freeze – will keep for 12 months.

VARIETIES

BULB VARIETIES

White-flesh onions
For all onion recipes.
Ailsa Craig – mild, large, excellent keeper.
Fen Globe – mild, large, very good keeper, general purpose.
Sturon – mid-strength, mid-sized, good keeper, juicy.
Stuttgarter – sweet, large, good keeper, yellow-skinned.

Red onions
Mild flavour. Most uses – ideal for roasting and onion gravy. Attractive served raw.
Long Red Florence – similar in shape to French shallot; mild, sweet, short keeper.
Red Baron – large, strong flavour, good keeper.

Shallots
Attractive when used whole in casseroles or sliced in tarts and omelettes. Generally milder than onions.
Picasso – French-type shallot. Pink-flecked with perhaps the finest flavour.
Yellow Moon – early variety with good bolting resistance. Stores well.
Golden Gourmet – large bulbs with good flavour. Stores well.

SALAD VARIETIES

Spring onions (scallions)
Mild flavour, ideal for salads, stir-fries and garnishes.
Furio and Redmate – tasty, attractive, red spring onions.

Guardsman – long white stems, good flavour.
White Lisbon – with cloches you can pick these all year round.

Welsh onions
A perennial bunching type similar to spring onions. Use in similar ways to spring onions; green tops can be used instead of chives.

PICKLING VARIETIES

For all pickling recipes and chutneys; can also be used in stews.
Silverskin – white-skinned, small, mild and round.

NO COOKING REQUIRED

Spring onions are generally eaten raw, chopped in salads and sandwiches. Serve trimmed of the darkest green sections of the bulbs as part of a ploughman's cheese lunch. Bulb onions can also be very thinly sliced and eaten raw, for example in tomato and onion salad or Greek salad. Grate raw onion to add flavour to coleslaws. To increase mildness, pour boiling water over slices, then dab dry with kitchen paper.

BASIC COOKING

Bulb onions: wash away dirt, trim off roots and stalk and peel off papery skin until you reach shiny white or red flesh.

To chop onion, cut in half lengthwise and place the cut side downwards on a board. Make cuts first downwards and then horizontally towards but not through the base. Finally chop downwards across the length of the onion and throw away the tough basal section.

FRIED ONIONS

Add thinly sliced, chopped or diced onions to a frying pan with 1 tbsp oil or butter for every onion. For serving as a side vegetable, fry sliced onions over medium-high heat, turning frequently, until soft, golden and lightly crisped: 10–15 minutes. For use in soups and casseroles, chop, slice or dice and sweat over low heat, turning occasionally, until soft and transparent but not coloured: 15–20 minutes.

BAKED ONIONS

Peel medium onions. Leave the root base intact. Blanch whole onions for 10 minutes, drain upside down on kitchen paper and dry. Sit the onions in a roasting tin and brush each one all over with oil; season. Bake at 200°C/gas mark 6 for 40 minutes, or until golden and tender. Good with roast lamb.

ROAST ONIONS

Cut each onion into 6 or 8 wedges, depending on size, and toss with oil and seasoning. Roast at 190°C/gas mark 5 for 30–45 minutes until golden and tender. Discard any very dry, blackened outer leaves.

ONION RECIPES

FRENCH ONION SOUP

This classic recipe with its delicious cheese-toast topping is a favourite with everyone.

Serves 4

3 onions	1 bay leaf
4 tbsp olive oil	1 tbsp flour
50 g (2 oz) butter	1 tsp Dijon mustard
3 cloves garlic	1 baguette
1 litre (1¾ pints) beef stock	150 g (5 oz) Gruyère
250 ml (8 fl. oz) white wine	

- Fry thinly sliced onions in 3 tbsp oil and the butter over medium-low heat to soften and tinge gold, then add 2 well-crushed garlic cloves and stir for a minute. Turn heat to very low and cook for 30 minutes, stirring occasionally.

- Add stock, wine and bay leaf, stir, bring to a simmer and cook for 40 minutes. Remove 3 tbsp of the soup, cool and mix with flour and mustard. Add this mixture to the pan, stir well until the soup thickens a little and simmer for a further 15 minutes.

- Combine remaining oil with well-crushed garlic clove and brush over the sliced baguette. Top with grated cheese and grill until bubbling. Serve soup with the cheese toasts on top.

ONION TART

One of the best savoury tarts you can make, this is an enticing combination of lightly set, smooth egg custard and soft onions inside a crumbly shell.

Serves 4

300 g (11 oz) shortcrust
  pastry (page 251)
3 onions
2 tbsp olive oil

25 g (1 oz) butter
2 eggs
200 ml (7 fl. oz) cream
100 ml (3½ fl. oz) milk

50 g (2 oz) grated Parmesan
2 tsp fresh thyme leaves
salt, black pepper

- Roll out pastry and line a 23 cm (9 in.) flan tin. Bake blind.

- Fry thinly sliced onions in oil and butter over medium-low heat to soften and tinge gold, then turn heat to very low and cook for a further 30 minutes until onions are soft and tender.

- In a bowl combine beaten eggs, cream, milk, cheese, thyme and seasoning, then stir in the onions. Spoon mixture into flan case and bake at 190°C/gas mark 5 for 25 minutes, or until golden and just set.

CREAMED SHALLOTS AND PEAS

A side dish that would be really good with salmon or white fish and also goes very well with lamb chops.

Serves 4

20 shallots
40 g (1½ oz) butter
300 g (11 oz) small tender peas
50 ml (2 fl. oz) vegetable stock
100 ml (3½ fl. oz) cream
½ tsp ground nutmeg
salt, black pepper

- Fry shallots in butter over medium-low heat, turning once or twice, for 15 minutes, or until tender and tinged gold all over.
- Add peas and stock. Cover and braise for 10 minutes. Add cream, nutmeg and seasoning, stir and cook for a further 2 minutes.

PISSALADIÈRE

The long, slow cooking of the onions in this famous French tart gives them a soft, smooth caramel texture which is really delicious. If you prefer, you can replace the pastry with a pizza base (page 251).

Serves 4

6 onions
5 tbsp olive oil
3 cloves garlic
salt, black pepper
375 g (13 oz) ready-rolled puff pastry
1 egg
50 g (2 oz) can anchovies
20 stoned black olives

- Fry thinly sliced onions in oil in a heavy-based pan over medium-low heat to soften and tinge gold, stirring occasionally. Add finely chopped garlic and seasoning. Turn heat down to very low and continue cooking for a further 45 minutes until the onions are reduced and very soft but still no more than a pale gold colour.
- Put pastry on a greased baking tray and with a very sharp knife score round edge 1 cm (½ in.) in, making sure not to cut all the way through to the tray. Spread onion evenly over pastry inside the scored line, then brush pastry edges with beaten egg.
- Arrange anchovies and halved olives over the top and bake at 200°C/gas mark 6 for 25 minutes, or until pastry edges are golden and the tart is cooked through. Serve warm.

ROAST ONIONS WITH CHEESE AND CIDER

Served with crusty bread, this makes an excellent supper dish.

Serves 4

8 onions, each no more than 125 g (4 oz)
2 tbsp olive oil
50 g (2 oz) butter
200 ml (7 fl. oz) dry cider
200 g (7 oz) cream cheese
salt, black pepper

- Cut each onion flat at the root end and make a deep cut crosswise at the top. Brush each onion thoroughly with oil and sit in a baking tray.
- Divide butter between onions, pressing into the cross cut. Pour cider over, season, cover with foil and roast at 190°C/gas mark 5 for 30 minutes. Remove foil, baste with juices and cook, uncovered, for a further 15 minutes, or until onions are golden and tender.
- Spread cheese over and into each onion and return to oven for 6–7 minutes to melt.

BATTERED ONION RINGS

Try these tasty rings as a starter with chilli and tomato salsa or sweet chilli sauce (pages 56 and 60), or have them on the side with steak or grilled chicken. Using water instead of eggs and milk for the batter makes it much crisper.

Serves 4

100 g (3½ oz) plain flour   1 large onion
1 tbsp cornflour   vegetable oil
1 tsp salt

- Combine flours and salt in a mixing bowl and then add ice-cold water until you have a thick batter. Allow to stand for 30 minutes.
- Cut onion into rings and separate each slice into 2-layer rings. Add to batter and stir well.
- Half fill a large pan with oil and heat to 180°C, or until a cube of bread dropped in turns golden in 30 seconds.
- Fry battered rings in the hot oil for 1–2 minutes until golden. Remove with a slotted spatula and drain on kitchen paper to serve.

The longer you store onions, the milder they tend to become and they will lose much of their ability to make your eyes water.

BAKED ONIONS WITH CREAM AND PARMESAN

The perfect dish to accompany roast leg of lamb.

Serves 4

20 small white onions or shallots
salt, black pepper
2 tsp fresh chopped sage

400 ml (14 fl. oz) cream
50 g (2 oz) breadcrumbs
50 g (2 oz) grated Parmesan

- Blanch onions for 5 minutes to soften, then drain and dry on kitchen paper. Arrange in a baking dish.
- Season well, sprinkle with sage and pour cream over. Combine breadcrumbs and cheese and sprinkle evenly over top. Bake at 180°C/gas mark 4 for 40 minutes until golden.

ONION RELISH

An easy, tangy relish. It's very good with beefburgers and grills, or as a cheese on toast topping. Use either red onions with red wine vinegar or white onions with white wine vinegar. The relish will keep for at least 2 weeks in an airtight container in the fridge.

Serves 4–6

2 onions
50 g (2 oz) butter
salt, black pepper

2 tbsp sugar
2 tbsp wine vinegar
1 tbsp balsamic vinegar

- Fry thinly sliced onions in butter over medium heat to soften and tinge gold. Season and stir in sugar, then fry until sugar is melted and onions are caramelized: approx. 5 minutes.
- Stir in vinegars and cook for a further 3 minutes, stirring. Add a little hot water if the pan gets dry.

SWEET AND SOUR SHALLOTS

You can use this easy recipe as a side dish for pork, gammon or lamb, or allow to cool and eat with cheese and biscuits.

Serves 4

20 shallots
50 g (2 oz) butter

3 tbsp soft light brown sugar
3 tbsp cider vinegar

- Halve large shallots, leave smaller ones whole. Fry in butter over low heat for approx. 15 minutes, shaking the pan and turning shallots once or twice. When all are lightly coloured and tender, turn heat up to medium and stir in sugar, vinegar and 2 tbsp hot water.
- Cook to dissolve sugar, stirring until the sauce coats the shallots.

ONION AND RED WINE GRAVY

For this gravy to be a success, you need to give the onion plenty of time to cook over low-medium heat so that it is nicely coloured and cooked through but not at all crisp. Beef stock gives the richest gravy, but you can also use chicken or vegetable. Great with sausages and toad in the hole.

Serves 4

2 onions
25 g (1 oz) butter
1 tbsp olive oil
1 tbsp flour
100 ml (3½ fl. oz) fruity red wine

2 tsp fresh thyme leaves
250 ml (8 fl. oz) stock
salt, black pepper

- Fry thinly sliced onions in butter and oil over medium heat to soften and brown, stirring occasionally. If the onions begin to look dry, add a dash of stock.
- When they are thoroughly soft, stir in the flour for a minute, then add wine and thyme. Stir again for 2 minutes.
- Add stock, stir and simmer for 10 minutes. Season.

ONION BHAJIS

Surprisingly easy to make, these make a tasty appetizer or part of an Indian meal. Serve with mango chutney or cucumber raita (page 80). Traditionally, gram (chick pea) flour is used and is becoming much easier to find, but wheat flour will be fine.

Makes 8–12 bhajis/serves 4

1 large onion
2 cloves garlic
75 g (3 oz) flour
2 tsp ground ginger
½ tsp each turmeric, chilli powder, ground cumin and ground coriander seed
salt, black pepper
1 egg yolk
2 tbsp fresh chopped coriander leaves
vegetable oil

- Combine thinly sliced onions and chopped garlic with flour, all the dry spices and seasoning. Stir in beaten egg yolk with a little water to make a thick batter, then stir in coriander leaves. Cover and set aside for 30 minutes.
- Half fill a large pan with oil and heat to 180°C, or until a cube of bread dropped in turns golden in 30 seconds. Drop large spoonfuls of mixture into the oil and fry for 2 minutes or until golden. Remove with a slotted spoon and drain on kitchen paper. Serve hot.

RED ONIONS STUFFED WITH BACON AND MUSHROOMS

This easy dish is a meal in itself with salad and bread, or half quantities would make a good starter.

Serves 4

125 ml (4 fl. oz) red wine
125 ml (4 fl. oz) chicken stock
25 g (1 oz) dried wild mushrooms
4 large red onions
3 tbsp olive oil
4 slices bacon
200 g (7 oz) mushrooms
8 spring onions
2 tbsp fresh chopped parsley
salt, black pepper

- Combine red wine and stock, then pour some over dried mushrooms to just cover. Leave for 20 minutes, then drain and chop. Reserve liquid.

- Halve onions lengthwise and scoop out half of the centre layers from each; finely chop these layers. Brush outer sides of onion halves with some of the oil and lay hollow side up in a roasting tin.

- Fry finely chopped onion and bacon in remaining oil over medium heat for 3 minutes. Add chopped mushrooms and dried mushrooms and cook for a further 3 minutes. Stir chopped spring onions, parsley and seasoning into the pan.

- Spoon mushroom mixture into onion halves. Pour stock and wine mixture (including mushroom-soaking liquid) into pan around onions. Cover with foil and bake at 190°C/gas mark 5 for 30 minutes.

- Remove foil, baste onions and cook for a further 20 minutes, uncovered, basting twice more, until the onions are tender and the sauce reduced.

SPRING ONION AND CHIVE FRITTATA

A no-fuss supper full of rich, satisfying flavour. Serve with green salad and sliced tomatoes.

Serves 4

3 slices bacon
2 tbsp olive oil
16 spring onions
300 g (11 oz) cooked new potatoes
2 tbsp fresh chopped chives
salt, black pepper
75 g (3 oz) Cheddar
6 eggs

- Fry bacon in oil over medium-high heat until just crisp. Push to the side and stir-fry sliced spring onions for a minute. Remove pan contents with a slotted spoon, crumble bacon and set aside.

- Slice potatoes and add to the pan evenly. Sprinkle bacon, spring onions, chives and seasoning over the top with half the grated cheese.

- Beat eggs with seasoning and pour into the pan. Cook over medium-low heat until the underside is golden and the top not quite set. Sprinkle remaining cheese over and put pan under a hot grill (handle outwards) for 1–2 minutes to brown the top.

ONION BREAD

An easy soda loaf which needs eating within a day of making – but that won't be a problem. You can add chopped olives or sun-dried tomatoes if you like.

Serves 8

1 onion
1 tbsp olive oil
450 g (1 lb) strong plain flour
1 tsp bicarbonate of soda
150 g (5 oz) Cheddar
300 ml (½ pint) natural yogurt

- Sweat finely chopped onion in oil over low heat to soften but not colour.

- Sift flour and bicarbonate of soda into a mixing bowl. Stir in most of the grated cheese and the cooked onions.

- Stir 50 ml (2 fl. oz) water into yogurt and combine with flour mixture to form a soft dough.

- Knead on a floured surface until dough is smooth and pliable. Shape into a round and place on a greased baking sheet. Mark out 8 wedges with a sharp knife. Sprinkle remaining cheese over.

- Bake at 220°C/gas mark 7 for 20 minutes.

Folklore is full of advice on how to stop onions making you cry as you peel them. Suggestions include chewing gum, lighting a candle or even putting a piece of bread in your mouth.

PARSNIP

Parsnips are from the same family as carrots and are also sweet, but with a distinctive nutty flavour. Reasonably easy to grow, they are winter-hardy and therefore an important vegetable in the kitchen during the colder months.

Parsnips are under-used in kitchens today, which is a shame, as they lend themselves to a variety of dishes and can be used instead of potatoes – for example, as a mash topping for cottage pie. Roasted, they are delicious with any joint and go especially well with strong meats such as beef, game and turkey.

STORING

Parsnips can be left in the ground over winter and dug up as required. In harsh winters, lift, allow to dry and remove dirt with a soft brush. Don't wash. Cut leaves 1 cm (½ in.) above the crowns and place between layers of sand or dry compost in boxes. Store in a dry shed. Inspect every month: should keep until March.

Parsnips will store for up to 2 weeks in plastic bags in the fridge – airholes in the bags will help. They can also be puréed and frozen, or peeled, chopped and blanched for 2 minutes, then bagged for freezing.

NO COOKING REQUIRED

Grate tender young parsnip into winter salads with carrot and beetroot.

BASIC COOKING

Cut away the top of the parsnip until the dark central core no longer shows. Trim off thin end roots. Young, unblemished parsnips can simply be washed and scrubbed before use, but older ones should be peeled and the central core removed.

BOILED PARSNIPS

Cut parsnips into chunks and boil in salted water for 6–10 minutes, depending on size. Drain and stir in a knob of butter.

STEAMED PARSNIPS

Cut into slices, place in a steamer over boiling water and steam for 8–12 minutes until tender. Season.

MASHED PARSNIPS

Boil chunks of parsnip, then mash with 10 g (¼ oz) butter for every 100 g (3½ oz) parsnip. Season and thin with a little milk.

FRIED PARSNIPS

Fry tender young parsnip slices or thin batons in oil over medium-high heat, turning occasionally, until golden and tender. Blanch older parsnips for 2–3 minutes to soften before frying.

ROAST PARSNIPS

Use small whole parsnips or cut larger ones into quarters or thick batons. Toss in vegetable oil and seasoning and roast at 190°C/gas mark 5 for 30–40 minutes until golden and tender.

PARSNIP CRISPS

Finely slice parsnips lengthwise and pat dry. Half-fill a large pan with oil and heat to 180°C, or until a cube of bread dropped in turns golden in 30 seconds. Fry parsnip slices in batches for 2 minutes, or until golden, stirring occasionally. Drain cooked crisps on kitchen paper.

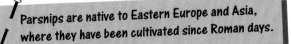

Parsnips are native to Eastern Europe and Asia, where they have been cultivated since Roman days.

PARSNIP RECIPES

PARSNIP GRATIN

One of the best accompaniments for roast beef, this can also make a good supper dish.

Serves 4

4 parsnips (approx. 800 g/1¾ lb)
400 ml (14 fl. oz) milk
100 ml (3½ fl. oz) cream
100 ml (3½ fl. oz) vegetable stock
3 tsp Dijon mustard
½ tsp ground nutmeg
50 g (2 oz) Cheddar
salt, black pepper
50 g (2 oz) grated Parmesan

- Thinly slice parsnips and blanch for a minute. Drain and pat dry. Arrange in a shallow ovenproof dish.

- Combine milk, cream, stock, mustard, nutmeg, grated Cheddar and seasoning and pour over parsnips.

- Sprinkle Parmesan on top and bake at 190°C/gas mark 5 for 30–40 minutes until parsnips are tender and the top is bubbling.

SPICY PARSNIP SOUP

One of the best warming winter soups you can find – and really quick and easy to make.

Serves 4

4 parsnips (approx. 800 g/1¾ lb)	2 tsp curry powder
1 onion	600 ml (1 pint) chicken stock
50 g (2 oz) butter	600 ml (1 pint) milk
	salt, black pepper

- Fry chopped parsnips and onion in butter in a lidded pan over low heat for 5 minutes to soften but not colour. Add curry powder and stir for a minute.
- Add stock, milk and seasoning, bring to a simmer, cover and cook for 20 minutes. Allow to cool a little.
- Blend in a blender until smooth. Reheat and check seasoning.

PARSNIP AND APPLE MASH

The perfect side dish for pork chops, sausages or roast pork. Bramley apples are ideal as they naturally break up on cooking and mash easily.

Serves 4

1 large cooking apple	50 g (2 oz) butter
¼ tsp ground nutmeg	100 ml (3½ fl. oz) milk
¼ tsp ground cinnamon	salt, white pepper
4 parsnips	

- Cook the peeled, chopped apple in a pan with 1 tbsp water and the spices for 5 minutes, stirring frequently, until soft and breaking up. Mash well.
- Boil chopped parsnips until tender. Mash with butter, milk and seasoning.
- Combine apples and parsnips thoroughly until you have a smooth mash.

HONEY-ROAST PARSNIPS

Honey brings out the sweetness of parsnips. Try this with a gammon joint or lamb.

Serves 4

4 parsnips	5 tbsp runny honey
4 tbsp vegetable oil	salt, black pepper

- Cut parsnips into thick batons and blanch for 2 minutes. Drain and pat dry.
- Toss in a roasting tin with oil. Warm honey a little until it is very runny and pour over parsnips. Toss and season. Roast at 190°C/gas mark 5 for 30 minutes, turning once or twice, until dark golden and sticky.

PARSNIP AND APPLE SOUP

Parsnips marry very well with apples, so give this soup a try. To serve, sprinkle some croutons on top.

Serves 4

4 parsnips (approx. 800 g/1¾ lb)
1 large cooking apple
25 g (1 oz) butter
1.2 litres (2 pints) chicken stock
3 fresh sage leaves
2 cloves
125 ml (4 fl. oz) cream
salt, black pepper

- Fry chopped parsnips and apple in butter in a lidded pan over low heat for 5 minutes to soften but not colour.
- Add stock, sage and cloves. Bring to a simmer, cover and cook for 20 minutes. Allow to cool a little.
- Remove sage leaves and cloves. Blend in a blender until smooth. Stir in cream, reheat and season.

WARM PARSNIP AND ONION SALAD

The tasty salad dressing is absorbed well because the vegetables are warm. Try this with chicken or game. The handful of rocket adds a good colour and a hint of pepper, but if you don't have any to hand use any strong-flavoured salad leaf.

Serves 4

4 parsnips
2 red onions
4 tbsp olive oil
1 tbsp maple syrup
2 tbsp white wine vinegar
1 tsp Dijon mustard
salt, black pepper
25 g (1 oz) rocket leaves
2 tsp sesame seeds

- Cut parsnips into thick wedges, quarter onions and put in a roasting tin. Toss with half the oil and roast at 200°C/gas mark 6 for 30 minutes, turning occasionally, until tender and the parsnips are light gold.
- Combine remaining oil with maple syrup, vinegar, mustard and seasoning. Toss cooked warm vegetables in dressing, lightly combine with rocket and sprinkle with sesame seeds.

Parsnips make a sweet, refreshing drink when juiced with apples.

CURRIED PARSNIP AND CHICKEN PIE

This pie is something special. It takes a while to make but is very easy, and is good for a family supper or a dinner party.

Serves 4

3 skinless chicken breast fillets
2 tbsp sunflower oil
2 parsnips
1 leek
1 carrot
1 tsp each chilli powder, turmeric and ground cumin
1 tbsp garam masala
100 g (3½ oz) cooked peas

75 g (3 oz) butter
1 tbsp plain flour
300 ml (½ pint) chicken stock
100 ml (3½ fl. oz) thick coconut milk
3 tbsp fresh chopped coriander
8 sheets filo pastry

- Cut chicken into bite-sized pieces and fry in half the oil over medium-high heat for a few minutes to brown on all sides. Remove and place in a pie dish.

- Add remaining oil to pan and fry chopped parsnips, leek and carrot over medium-low heat for 10 minutes, stirring frequently, to soften and lightly colour. Add spices for last minute of cooking and stir well. Transfer to the pie dish with the cooked peas.

- Melt 25 g (1 oz) of the butter in the same pan over medium heat. Add flour and stir for a minute. Gradually stir in stock to make a smooth sauce, then add coconut milk and coriander. Pour into pie dish.

- Brush each filo layer in turn with melted butter, then scrunch up a little and lay on top of the pie, tucking the edges into the sides and finishing with butter. Bake at 190°C/gas mark 5 for 25 minutes until the top is golden.

PARSNIP AND TOMATO BAKE

Parsnips go well with tomatoes – the sweet acidity of the fruit lifts the parsnip flavour. Cheese and crumbs are added for a complete supper or a side dish with meat or poultry for a hearty meal.

Serves 4

4 parsnips
50 g (2 oz) butter
6 tomatoes
salt, black pepper

½ tsp paprika
a little tomato juice
100 g (3½ oz) mature Cheddar
50 g (2 oz) breadcrumbs

- Slice parsnips quite thinly lengthwise and boil until just tender. Drain and pat dry.

- Place half the parsnips in a greased ovenproof dish, then add half the peeled and chopped tomatoes, the seasoning and paprika. Pour a little tomato juice over (you may not need this if the tomatoes are very juicy).

- Repeat the layer, then combine grated cheese with breadcrumbs and sprinkle on top. Bake at 190°C/gas mark 5 for 30 minutes, or until the top is golden.

PARSNIP SPONGE CAKE

Parsnips are as sweet as carrots and make just as good an ingredient in cakes.

Makes 10 slices

175 g (6 oz) butter
250 g (9 oz) soft brown sugar
100 ml (3½ fl. oz) runny honey
3 large eggs
250 g (9 oz) self-raising flour
2 tsp baking powder
1 tsp mixed spice
250 g (9 oz) parsnips
1 dessert apple
1 orange
200 g (7 oz) cream cheese icing (page 250)
1 tbsp icing sugar

- Grease two 20 cm (8 in.) sandwich tins with some of the butter and line with lightly greased baking parchment.

- Stir butter, sugar and honey in a pan over medium-low heat until all sugar is dissolved. Cool a little.

- Combine thoroughly with beaten eggs. Stir in flour, baking powder and spice. Stir in grated parsnips and apple, orange juice and grated zest. Divide between tins and bake at 180°C/gas mark 4 for 25–30 minutes until a metal skewer inserted in the centre comes out clean.

- Cool cakes, then turn out on wire racks to cool completely. Spread icing over one cut half and sandwich the other on top. Dust with icing sugar.

PEA

Peas are one of the great seasonal delights for the cook. The first pickings brought into the kitchen herald summer, the season of salads and light meals. They are also one of the few vegetables that almost all children enjoy!

The sweetness of young peas is a good foil for several foods, including eggs, lamb, ham and fish. They also add colour and taste to dishes such as fried rice, kedgeree, paella, omelettes and curries. Their flavour is enhanced by several fresh herbs: mint, summer savory and parsley. If peas are left to grow in the pod for too long, the sugars turn into starch and they become tougher and lose their delicate sweetness.

Peas are members of the legume family and nowadays we also often grow them to eat in their pods – either as mangetout or sugar snaps, so expanding their repertoire.

It is a good idea to dry some peas for winter use in soups, stews and as purées.

STORING

Peas are best eaten as fresh as possible, but they can be picked in the pod and stored in a plastic bag in the fridge for a day or two. Once podded, eat the same day.

Peas freeze well: pod, blanch for 1 minute, drain and freeze in plastic bags. Once defrosted they can be used in any recipe apart from those that require raw peas.

To dry peas, leave the pods on the plant until they start to shrivel (in wet weather lift plants and hang in bundles in a greenhouse or shed until ripe), pod them and lay them out on paper-covered trays in a warm, airy place to dry; a very cool oven can be used to hasten the process. Store in airtight jars.

NO COOKING REQUIRED

Tender young fresh peas are delicious eaten raw. Try them as a snack instead of sweets, or toss them into a green salad or over a strong cheese salad.

BASIC COOKING

Pop pods open using thumb and forefinger – if the pods are fresh and the peas small they should snap and open easily. Discard any large, starchy peas (often these have a square shape) or discoloured ones; check for maggots. Top and tail mangetout and sugar snaps, then wash if necessary

BOILED PEAS

Boil peas in lightly salted water – sprigs of mint can be added. Petits pois will take 2–3 minutes and fresh peas should cook in 3–4 minutes. Mangetout will take a minute longer and sugar snaps 2 minutes longer, on average. Drain and add a knob of butter – chopped mint is optional.

STEAMED PEAS

Put peas in a steamer over a pan of boiling water and steam for 4–6 minutes, depending on their size. Allow 1–2 minutes longer for mangetout and sugar snaps. Drain, season, and add a knob of butter to enhance flavour.

PEAS IN BUTTER

Boil peas until tender, drain and put them back in the pan. Add 15 g (½ oz) butter for every 100 g (3½ oz) peas and ½ tsp sugar, then stir over high heat for 2 minutes. Serve sprinkled with chopped herbs.

PURÉED PEAS

Boil peas, drain, add 10 g (¼ oz) butter and 1 tsp finely chopped mint for every 100 g (3½ oz) peas, season and mash with a fork, or purée in a blender for a smoother finish.

BOILED DRIED PEAS

Simmer in water for 30 minutes, drain and use in your recipe. Leave dried and add to soups and casseroles; they should be cooked in approx. 30 minutes.

PEA RECIPES

PEAS À LA FRANÇAISE

The flavour combinations in this classic French side dish are beautiful. If you don't have shallots to hand, use large spring onions as a substitute. Try it served with any roast meat or game.

Serves 4

800 g (1¾ lb) peas	**1 bouquet garni**
1 soft lettuce	**1 tsp sugar**
12 small shallots	**salt, black pepper**
75 g (3 oz) butter	

- Put peas in a pan with shredded lettuce, peeled shallots, 50 g (2 oz) of the butter, and the remaining ingredients. Add 4 tbsp water.

- Bring to a simmer and cook, covered, on very low heat for 30 minutes. When everything is tender, remove bouquet garni, stir in remaining butter and serve.

PEA AND HAM SOUP

In the UK this is the traditional soup to make with peas – ideal for a cold winter's day if you have any peas left in the freezer. Ham stock cubes are easy to find in the supermarket, or you can make your own stock.

Serves 4

1 onion	1 litre (1¾ pints) ham
2 cloves garlic	stock
4 rashers unsmoked	800 g (1¾ lb) peas
streaky bacon	salt, black pepper
25 g (1 oz) butter	75 g (3 oz) lean ham

- Sweat finely chopped onions, garlic and bacon in butter over low heat to soften but not colour – approx. 15 minutes.
- Add stock, bring to a simmer and cook, covered, for 30 minutes, adding peas for the last 10 minutes of cooking time.
- Allow soup to cool a little, then blend in a blender until smooth. Reheat, season and serve garnished with finely chopped ham.

MUSHY PEAS

Mushy peas have been a part of the British diet – particularly in the north of England – for hundreds of years and are traditionally served with ham or fried fish and chips. Once cooked, mushy peas freeze well.

Serves 4

225 g (8 oz) dried peas	40 g (1½ oz) butter
1 tsp bicarbonate	salt, black pepper
of soda	

- Soak peas overnight in 750 ml (1¼ pints) water with the bicarbonate of soda added.
- Drain and rinse, then put in a pan and cover with water. Bring to a simmer and cook for an hour, or until soft – depending on age, this may take much longer. Stir occasionally.
- The peas should break up as they cook and there should be no liquid left, but the peas should be mushy – moist, soft and purée-like. Beat in butter and seasoning.

In early times peas were mainly eaten in their dried form. In Britain and France it wasn't until around the 17th century that they were eaten fresh.

EASY PAELLA WITH PEAS

Spanish paella doesn't have to be a drawn-out dish to prepare – here's an easy version. You can find paella rice and packs of frozen mixed seafood in the supermarket. If you don't want to use chorizo (Spanish spicy sausage), use cooked chicken instead.

Serves 4

1 large leek
1 tbsp olive oil
125 g (4 oz) chorizo
1 tsp sweet paprika
300 g (11 oz) paella rice
1 litre (1¾ pints) chicken stock
250 g (9 oz) peas
400 g (14 oz) pack mixed seafood

- Sweat finely chopped leek in oil over low heat to soften but not colour. Add chopped chorizo, turn heat up to medium and fry, stirring occasionally, for 3–4 minutes.
- Stir in paprika and rice for a minute, then pour in stock. Bring to a simmer and cook for 20 minutes, stirring from time to time.
- Add peas and defrosted seafood and cook for a further 10 minutes, or until the rice is tender but still moist. Check seasoning and serve immediately.

SPLIT PEA SOUP

A great recipe for a cold day. You can use vegetable stock instead of chicken if you prefer.

Serves 4

2 onions
2 carrots
2 stalks celery
2 cloves garlic
2 tbsp vegetable oil
200 g (7 oz) dried peas
1 litre (1¾ pints) chicken stock
1 bay leaf
salt, black pepper

- Sweat chopped onions, carrots, celery and garlic in oil over low heat to soften but not colour.
- Stir in peas, stock and bay leaf, bring to a simmer, cover and cook for 1–2 hours, or until peas are tender, stirring occasionally.
- Allow to cool a little, remove bay leaf and blend in a blender. Return to pan, season and reheat.

PEA AND POTATO PASTIES

These are like a British version of Indian pea samosas, but they are less fiddly to make, creamier and not spicy. They are good hot or cold and make nice picnic pies.

Serves 4

100 ml (3½ fl. oz) Mascarpone
25 ml (1 fl. oz) milk
200 g (7 oz) cooked potato
6 spring onions
150 g (5 oz) peas
1 tbsp fresh chopped mint
1 tbsp fresh chopped parsley
50 g (2 oz) Cheddar
salt, black pepper
300 g (11 oz) shortcrust pastry (page 251)
1 egg

- Thin the Mascarpone with a little of the milk, then stir in chopped potato and diced spring onions, followed by cooked peas, herbs, grated cheese and seasoning.
- Roll out pastry very thin and cut into 4 pieces. Divide filling between the centres of each piece.
- Brush edges of pastry with remaining milk, then bring all the edges up and press them firmly together to make a parcel. Brush parcels with beaten egg, place on a lightly greased baking sheet and cook at 200°C/gas mark 6 for 25 minutes, or until golden.

PEA AND LEMON DIP

If you have a glut of fresh peas, make this dip instead of buying hummus – it tastes really fresh and tangy. Or use it as a sauce-cum-side-dish with grilled fish. Try to use a good extra-virgin olive oil.

Serves 4

500 g (1¼ lb) peas	1 tsp ground cumin
3 cloves garlic	1 tsp ground coriander
1 tbsp light tahini	2 tbsp olive oil
juice of 1 lemon	salt, black pepper

- Boil peas, drain and add to a blender with remaining ingredients. Blend until just smooth but still with some texture. Chill if using as a dip.

PEA AND FETA TART

The sweetness of the peas is very good with the sharpness of the cheese in this easy-to-make tart.

Serves 4

300 g (11 oz) shortcrust pastry (page 251)	200 g (7 oz) feta cheese
500 g (1¼ lb) peas	salt, black pepper
2 eggs	75 g (3 oz) grated
300 ml (½ pint) cream	Parmesan
1 tbsp fresh chopped parsley	

- Line a 23 cm (9 in.) tart tin with the pastry and bake blind.
- Boil peas, drain and crush lightly. Combine with beaten eggs, cream, parsley, crumbled feta and seasoning.
- Pour mixture into the tart case, sprinkle Parmesan over and bake at 200°C/gas mark 6 for 30 minutes, or until filling is lightly set. Allow to cool a little and then eat either warm or cold.

CHINESE STIR-FRIED SUGAR SNAPS

Try these served with salmon or grilled chicken.

Serves 4

450 g (1 lb) sugar snaps	2 cloves garlic
2 tbsp toasted sesame oil	small piece ginger
100 g (3½ oz) spring onions	1 tbsp soy sauce
1 red chilli	

- Heat oil in a wok or large pan and stir-fry sugar snaps over high heat for 3 minutes.
- Halve spring onions lengthwise, finely chop chilli and garlic, peel and chop ginger. Add to pan and stir for a further 2 minutes.
- Add soy sauce and stir to combine.

POTATO

The potato is our most popular vegetable – for millions of families it would be a strain to exist for two days without having at least one potato dish. There are many hundreds of recipes, but most of us use a very limited range. Chips, crisps and mashed potatoes are the everyday standbys, with roast, baked and boiled as popular occasional methods of preparation.

Some experts feel that it is a waste of time to grow potatoes – there are much more valuable ways of using limited garden space. There is an argument for this view if we are thinking of Maincrop potatoes, but growing Earlies for cooking straight from the garden as new potatoes is certainly worthwhile for everyone.

STORING

Ensure tubers are bone dry and store them in a cool, dark and dry place. Good ventilation is necessary – a slatted shelf is ideal. If exposed to light, the tuber skins/outer flesh may turn green; these parts are poisonous and shouldn't be eaten. Check the potatoes now and then and remove any with soft, mouldy or wet patches. Maincrops should keep for several months but Earlies should be used after a week or two.

VARIETIES

EARLIES

First Earlies are harvested in June or July. They do not produce high yields, but all produce **new potatoes** when shop prices are high. A new potato is not stored before use. The skin can be rubbed off with your finger. **Second Earlies** bridge the gap between the First Earlies of July and the Maincrops of autumn. Most are suitable for boiling, but only a few (e.g. Maris Peer) are used as new potatoes.

MAINCROPS

Maincrops provide the heaviest yields – these **old potatoes** are stored for winter use. The earliest are ready for lifting at the beginning of September.

WAXY FLESH

Waxy potatoes are low in starch and high in water content – they hold their shape after boiling. The very waxy ones are **salad potatoes**; these varieties are ideal for potato salad and for boiling as new potatoes, even though not all are Early varieties. Examples of salad potatoes are Charlotte, Anya and Pink Fir Apple.

FLOURY FLESH

Floury potatoes are high in starch and low in water content – they become fluffy when cooked. This property makes them the first choice for baking and mashing, but they are not a good choice for boiling.

BASIC COOKING

FRIED POTATOES

Peel and cut old potatoes into even-sized matchsticks or chips; dry thoroughly. Fill a chip pan one-third full with vegetable oil. Heat to 190°C, or until one chip dropped in rises to the surface and the oil bubbles. Cook chips in batches, filling the pan basket to one-third full and reheating the oil between batches. Fry until golden: 3–8 minutes, depending on thickness. Drain cooked chips on kitchen paper.

	approx. 0.3 cm (1/8 in.) wide	approx. 0.6 cm (1/4 in.) wide	approx. 1.2 cm (1/2 in.) wide
FRANCE	Pommes allumettes	Pommes frites	Pommes Pont-Neuf
GREAT BRITAIN	Matchstick potatoes	Chips	Chips
U.S.A.	Shoestring potatoes	French fries	French fries

BOILED POTATOES

Potatoes should be about the same size – cut if necessary. Put into a pan of boiling salted water; the water should just cover the potatoes. Cover and boil for about 20 minutes until tender. Boiled potatoes are cooked when a sharp knife will pierce through to the centre with no resistance. Drain, then shake in pan for a minute to dry before serving.

BAKED POTATOES

Wash and dry medium–large floury potatoes; prick all over with a fork. Brush lightly with oil and bake directly on an oven rack at 200°C/gas mark 6 for 50–60 minutes. When ready, a metal skewer should go through the centre with no resistance. Serve split open with butter. For ultra-quick 'baking' simply microwave on high for approx. 8 minutes (1 medium potato) or 12 minutes (2 medium potatoes).

ROAST POTATOES

Peel and cut old potatoes – floury varieties are best – into 5 cm (2 in.) chunks. Parboil for 5 minutes, drain and shake the pan for a minute to dry them off. Heat 1 tbsp oil for every 200 g (7 oz) potatoes in a roasting tin, tip in potatoes and baste. Roast at 200°C/gas mark 6 for 50 minutes, turning halfway through, until crisp and golden. Potatoes are also excellent roasted in goose or duck fat.

Chips (French fries) are the only foodstuff which all races find palatable.

STEAMED POTATOES

Wash small new potatoes and steam for 8–10 minutes or until tender. Serve tossed in butter or olive oil.

SAUTÉED POTATOES

Slice boiled potatoes into 0.5 cm (¼ in.) rounds. Fry in 1–2 tbsp oil over high heat until undersides are golden – approx. 4 minutes. Turn and cook for 2–3 minutes more. Season.

OVEN WEDGE POTATOES

Cut medium floury potatoes (skin on) lengthwise into 8 wedges, pat dry with kitchen paper and toss in a bowl with olive oil, salt and pepper, adding 1 tsp Italian or Mexican seasoning (pages 248 and 249) if liked. Spread on a tray and bake at 200°C/gas mark 6 for 25–30 minutes until golden and crisp outside and fluffy inside.

MASHED POTATOES

Peel and boil old potatoes, drain, add 15 g (½ oz) butter and 50 ml (2 fl. oz) milk for every 250 g (9 oz) potatoes, and season. Mash with a potato masher or fork until fluffy; check seasoning. For extra richness, add cream instead of milk. The flesh from baked potatoes can be used in the same way.

ANNA POTATOES

Oil a 20 cm (8 in.) cake tin and line with greaseproof paper. Thinly slice peeled, waxy potatoes and arrange overlapping layers in the tin, sprinkling each new layer with seasoning and a little melted butter. Press potatoes down well. Continue until tin is full. Cover with greaseproof paper and foil. Bake for 1 hour at 190°C/gas mark 5.

HASH BROWNS

Parboil peeled floury 5 cm (2 in.) potato chunks for 4 minutes. Drain well and cool, then grate into a mixing bowl and season. Heat butter to cover the base of a frying pan, form the grated potato into patties and fry for 3–4 minutes, turning halfway, until crisp and golden.

CHATEAU POTATOES

Cut small, waxy, peeled potatoes into rugby-ball shapes 2.5 cm (1 in.) thick and parboil for 3 minutes. Drain and put in a frying pan with 25 g (1 oz) butter for every 250 g (9 oz) potatoes, 1 tbsp oil, salt and black pepper. Fry over medium-high heat for 4 minutes, turning occasionally, until golden. Turn heat down, put lid on and cook for 15 minutes until potatoes are tender.

POTATO PANCAKES

Try these topped with smoked mackerel and horseradish sauce or bacon and maple syrup.

Serves 4

200 g (7 oz) potatoes
1 egg
25 g (1 oz) plain flour
salt, black pepper
50 ml (2 fl. oz) milk
1 tbsp vegetable oil
10 g (¼ oz) butter

- Boil potatoes and mash with beaten egg. Mix with flour and seasoning. Stir in milk and combine.
- Heat oil and butter in a frying pan, add separate tablespoons of mixture to make 8 mini pancakes and cook for 1–1½ minutes over medium heat until golden. Turn and cook for 1 minute more.

Potatoes came to Europe in the 16th century, but it was a struggle to get them accepted. In Germany armed soldiers had to be called in to force the peasants to eat them. It was not until the 19th century that the universally loved potato became a staple food across Europe.

DUCHESSE POTATOES

An impressive way to turn ordinary mashed potatoes into something special.

Serves 4

500 g (1¼ lb) potatoes   ¼ tsp ground nutmeg
1 egg   salt
50 g (2 oz) butter   a little oil for greasing

- Boil potatoes and beat egg. Mash together while still hot with butter, nutmeg and salt until really smooth.
- Fill a piping bag with the potato and pipe 8 rosettes on to a lightly greased baking tray. If you don't have a piping bag you can cut a 0.5 cm (¼ in.) corner off a strong plastic food bag and use it to pipe the mashed potato. Bake at 200°C/gas mark 6 for 25 minutes until golden.

POTATO RECIPES

LYONNAISE POTATOES

Try these with liver and bacon or lamb chops.

Serves 4

800 g (1¾ lb) potatoes   salt, black pepper
2 onions   2 tbsp fresh chopped
3 tbsp olive oil   parsley
15 g (½ oz) butter

- Boil potatoes and cut into 0.5 cm (¼ in.) slices. Cut onions into thin rings and fry in 2 tbsp oil over medium-low heat for 10 minutes to soften and tinge gold. Season, remove from pan and keep warm.
- Add remaining oil, the butter and potatoes, season and cook until golden brown, turning once.
- Arrange potatoes in a serving dish in alternate layers with the onion and more seasoning to taste. Sprinkle with parsley.

POTATO AND LEEK SOUP

This soup can be served hot in winter or chilled in summer, when it is often called 'vichyssoise'.

Serves 4

4 large leeks   salt, white pepper
1 onion   500 ml (17 fl. oz)
25 g (1 oz) butter   vegetable stock
400 g (14 oz) floury   500 ml (17 fl. oz) milk
   potatoes   2 tbsp cream

- Clean and chop white and pale green parts of leeks only. Melt butter in a large saucepan and sweat leeks and chopped onion over low heat for 10 minutes to soften but not colour.
- Add peeled and diced potatoes to pan with seasoning and stock. Cover and simmer for 20 minutes, then add milk and liquidize in a blender.
- Add more seasoning to taste. Swirl in cream.

SPANISH OMELETTE (Tortilla)

This is the simple, classic version of a flat omelette. Some people like to add cooked peas.

Serves 3

350 g (12 oz) waxy potatoes   **6 eggs**
1 onion   **salt, black pepper**
2 tbsp olive oil

- Peel and slice potatoes into 0.5 cm (¼ in.) rounds and boil for 5 minutes.
- Fry thinly sliced onion over medium-low heat in 2 tbsp of the oil in a medium (23 cm/9 in.) frying pan for 10 minutes to soften and tinge gold, stirring occasionally. Add potatoes and cook for 1 minute.
- Beat eggs in a bowl, season, then pour over the onion/potato mixture and stir.
- Turn heat to low and cook for 8 minutes until underside is golden. Put pan under a hot grill (handle outside) for 1–2 minutes to cook and brown the top. Serve hot or cold, cut into wedges.

COLCANNON

A simple Irish dish with many variations.

Serves 4

800 g (1¾ lb) floury potatoes   salt, black pepper
100 ml (3½ fl. oz) milk   400 g (14 oz) cabbage
50 g (2 oz) butter   bunch spring onions

- Peel and boil potatoes and mash with milk, butter and seasoning.
- Steam thinly sliced cabbage until tender, finely chop spring onions and stir all vegetables together. Serve hot.

POTATOES BOULANGÈRE

A good dish to make when you have the oven on for a roast. *Boulangère* is the French word for a baker's wife. Villagers would take their dishes of potatoes to the bakery to cook in the residual heat of the oven.

Serves 4

800 g (1¾ lb) potatoes   salt, black pepper
1 onion   approx. 300 ml (½ pint)
25 g (1 oz) butter   vegetable stock

- Peel and thinly slice potatoes and onion. Butter a 1 litre (1¾ pint) ovenproof dish and layer the vegetables in it, seasoning as you go.
- Pour over enough stock to just cover vegetables, dot with remaining butter and cover dish with foil. Bake at 170°C/gas mark 3 for 1 hour. Remove foil and cook for a further 30 minutes until potatoes are tender and top is browned.

POTATOES DAUPHINOISE

Great with steak or roast lamb, this is rich and delicious – but very easy to make.

Serves 4–6

900 g (2 lb) waxy potatoes   approx.100 ml
40 g (1½ oz) butter   (3½ fl. oz) milk
2 cloves garlic   pinch ground nutmeg
500 ml (17 fl. oz)   salt, black pepper
   double cream   50 g (2 oz) Gruyère

- Peel and thinly slice potatoes (no more than 0.3 cm/⅛ in. thick) and layer evenly in a 1 litre (1¾ pint) dish, greased with some of the butter.
- Combine finely chopped garlic with cream, milk, nutmeg and seasoning, then pour over potatoes. If it doesn't just cover them, add a little more milk.
- Dot with small knobs of butter and grate cheese over. Bake at 170°C/gas mark 3 for 1½ hours or until potatoes are tender when pierced with a sharp knife.

POTATO CROQUETTES

A family favourite that makes a change from chips.

Serves 4

500 g (1¼ lb) potatoes   2 tbsp flour
2 eggs   75 g (3 oz) stale
2 tsp fresh chopped parsley   breadcrumbs
salt, black pepper   2 tbsp vegetable oil

- Boil potatoes and beat eggs. Mash potatoes with half the egg, then add parsley and seasoning.
- Form potato mixture into 8 sausage shapes. Put flour, remaining egg and breadcrumbs in separate shallow dishes. Dip each croquette in flour, then egg, then breadcrumbs so each is completely covered.
- Fry croquettes in oil over medium-high heat, turning occasionally, for 5 minutes until golden. Drain on kitchen paper to serve.

POTATO RÖSTI

A classic Swiss dish to accompany meat.

Serves 4

800 g (1¾ lb) floury potatoes   1 onion
75 g (3 oz) butter   salt, black pepper

- Boil potatoes in their skins until barely cooked, drain and put in fridge for at least 2 hours. Remove skins, then grate into a bowl.
- Melt 25 g (1 oz) butter in a frying pan and sweat thinly sliced onion over low heat for 5 minutes to soften but not colour. Stir into potato. Season.
- Melt remaining butter, add potato mixture to pan and flatten gently over the whole base to form a cake. Fry over medium-high heat until underside is golden. Flip over and brown other side. Cut into wedges to serve.

POTATO SALAD

Excellent with ham or salmon.

Serves 4

600 g (1 lb 6 oz) potatoes   juice of ½ lemon
4 tbsp mayonnaise   salt, black pepper
2 tbsp natural yogurt   1 tbsp fresh
1 tsp French mustard   chopped chives

- Boil peeled potatoes; cool. Cut into small chunks.
- Combine mayonnaise, yogurt, mustard, lemon juice and seasoning. Stir into potato with chives.
- For a warm salad toss cooked new potatoes in French dressing (page 250) with chopped parsley and mint.

CHEESE AND BACON STUFFED POTATOES

An ideal family supper served with side salad.

Serves 4

4 medium–large floury potatoes	100 g (3½ oz) butter
2 tbsp vegetable oil	bunch spring onions
4 rashers lean rindless back bacon	75 ml (2½ fl. oz) milk
	salt, black pepper
	100 g (3½ oz) Cheddar

- Rub potato skins with oil and bake on a tray at 200°C/gas mark 6 for 1 hour. Add bacon to tray for final 12 minutes to crisp lightly, then crumble.

- Melt 15 g (½ oz) butter in a saucepan, add chopped onions and fry over medium-low heat for 2 minutes to soften and tinge gold.

- Halve potatoes lengthwise. Remove all but a 1 cm (½ in.) layer of flesh with a spoon, taking care not to pierce skins, and roughly mash with remaining butter, milk and seasoning. Grate cheese – add half with bacon and onions to the potatoes.

- Spoon mixture into skins, sprinkle with remaining cheese and put back in oven on baking tray for 10 minutes to brown (or under a hot grill for 2 minutes).

CHICKEN AND POTATO TRAYBAKE

This easy all-in-one makes a good alternative to a classic roast meal or a good mid-week dish for winter. If you happen to have any, you could add diced aubergine or courgette to the pan, with a little extra oil.

Serves 4

8 chicken thighs/ drumsticks	1 tbsp fresh chopped thyme
3 tbsp olive oil	1 tbsp fresh chopped rosemary
4 floury potatoes	salt, black pepper
4 red onions	200 ml (7 fl. oz) chicken stock
8 skin-on cloves garlic	
juice of 1 lemon	

- Brown chicken in 1 tbsp oil. Peel and cut potatoes into 1 cm (½ in.) rounds, quarter onions and toss vegetables in remaining oil.

- Arrange chicken and vegetables in a roasting tin with whole garlic cloves, sprinkle over lemon juice, herbs and seasoning, and bake at 190°C/gas mark 5 for 15 minutes.

- Pour stock into pan, stir, turn heat down to 170°C/gas mark 3 and cook for a further 45 minutes, adding a little water if the pan looks dry – you want to end up with several spoonfuls of pan juices to serve with the dish.

MEXICAN CHICKEN AND POTATO SUPPER

Potatoes are well suited to the spicy Mexican flavours in this hearty meal.

Serves 4

800 g (1¾ lb) potatoes
4 skinless chicken breast fillets
2 tbsp fajita spice mix
2 onions
2 red peppers
2 tbsp vegetable oil
4 tomatoes
200 g (7 oz) cooked red kidney beans
200 ml (7 fl. oz) passata (page 153)
4 tbsp sour cream
4 tbsp fresh coriander leaves

- Peel and boil potatoes until barely cooked, then dice. Thinly slice chicken and mix in a bowl with potatoes and fajita spice.

- Stir-fry chopped onions and peppers in oil over medium heat for 4 minutes to soften and brown, then add potato mixture and stir-fry for a further 3 minutes.

- Add chopped tomatoes with kidney beans, passata and 50 ml (2 fl. oz) water, put lid on and simmer for 15 minutes. Serve with sour cream and coriander garnish.

RADISH

Radish is a familiar salad vegetable – a favourite with children because they are ready to harvest so quickly and look so bright. Their crisp, refreshing texture and peppery flavour are also popular with adults and are why radishes are usually eaten raw.

Varieties are either round or bullet-shaped and can vary in colour from white through to dark red. Young, undamaged radish leaves are edible when lightly cooked in a similar way to spinach, but do not eat them raw – the hairy leaves can irritate the mouth or cause a skin rash when touched.

STORING

It's best to dig and eat as required, but radishes will keep in a plastic bag in the fridge for a day or two – remove tops before storage. Not suitable for freezing.

NO COOKING REQUIRED

Ideal to pep up cheese or ham sandwiches, but they also make a good sandwich filling with some salt and plenty of butter. Slice them into salads or use as a garnish. Or make a dip and use radish slices to scoop it up.

RADISH FANS

Top and tail radishes and lay on a chopping board with the top to your left and the tail to your right. With a sharp knife, cut to the middle of the radish lengthwise from left to right, making sure you don't cut as far as the tail. Rotate the radish slightly and continue making cuts all the way round. Drop cut radishes into iced water and soak for several hours, by which time they will be fanned out. Dry to serve.

RADISHES WITH CHEESE AND CHIVE DIP

Choose very fresh and crisp French long radishes and soak them in ice-cold water for 15 minutes before use – this helps them firm up.

Serves 4–6

200 g (7 oz) soft cheese
50 ml (2 fl. oz) mayonnaise
50 ml (2 fl. oz) mild natural yogurt
50 g (2 oz) mature Cheddar
3 tbsp fresh chopped chives
salt, black pepper
12 long radishes

- Grate cheese and combine all ingredients except radishes. Chill for an hour.
- Cut each radish into four lengthwise. Put dip in a serving dish or plate and surround with radish slices.

RED SALAD WITH RADISHES AND ONION

A salad that goes well with a strong cheese. It can also accompany a roast or tandooried chicken or fish.

Serves 4

1 red chilli
2 tbsp light olive oil
juice of 1 lime
salt, black pepper
16 radishes

1 red onion
1 red pepper
2 tbsp fresh chopped coriander

- Combine very finely chopped chilli, oil, lime juice and seasoning and set aside for 30 minutes.
- Thinly slice vegetables and arrange on a serving plate. Pour dressing over, then garnish with coriander.

Radishes were eaten in ancient Egypt and Greece, but were not cultivated in Britain until the 16th century.

RADISH, CUCUMBER AND GOAT'S CHEESE SALAD

A good light lunch for a summer's day. Serve with some French bread.

Serves 4

16 radishes
1/3 cucumber
400 g (14 oz) log goat's cheese
4 tbsp French dressing (page 250)
100 g (3½ oz) walnut pieces
4 semi-dried apricots

- Thinly slice radishes and cucumber and arrange around outer edges of breakfast-sized plates.
- Slice goat's cheese into 8 rounds and grill on an oiled grill-pan base for 3 minutes, or until bubbling. Add to centre of plates.
- Spoon dressing over, then sprinkle with walnut pieces and finely chopped apricot.

BASIC COOKING

Wash (scrub if necessary), trim off tops and tails (be careful, as some people are allergic to the hairy leaves). Small radishes are nice left whole – just pick up and eat with your fingers, or halve or slice as required. If you find radishes too hot, peel them – most of the pungency is in the skin. Prepare radishes as near to eating as you can, as they soon go soft and lose that nice crunch.

SAUTÉED RADISHES

Slice radishes and fry in oil over medium-high heat for 2–3 minutes until slightly coloured. Salt to taste.

RADISH RECIPES

ROAST RADISHES WITH SOY SAUCE AND SESAME SEEDS

Here's a good way to use up a glut of radishes before they become too big and woody. If you have no sesame oil, use more vegetable oil instead.

Serves 4

30 medium radishes	1½ tbsp soy sauce
1 tbsp vegetable oil	1 red onion
1 tbsp sesame oil	1 tbsp toasted sesame seeds

- Quarter radishes and put in a small roasting dish. Toss in the oils and ½ tbsp of the soy sauce. Roast at 190°C/gas mark 5 for 20 minutes, turning once.
- Thinly slice onion and separate layers, then stir into the radishes. Roast for a further 5–10 minutes until radishes are quite tender and onion is golden. Stir in remaining soy sauce and sprinkle with sesame seeds. Serve hot.

RADISH CURRY

Try this spicy radish dish as part of a meal with rice and curried beef or chicken. In India the chopped radish leaves are added to the dish with the spices.

Serves 4

30 radishes	1 tsp turmeric
1 onion	1 tsp coriander seeds
2 tbsp vegetable oil	½ tsp mustard powder
2 cloves garlic	2 tomatoes
3–4 chillies	salt, black pepper

- Slice radishes quite thinly and slice onion very thinly. Stir-fry in oil over medium-high heat for 3 minutes, then add finely chopped garlic and chillies, turmeric, crushed coriander seeds and mustard. Stir for a further minute.
- Stir in chopped tomatoes and seasoning, combine well, turn heat down, cover and cook over low heat for 10 minutes.

RHUBARB

Rhubarb has been grown for centuries in the British garden but originates in northern Asia. Often thought of as a fruit, the stalks of this vegetable can be pulled from the garden from early spring to summer and, although naturally sour, become delicious with the addition of sugar. Rhubarb can be used in many ways, including in desserts, pies, puddings, pancakes, cakes, chutney, jam and as a side dish for savouries.

There are several varieties of rhubarb, ranging from mainly green-stalked through to bright red. In general, the redder the stalk, the tastier and more tender it is and the less inclined to stringiness. Young forced stalks are sweeter than older stalks so need less sugar, and should not need peeling.

Note: Both the leaves and the roots of rhubarb contain oxalic acid, which is poisonous, so these parts of the plant should never be eaten.

STORING

Rhubarb is best picked throughout the season as required, but it will keep for several days in a plastic bag in the fridge. Once the stalks are too limp to snap, they aren't worth using. Stalks freeze well – wash, dry, chop into sections and open-freeze on a tray, then put in strong plastic bags.

> Timperley Early has thin stems and is a good variety of rhubarb for forcing.

> Stockbridge Arrow is a fine stringless variety of rhubarb.

> Prolonging the season, Victoria rhubarb is an excellent late variety of rhubarb.

NO COOKING REQUIRED

It is possible to eat tender young rhubarb raw – preferably dipped in sugar – but in the UK it is usually cooked.

BASIC COOKING

Cut off leaf and any green stalk near the leaf. Wash. Peel older stalks as necessary to remove string. Chop or cut into lengths as required.

POACHED RHUBARB

Put rhubarb chunks in a saucepan with 1 tbsp sugar for every 100 g (3½ oz) rhubarb (1 average stalk), plus 1–2 tbsp water – spices or vanilla can be added. Cover and cook very gently for 10 minutes until rhubarb is tender.

BAKED RHUBARB

Put rhubarb chunks in a shallow baking dish, sprinkle with soft brown sugar (1 tbsp for every stalk rhubarb). Vanilla, or a small glass of sweet wine or orange juice with ginger or cinnamon, can be added to the baking dish. Cover with foil and roast at 200°C/gas mark 6 for 15 minutes until the rhubarb is just tender and you have a sweet, thin sauce. Cook, uncovered, for a further 5 minutes to reduce the sauce.

CARAMELIZED RHUBARB

Fry rhubarb chunks in 15 g (½ oz) butter for every stalk rhubarb over medium heat until barely soft, turning once. Add soft brown sugar (1 tbsp for every stalk of rhubarb) – a pinch of cinnamon can be added. Allow to dissolve. Cook, turning gently once or twice, until you have a caramel sauce and the rhubarb is tender but not broken up.

RHUBARB RECIPES

RHUBARB FOOL

A fruit fool is an easy but tempting summer dessert – rhubarb is one of the best fruits to use. Ready-made custard is fine.

Serves 4

300 g (11 oz) rhubarb   **150 ml (¼ pint) custard (page 250)**
40 g (1½ oz) sugar   **50 g (2 oz) chopped nuts**
150 ml (¼ pint) whipping cream

- Poach chopped rhubarb with sugar and 1 tbsp water until tender and breaking up. Leave to cool.

- Lightly whip cream, fold in custard and rhubarb, then spoon into serving glasses. Top with nuts. Chill for an hour before serving.

RHUBARB COMPOTE

Rhubarb is a good accompaniment for fatty and strong meats, poultry and game. Try this with roast duck or goose.

Serves 4

1 small onion
15 g (½ oz) butter
300 g (11 oz) rhubarb
2 tsp fresh chopped ginger
½ tsp ground mixed spice
½ orange

- Sweat finely chopped onion in butter over low heat to soften but not colour. Cut rhubarb into 4 cm (1½ in.) lengths.
- Add ginger and spice to pan and cook for a further minute, then add rhubarb, orange juice and grated zest and cook gently until rhubarb is tender: approx. 10 minutes.

RHUBARB PLATE PIE

An old-fashioned rhubarb pie on a plate. Serve with custard, cream or ice cream for a real treat. Adding a little cornflour thickens the rhubarb juices.

Serves 6

300 g (11 oz) shortcrust pastry (page 251)
500 g (1¼ lb) rhubarb
75 g (3 oz) sugar
½ orange
2 tsp cornflour
1 egg

- Roll out pastry and cut 2 circles to fit a 23 cm (9 in.) pie plate. Put the first round on the plate, then top with the chopped rhubarb, sugar and orange juice and grated zest. Sprinkle in the cornflour.
- From the leftover pastry cut a 1 cm (½ in.) strip to fit on the rim of the plate. Wet this strip with water and press it on to the rim, wet side down. Now wet the top side and put the second pastry round on to form a lid, pressing firmly into the pastry strip.
- Make a hole in the centre of the pastry lid and brush the surface with beaten egg. Bake at 200°C/gas mark 6 for 25 minutes, or until the pastry is golden and the rhubarb tender.

> Rhubarb goes well with spices such as ginger and cinnamon, and is also a good partner for orange juice and strawberries. Both cream and custard reduce its tendency to sharpness.

RHUBARB CRUMBLE

The simplest, and to many minds the best, way to eat rhubarb is in a crumble. This topping is extra good – a bit like a flapjack.

Serves 4

500 g (1¼ lb) rhubarb
50 g (2 oz) sugar
½ tsp ground ginger
75 g (3 oz) demerara sugar
75 g (3 oz) porridge oats
100 g (3½ oz) self-raising flour
100 g (3½ oz) butter
2 tbsp golden syrup

- Put chopped rhubarb, sugar and ginger in a pie dish with 1 tbsp water.
- Mix demerara sugar, oats and flour in a bowl. Melt butter with syrup in a pan and stir into the dry mixture. Mix thoroughly.
- Spoon topping over rhubarb. Bake at 180°C/gas mark 4 for 30–40 minutes until golden.

STEAMED RHUBARB PUDDING

If you've never made a steamed sponge pudding, try this. All the family will love it. It goes very well with single cream or pouring custard.

Serves 6

400 g (14 oz) rhubarb	**2 eggs**
200 g (7 oz) caster sugar	**175 g (6 oz) self-raising**
125 g (4 oz) butter	**flour**
1 tsp vanilla extract	**25 ml (1 fl. oz) milk**

- Poach chopped rhubarb with 75 g (3 oz) of the sugar for 3 minutes until partially softened. Remove from heat.
- Grease a 900 ml (1½ pint) pudding basin. Put butter and remaining sugar in a bowl and cream together. Stir in vanilla extract, then gradually beat in eggs. Fold in sifted flour. Add milk to give a dropping consistency.
- Spoon rhubarb into basin, then spoon sponge mixture on top and level off.
- Butter a piece of greaseproof paper slightly bigger than the top of the basin. Make a pleat in the centre and secure it over the top of the basin. Repeat with a piece of foil. Secure with string.
- Place the basin in a pan on an inverted heatproof saucer or similar. Half fill the pan with boiling water, cover and cook for 1½ hours, adding fresh boiling water once or twice so the pan doesn't boil dry.
- Remove cover, turn out pudding on to a plate, then lift off the basin.

RHUBARB AND CUSTARD TART

This is perfect after a light main course. Try serving with a little rhubarb purée on the side. You can buy dessert pastry (containing sugar) in supermarkets.

Serves 4

300 g (11 oz) sweet
   shortcrust pastry
   (page 251)
150 ml (¼ pint) cream
150 ml (¼ pint) milk

1 tsp vanilla extract
75 g (3 oz) caster sugar
3 eggs
500 g (1¼ lb) caramelized
   rhubarb (page 128)

- Line a 23 cm (9 in.) tart tin with rolled-out pastry and bake blind.
- Combine cream, milk and vanilla in a jug. Beat sugar and eggs together in a large bowl, then, whisking continually, pour in the cream mixture.
- Arrange rhubarb in the pastry case, put tin on a baking tray and slowly pour in the custard.
- Bake for 30–40 minutes at 190°C/gas mark 5 until the custard is just set. Serve warm or cold.

RHUBARB BETTY

A cross between a crumble and a suet pudding, and very easy to make.

Serves 4

500 g (1¼ lb) rhubarb
50 g (2 oz) sugar
½ orange
100 g (3½ oz) breadcrumbs

75 g (3 oz) demerara sugar
75 g (3 oz) shredded suet
15 g (½ oz) butter

- Grease a 900 ml (1½ pint) ovenproof dish. Put in half the chopped rhubarb, sugar and grated orange zest.
- Combine breadcrumbs, demerara sugar and suet. Sprinkle half this mixture on the rhubarb. Repeat the layers. Dot with butter and bake at 180°C/gas mark 4 for 35–40 minutes until fruit is bubbling and top golden.

RHUBARB TRIFLE

This looks lovely made with young, pink, forced rhubarb.

Serves 4–6

500 g (1¼ lb) rhubarb
50 g (2 oz) sugar
1 tbsp sweet sherry
2 tbsp strawberry jam
10 sponge fingers

500 ml (17 fl. oz) custard
   (page 250)
200 ml (7 fl. oz) whipping
   cream
50 g (2 oz) walnut pieces

- Poach chopped rhubarb with sugar, sherry and 1 tbsp water until tender. Stir in jam and allow to cool.
- Layer rhubarb, sponge fingers and custard in a glass serving bowl. Top with lightly whipped cream and sprinkle walnut pieces over. Chill for an hour.

RHUBARB AND STRAWBERRY MERINGUES

A good alternative to a pavlova and they look great – especially if you have toughened glass ramekins to show off the pretty fruit colour. Use the leftover egg yolks to make a quiche.

Serves 4

300 g (11 oz) rhubarb
½ lemon
100 g (3½ oz) caster
   sugar

100 g (3½ oz) strawberries
1 tbsp strawberry jam
2 eggs

- Poach chopped rhubarb with grated lemon zest and 1 tbsp water until tender. Drain off any excess liquid. Stir in 40 g (1½ oz) sugar until dissolved, then stir in sliced strawberries and jam. Divide between four ovenproof ramekins.
- Separate eggs and whisk whites until stiff. Fold in half the remaining sugar, whisk again, then fold in remaining sugar. Pile the meringue on top of the rhubarb pots.
- Bake at 180°C/gas mark 4 for 10 minutes until the meringue is golden. Serve immediately.

RHUBARB BREAKFAST

This can, of course, also be used as a dessert.

Serves 4

400 g (14 oz) rhubarb
40 g (1½ oz) sugar
juice of ½ orange
½ tsp ground cinnamon
500 ml (17 fl. oz) Greek yogurt
65 g (2½ oz) rolled oats
2 tbsp runny honey

- Poach rhubarb with sugar, orange juice and cinnamon. Allow to cool.
- Divide yogurt between serving glasses and fold rhubarb, oats and honey through. Chill to serve.

SALSIFY AND SCORZONERA

Familiar in Belgian and Dutch homes, but neglected in UK gardens and kitchens for decades, salsify and its close relative scorzonera are becoming more popular. Deservedly so, as they have a delicious flavour which has been likened to oysters, artichoke hearts, asparagus and Jerusalem artichoke. Salsify has a pale beige skin while scorzonera has black skin. Both have the texture of a parsnip with creamy white flesh and look similar, but thinner and longer. They belong to the dandelion family and are native to the eastern Mediterranean area. Eat when fairly young, as they can be tough and woody when older. They can be boiled, mashed, sautéed or used in soups and stews, and are in season from October through winter.

Young leaves can be eaten. In autumn cut off old leaves, cover roots with several inches of soil and new, blanched shoots will push through. Treat like chicory. The flowers are also edible and can be added to salads.

Salsify and scorzonera are interchangeable in most recipes, including all those here.

STORING

Harvest before the frosts as salsify and scorzonera break easily when dug out of hard ground. Cut off leaves, dry and store in boxes between layers of compost, or refrigerate in a plastic bag and use within a week. The sweet flavour diminishes during storage.

NO COOKING REQUIRED

Grate and add to winter slaws and salads.

> During the Middle Ages, scorzonera was said to have anti-venom properties, hence its common name, 'viper grass'.

BASIC COOKING

Top and tail, then scrub well under running water. The skin is not edible, so either boil or steam with skin on and remove it later (this makes the job easier and you retain more of the flesh) or, if the recipe requires it, peel before cooking. For bulk peeling/preparation before cooking, put into water with 1–2 tsp lemon juice to avoid discolouring. Take care when cooking and remove from heat as soon as the 'tender' point is reached – the flesh quickly turns to mush with longer cooking.

BOILED SALSIFY

Leave whole or cut into long lengths and simmer in salted water for 10–15 minutes until tender. Peel.

STEAMED SALSIFY

Steam over a pan of boiling water for 15–20 minutes, or until tender. Peel and season. Serve with melted butter and lemon juice.

MASHED SALSIFY

Cook, peel and mash with 15 g (½ oz) butter for every 100 g (3½ oz) salsify. Season well.

SAUTÉED SALSIFY

Parboil or steam, peel, cut into slices and fry in 10 g (¼ oz) butter or oil for every 100 g (3½ oz) salsify, turning once or twice, until tender. Season.

ROAST SALSIFY

Peel, cut into chunks, toss in lemon juice and seasoning and roast in olive oil for 45 minutes at 190°C/gas mark 5, turning halfway through.

SALSIFY SALAD

Dress cooked cold salsify with lemon juice, seasoning and chopped parsley, and toss. Serve with fish or chicken.

SALSIFY/SCORZONERA RECIPES

CREAM OF SALSIFY SOUP

This has superb flavour and texture, so try it for lunch when you have friends round.

Serves 4

1 onion	500 g (1¼ lb) salsify
50 g (2 oz) butter	salt, black pepper
1 litre (1¾ pints) chicken stock	pinch cayenne pepper
	125 ml (4 fl. oz) cream
juice of ½ lemon	½ tsp ground nutmeg

- Sweat chopped onion in butter over low heat to soften but not colour. Add stock, lemon juice, peeled and chopped salsify and seasoning. Bring to a simmer, cover and cook until salsify is tender.
- Allow to cool and blend in a blender. Stir in cream and nutmeg and reheat gently.

SAUTÉ OF SALSIFY AND SHALLOTS

This flavourful side dish goes well with game, beef or duck. Instead of parsley, you can use chives.

Serves 4

8 salsify roots	3 tbsp fresh chopped parsley
8 shallots	juice of ½ lemon
50 g (2 oz) butter	salt, black pepper

- Boil or steam salsify until tender. Drain, peel and slice.
- Fry sliced shallots in butter over medium-low heat to soften and tinge gold. Add salsify, parsley, lemon juice and seasoning and cook on medium heat for 2 minutes, stirring occasionally.

SALSIFY GRATIN

If you don't have enough salsify, substitute potatoes or Jerusalem artichokes for half the quantity.

Serves 4

10 salsify roots	200 ml (7 fl. oz) cream
200 g (7 oz) spring greens	
200 ml (7 fl. oz) vegetable stock	salt, black pepper

- Boil or steam salsify until tender. Drain, peel and cut into 5 cm (2 in.) lengths.
- Steam thinly sliced greens until wilted. Combine stock, cream and seasoning.
- Arrange greens and salsify in a shallow, greased, ovenproof dish. Pour the cream mixture over and bake at 180°C/gas mark 4 for 45–60 minutes until brown and bubbling.

BRAISED HONEYED SALSIFY

A very good alternative to roast or new potatoes for serving with lamb or pork.

Serves 4

10 salsify roots	1 tbsp runny honey
50 g (2 oz) butter	salt, black pepper
1 tsp fresh thyme leaves	1 tbsp fresh chopped parsley
2 tsp fresh chopped sage	
100 ml (3½ fl. oz) vegetable stock	

- Boil or steam salsify until barely tender. Drain, peel and chop each into four.
- Fry salsify in butter with herbs over medium heat for 3–4 minutes to colour, turning occasionally.
- Pour in stock, bring to a simmer and cook, uncovered, for 10 minutes until stock has nearly all evaporated. Stir in honey and seasoning. Sprinkle with parsley to serve.

SALSIFY AND SMOKED MACKEREL PATTIES

These rich little patties make a good change from ordinary fishcakes for a midweek supper. Serve with green salad or vegetables and potato wedges.

Serves 4

6 salsify roots	200 g (7 oz) smoked mackerel fillet
40 g (1½ oz) butter	
2 tsp lemon juice	100 g (3½ oz) flour
salt, black pepper	2 tbsp vegetable oil

- Steam, peel and mash salsify with butter, lemon juice and seasoning.
- Take mackerel fillet off its skin and flake, checking for bones. Stir mackerel into the mash.
- Shape into 8 flat patties. Put the flour on a plate and coat the patties in it.
- Fry patties in oil over medium-high heat until golden, then turn over to brown the other side.

SEED SPROUTS

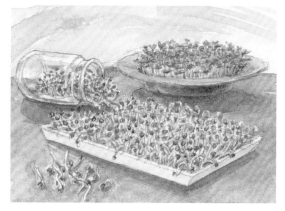

As seed sprouts are quite expensive to buy, it makes sense to grow your own. There are several varieties of seed which can be easily sprouted and which make welcome additions to both salads and cooked dishes such as stir-fries and chow mein.

Taste, size and colour vary according to the seed you use. Adzuki and chick pea sprouts have a nutty flavour; mustard, radish and rape cress are peppery and will really liven up your dish. Seeds can be sprouted in a jar or on a tray and are ready to eat when the sprout shoots are 2–6 cm (¾–2¼ in.) long, depending on variety, and the seeds still bright and with no signs of brown on the shoots.

STORING

When sprouts are ready they should be harvested and eaten as soon as possible, though they will store in a plastic bag in the fridge for a day or two once picked.

NO COOKING REQUIRED

Seed sprouts can be eaten raw, and indeed this is the way they are most often consumed. Mix several varieties together for a nutritious salad with French dressing (page 250). Mix together crunchy sprouts such as mung beans with softer ones such as mustard and cress for interesting texture, or add them to a plain green salad.

SEED SPROUT AND CARROT SLAW

As sprouted seeds will grow indoors all year round, you can always have them to hand in the kitchen, no matter how cold outside, making this slaw recipe ideal for winter months.

Serves 4

1 large carrot	2 tbsp toasted
1 red onion	pumpkin seeds
175 g (6 oz)	4 tbsp French dressing
seed sprouts	(page 250)

- Grate carrot and onion and combine with seed sprouts, seeds and dressing.

> Mung sprouts are the classic multi-purpose 'beansprouts' but fenugreek sprouts are also delicious multi-purpose sprouts. Mustard, cress, radish and rape cress sprouts are all excellent in salads and sandwiches.

> Chick pea, green lentil and radish sprouts are good for stir-fries. Use adzuki sprouts for Japanese recipes.

SEED SPROUT SALAD WITH SOY DRESSING

A simple salad that can be served with cold poultry, duck or beef.

Serves 4

300 g (11 oz) seed sprouts	4 tbsp light olive oil
1 carrot	1 tbsp wine vinegar
½ cucumber	1 tbsp soy sauce
1 clove garlic	2 tsp caster sugar
1 tsp fresh chopped ginger	salt, black pepper

- Combine seed sprouts in a serving bowl with grated carrot and finely chopped, de-seeded cucumber.
- Combine finely chopped garlic with remaining ingredients and stir into the seed sprouts.

SPICED SEED SPROUT PITTAS

These colourful pittas with their unusual filling will be popular with all the family. If you don't have alfalfa, use whatever sprouts you do have.

Serves 4

1 carrot	2 tbsp mayonnaise
2 tomatoes	2 tbsp natural yogurt
¼ cucumber	salt, black pepper
1 tsp curry powder	100 g (3½ oz) alfalfa sprouts
1 tsp mango chutney	4 pittas

- Cut carrot, tomatoes and cucumber into small cubes.
- Combine curry powder, chutney, mayonnaise, yogurt and seasoning.
- Mix all vegetables with the dressing and half the sprouts, then stuff into halved pittas. Garnish with remaining sprouts.

BASIC COOKING

Rinse seed sprouts in a colander to remove any clinging compost. Dry gently in clean kitchen paper or a tea-towel unless they are to be cooked immediately with moisture (e.g. steamed or added to a soup).

BOILED SEED SPROUTS

Add to a pan containing 3 tbsp water for every 100 g (3½ oz) sprouts. Boil for 1 minute, or until just tender. Drain and serve.

STEAMED SEED SPROUTS

Place in a steamer tray and cook over boiling water for 2–3 minutes until just tender.

STIR-FRIED SEED SPROUTS

Fry crunchy varieties in 1 tbsp vegetable oil for every 150 g (5 oz) sprouts over high heat for 2 minutes, or until just tender but retaining some bite. This method is not suitable for mustard, cress and any other very soft variety.

SEED SPROUT RECIPES

EGG-FRIED RICE WITH SEED SPROUTS

The seed sprouts give this traditional dish another dimension, making it much more interesting and light. Mung sprouts work best. You could include cooked prawns or sweet corn.

Serves 4

200 g (7oz) long-grain rice	4 spring onions
2 eggs	2 tbsp vegetable oil
1 tbsp sesame oil	150 g (5 oz) seed sprouts
100 g (3½ oz) small cooked peas	1 tbsp soy sauce
	black pepper

- Cook rice, drain and leave to cool.
- Beat eggs and scramble in sesame oil until just cooked – don't over-stir, as you want large, soft pieces of egg.
- Stir-fry rice, peas and chopped spring onions in vegetable oil over high heat for 3 minutes, then stir in seed sprouts and cook for a further minute.
- Add egg, soy sauce and pepper. Stir for a minute.

SHREDDED PORK AND SEED SPROUTS

A perfect dish to serve as part of a buffet-style Chinese meal – it is much quicker to cook than ordering a takeaway. If you don't have any leftover roast pork, use pork fillet and stir-fry for 3–4 minutes before adding to the dish.

Serves 4

300 g (11 oz) lean roast pork	250 g (9 oz) seed sprouts
2 tbsp medium-dry sherry	salt, black pepper
1 tsp Chinese five-spice powder	½ tsp sugar
2 tbsp sesame oil	4 spring onions

- Shred pork and marinate in sherry and five-spice powder for 30 minutes.
- Remove pork from marinade with a slotted spoon and stir-fry in oil over high heat for 2 minutes. Add seed sprouts and stir for a further 30 seconds.
- Add marinade, seasoning and sugar and stir for a minute.
- Serve garnished with chopped spring onions.

CHICKEN CHOW MEIN

Chow mein means 'stir-fried noodles' in Chinese. The addition of seed sprouts is common and gives the dish more crunch and freshness.

Serves 4

2 skinless chicken breast fillets
2 tbsp soy sauce
1 tsp Chinese five-spice powder
1 tsp sweet chilli sauce (page 60)
4 nests (200 g/7 oz) medium egg noodles
4 tbsp sesame oil

1 large carrot
8 spring onions
2 cloves garlic
1 red chilli
2 tsp fresh chopped ginger
300 g (11 oz) seed sprouts

- Cut chicken into thin slices and marinate for 30 minutes with soy sauce, five-spice powder, chilli sauce and 1 tbsp water. Drain and reserve marinade.

- Cook noodles according to packet instructions – usually 3–4 minutes. Toss with half the sesame oil and keep warm.

- Cut carrot and spring onions into thin strips and chop garlic and chilli. Stir-fry with ginger and chicken in remaining oil over high heat for 3 minutes.

- Stir in seed sprouts. Cook for 1 minute, then stir in marinade. Cook for 30 seconds, then add noodles and stir through.

SPRING ROLLS

Spring rolls acquired their name because traditionally they mark the coming of spring in China, although they are eaten all year round. If you can't find spring roll wrappers in the supermarket, use 6 halved sheets of filo pastry instead. As a starter or snack these are great with sweet chilli sauce (page 60).

Makes 12

50 g (2 oz) dried mushrooms	2 tbsp soy sauce
1 red pepper	1 tsp hot chilli sauce
1 tbsp sesame oil	salt, black pepper
150 g (5 oz) peeled prawns	12 spring roll wrappers
200 g (7 oz) seed sprouts	cornflour
	vegetable oil

- Soak mushrooms for 20 minutes in enough hot water to just cover, then finely chop.
- Shred red pepper and stir-fry in oil over high heat for 2 minutes. Add chopped prawns, seed sprouts, soy sauce, chilli sauce and seasoning. Stir for a minute, then allow to cool.
- Place spoonfuls of the mixture on wrappers. Roll up and tuck in either end, using cornflour mixed with a little cold water to seal.
- Half fill a large saucepan with vegetable oil and heat to 180°C, or until a cube of bread dropped in turns golden in approx. 30 seconds. Fry rolls in two batches until golden. Remove and drain on kitchen paper, then serve.

SHRIMP NOODLE SOUP

A delicious, strongly flavoured soup which is nevertheless light enough to be a starter. Soba noodles are Japanese buckwheat noodles and are sold in most supermarkets.

Serves 4

150 g (5 oz) soba noodles	1 litre (1¾ pints) vegetable stock
2 tbsp vegetable oil	2 tbsp soy sauce
1 red pepper	2 tbsp medium-dry sherry
100 g (3½ oz) baby corn	75 g (3 oz) seed sprouts
2 spring onions	200 g (7 oz) cooked shrimps or small prawns
100 g (3½ oz) mushrooms	
1 tbsp fresh grated ginger	
2 cloves garlic	
1 red chilli	

- Cook noodles according to packet instructions – usually 5–6 minutes. Toss with half the vegetable oil and keep warm.
- Cut pepper into julienne strips. Cut corn and spring onion into diagonal slices. Stir-fry with thinly sliced mushrooms and ginger, chopped garlic and chilli in remaining oil over high heat for 3 minutes.
- Add stock to pan with soy sauce and sherry, and bring to the boil. Turn heat down and simmer for 3 minutes. Stir in seed sprouts and shrimps, then cook for a further minute.
- Divide noodles among serving bowls. Ladle soup on top and serve immediately.

CHICKEN, CASHEW AND SEED SPROUT STIR-FRY

A quick supper full of flavour and stickiness. Serve with rice or noodles.

Serves 4

4 skinless chicken breast fillets	juice of 1 lemon
2 tbsp soy sauce	125 g (4 oz) cashew nuts
2 tbsp runny honey	1 head pak choi
2 tbsp vegetable oil	150 g (5 oz) seed sprouts

- Slice chicken and marinate for at least 5 minutes in a bowl with soy sauce, honey, half the oil and half the lemon juice.
- Stir-fry chicken in remaining oil over medium-high heat for 3–4 minutes until cooked through.
- Add nuts and any marinade juices remaining in the bowl, then stir-fry over medium heat for a further 2 minutes until chicken and nuts are sticky and golden. Add sliced pak choi, seed sprouts and remaining lemon juice and stir for 30 seconds.

SEED SPROUT, PEPPER AND BROCCOLI STIR-FRY

An ideal side dish for steak, grilled chicken or chops.

Serves 4

250 g (9 oz) broccoli	1 green chilli
1 yellow pepper	200 g (7 oz) seed sprouts
2 tbsp olive oil	1 tsp sesame seeds
2 cloves garlic	

- Divide broccoli into small florets and finely slice pepper. Stir-fry in oil over high heat for 3–4 minutes until just tender.
- Add finely chopped garlic and chilli and stir-fry for a further minute, then add seed sprouts and sesame seeds and stir-fry for 30 seconds.

Wheat sprouts are exceptionally nutritious and are good for juicing.

SPINACH

The bright green leaves of spinach have a strong, distinctive flavour which is something of an acquired taste – and if over-cooked to a mush they can be unpleasant. But the reputation spinach has as a vegetable eaten for health rather than pleasure is unjustified. Whether it is small leaves eaten raw in a salad, or larger leaves used in sauces, pasta dishes, soup, omelettes, curries and pies, if properly cooked the vegetable is versatile and delicious. And if you grow summer and winter varieties you can have fresh spinach almost all year round.

STORING

Spinach is best picked young and eaten soon afterwards, but the leaves will keep in a plastic bag in the fridge for a day or two. To freeze, blanch leaves for a minute until wilted, then drain and freeze in plastic bags.

NO COOKING REQUIRED

Use small, young summer leaves in a mixed green salad, or in a variety of other ways – the flavour goes well with watercress, rocket, lamb's lettuce, bacon, nuts, eggs and cheese. Older leaves become a bit too stringy to eat raw, and winter leaves tend to be coarser.

SPINACH, FETA, PEAR AND WALNUT SALAD

Combine 4 tbsp walnut oil with the juice of ½ lemon and season. Peel and core 2 pears, cut each into thin slices and toss in half the dressing. Arrange 150 g (5 oz) baby spinach leaves on plates with pear slices, crumble 175 g (6 oz) feta cheese over and sprinkle with 75 g (3 oz) walnut pieces. Drizzle remaining dressing over to serve.

BABY SPINACH, AVOCADO AND BACON SALAD

Combine 300 g (11 oz) baby spinach leaves and 50 g (2 oz) watercress in a bowl with 2 peeled, stoned and sliced avocados. Grill or dry-fry 6 rashers back bacon until golden and slightly crisp. Crumble and add to the salad. Toss with 6 tbsp French dressing (page 250) and serve immediately.

BASIC COOKING

Wash thoroughly in cold water to remove grit, sand and dirt. Remove any larger stalks and slice large leaves, discarding any that are yellow or look too big. If the recipe calls for dried leaves, shake in a salad spinner to remove moisture or pat dry on a tea-towel or kitchen paper.

BOILED SPINACH

Leave washed spinach with water clinging to its leaves, place in a saucepan with no more than 1 tbsp water, bring to the boil and allow to wilt, stirring several times. This will take 2–4 minutes. Drain off surplus moisture. For a drier finish required by some recipes, press out more moisture with a wooden spoon. Add a knob of butter and seasoning.

STEAMED SPINACH

Place washed leaves in a steamer over boiling water and cook for 3–4 minutes until wilted. Season.

STIR-FRIED SPINACH

Chop as necessary; leave small leaves whole. Stir in hot oil for a minute until wilted – don't over-cook. Season.

SPINACH RECIPES

FLORENTINE POACHED EGGS

One of the very best, and easiest, spinach recipes. It makes a great lunch, or half quantities make a starter.

Serves 4

900 g (2 lb) spinach	**25 g (1 oz) butter**	**500 ml (17 fl. oz) white sauce (page 251)**
salt, black pepper	**8 eggs**	**100 g (3½ oz) Gruyère**

- Boil or steam spinach until just tender, then chop any large leaves. Stir in seasoning and butter. Arrange in 4 small or 1 large ovenproof dish, making a well for each egg.

- Break an egg into each well. Gently pour warmed white sauce over to cover and sprinkle on grated cheese.

- Bake at 190°C/gas mark 5 for 12 minutes.

CREAMED SPINACH

Cream reduces the strong taste of spinach and gives it a lovely texture. This is ideal with fish.

Serves 4

750 g (1 lb 10 oz) spinach
200 ml (7 fl. oz) thick cream
½ tsp ground nutmeg
salt, black pepper

- Boil or steam spinach and press out as much water as you can. Blend lightly in a blender with the remaining ingredients.
- Return to the pan and reheat gently without boiling.

SPINACH SOUP

You won't find a prettier green soup than this. It's also very tasty and good for a dinner-party starter. A short cooking time for the spinach helps retain its colour.

Serves 4

1 onion
2 cloves garlic
50 g (2 oz) butter
2 potatoes
1 litre (1¾ pints) chicken stock

500 g (1¼ lb) spinach
½ tsp ground nutmeg
salt, black pepper
100 ml (3½ fl. oz) cream

- Sweat finely chopped onion and garlic in butter over low heat to soften but not colour.
- Stir in peeled, chopped potatoes and stock, then simmer for 20 minutes.
- Add spinach and nutmeg. Simmer for 2 minutes. Allow to cool a little, then blend in a blender until smooth. Return to the pan to reheat. Season and stir in cream.

SPINACH WITH PINE NUTS AND RAISINS

Serve this as a side dish with oily fish such as sardines, toss it through pasta, or serve it as part of a Spanish tapas.

Serves 4–6

2 shallots
3 tbsp olive oil
100 g (3½ oz) raisins
75 g (3 oz) pine nuts

900 g (2 lb) spinach
1 tbsp wine vinegar
salt, black pepper

- Sweat chopped shallots in oil over low heat to soften but not colour. Add raisins, turn heat to medium and fry for 2 minutes.
- Add pine nuts and cook until golden, then add spinach to pan and stir-fry until wilted. Pour in vinegar and season.

SPINACH AND RICOTTA FILO PIE

This classic Greek pie – called *spanakopita* – can be eaten warm or cold and is delicious. You can also use the filling to make individual pasties.

Serves 4–6

2 onions
2 cloves garlic
6 tbsp olive oil
900 g (2 lb) spinach
4 tbsp fresh chopped parsley

salt, black pepper
2 eggs
150 g (5 oz) Ricotta
200 g (7 oz) feta cheese
8 sheets filo pastry

- Fry finely chopped onions and garlic in half the oil over medium-low heat to soften and tinge gold.
- Stir in spinach, parsley and seasoning and cook until spinach is wilted. Remove from heat.
- Combine beaten eggs, Ricotta, feta and seasoning in a large bowl. Stir in the spinach mixture.
- Lay 4 sheets pastry in an oiled 23 cm (9 in.) baking tin, brushing each sheet lightly with olive oil. The sheets will hang over the edge of the tin.
- Spread on the spinach mixture and fold the filo over the top. Brush with oil. Layer remaining oiled filo on top, tucking overhanging filo down into the sides of the tin to seal. Bake at 190°C/gas mark 5 for 25–30 minutes, or until golden.

SPINACH, CHICK PEA AND POTATO CURRY

One of the nicest combinations for an Indian vegetable curry. Try this easy version of Saag Aloo with rice for a non-meat meal, or serve it with a meat curry and Indian bread.

Serves 4

1 large onion
2 tbsp vegetable oil
1 clove garlic
2 tbsp balti curry paste
500 g (1¼ lb) cooked potatoes
200 g (7 oz) canned chick peas

300 ml (½ pint) vegetable stock
1 tbsp tomato purée
400 g (14 oz) spinach
2 tsp garam masala

- Fry sliced onion in oil over medium-low heat to soften and tinge gold. Add chopped garlic and curry paste and stir for a minute to release aroma.
- Stir in cubed potatoes and chick peas. Stir in stock and tomato purée, bring to a simmer and cook for 20 minutes, uncovered.
- Add spinach and garam masala and cook for a further 3 minutes until spinach is wilted.

SPINACH LASAGNE

You can't make a better meat-free lasagne than this rich spinach version. The unbaked lasagne will freeze.

Serves 4

2 onions
4 cloves garlic
2 tbsp olive oil
750 g (1 lb 10 oz) spinach
½ tsp ground nutmeg
150 g (5 oz) Mozzarella
150 g (5 oz) mild soft
  blue cheese
100 g (3½ oz) toasted
  pine nuts

250 ml (8 fl. oz) sour
  cream
salt, black pepper
600 ml (1 pint) white
  sauce (page 251)
150 ml (¼ pint) milk
12 no-pre-cooking
  lasagne sheets
75 g (3 oz) grated
  Parmesan

- Sweat finely chopped onion and garlic in oil over low heat to soften but not colour.

- Add spinach and nutmeg and stir until spinach is wilted. Cut half the Mozzarella into small cubes and stir into spinach with blue cheese, pine nuts and cream. Season.

- Grate remaining Mozzarella and stir into warmed white sauce. Thin sauce down with milk, then pour a little into a square, greased, ovenproof dish.

- Cover with a third of the spinach mixture and top with 4 lasagne sheets. Repeat spinach and lasagne layers twice more.

- Pour remaining white sauce over and sprinkle with Parmesan. Bake at 190°C/gas mark 5 for 40 minutes, or until bubbling and golden on top.

SPINACH AND MUSHROOM QUICHE

Spinach and mushrooms are excellent partners in this soft-set tart.

Serves 4

300 g (11 oz) shortcrust
  pastry (page 251)
1 onion
2 cloves garlic
2 tbsp olive oil
200 g (7 oz) mushrooms
250 g (9 oz) spinach

2 eggs
200 ml (7 fl. oz) cream
100 ml (3½ fl. oz) milk
¼ tsp ground nutmeg
1 tsp Dijon mustard
salt, black pepper

- Line a 20 cm (8 in.) quiche tin with pastry and bake blind.

- Fry finely chopped onion and garlic in oil over medium-low heat to soften and tinge gold.

- Add sliced mushrooms and stir for a minute. Add spinach and wilt very lightly. Spoon off any moisture and discard. Spoon pan contents into pastry case.

- Combine beaten eggs with remaining ingredients and pour into case. Bake at 190°C/gas mark 5 for 30 minutes, or until golden.

SPINACH WITH PASTA, LEMON, GARLIC AND BREADCRUMBS

One of the nicest quick pasta dishes you can make.

Serves 4

50 g (2 oz) breadcrumbs
½ lemon
4 tbsp fresh chopped parsley
salt, black pepper
400 g (14 oz) pasta shapes
1 tbsp olive oil
300 g (11 oz) baby spinach leaves
2 cloves garlic
200 ml (7 fl. oz) sour cream

- Spread breadcrumbs in an oiled, non-stick frying pan and cook for 2–3 minutes, stirring once or twice, until golden. Tip into a bowl and combine with grated lemon zest, parsley and seasoning.

- Cook pasta in boiling salted water, drain, return to pan and stir in oil.

- Leaving the pasta pan over very low heat, add spinach, well crushed garlic and lemon juice. Stir gently until leaves are wilted and garlic releases its aroma.

- Stir in cream and half the breadcrumb mixture, then serve with remaining crumbs sprinkled over.

SQUASH AND PUMPKIN

Do not dismiss the pumpkin family as merely Halloween decoration – there is more to these gourds than meets the eye. There are three types of these relatives of cucumbers and marrows – **summer squash** (soft-skinned, summer harvest), **winter squash** (hard-skinned, autumn harvest) and **pumpkin** (hard-skinned, autumn harvest).

The different varieties have flesh varying from white or cream through to yellow, gold and orange – generally, the more colour, the better the flavour and sweetness. There's often a nutty hint, and the flesh is smooth and tender when cooked.

Size can vary from tennis ball to football or larger, depending on variety and how grown. Big or small, they can be used in a variety of ways. From soups to stews, purées, curries, bakes, pasta dishes, desserts and much more, pumpkins and squashes are versatile and easy to cook. Summer squashes tend to be delicate both in flavour and texture and don't need as much cooking as later fruits. Larger fruits have a very high water content – use minimal water for cooking, or methods that require no water. They lose much of their flavour and texture when boiled. Very large fruits can be tasteless – save them for carving.

STORING

Summer squashes do not have a thick rind and should be consumed within a week of picking. Store in the fridge. The larger winter squashes and pumpkins have thicker skin – sometimes very thick – and, if properly dried, can be stored in a cool, dry place over winter and into the following early spring. Once harvested, remove surplus stalk, wipe to remove dirt, but don't wet. If only part of the fruit is required, store the surplus as a whole piece in the fridge – it will keep 2–3 days. Remove any discoloured flesh from cut sides before use.

To freeze squash and pumpkin: peel, cut into chunks, steam for 1 minute to blanch, then bag and freeze.

Perhaps the best pumpkin variety for flavour is Crown Prince. Moschata pumpkins are excellent for purée and pumpkin pie. The size, bright orange skin and firm flesh of Spellbound pumpkins make them good for cooking and for Halloween.

Good winter squash varieties include Butternut Sprinter, Spaghetti Squash, Sweet Lightning and Turks Turban. Good summer varieties include Gemstore and Patty Pan (also called Custard Squash or Scallopino).

NO COOKING REQUIRED

Squashes and pumpkins are cooked before they are eaten, but the seeds can be eaten raw.

BASIC COOKING

Wash and wipe dry. Although the skin is edible on all but the toughest fruits, most people prefer to remove it – an exception is when baking it whole or in halves.

Small fruits can be baked whole, or halved with the pips removed before stuffing. Larger fruits can be halved, de-seeded using a spoon, sliced and roasted.

The best way to prepare large fruits is to halve them using a cleaver or similar, scoop out the seeds and pith, place the cut side on the chopping board and slice through using a long-bladed, long-handled knife – take care. Then peel using a smaller knife. The peel can be very tough on long-store pumpkins and squashes.

STEAMED SQUASH OR PUMPKIN

Peel, de-seed, cut into chunks and steam over boiling water for 6–10 minutes until tender. Add butter or olive oil and seasoning.

BAKED SQUASH OR PUMPKIN

Place on a baking tray and bake whole de-seeded small fruit, or halve and de-seed larger fruit and brush with oil on cut side. Bake at 190°C/gas mark 5 until tender. This will take 30–60 minutes, depending on size. Season and serve with butter.

ROAST SQUASH OR PUMPKIN

Peel, de-seed and cut into chunks. Toss in olive or vegetable oil and seasoning, put in a roasting tin and roast at 190°C/gas mark 5 for 25–45 minutes, depending on size of chunks and variety of vegetable.

PURÉED SQUASH OR PUMPKIN

Bake whole or halved de-seeded fruit in skin, then scoop out flesh and purée in a blender until smooth, or mash thoroughly with a potato masher. Butter/olive oil and seasoning can be added.

SQUASH AND PUMPKIN RECIPES

CREAM OF PUMPKIN SOUP

A winter soup with a fine flavour and smooth texture. Serve with wholemeal bread for lunch.

Serves 4–6

1 kg (2¼ lb) orange-fleshed pumpkin
2 tbsp vegetable oil
2 onions
750 ml (1¼ pints) vegetable stock
400 ml (14 fl. oz) milk
½ tsp ground nutmeg
salt, black pepper
100 ml (3½ fl. oz) cream
4 tbsp Cheddar

- Peel pumpkin and cut into chunks. Sauté in oil in a large, lidded pan over medium heat for 10 minutes to soften and colour.
- Turn heat down to low, push pumpkin to edges and sweat chopped onion in the same pan to soften but not colour. (Add a little more oil if necessary.)
- Add stock, milk, nutmeg and seasoning, stir, bring to a simmer and cook, covered, for 20 minutes.
- Cool a little, then blend in a blender until smooth, adding water if too thick.
- Reheat, stir in cream and check seasoning. Serve sprinkled with grated cheese.

PUMPKIN PIE

There is a great tradition of serving pumpkin pie on Thanksgiving Day in both the United States and Canada. The sweet, creamy, spicy filling is really tasty. Tip: if the top of the pastry crust is browning too much before the filling is cooked, cover it with a strip of foil. Serve with cream.

Serves 6

600 g (1 lb 6 oz) pumpkin purée (page 143)
400 g (14 oz) shortcrust pastry (page 251)
3 eggs
400 g (14 oz) can evaporated milk

125 g (4 oz) soft light brown sugar
1 tsp ground cinnamon
½ tsp ground ginger
¼ tsp ground cloves
¼ tsp ground nutmeg
½ tsp salt

- If pumpkin purée seems a bit watery, drain overnight in a colander and discard any water that collects.

- Line a deep 23 cm (9 in.) tart tin with rolled-out pastry and bake blind.

- Thoroughly combine beaten eggs with pumpkin purée, milk, sugar, spices and salt.

- Put tart tin on a baking tray. Pour pumpkin filling into pie and bake at 180°C/gas mark 4 for 35–45 minutes, or until filling is set but still a bit quivery. Serve warm or cold.

SPICED SQUASH AND COCONUT SOUP

A can of coconut milk brings out the nuttiness of the butternut squash and is a perfect foil for the warm spices.

Serves 4

1 large (approx. 800 g/1¾ lb) butternut squash
1 onion
3 tbsp vegetable oil
3 cloves garlic
2 red chillies
2 tsp fresh chopped ginger
1 tsp coriander seed
1 litre (1¾ pints) vegetable stock
2 tbsp Thai fish sauce
400 ml (14 fl. oz) can coconut milk
juice of 1 lime
salt, black pepper
4 tbsp fresh coriander leaves

- Peel squash and cut into chunks. Sauté with chopped onion in 2 tbsp of the oil in a lidded pan over medium heat for 10 minutes to soften and colour.
- Using a mortar or a blender, pound garlic, chillies, ginger and coriander with remaining oil until you have a paste. Add to pan and stir-fry for a minute to release aromas.
- Stir in stock, bring to a simmer, cover and cook for 10 minutes. Add fish sauce and three-quarters of the coconut milk. Cook for a further 5 minutes, or until the squash is tender.
- Add lime juice, allow to cool a little, then blend in a blender until smooth. Reheat, season, drizzle remaining coconut milk over and sprinkle with coriander leaves.

> Roast savoury pumpkin seeds make a tasty snack. Collect 100 g (3½ oz) of flesh-free seeds – wash, pat with a tea-towel and place on a baking tray to dry. Leave for 24 hours. Toss seeds in a mixture of 1 tsp celery salt, ½ tsp paprika, 1 tbsp olive oil and a little black pepper. When thoroughly coated, spread out seeds on the baking tray and toast at 180°C/gas mark 4 for 10 minutes, turning halfway through. Store in an airtight tin – will keep for several weeks.

SAUTÉED PUMPKIN WITH BACON AND HERBS

Bacon is a perfect foil for the sweet nuttiness of pumpkin. Here's a quick midweek supper.

Serves 4

800 g (1¾ lb) pumpkin
2 tbsp olive oil
4 shallots
8 rashers smoked streaky bacon
25 g (1 oz) butter
juice of ½ lemon
2 tbsp fresh chopped parsley
salt, black pepper

- Sauté peeled, chopped pumpkin in oil in a large frying pan over medium heat until nearly tender and turning gold.
- Push pumpkin to the edges, add thinly sliced shallots and diced bacon to the pan and cook for a further 5 minutes, or until bacon is golden and shallots are tender.
- Add butter, lemon juice, parsley and seasoning to the pan and stir everything together for 1 minute.

SQUASH WITH RICE STUFFING

The beans are protein-rich, so this makes a complete meal for the Indian food enthusiast.

Serves 4

2 large squash
2 tbsp olive oil
3 shallots
2 tsp harissa paste
1 tsp garam masala
1 tomato
1 tbsp tomato purée
100 ml (3½ fl. oz) vegetable stock
100 g (3½ oz) cooked red kidney beans
100 g (3½ oz) cooked red lentils
100 g (3½ oz) cooked brown rice
salt, black pepper
4 tbsp Cheddar

- Halve squashes and remove seeds. Brush with oil and bake at 190°C/gas mark 5 for 25 minutes.
- Fry chopped shallots in remaining oil for 3 minutes to soften, then add harissa and garam masala. Stir for a minute.
- Chop tomato and add to pan with all the remaining ingredients except the cheese. Mix thoroughly. Stuff squash halves with the mixture. Sprinkle grated cheese over and return to the oven for 20 minutes.

SWEDE

Swede is a member of the brassica family and closely related to the turnip, but with a sweeter flavour and yellow/orange flesh. Very easy to grow and store, it is an extremely useful winter root but is sadly under-used in the kitchen. Swede has plenty of uses – not just in meat stews and vegetable soups but in a range of other dishes too. Harvest before the roots get too large, otherwise they can become tough and woody and lose their sweetness.

STORING

Swedes can be left in the ground and dug up as required, when the weather allows. Or dig up, twist off leaves, dry and store in peat or compost, or between layers of newspaper in boxes in a cool, dry place. They can also be brought inside and will store in a vegetable rack for a week or two, or can be kept unpeeled in a plastic bag in the fridge for up to 2 weeks. Blanch and freeze peeled chunks in a plastic bag. Mashed swede can also be bagged and frozen.

NO COOKING REQUIRED

Swede is not usually eaten without cooking.

BASIC COOKING

Wash, peel and cut into chunks.

BOILED SWEDE

Boil chunks of swede in salted water for 15 minutes, or until tender. Drain.

STEAMED SWEDE

Steam chunks of swede over a pan of boiling water for 15–20 minutes, or until tender. Season.

MASHED SWEDE

Add 15 g (½ oz) butter and plenty of seasoning to every 100 g (3½ oz) boiled or steamed swede, and mash using a potato masher or blender until smooth.

BASHED NEEPS

Boil swede chunks in vegetable stock until tender. Drain and retain liquid. Return swede to pan over low heat. Add 10 g (¼ oz) butter, 1 tbsp of the stock, a pinch ground nutmeg and ½ tsp sugar for every 100 g (3½ oz) swede. Use a potato masher to make a coarse mash. Serve with haggis!

ROAST SWEDE

Cut peeled swede into slices approx. 1.5 cm (½ in.) thick. Toss in olive oil and seasoning and roast at 190°C/gas mark 5 for 40–45 minutes, or until golden and tender. Turn halfway through.

'Swede' is short for Swedish turnip and has several other names abroad. In the USA it is 'rutabaga'. In Scottish dialect it is a 'neep' and is traditionally served on Burns Night as an accompaniment to haggis.

SWEDE RECIPES

SWEDE, CARROT AND BARLEY SOUP

A healthy, hearty traditional British soup and very
easy to make. You could serve it topped with
cheese toasts (like those for French onion soup), or
serve with cheese scones.

Serves 4

1 small swede (approx. 400 g/14 oz)
2 carrots
1 onion
1 stalk celery
25 g (1 oz) butter
1.2 litres (2 pints) vegetable stock
125 g (4 oz) pearl barley
salt, black pepper
3 tbsp fresh chopped parsley

- Chop all vegetables and sauté in butter in a large
  lidded pan over medium-low heat for 5 minutes
  to soften.
- Add stock and barley, bring to a simmer and
  cook, covered, for 45 minutes on low heat.
- Season, then sprinkle on parsley to serve.

STOVE-TOP CHICKEN, BACON AND SWEDE SUPPER

Sweet swede and salty bacon go very well together.
Try them with tender chicken and lemony stock for a
tasty supper.

Serves 2

1 small swede (approx. 400 g/14 oz)
2 skinless chicken breast fillets
4 rashers bacon
2 tbsp olive oil
2 cloves garlic
½ tsp ground cumin seeds
juice of 1 lemon
100 ml (3½ fl. oz) chicken stock
2 tbsp fresh chopped parsley
salt, black pepper

- Boil chopped swede and drain. Dry out thoroughly
  by placing pan on low heat for a minute.
- Fry sliced chicken and bacon in oil over high heat
  for 2 minutes to brown. Add swede, finely chopped
  garlic and cumin. Turn heat to medium-high and
  cook for a further 5 minutes, or until swede is light
  golden and chicken cooked through.
- Add lemon juice, stock, parsley and pepper, then
  stir over high heat for 1–2 minutes until bubbling
  and stock has thickened slightly. Check
  seasoning, adding a little salt if necessary.

SWEDE CHIPS WITH PARMESAN

Swede chips make a change from potato chips and
are good with steak, gammon or chicken.

Serves 4

1 swede (approx. 600 g/
   1 lb 6 oz)
2 tbsp olive oil
1 tsp Season-All seasoning

50 g (2 oz) finely
   grated Parmesan
salt, black pepper

- Cut swede into chips approx. 1.5 cm (½ in.) thick
  and 5 cm (2 in.) long. Toss in oil in a bowl,
  draining off any surplus oil.
- Add remaining ingredients to bowl and combine
  thoroughly.
- Arrange coated chips on a baking tray and bake
  at 200°C/gas mark 6 for 25–30 minutes, turning
  halfway through, until chips are golden and crisp
  on the outside and tender inside.

SWEDE AND POTATO MASH

Sweet, tangy swede gives mashed potato a real lift.
Try it with roast beef, lamb or pork. It is surprisingly
good as a fish pie topping.

Serves 4

400 g (14 oz) floury
   potatoes
1 small swede (approx.
   400 g/14 oz)

50 g (2 oz) butter
50 ml (2 fl. oz) cream
½ tsp ground nutmeg
salt, black pepper

- Boil peeled, chopped potatoes and swede, drain
  thoroughly and return to pan.
- Add remaining ingredients and mash until smooth.

SWEET CORN

Sweet corn, or corn on the cob, is in season from August to September. The small golden-yellow kernels on a tough core are sweet and juicy, and can be stripped from the core or left in place and the cob cooked whole or in chunks. The sugars in the kernels quickly turn to starch, so cobs should be eaten as fresh as possible when they are fully ripe but no later. Test for ripeness by pulling back the green sheath. Small, pale kernels are not yet ripe. If the end silks (silky threads) protruding from the sheath are brown, then the cob is ripe. Fresh kernels will release a milky liquid when pierced.

Corn kernels make a change from peas and are popular with children as well as adults. They are a good accompaniment to any savoury dish, either meat or fish. They can be used to stuff an omelette or quiche, mashed and made into fritters or added to salads and stir-fries.

Whole cobs can be cooked and eaten as a starter with melted butter and seasoning, or cut into 2–3 segments and roasted around chicken or with vegetables.

STORING

Once picked, use as soon as possible – but the cobs, in their sheaths will keep for a day or two in the fridge. To freeze, strip cobs of sheaths and silks, then blanch for 2 minutes, drain, put into strong plastic bags and freeze. Kernels freeze well: blanch for 1 minute, drain and bag.

NO COOKING REQUIRED

Small tender kernels can, like peas, be eaten raw as a snack, or added to a mixed salad. The 'milk' inside each kernel is a delicacy.

BASIC COOKING

Pull back sheath and strip away the silks to expose the kernels. Replace sheath if cooking whole, or cut off from base using a sharp knife. Rinse under cold running water if necessary. Cobs are tough to chop raw – it is easier to cook first and chop later.

To remove kernels, stand the base of the cob on a non-slip surface, hold the top with one hand and use a sharp knife to slice off kernels from top to bottom as close as possible to the core.

BOILED SWEET CORN

Cobs: Boil in unsalted water for 4–6 minutes until tender. Drain and serve with melted butter and seasoning.
Kernels: Boil in unsalted water for 2–4 minutes until tender. Drain.

STEAMED SWEET CORN

Cobs: Cook over boiling water for 10–12 minutes until tender.
Kernels: Cook over boiling water for 3–5 minutes until tender. Season.

GRILLED/BARBECUED SWEET CORN

Put cobs into barbecue ashes in their husks, or wrapped in foil, or put on a rack. Cook for 10 minutes, or until kernels are tender. Uncovered cobs can be brushed with olive oil and cooked for 7–10 minutes on the barbecue at least 5 cm (2 in.) away from the coals, or under the grill about the same distance from the heat source. Turn once.

ROAST SWEET CORN

Toss cobs in oil and season, then roast in a baking dish at 190°C/gas mark 5 for approx. 30 minutes, or until tender and golden, turning once.

SWEET CORN RECIPES

SWEET CORN FRITTERS

Try these with fried bacon or ham, or eat as a snack with a sweet pepper salsa (page 58). For a heartier snack, add some grated cheese to the mixture.

Serves 4

300 g (11 oz) sweet corn kernels
150 g (5 oz) flour
1 tsp baking powder
2 eggs

125 ml (4 fl. oz) milk
4 spring onions
salt, black pepper
1 tbsp vegetable oil

- Boil or steam sweet corn and drain. Whisk together flour, baking powder, eggs and milk. Stir in sweet corn and finely chopped spring onions. Season.

- Fry large spoonfuls of the mixture in oil over medium heat until the underside is golden. Turn and repeat.

SWEET CORN FRITTATA

All this tasty supper needs is a green salad and perhaps some bread.

Serves 3–4

200 g (7 oz) sweet corn kernels	1 green pepper
1 tbsp olive oil	3 mushrooms
1 onion	salt, black pepper
	6 eggs

- Boil or steam sweet corn; drain. Heat oil in a large frying pan and fry thinly sliced onion and pepper over medium-low heat to soften and tinge gold.
- Add sliced mushrooms, sweet corn and seasoning, then stir for a minute.
- Pour beaten eggs over and stir to ensure egg reaches base of pan. Cook over medium heat for 5 minutes, or until the base is golden, then place under a hot grill to brown the top.

SWEET CORN, BACON AND POTATO CHOWDER

A chowder is a thick, creamy soup from the USA – and one of the classic combinations is sweet corn and bacon.

Serves 4

300 g (11 oz) sweet corn kernels
250 g (9 oz) unsmoked bacon
1 tbsp vegetable oil
25 g (1 oz) butter
1 onion
1 stalk celery
350 g (12 oz) potato
600 ml (1 pint) chicken stock
400 ml (14 fl. oz) milk
1 bay leaf
½ tsp sweet paprika
1 level tbsp cornflour
salt, black pepper

- Boil or steam sweet corn and drain. Fry diced bacon in oil over medium-high heat until golden; remove with a slotted spoon. Turn heat down, add butter and sweat finely chopped onion and celery over low heat to soften but not colour.
- Stir in finely chopped potato, sweet corn, stock, milk, bay leaf and paprika. Bring to a simmer and cook for 20 minutes.
- Combine cornflour with 2 tbsp cold water then add to pan, stirring. Simmer for 3 minutes. Remove bay leaf and cool the soup a little.
- Blend a quarter of the soup in a blender, then return to the pan. Add bacon. Reheat and season.

MEXICAN CORN AND PEPPER SALAD

Sweet corn and bell peppers with added spice are a typical Central American side dish or salad. Try it, hot or cold, as an accompaniment to grilled chicken. You can use fresh chopped chilli instead of the cayenne pepper.

Serves 4

400 g (14 oz) sweet corn kernels	6 spring onions
1 green pepper	1 tbsp vinegar
1 red pepper	2 tsp sweet paprika
2 tbsp vegetable oil	1 tsp cayenne pepper
	salt, black pepper

- Boil or steam sweet corn and drain. Fry finely chopped peppers in oil over medium-low heat for 10 minutes until tender and tinged brown.
- Add chopped spring onions, sweet corn, vinegar, spices and seasoning, then stir for 2 minutes.

SWEET CORN, SALMON AND POTATO SALAD

An excellent, simple midsummer salad for those with sweet corn, shallots and new potatoes in the garden.

Serves 4

400 g (14 oz) waxy new potatoes	4 salmon fillets
5 tbsp olive oil	4 shallots
salt, black pepper	juice of ½ lemon
250 g (9 oz) sweet corn kernels	2 tbsp fresh chopped parsley

- Boil potatoes until tender, drain, halve, toss with 1 tbsp of the oil and the seasoning; keep warm. Boil or steam sweet corn and drain.
- Fry salmon fillets in 2 tsp of the oil until golden and just cooked through: approx. 3 minutes each side, depending on thickness. Clean pan.
- Stir-fry thinly sliced shallots in 1 tbsp of the oil over medium-high heat until golden and lightly crisp.
- Combine remaining oil with lemon juice, seasoning and 1 tbsp parsley. Stir in sweet corn.
- Cut each salmon fillet into four and arrange on serving plates with the potatoes. Spoon sweet corn dressing over. Top with crispy shallots and remaining parsley.

Christopher Columbus is said to have brought sweet corn to Europe from America, where it has been enjoyed as a food for 7,000 years.

> Sweet corn is not only eaten as cobs or kernels, but can be ground into corn meal and used like wheat flour in baking, sauces, etc.

TUNA AND SWEET CORN BURGERS

These burgers will become a firm family favourite and they are very easy to make. Serve with tomato wedges and green salad or vegetables.

Serves 4

450 g (1 lb) potatoes	300 g (11 oz) canned tuna
3 tbsp mayonnaise	3 tbsp fresh chopped
salt, black pepper	parsley
250 g (9 oz) sweet corn	50 g (2 oz) breadcrumbs
kernels	1 tbsp vegetable oil

- Boil chopped potatoes until tender. Drain and lightly mash with mayonnaise and seasoning.
- Boil or steam sweet corn, drain and stir into potato with the drained tuna, parsley and seasoning.
- Divide mixture into 8 burgers. Put breadcrumbs on a plate and cover each burger with crumb.
- Fry in oil over medium heat for 2–3 minutes each side.

SWEET CORN PUDDING

This isn't a dessert but a side dish to accompany grilled gammon steaks, baked ham or roast chicken.

Serves 6

600 g (1 lb 6 oz)	300 ml (½ pint) milk
sweet corn kernels	1 tbsp caster sugar
200 ml (7 fl. oz) cream	½ tsp baking powder
50 g (2 oz) butter	1 tsp salt
50 g (2 oz) flour	3 eggs

- Boil or steam sweet corn, drain and cool. Blend half in a blender with cream.
- Melt butter in pan and stir in flour over medium heat for a minute. Stir in milk gradually to make a thick sauce. Add sugar, baking powder and salt.
- Remove from heat and stir in sweet corn and blended corn mixture. Separate eggs and stir in beaten egg yolks.
- In a clean, dry, grease-free bowl, whisk egg whites until stiff. Fold into the sweet corn mixture.
- Pour into a greased ovenproof dish set in a roasting tin. Add 500 ml (17 fl. oz) water to the roasting tin. Bake at 180°C/gas mark 4 for 45 minutes, or until golden and puffed up.

CHICKEN AND SWEET CORN PIE

An easy pie to make, and a great late-summer family supper.

Serves 4

250 g (9 oz) sweet corn	50 ml (2 fl. oz) chicken
kernels	stock
150 g (5 oz) carrots	2 tbsp fresh chopped
500 g (1¼ lb) skinless	parsley
chicken breast fillets	300 g (11 oz) shortcrust
25 g (1 oz) butter	pastry (page 251)
400 ml (14 fl. oz) white	1 egg
sauce (page 251)	

- Boil or steam sweet corn kernels with diced carrot. Drain.
- Cut chicken into bite-sized pieces and fry in butter over medium heat, turning occasionally, until tinged with gold.
- Pour white sauce and stock into pan with chicken and stir thoroughly to combine. Stir in sweet corn, carrot and parsley.
- Tip mixture into a pie dish. Roll out pastry. Brush dish edges with water and cover with the pastry, trim and make a hole in the centre. Brush with beaten egg.
- Bake at 200°C/gas mark 6 for 25 minutes, or until pastry is golden.

SWEET CORN SALSA

A salsa made in a minute, which will enliven any plainly cooked meat, chicken or fish dish.

Serves 4

200 g (7 oz) sweet corn	1 lime
kernels	1 tsp Tabasco
1 red onion	2 tbsp fresh chopped
3 tbsp olive oil	coriander

- Boil or steam sweet corn, drain and cool. Combine with finely chopped onion and remaining ingredients. Allow to sit for an hour before serving.

TOMATO

One of the most indispensable vegetables (in fact – a fruit!) in the kitchen, tomatoes provide colour, flavour, bulk, moisture, sweetness, acidity and interest in a huge range of recipes. They are also our most popular vegetable for eating raw. No wonder they are now the world's most widely grown vegetable.

Today we have a broad range of colours, shapes, sizes and tastes from which to choose, from the small golden or bright red cherries through to plum and huge beefsteak types.

While tomatoes are an important ingredient in recipes where other vegetables or foods are the stars, they can easily take centre stage – grilled or fried, in soups and salads, stuffed, baked or in sandwiches.

STORING

Tomatoes should be stored at room temperature. Keeping them in the fridge impairs flavour. A fruit bowl in the kitchen is an ideal place for semi-ripe and even green tomatoes to continue to ripen.

Tomatoes turn to mush when frozen, but are suitable for cooked recipes, so freezing is a good choice for a glut. They can be left unpeeled. To freeze whole, just wash, dry, bag and freeze. The tomatoes will keep for 3 months and can be thawed to use in stews, soups, sauces, etc. If you blanch for 1–2 minutes they will keep for a year. To open-freeze, put small whole or larger halved tomatoes on a tray in the freezer. When frozen, bag or put in a container. These are ideal for recipes where only a few are required. Tomato juice/passata (page 153), fried tomatoes and tomato sauce (page 156) all freeze well.

Tomatoes are a key ingredient for many chutneys and preserves – see pages 240–241.

VARIETIES

STANDARD

Medium-sized, round tomatoes. All-purpose. Good varieties include Shirley, Ailsa Craig and Golden Sunrise.

PLUM

Plum-shaped tomatoes with more flesh and less pip. Ideal for sauces, freezing, pickling, preserves and for grilling on skewers. Good varieties include Roma, Agro and the mini Yellow Pear.

CHERRY

Small, sweet tomatoes. Use for salads, sauces, roasting and kebabs. Good varieties include Gardeners Delight, Sweet Million and Golden Cherry.

BEEFSTEAK

Very large, fleshy tomatoes. Use for stuffing, slicing and frying. Good varieties include Big Boy and Red Brandywine.

NO COOKING REQUIRED

Eat raw on their own or with French dressing (page 250), olive oil or balsamic vinegar.

THICK TOMATO JUICE/PASSATA

It is easy to make your own tomato juice. Store in the fridge and drink within 2 days, or freeze. Use this when passata is required. You can add other ingredients to the basic recipe – chopped onion, celery or carrot – and spice it up with Tabasco and/or celery salt. Ready-made passata is available from supermarkets.

ripe tomatoes	1 tsp caster sugar for
juice of ½ lemon for	every 4 tomatoes
every 4 tomatoes	salt, black pepper

- Chop tomatoes and put in a blender with lemon juice, sugar and seasoning. Blend until smooth. If too thick, add water and blend again. Straining through a sieve over a large bowl is an optional extra. Chill.

RAW TOMATO SAUCE FOR PASTA

You don't need to cook ripe tomatoes to make a great sauce. If the pasta is piping hot, it will warm the sauce when it is stirred through. Try this one with spaghetti or fusilli. Grated cheese or Mascarpone can be added.

Serves 4

6 tomatoes	2 tbsp fresh
2 cloves garlic	chopped basil
salt, black pepper	4 tbsp olive oil
2 tbsp fresh chopped parsley	1 tbsp red wine vinegar

- Chop peeled or unpeeled tomatoes and put in a bowl.
- Crush garlic with salt until you have a paste (use a pestle and mortar to make this easy). Stir in remaining ingredients and combine well, then toss thoroughly with the tomatoes. Cover and leave to stand for 15 minutes (not in the fridge).

TOMATO, TUNA AND BEAN SALAD

A perfect combination of flavours for summer.

Serves 4

500 g (1¼ lb) tuna	2 shallots
6 tomatoes	4 tbsp French dressing
300 g (11 oz) cooked	(page 250)
cannellini beans	1 tbsp fresh chopped chives

- Grill tuna for 2 minutes each side or until golden on the outside and slightly pink inside. Allow to cool until just warm, then cut into bite-sized chunks.
- Combine with sliced tomatoes, well-drained and rinsed beans, thinly sliced shallots and dressing. Sprinkle chives over to serve.

PANZANELLA

A famous tomato and bread salad from Italy. Good made with ciabatta, but any crusty white bread will do.

Serves 4

4 thick slices	1 red onion
slightly stale bread	3 tbsp fresh
6 tomatoes	chopped basil
12 stoned black	1 clove garlic
olives	100 ml (3½ fl. oz) French
¼ cucumber	dressing (page 250)

- Toast bread until deep golden, cut into cubes and mix with roughly chopped tomatoes, olives and cucumber, thinly sliced onion and the basil.
- Thoroughly crush the garlic and combine with French dressing. Toss salad in dressing.

TOMATO PESTO STACKS

A brilliant supper-party starter as they are easy to prepare and need no cooking, but still look elegant.

Serves 4

25 g (1 oz) toasted	1 tbsp capers
pine nuts	4 large tomatoes
4 tbsp basil pesto	1 tbsp French dressing
(page 161)	(page 250)
4 spring onions	basil leaves

- Very lightly crush pine nuts in a bowl and combine with pesto, finely chopped spring onions, and drained and rinsed capers.
- Cut a slice off the bottom of each tomato so it will sit on a serving plate. Cut each tomato into 5 horizontal slices, then re-assemble, layering each slice with a little of the pesto filling.
- Drizzle a small amount of dressing over each tomato and garnish with basil leaves.

BASIC COOKING

Rinse if necessary; dry. Some recipes require seeds to be removed: halve tomatoes, and scoop out seeds and membrane with a small spoon. Any green, tough section near the stalk end can be removed with a small, sharp knife. Small tomatoes can be left on the vine stalk to roast, barbecue or grill.

To peel tomatoes: Make a cross in the stalk end with a sharp knife. | Put into boiling water for 1 minute. Drain. | Plunge into cold water for a few seconds. Drain. | Peel off skin. It should come away easily.

FRIED TOMATOES

Quarter or slice large tomatoes, halve smaller ones or leave whole. Fry with seasoning and/or fresh chopped herbs in oil over medium heat. A dash of balsamic vinegar or sugar improves less tasty varieties or under-ripe tomatoes.

ROAST TOMATOES

Halve tomatoes if too large, put in a roasting tin, brush with oil, season and cook at 190°C/gas mark 5 for 20 minutes, or until slightly browned.

GRILLED TOMATOES

Halve tomatoes, season and grill for 3–5 minutes, turning once.

DRIED TOMATOES

If you have a glut, it is worth trying to dry tomatoes in the oven, but as it is hard to remove all the moisture content they may not keep as long as shop-bought dried tomatoes. Quarter and de-seed them and sprinkle the insides with salt and a little caster sugar. Place cut side up on a baking tray and put in the oven on the lowest heat for 3–4 hours. Check every hour after the first 2 hours. The dried tomatoes should be dark red, moisture-free but still pliable. They will keep in an airtight container for several weeks (check weekly) and for longer in a sterilized jar, covered with oil, in the fridge. Their rich, concentrated flavour makes them good for adding to pasta sauces and stews. See also semi-dried tomatoes (right).

SOUTHERN-STYLE FRIED GREEN TOMATOES

If you have any tomatoes that don't want to ripen, give this recipe a try – it is delicious. Serve with bacon or grilled meat.

Serves 4

4 large green tomatoes
salt, black pepper

100 g (3½ oz) polenta flour
2 tbsp vegetable oil

- Cut tomatoes into 1 cm (½ in.) thick rounds. Season. Spread flour on a plate and dip slices in until coated.
- Fry in oil over medium-high heat until golden on both sides: approx. 5 minutes.

> The Aztec word *tomatl* translates as 'plump fruit' – a name changed to *tomate* by the Spanish explorers in the 16th century.

SEMI-DRIED TOMATOES WITH HERBS

Try these drained and chopped in a salad. Or cook them with some of their oil, purée and use to enrich tomato sauces. Store in the fridge and use within a month.

Serves 4–8

12 ripe tomatoes
salt, black pepper
1 tbsp finely chopped oregano

2 tsp fresh thyme leaves
olive oil

- Halve tomatoes, scoop out seeds, then quarter them. Arrange on a baking tray. Sprinkle with seasoning and herbs, and drizzle a little oil over.
- Put in the oven on the lowest heat until most of the moisture has gone: 3–4 hours.
- Put tomatoes in a sterilized jar and cover with olive oil.

TOMATO RECIPES

CREAMY TOMATO AND PASTA BAKE

A very easy supper for the family. Serve with a green salad.

Serves 4

300 g (11 oz) pasta shapes	**500 g (1¼ lb) small tomatoes**	**75 g (3 oz) grated**
75 g (3 oz) Cheddar	**3 tbsp fresh chopped parsley**	**Parmesan**
500 ml (17 fl. oz) white sauce (page 251)	**6 spring onions**	

- Cook pasta in boiling salted water, drain and tip into an ovenproof dish.

- Add grated Cheddar to warmed white sauce. Halve tomatoes and add to pasta with sauce, parsley and finely chopped spring onions.

- Sprinkle Parmesan on top and bake at 190°C/gas mark 5 for 25 minutes, or until golden and bubbling.

TOMATO SAUCE

A recipe which you will use time and again in many other recipes. It will freeze in sturdy plastic bags or containers. You can add flavourings to the basic sauce – for example, chopped chillies or herbs for a pasta sauce. For a smoother sauce, purée it in a blender. Ready-made tomato sauce is available from supermarkets.

Makes 400 ml (14 fl. oz)

1 onion
1 tbsp olive oil
1 clove garlic
500 g (1¼ lb) tomatoes
2 tsp tomato purée
1 tsp soft brown sugar
juice of ½ lemon
salt, black pepper

- Sweat finely chopped onion in oil over low heat to soften but not colour. Add finely chopped garlic and stir for a minute.

- Add chopped tomatoes and remaining ingredients, bring to a simmer and cook, uncovered, for 30 minutes, stirring from time to time, until you have a rich sauce.

TOMATO KETCHUP

Your own home-made ketchup isn't hard or time-consuming to make and it is a good way to use up a glut. It will keep for around 2 weeks in the fridge. If you want to store it for longer, bottle and sterilize as for bottled fruit (page 239).

Makes approx. 300 ml (½ pint)

1 onion
1 kg (2¼ lb) ripe tomatoes
2 cloves garlic
250 ml (8 fl. oz) white wine vinegar
1 tsp whole black peppercorns
½ tsp each ground cloves, cinnamon, allspice and cayenne pepper
125 g (4 oz) soft light brown sugar
1 tbsp treacle

- Put chopped onion, tomatoes and garlic in a large saucepan over low heat until tomato juices begin to run. Turn heat to medium and cook, uncovered, for 45 minutes until you have a thick sauce.

- Pour vinegar into another pan, add all the spices and warm over a low heat for 15 minutes.

- Rub tomato and onion pulp through a nylon sieve into a clean pan, pushing through as much as you can. Strain vinegar into the pan, add sugar and treacle, stir well and simmer over low heat for 20 minutes, or until thick.

> *Tomatoes are perfect partners for basil, oregano, cheese, eggs and white fish.*

WARM TOMATO, MOZZARELLA AND BASIL SALAD

Popped under the grill, this salad makes lots of delicious juices for which you need plenty of crusty bread for mopping up. Try to use buffalo rather than cow's Mozzarella, as it is much more tasty and tender.

Serves 4

6 large tomatoes
3 x 125 g (4 oz) balls buffalo Mozzarella
4 tbsp fresh chopped basil
4 tbsp French dressing (page 250)
2 tsp basil pesto
several whole basil leaves

- Divide thinly sliced tomatoes and Mozzarella between 4 individual gratin dishes, arranging them in overlapping layers.

- Sprinkle with chopped basil. Combine French dressing with pesto and pour over.

- Place under a hot grill for 4 minutes, or until the Mozzarella has melted. Sprinkle with torn basil leaves and serve immediately.

CREAM OF TOMATO SOUP

Another good way of using a glut of tomatoes. This soup will freeze.

Serves 4

1 onion	**1 bay leaf**
25 g (1 oz) butter	**600 ml (1 pint) vegetable**
1 clove garlic	**stock**
1 tsp paprika	**150 ml (¼ pint)**
1 tbsp tomato purée	**double cream**
1 kg (2¼ lb) tomatoes	**salt, black pepper**
2 tsp sugar	

- Sweat chopped onion in butter over low heat to soften but not colour. Put in chopped garlic and paprika about a minute before adding tomato purée and cook for a further 2 minutes.

- Add chopped tomatoes, sugar, bay leaf and stock. Bring to a simmer and cook for 20 minutes.

- Remove bay leaf and allow to cool a little. Blend in a blender until smooth.

- Stir in two-thirds of the cream. Reheat, season and serve with remaining cream drizzled over.

PIPERADE

An easy alternative to scrambled eggs or omelette for lunch. Serve with crusty bread or on toast.

Serves 4

4 spring onions	2 tsp fresh chopped
1 chilli	mixed herbs
1 clove garlic	salt, black pepper
30 g (1¼ oz) butter	6 eggs
400 g (14 oz) tomatoes	50 ml (2 fl. oz) cream

- Combine chopped onions, finely chopped chilli and garlic. Fry in butter over medium heat for a minute. Add chopped tomatoes, herbs and seasoning; stir.
- Beat eggs with cream and seasoning, pour into the pan and cook, stirring frequently, until egg is set but still soft and creamy.

TOMATO UPSIDE-DOWN TART

Plum tomatoes work well here as they contain less moisture than some other types.

Serves 4

50 g (2 oz) butter	2 tsp fresh chopped
salt, black pepper	oregano
2 tsp caster sugar	300 g (11 oz) ready-
juice of ½ lemon	rolled puff pastry
500 g (1¼ lb) tomatoes	

- Soften butter and spread over the base of a flan tin. Sprinkle with seasoning, sugar and lemon juice.
- Slice tomatoes into rounds and arrange in a thick layer on top of the butter.
- Sprinkle on oregano. Roll out pastry to fit the tin and press edges down inside.
- Bake at 200°C/gas mark 6 for 20 minutes, or until pastry is golden. Cool a little, invert the tin on to a serving plate and serve.

MUSHROOM AND BACON STUFFED TOMATOES

One beefsteak tomato filled with a rich stuffing is a light meal in itself – all you need is a green salad on the side. Or you could use the mixture to stuff smaller tomatoes for a starter or part of a buffet.

Serves 4

4 beefsteak tomatoes	4 mushrooms
100 g (3½ oz) rice	2 shallots
1 tsp saffron strands	2 tbsp fresh chopped
salt, black pepper	parsley
4 rashers back bacon	25 g (1 oz) butter
2 tbsp olive oil	

- Slice tops off tomatoes and scoop out seeds and membrane, leaving flesh walls intact. Keep the tops and any pulpy juice.
- Cook rice with saffron and seasoning until tender. Fry bacon in a little of the oil until golden and crisp; crumble. Chop mushrooms and add to pan with a little more oil. Stir-fry for a minute to colour.
- In a bowl, combine rice with bacon, mushrooms, finely chopped shallots, parsley and juice from tomatoes.
- Stuff tomatoes with the mixture and put tops on. Put in a greased baking dish and dot with butter. Bake at 190°C/gas mark 5 for 20 minutes, or until tomatoes are tender.

TOMATO AND CHEDDAR MUFFINS

Great served as a bread with any meal, and also good on their own for breakfast. Use dried tomatoes (page 154) – or you can use fresh tomatoes, decreasing the milk to 200 ml (7 fl. oz).

Makes 12

250 g (9 oz) plain flour
1 tbsp baking powder
1 tsp salt
3 eggs
250 ml (8 fl. oz) milk
100 g (3½ oz) butter
20 pieces dried tomatoes
100 g (3½ oz) Cheddar

- Sift flour, baking powder and salt into a bowl.
- In a separate bowl, beat eggs with milk and melted butter. Stir in chopped tomatoes and grated cheese.
- Fold flour into the wet mixture and combine well.
- Spoon into muffin cases in a tray, filling just to the top. Bake at 200°C/gas mark 6 for 20–25 minutes until risen and golden brown.

TURNIP

Turnips are much neglected in the kitchen, but they are very versatile and many varieties come without the classic slightly bitter flavour. Early-season, quick-growing types for summer and autumn eating can be pulled when not much larger than a radish, and eaten in a similar way, while the larger, more fibrous maincrop varieties are ideal for stews and roasting. Turnip tops are a useful green vegetable – cook them in a similar way to spring greens: slice and boil, steam or stir-fry until tender. Small leaves can also be eaten raw. Several colours are available – the usual creamy-white through to gold, and varieties with purple or green tops – but all have white flesh. As well as the globe shapes, there are also flat-topped and cylindrical types.

STORING

Early turnips can be kept in a plastic bag in the fridge for a few days, but are best eaten straight after harvesting. Maincrops can be pulled in November for winter use. Cut off the tops to within 2.5 cm (1 in.) of the root, dry and store in peat or compost, or between thick layers of newspaper in boxes in a dry, cool, dark place. Freeze small turnips, peeled if necessary. Slice/cut into chunks; blanch for 2 minutes; freeze in plastic bags.

Early-season turnips include Aramis, good for salads or roasting whole; Scarlet Queen, excellent eaten raw when radish-sized; and Snowball, which is delicious roasted or grated raw. The flat-topped Purple Top Milan turnip – one of the earliest to harvest – is good eaten raw, steamed or baked.

Maincrop turnips include Golden Ball, good mashed or baked whole; Green Top Stone, a good all-rounder; and Noir d'Hiver, an unusual black-skinned turnip with sweet flesh and great flavour when roasted or steamed.

NO COOKING REQUIRED

Early-season turnips can be eaten raw. Grate or thinly slice and use in salads, coleslaw or cheese sandwiches.

BASIC COOKING

Top and tail, wash and dry. Earlies should not need peeling. Small earlies: leave whole with 2–3 cm (¾–1¼ in.) stalk intact. Larger earlies: chop if necessary. Maincrop: peel and cut into chunks.

BOILED TURNIP

Boil in lightly salted water for 10–15 minutes (depending on size and age) until tender; drain.

STEAMED TURNIP

Steam over boiling water for 12–20 minutes until tender. Season.

MASHED TURNIP

Mash boiled or steamed turnips with 10 g (¼ oz) butter per 100 g (3½ oz). Season.

FRIED TURNIP

Slice and parboil for 3 minutes. Dry, then fry in vegetable oil over medium-high heat until tender: 3–4 minutes each side. Season.

ROAST TURNIP

Parboil for 3 minutes (small, whole) or 5 minutes (maincrop, chunks). Drain and toss with vegetable oil and seasoning. Roast at 190°C/gas mark 5 for 45 minutes, turning once, until tender and golden.

BAKED TURNIP

Place small whole turnips on a baking tray. Brush with vegetable oil, season and bake at 200°C/gas mark 6 for 30 minutes, or until tender.

TURNIP RECIPES

TURNIP GRATIN

Extremely more-ish dish to go with a pork, gammon or chicken roast.

Serves 4

300 ml (½ pint) cream
100 ml (3½ fl. oz) medium-dry cider
salt, black pepper
1 tbsp Dijon mustard
4 turnips (approx. 800 g/1¾ lb)
25 g (1 oz) grated Parmesan

- Pour cream and cider into a frying pan and reduce over medium heat for 5 minutes, stirring once or twice. Add seasoning and mustard.
- Stir in thinly sliced turnips to coat, then tip pan contents into a shallow ovenproof dish and sprinkle cheese over. Bake at 190°C/gas mark 5 for 40–45 minutes, or until golden, bubbling and tender.

SAUTÉED BABY TURNIPS AND BACON

Try to use turnips no bigger than a large radish. Halve larger ones before cooking.

Serves 4

6 rashers smoked back bacon
1 tbsp olive oil
500 g (1¼ lb) small turnips
25 g (1 oz) butter
1 clove garlic
juice of 1 lemon
3 tbsp fresh chopped parsley
salt and pepper

- Fry chopped bacon in oil in a large pan over medium-high heat until golden and just crisp. Remove with a slotted spoon, cool a little and crumble.
- Add turnips to pan with butter and sauté over medium-high heat for 3–4 minutes until golden.
- Add chopped garlic to pan and stir for a minute, then add lemon juice, 2 tbsp parsley and the seasoning. Turn heat to low and cook until turnips are tender. Season again, stir in bacon for a minute, then serve sprinkled with remaining parsley.

Before the USA took over the idea of carving pumpkins into jack o' lanterns for Halloween, the British used turnips or swedes to make lanterns and left them on the doorstep to ward off evil spirits.

BRAISED TURNIPS WITH MUSTARD

Good with a roast – but if you don't have the oven on you can cook the dish on the hob in a lidded pan.

Serves 4

500 g (1¼ lb) small– medium turnips	salt, black pepper
2 shallots	200 ml (7 fl. oz) vegetable stock
25 g (1 oz) butter	2 tbsp fresh chopped
2 tsp mustard powder	parsley

- Slice turnips approx. 0.5 cm (¼ in.) thick and sweat with finely chopped shallots in butter in a flameproof casserole over low heat for 10 minutes.
- Stir in mustard and seasoning, then add stock and parsley. Bring to a simmer, put lid on and cook at 170°C/gas mark 3½ for 45 minutes, or until tender.

TURNIP, POTATO AND CELERIAC MASH

A combination that really works and is full of flavour because the vegetables are mashed with some of the cooking liquid. Try it with baked gammon or roast lamb. A similar mash, without the celeriac and including chives, is the Scottish 'clapshot'.

Serves 4

2 turnips (approx. 400g/14 oz)	200 ml (7 fl. oz) milk
1 small–medium celeriac	1 bay leaf
2 potatoes	25 g (1 oz) butter
	salt, black pepper

- Chop all vegetables into fairly small cubes and put into a saucepan. Add milk and bay leaf, then pour in boiling water so that the vegetables are just covered. Add salt. Simmer for 20 minutes, or until everything is tender.
- Drain off liquid into a jug, removing bay leaf. Add butter and seasoning and 2 tbsp of the cooking liquid. Mash thoroughly, adding more cooking liquid as necessary.

CHAPTER 4
HERBS

Herbs – which can be leaves, stems, bulbs or seeds of the plant – are generally used to enhance other foods by providing aroma, flavour and colour. Many of the herbs in our gardens grow wild in the countries bordering the Mediterranean and have been used there widely and abundantly since Greek and Roman times. Some herbs have a special affinity for certain foods which are a feature of the cuisine of the area. Sweet basil, for example, which grows wild in Italy, is widely used in Italian cooking.

Herbs are best picked as needed and used fresh, but some can be dried for use throughout the year – individual drying notes appear in the A–Z.

The herbs described in the A–Z are the ones most often grown in the garden and used in the kitchen, rather than the herbs grown and used for non-culinary purposes such as pot-pourri.

USING HERBS

MIXED HERBS A mixture of finely chopped, strongly flavoured fresh or dried herbs that often includes sage, thyme, marjoram and parsley. Use to flavour casseroles or sprinkle over meat or poultry before roasting.

FINES HERBES A mixture of finely chopped, delicately flavoured (*fine*) fresh herbs that often includes chervil, parsley, chives and tarragon in equal quantity. Use to flavour omelettes, scrambled egg, chicken or fish. It can also be used in herb butter – see below.

BOUQUET GARNI A bunch of fresh herbs tied together with string or put into a small muslin bag. The classic combination is parsley, thyme and bay leaf, although chervil can replace parsley. Add to stocks, casseroles or other dishes during cooking; remove before serving.

HERB BUTTER Butter blended with finely chopped herbs. A single herb is usually used – e.g. parsley, chives, garlic or dill – but mixtures are also good. Beat 1–2 tbsp of the chopped herb into 100 g (3½ oz) softened butter. Form into small patties and chill. Use to garnish grilled meats, fish or vegetables.

HERB PASTE Herb leaves pounded to a paste, using a pestle and mortar for a rough paste or a food processor for a smoother finish, with other ingredients including oil and seasoning. Use instead of fresh herbs in curries, casseroles, stir-fries and soups.

HERB PESTO The name pesto is from the Italian word *pestare* – to pound or crush. A pesto is traditionally made of fresh herb leaves pounded with garlic, nuts, seasoning and olive oil; often Parmesan or Pecorino cheese is added. The most familiar pesto is made with basil (page 161). Other suitable herbs include coriander leaf, mint or parsley. Use to flavour fish, pasta, soup and other dishes.

HERB OIL The flavour of olive or vegetable oils can be enhanced by steeping fresh herbs in them. Add a large handful of unchopped herbs to 500 ml (17 fl. oz) oil, seal and leave to marinate for a month; strain and bottle. Some popular flavoured oils include basil, garlic, rosemary and thyme. Use sparingly in sauces or salad dressings and for cooking, using the flavoured oil which will enhance the food best (e.g. basil oil for tomato salad or rosemary oil for lamb chops).

HERB VINEGAR Add a handful of herb sprigs or leaves to 500 ml (17 fl. oz) warm vinegar of choice, leave to stand for 3 weeks, shaking occasionally, then strain and bottle. Suitable herbs include tarragon, mint and rosemary.

HERB TEA A hot drink made with various herbs, including mint (digestive), chamomile (calming) and lemon balm (refreshing). Chop 1 tbsp fresh leaves, add 300 ml (½ pint) boiling water, then steep for 5 minutes and strain.

STORING

Once dried, herbs should be kept in an opaque container in a dark place. In the light they will lose colour, aroma and flavour. Many herbs can also be frozen. Sage and parsley freeze particularly well simply chopped and frozen in bags. Thyme and rosemary stalks can be frozen whole – the leaves conveniently drop off. Herbs for use in sauces, casseroles, etc., can be chopped, put into ice-cube trays and covered with water. When required simply remove a cube and use it in your recipe.

Sterilized containers are recommended for the storage of fresh herbs – see the section on Sterilizing Jars, page 235.

ANGELICA

The young green stalks of this perennial are well known as a candied decoration for cakes, jellies and desserts. Leaves and stalks can be added to tart fruits such as rhubarb and gooseberries to make them less acidic. Angelica is also made into a liqueur.

To make candied angelica: cut young angelica stems into 15–20 cm (6–8 in.) lengths. Soak in water for 3 hours, then blanch in boiling water for 1–2 minutes, or until stems soften. Drain, cool and remove any pithy string. Make a syrup using 225 g (8 oz) sugar to 300 ml (½ pint) water and boil together until syrupy. Add stems and leave for 24 hours. Repeat the process three times. Lay the pieces of angelica on a baking tray, dust with icing sugar and dry in the oven at 120°C/gas mark ½ for 3 hours.

BASIL

Used extensively in Asia, Greece, Egypt and Italy for centuries, basil was introduced to Western Europe in the 16th century but has only recently become one of our most popular culinary herbs. Sweet (common) basil is now a familiar sight on window sills, but there are several other forms – lettuce-leaved, ruffled, purple, lemon and Thai (with a hint of pepper). There is also bush basil, a smaller-leaved and slightly hardier version of sweet basil with a similar aroma and flavour.

Basil is best eaten raw, or added at the very end of a cooked recipe as the colour, flavour and aroma quickly disappear when heated. It marries especially well with tomatoes – a salad of sliced tomatoes, olive oil and a scattering of torn basil leaves is a treat. It enhances soft cheeses, particularly Mozzarella, and the hard Italian cheeses such as Parmesan, and is good with pasta. It is even good torn and stirred into a dish of sliced strawberries. The delicate leaves are easily bruised, so handle carefully and tear just before eating.

Basil doesn't dry or freeze well. Store it by packing leaves into a clean airtight jar, then fill with olive oil, seal and keep in the fridge for a month. You can also use it to make pesto.

To make basil pesto: using a pestle and mortar, pound 3–4 cloves peeled garlic with 1 tsp salt until creamy. Add 50 g (2 oz) pine nuts and pound again until crushed. Add 6 handfuls fresh basil leaves and 4 tbsp olive oil, and pound into a rough green paste. Stir in grated Parmesan (optional). Check seasoning. Stir into cooked pasta or thin down with oil and drizzle over chicken, salmon, or a tomato and Mozzarella salad. Keeps for 2–3 months. Basil pesto is available in supermarkets.

BAY

Bay leaves come from the sweet bay tree – *Laurus nobilis* – which can reach 15 metres (50 feet) growing wild in the Mediterranean area. In most gardens, however, it will be no more than a metre (3 feet) tall and easily contained in a pot. The aromatic, slightly bitter leaves are evergreen and so can be picked all year round.

Bay is essential to the classic bouquet garni and is excellent at drawing out the flavours of different ingredients in a meal. Because of its intense flavour, leaves are generally used singly – lightly torn if you like. Too many may make the dish taste bitter.

Some uses for bay leaves:
- Use in beef or lamb stew.
- Add to chicken fricasee.
- Stir into meat, chicken or fish stock.
- Use in fish pie or for other fish dishes – it goes very well with oily fish such as salmon.
- Add it when cooking rice.
- Prepare custard or rice pudding: steep a bay leaf in warm milk for 30 minutes before proceeding with the recipe.

Remove whole bay leaves from your dish before serving.

Bay leaves are much more pungent fresh than dried. They will dry easily – simply hang up branches or twigs in a warm, dry room. Leave on the branch, or pick and put into a jar. Use within 6 months, preferably sooner. You can also grind the dried leaves and use a pinch or ½ tsp in your dishes.

Note: Don't confuse bay with common laurel – *Prunus laurocerasus* – grown for hedging. Laurel leaves look similar but are larger and are poisonous.

BERGAMOT

A perennial plant with flowers and leaves that have an orange perfume and flavour, bergamot grows wild in North America and was used by both Amerinds and settlers. It is said that the leaves were used as a substitute for Indian tea after the Boston Tea Party.

Today the leaves are used in savoury and sweet dishes, including pork, veal, vegetarian and fruit dishes, and ices. They are a classic ingredient of an American meat loaf. The thin flower petals can be added to salads, or whole flower heads used as a garnish for trifles and jellies.

To dry – spread out petals or leaves on a tray and leave in a hot, dry room or very low oven until dry, turning occasionally. Store in a jar.

BORAGE

A robust annual plant, native to the Middle East, with thick soft stems and large leaves covered in 'hairs' (which can produce a rash when touched). The small, star-shaped blue or occasionally pink flowers are full of nectar which bees love. The flowers have given borage its common name, starflower, and these are the source of starflower oil.

The flowers may be used as they are or dipped in egg white and caster sugar as a garnish for cold drinks such as fruit punch or cocktails, fruit salads, cakes and desserts. The leaves are similar to cucumber in flavour – finely chop and use in salads.

The flowers and leaves are best used fresh rather than dried, which will reduce flavour.

CARAWAY

Every part of the biennial caraway can be eaten – its carrot-like leaves, its tiny white-to-pale-pink flowers, its seeds and even its roots. The seeds have a distinctive, strong flavour, but other parts are milder. The leaves taste like parsley.

Some uses for caraway:
- Harvest leaves throughout the season for use in salads, or cook like spinach.
- Pick flowers and add to salads.
- Cut seed heads when brown and ripe and use in seed cake, sprinkle over bread before baking, sprinkle over leaf salads or coleslaw, add to stewed or baked apples, or add to meat or vegetable sauces and soups.

Leaves are best preserved using the ice-cube method (page 160). Store seeds whole in an airtight container.

CHERVIL

Nicknamed 'gourmet parsley', chervil is a small, delicate biennial herb native to the Continent and introduced into England by the Romans. It tastes like mild aniseed, and is one of the herbs commonly used for *fines herbes*.

Cooking destroys the mild flavour, so chervil is best used raw. Add it to a green or herb salad to go with fish and egg dishes, or chop as a garnish for soups and vegetables such as carrots and peas. It makes a good herb butter for steak and grilled chicken.

The leaves soon wilt, so pick just before use.

Chervil can be dried, although it loses much of its flavour. It is best preserved by picking off the leaves and freezing using the ice-cube method (page 160).

CHAMOMILE

A low-growing perennial or small annual, native to countries around the Mediterranean. The name 'chamomile' comes from the Greek word meaning 'ground apple'. In Medieval England it was scattered around the home to mask unpleasant odours.

Chamomile flowers can be added to salads for fragrance and as a garnish. Dried, they can be made into a tea. It has a pungent yet sweet taste – try it with honey and lemon.

Pick the flower heads on a sunny, dry day, spread them out on a tray and leave in a hot, dry room or very low oven until dry, turning occasionally. Store in a jar.

CHIVES

Chives were discovered and eaten more than 3,000 years ago in China and the Mediterranean area. These perennial plants resemble clumps of grass but are members of the allium family, which includes onions and leeks. The leaves have a mild, pleasant onion flavour. Garlic chives are a similar plant with a definite garlicky taste. In summer, chive clumps are covered with pretty, thistle-like pink–mauve flowers which make a good garnish for salads. If cut back when they flower, they will soon produce many new tasty leaves.

Chives are an essential ingredient in *fines herbes*. They are best eaten raw or barely cooked. Use whole or chopped (or snipped with scissors) in a variety of dishes.

Some uses for chives:
- Sprinkle over new or boiled potatoes before serving.
- Beat with butter and toss with peas or serve with baked potato.
- Stir into a leek, pea or potato soup just before serving.
- Make into a dip with cream cheese.
- Add to the dough when making dumplings.
- Mash with potatoes and olive oil.
- Sprinkle over an omelette before folding.
- Stir into a quiche before baking.
- Add to a tomato salad to go with cheese.
- Use whole as a garnish for grilled fish, hard-boiled eggs, chicken and canapés.

Chives are best used fresh, rather than dried, when they will lose flavour and colour. They may be chopped, bagged and frozen for use in most recipes – but they will not be so good for garnish once defrosted.

CORIANDER

Twenty or thirty years ago coriander plants – known as cilantro in the USA and sometimes called Chinese parsley – were rarely seen in British kitchen gardens, but now coriander has become one of the most popular herb seeds in the catalogues. The fragrant, slightly metallic-smelling serrated leaves, stalks and seeds are all valuable additions to the modern kitchen and even the roots can be used (for example, as a coffee substitute). The flavour of coriander is unique – varyingly described, by some as citrusy and others as like soap!

A half-hardy annual, it is an important addition to many Indian, Thai, Chinese, Mexican and other ethnic cuisines and is best added towards the end of cooking time as the flavour is most potent when the leaves are raw or barely cooked.

The plants go readily to seed even if you keep picking. Let some of these seeds ripen and turn light brown, when you can use them, lightly crushed or ground, in curries, tagines and other spiced dishes, or use whole as a pickling spice.

Some uses for coriander leaf:
- Prepare pesto (see basil pesto, page 161).
- Add to stir-fries just before serving.
- Chop with stalks and stir into a tomato, onion or cucumber salsa.
- Scatter over a curry, a stir-fry or chilli con carne.
- Crush as the basis of Green Thai paste, combined with garlic, chillies, ginger and cumin.

The leaves don't dry very well, losing aroma, so preserve using the ice-cube method (page 160). Store the seeds in an airtight container. To retain maximum aroma and flavour, never grind until you need them.

DILL

Dill is a versatile herb with little waste as the leaves, seeds and flowers can all be used in the kitchen. A half-hardy perennial usually grown as an annual, its feathery frond leaves are commonly called 'dill weed' and have a distinctive, aniseedy flavour which goes particularly well with fish, eggs, cucumber and potatoes.

It is best eaten raw or barely cooked to preserve its flavour and bright colour.

Dill weed is better chopped with scissors than with a knife. The seeds are a better option than dill weed to flavour long-cook dishes such as fish soups and casseroles.

Some uses for dill weed:
- Chop and combine with mayonnaise and a few capers for a potato salad.
- Make a low-fat dressing with thick natural yogurt, dill weed and French mustard.
- Stir into scrambled egg before serving, or add to omelette.
- Mix into sour cream for a quick dip and serve with cucumber batons.
- Add to cucumber sandwiches.
- Combine with diced cucumber, white wine vinegar and seasoning for a salad to accompany fish.
- Make into a herb butter to go with salmon or new potatoes.
- Mix with cream cheese and serve on crackers.
- Add to béchamel sauce with a little lemon juice to serve with salmon or for a fish pie.

Try tossing dill flowers into a leaf and herb salad or use for garnishing fish, egg and other dishes. The seeds can be used whole or ground in breads, sprinkled lightly over cheese salad or added to salad dressings. Add seeds to white wine or cider vinegar (page 160). Dill seeds are also commonly used in pickles, often referred to as 'dill pickles'.

Dill weed dries reasonably well in a low oven or warm, airy place, but is best preserved using the ice-cube method (page 160).

FENNEL

A tall perennial plant with graceful, frondy, drooping leaves, fennel can be green (common fennel) or bronze. The green type is usually used in the kitchen, although the bronze leaves are perfectly edible and a little milder in taste. The seeds – and smaller stems – are also used.

Fennel has a similar aniseed/liquorice taste to dill, and can be used to replace dill in recipes (and vice versa). The herb is closely related to Florence fennel, which also has an aniseed flavour. It originated in Asia, where the seeds are chewed after a meal as a breath freshener.

The tiny yellow flowers appear on flat heads in late summer and the yellowy-brown seeds should be harvested in autumn when ripe. They are good added to mackerel or other oily fish dishes, sprinkled sparingly on salads, or added to bread before baking. Try stirring them into savoury rice dishes.

Some uses for fennel:
- Toss leaves or seeds into the pan when braising fish.
- Make a foil parcel for salmon or sardines, add lemon juice, oil and fennel (seed or leaf), wrap loosely, then bake.
- Flavour a shellfish risotto with crushed fennel seeds.
- Stir fennel leaves into fish soup (e.g. bouillabaisse) for the last few minutes of cooking time.
- Add fennel leaves to the pan juices when cooking pork to counteract the richness and fattiness of the meat.
- Lay a whole fish on a bed of fennel branches, sprinkle with oil and seasoning and roast.
- Stuff small whole fish (e.g. sea bass, sardines) with chopped fennel mixed with lemon juice, oil and breadcrumbs before cooking.

Fennel leaves lose flavour, colour and aroma when dried but they can be preserved by using the ice-cube method (page 160), or simply chop, bag and freeze. Store the dried whole seeds in an airtight container.

GARLIC

Garlic is a bulb, native to Asia, which has long been popular in the kitchens of the Mediterranean area and is becoming a very familiar sight in our kitchen gardens. A member of the allium family, it is related to onion, leeks and chives. Each round bulb, with its white, papery covering, is made up of several wedge-shaped 'cloves' which are usually peeled and chopped for recipes but can also be used unpeeled or whole.

Raw and freshly chopped, garlic has a powerful, almost overwhelming pungency. Once cooked it becomes mild and with long cooking it is difficult to detect, but it brings out the flavour in other foods extremely well. It can be used in many ways in a wide variety of savoury dishes. Regular garlic-users find that the notorious 'garlic breath' disappears as the body adapts to processing its compounds.

You can add a clove or two of chopped garlic to almost any soup, stew, pasta sauce or dip (it will soon become addictive).

Some uses for garlic:
- Make basil pesto (page 161).
- Add well-crushed garlic to tzatziki (page 80).
- Prepare the Italian sprinkle-seasoning *gremolata* – to serve 4, crush 4 cloves garlic and mix with juice and zest of a lemon, 2 handfuls fresh chopped parsley, 50 ml (2 fl. oz) olive oil and seasoning. Sprinkle over grilled meats, fish or pasta.
- Stuff a roasting chicken with unpeeled cloves, a halved lemon and some butter and seasoning. When the bird is ready, serve the cloves on the plate – the flesh should be soft, mild and delicious, and slip easily from the skin.

- Use to make garlic bread – finely chop 4–6 peeled cloves, beat with 125–150 g (4–5 oz) softened butter, cut a French loaf and spread butter in between each cut side – wrap in foil, bake until butter is melted.
- Roast garlic – cut root side flat so the whole bulbs can sit upright in a roasting tin. Brush with olive oil and roast at 180°C/gas mark 4 for about 25 minutes.

In a good sunny summer, garlic will produce heads that will store well through the winter if kept in an airy, dry place. String them up as for onions, or store in trays layered with paper.

HOP

The hop is a large, climbing perennial, belonging to the same family as cannabis, and has been used for centuries in beer-making. The pretty flower clusters can also be used to make a tea: add 2 tbsp flower heads to 300 ml (½ pint) boiling water, steep for 5 minutes, then strain. The leaves can be boiled and used as a vegetable in a similar way to spinach.

Hop flowers can be laid out on a tray or hung up and dried, but lose their potency after several months' exposure to light.

HORSERADISH

A perennial plant of the mustard family, with large leaves and long, thick roots, used to provide a hot, sharp flavour in sauces and dressings. To reduce its eye-watering effect scrub and peel in a bowl of water. Wear rubber gloves while grating.

To make horseradish sauce – traditionally served with roast beef and good with grilled or smoked mackerel: to serve 4, combine 2 tbsp grated horseradish with 2 tsp lemon juice or vinegar, 2 tsp caster sugar, a pinch of mustard powder and 125 ml (4 fl. oz) whipped cream.

Roots will store over winter in boxes filled with sand.

HYSSOP

Hyssop is a small, hardy shrub from the Mediterranean area with an aroma similar to mint and a strong flavour similar to a mixture of rosemary and lavender. Both the flowers and the leaves can be used. Since the Middle Ages it has been popular as a flavouring for soups and stuffings. It goes well with pork and can be used in any recipe requiring rosemary. It is used in making liqueurs such as Chartreuse.

Try fresh leaves or flowers scattered into salads, or use flowers as a soup, jelly or cold drink garnish. The leaves also make a refreshing tea: add 1 tbsp fresh or dried leaves to 300 ml (½ pint) boiling water, steep for 5 minutes, then strain.

As the plant is semi-evergreen, you can pick leaves for most of the year or dry them.

LEMON BALM

Lemon balm (*Melissa*) is a hardy perennial native to southern Europe. Its soft leaves have a pleasant, lemon aroma and taste. They make an excellent tea: add 2 tbsp whole or chopped leaves to 300 ml (½ pint) boiling water, steep for 5 minutes, then strain. Drink hot or cold with slices of lemon.

Some uses for lemon balm:
- Stir small leaves into fruit salad 30 minutes before serving.
- Use as a garnish for summer drinks.
- Add a few whole leaves to milk puddings and custards before baking. Remove before serving.
- Chop and stir into natural yogurt as an accompaniment to curry or as a dip.
- Add to summer lamb casserole and any fish dish.

The leaves can be dried but will lose some aroma and flavour.

LEMON VERBENA

Introduced to England from South America in the 18th century, the lance-shaped leaves of this fairly tender small shrub have the strongest lemon aroma and flavour of all the 'lemon' herbs. Use sparingly, picking leaves individually to add to a dish whenever a lemon flavour is required. Remove before serving.

Some uses for lemon verbena:
- Use to flavour milk and cream-based desserts such as custard and mousses.
- Make flavoured oil: steep leaves in mild olive oil for 3 weeks, strain and use to drizzle over fish or chicken, or in a salad dressing.
- Prepare an aromatic tea, either alone or mixed with mint leaves.

The leaves dry well – dry on the stalks, then pick off and store in an airtight jar.

LOVAGE

Sometimes known as 'sea parsley', lovage is a tall, perennial plant related to carrots and angelica. Its flavour is much like celery and somewhat like parsley, with a hint of pepper. The leaves, tender stems and seeds can all be used.

Some uses for lovage:
- Add chopped leaves to salads or use to garnish soup.
- Add chopped tender stems to stir-fries, casseroles and soups.
- Make soup by simmering leaves in chicken stock.
- Blanch the larger stem bases for 2 minutes and braise as for celery.
- Use seeds as a substitute for celery seed in cooking and baking.

The leaves don't dry well, but can be preserved using the ice-cube method (page 160).

MARJORAM/OREGANO

Marjoram – *Origanum marjorana* – is a small bush with tiny white or pink flowers and small, soft, grey-green leaves that have a similar but milder aroma and flavour to oregano. *Origanum vulgare* is the wild Mediterranean oregano that can be seen growing on all the hills in Greece and elsewhere. For most uses, marjoram and oregano are interchangeable.

The herb is one of the most useful in the kitchen, lending a deep and unique aroma to casseroles, stuffings, pasta and meat dishes (particularly lamb), pizza and other savoury dishes. It is a common ingredient in mixed herbs.

Some uses for marjoram/oregano:
- Make slits in a lamb joint, stuff with chopped marjoram and garlic before roasting.
- Use instead of sage in a stuffing mixture for pork or turkey.
- Finely chop and sprinkle over pizza before cooking.
- Add chopped to a tomato or meat sauce for pasta, lasagne or moussaka.
- Steep oregano stalks in olive oil with garlic to make a flavoured oil ideal for lamb chops.
- Add chopped to a pan of chicken fillet sautéed in olive oil and lemon juice.

The leaves dry well and retain much of their characteristic fragrance. Hang up bunches in a dry, airy room, then strip stems and store in an airtight container.

MINT

Mint – along with parsley – is the most popular herb grown in the UK for kitchen use. Cut back this hardy perennial two or three times during the growing season for fresh aromatic and delicious leaves for at least six months of the year. Native to the Mediterranean area, where it was used as an insect repellent, digestive aid and breath freshener as well as to enhance food. It was brought to Britain by the Romans.

There are several common varieties – spearmint, the most popular, which is the 'mint sauce' herb; peppermint, used to make essential oils and good in sweet dishes or as a tea; and applemint, with round, soft leaves similar in appearance to lemon balm – a good all-purpose mint and some say the best taste of all.

Mint goes well with lamb, veal and rabbit, potatoes, broad beans, peas, many fruits, and chocolate, and can be added to desserts or made into a refreshing tea. Traditionally mint sauce (or jelly, page 238) is used as an accompaniment to lamb.

To make mint sauce: to serve 4, finely chop 3 tbsp fresh mint. Add 1 tbsp boiling water to ½ tbsp caster sugar in a dish, stir to dissolve. Stir in the mint and 1 tbsp malt or wine vinegar or to taste. Stir well and leave for an hour.

Some uses for mint:
- Add sprigs to new potatoes, peas or broad beans before boiling. Remove mint and serve vegetable garnished with fresh chopped mint.
- Snip leaves into fruit salads – great with strawberries, apples, limes, pineapple, melon.
- Add finely chopped mint to rice dishes such as stuffed vine leaves.
- Prepare the Lebanese bulghar wheat salad *tabbouleh*: to serve 4, reconstitute 125 g (4 oz) dry weight bulghar wheat in boiling water. Stir in 2 tbsp each chopped mint, parsley and spring onions. Add 4 tbsp chopped cucumber and stir in a dressing of olive oil, lemon juice and seasoning.
- Use to flavour drinks, such as a Cuban Mojito cocktail, or as a drink garnish.
- Use instead of basil in a herb pesto, or make a sweet pesto with crushed mint, nuts, honey and vanilla extract.
- Stir into chocolate cake before baking, or as a sauce for ice cream.

Preserve using ice-cube method (page 160), or dry (see Bay), though it will lose some colour and aroma over time.

PARSLEY

Parsley – a hardy biennial – is probably the most widely used culinary herb in the world. Its curly, crisp (common parsley) or flat (Italian parsley) bright green leaves are a familiar garnish for meats and salads, or tossed into cooked vegetables (perhaps as a herb butter). The flavour is distinctive and refreshing and goes well with ham, bacon, other meats, eggs, beans and peas, pasta, pulses or rice.

A classic ingredient in French cooking, it is a vital component of bouquet garni, *fines herbes* and mixed herbs, and the Italian *gremolata* (see Garlic). It is also used extensively in Middle Eastern cooking chopped into salads, including the Lebanese dish *tabbouleh* (see Mint), and falafel patties, and added to egg dishes, stews and tagines.

In the UK, parsley is familiar in a sauce served with ham, broad beans or fish. To serve 4, stir 6 tbsp finely chopped parsley into white sauce (page 251). Cook for a minute.

The herb is excellent in stuffing: follow sage and onion stuffing recipe (see Sage), replacing sage with parsley. Stuff chicken or bake separately. Curly parsley is easier to chop when slightly wet.

Some uses for parsley:
- Stir-fry broad beans and bacon with plenty of chopped parsley and mint – great with chicken.
- Add 1–2 tbsp to leek, pea or spinach soup during cooking.
- Make a pesto with the flat-leaf variety, as a basil substitute. Drizzle over tomato salad or pasta.
- Deep fry the curly variety and serve with meats and fish, as they do in France.
- Add a good bunch to a potato, onion and milk soup base – blend for delicious soup.
- Add, finely chopped, to French dressing (page 250), or to olive oil and lemon juice for a fish marinade.
- Sauté 3–4 tbsp chopped parsley with prawns, garlic and butter as an easy starter.
- Chew on a raw sprig of parsley after eating garlic to neutralize the odour.

Cut parsley stalks keep well in a jar of water or in a plastic bag in the fridge. Preserve chopped parsley using the ice-cube method (page 160), or pack into a jar and cover completely with oil. It will keep for weeks in the fridge.

ROSEMARY

Rosemary is a small, evergreen, hardy perennial bush with dark green, pine-like leaves and pretty mauve or white flowers in summer. Its taste is strong, so it should be used sparingly. It is commonly used to add flavour and aroma to meat, and goes particularly well with lamb, pork, chicken, veal and rabbit. Tomatoes, garlic and oily fish are also good partners, and the herb is used in many Italian sauces and dishes.

To flavour roast meats, make slits about 2.5 cm (1 in.) deep with a sharp knife in several places on the joint and fill with sprigs of rosemary, slivers of garlic and a little oil or butter. Or place 2 rosemary stalks under the joint in the baking dish, or in the cavity of poultry.

Some uses for rosemary:
- Add finely chopped leaves to game or pork paté.
- Put sprigs in a casserole during cooking; remove before serving.
- Finely chop leaves and sprinkle over tomato pizza, or stir into tomato pasta sauces.
- Add leaves to a marinade for fish (e.g. monkfish or mackerel) or chicken breasts with olive oil, garlic and lemon juice.
- Use in a savoury stuffing: add 1 tsp finely chopped leaves to every portion of crumb, rice or sausage meat stuffing before cooking.
- Use de-leafed straight stalks as barbecue kebab sticks for meat or fish kebabs.
- Add chopped rosemary to vegetable traybakes such as potato, parsnip and squash.
- Add some finely chopped leaves to a pan of sautéed potatoes during cooking.

You can also make a rosemary oil or vinegar (page 160). The herb dries better than most – hang up stems in bunches in a warm, dry, airy place, then de-leaf the stalks and put in an airtight container. Keep the stalks.

SAGE

A virtually hardy small shrub which grows wild throughout the Mediterranean area and is semi-evergreen. The grey-green leaves of common sage are useful in a range of recipes, but the purple and variegated varieties are normally not used in the kitchen as they are less aromatic.

Sage is an ingredient of mixed herbs where its strong flavour counteracts the rich fattiness of meats such as pork, goose and game. It is often used in stuffing mixtures for such roasts. To make sage and onion stuffing: to serve 4, finely chop an onion, sweat over low heat in a little oil until softened, then combine with 25 g (1 oz) melted butter, 100 g (3½ oz) breadcrumbs, 1 tbsp fresh chopped sage and seasoning. Bind with a beaten egg. Stuff a roast or cook in a tin at 180°C/gas mark 4 for 25 minutes until golden.

Some uses for sage:
- Chop very finely and add to egg and cheese dishes.
- Use sparingly in stews and soups – too much can make them bitter.
- Use de-leafed branches and stalks on barbecue coals for a wonderful aroma.

Sage leaves dry very well. Hang up twigs to dry, then remove leaves and store.

SALAD BURNET

This neat, weeping and pretty-leaved little evergreen perennial grows wild throughout the Mediterranean area but is not that familiar in Britain nor common in herb gardens. However, it has several uses in the kitchen.

The leaves have a flavour like cucumber and can be used wherever such a taste is required.

Some uses for salad burnet:
- Use as a garnish on grilled meats, fishes and soup.
- Stir into natural yogurt for a simple sauce to accompany fish or lamb.
- Beat with cream cheese or sour cream to make a dip, or a spread for crackers, topped with smoked salmon.
- Add to punch drinks or to lemonade.

Pick leaves as required, just before use. In normal years you should have a year-round supply.

SAVORY

Savory was introduced to Britain by the Romans. There are two types: winter savory is a small, evergreen perennial bush with glossy, narrow leaves, while summer savory is an annual with a slightly finer flavour than the winter plant. Both have a fine, slightly peppery flavour which enhances other foods.

Savory goes very well with most pulses and with broad beans and can be used in any recipe as a substitute for sage. For example, finely chop and use in stuffings, sprinkle over roasting vegetables, or stir into rice. Add chopped leaves to sauces for pork or seafood, stir into lentil soup or into sautéed broad beans. With summer and winter savory you should have a year-round supply, but the leaves of summer savory can be preserved using the ice-cube method (page 160); the winter version can be dried as for rosemary.

SORREL

This hardy perennial has leaves which look similar to spinach – and the French sorrel (the cultivated version of the basic wild sorrel) looks somewhat like red-veined chard. The leaves are best harvested young, when they have a sharp but pleasant flavour of lemon; when older they become more bitter – the name sorrel comes from the Greek word for sour.

Some uses for sorrel:
- Use the leaves as for spinach – wilted in a pan with a tbsp of water and a knob of butter as a side vegetable.
- Toss baby leaves into a salad, or chop into omelette or scrambled eggs.
- Chop and stir into a béchamel sauce to accompany fish or chicken.
- Make the classic sorrel sauce for fish: to serve 4, sweat 100 g (3½ oz) sorrel leaves in 15 g (½ oz) butter, blend in a blender, stir in 100 g (3½ oz) crème fraîche and season to taste.
- Cook lightly with chicken stock and cream and blend to make soup.

The leaves should be harvested as needed, as they do not last long once picked – but they are very hardy and should provide leaves for much of the year.

TARRAGON

Tarragon, with its lance-shaped leaves on long, tangled stems, is not a particularly attractive herb for the garden, but its strong aniseed flavour is hard to replace in classic recipes. Always choose French tarragon ('the king of herbs'), not the Russian variety, which is hardier and larger but virtually tasteless. Tarragon is used in many chicken and fish dishes, is good with eggs and is a component of *fines herbes*, sauce Béarnaise (a buttery sauce for steak made using egg yolks, shallots and tarragon) and remoulade sauce (mayonnaise combined with tarragon, capers and French mustard – serve with fish).

Some uses for tarragon:
- Prepare roast tarragon chicken. Make a tarragon butter (see Herb Butter, page 160) and push it between the breast meat and skin before roasting; stuff stalks and leaves into the cavity. Use meat juices in the pan as the base for a tarragon gravy.
- Make a tarragon cream sauce for salmon or chicken: to serve 4, sauté meat or fish in butter, remove, add 2 tbsp each white wine and fish or chicken stock to pan juices with 2 tbsp chopped tarragon. Boil for a minute. Stir in 75 ml (2½ fl. oz) double cream or crème fraîche. Season.
- Chop and add to omelette or eggs baked in cream.
- Chop into a French dressing (page 250) for a leaf salad.
- Use for herb oil or vinegar (page 160).

Tarragon does not dry very well – it loses flavour. Use the ice-cube method (page 160) to preserve.

SWEET CICELY

Also known as Spanish chervil or garden myrrh, sweet cicely is a hardy perennial which grows wild in the UK. A thick, tap-rooted plant, its ferny leaves have a liquorice-like flavour and pleasant, sweet aroma, and the seeds have a spicy taste.

Sweet cicely can be cooked with tart fruits such as rhubarb, blackcurrants, gooseberries and damsons to reduce the acidity. It enables you to cut down on added sugar by up to 50 per cent. It can also be chopped and added to salads or omelettes. The leaves make a pleasant aniseedy-tasting tea: add 1 tbsp leaves to 300 ml (½ pint) boiling water, steep for 5 minutes, then strain.

The seeds can be chewed or sprinkled over desserts. Even the roots (a digestive aid once commonly offered to the elderly) can be dug up, scrubbed, chopped and boiled as for carrots.

THYME

A basic ingredient of bouquet garni and mixed herbs, thyme is one of our better-known herbs. Its tiny round leaves pack a punch and should be used sparingly to enhance the flavour of a variety of foods, including meat, rabbit and poultry casseroles and roasts, meat sauces, stuffings, eggs, lentils and tomatoes. Too much may overpower fish, but a little sprinkled into fish marinades or bakes can be good.

Thyme also makes a good accompaniment to dishes that use a lot of butter or fat. Include it in meat and poultry marinades, and add to chicken breast parcels baked in foil with lemon juice and olive oil.

As well as common thyme, you can also grow lemon thyme for kitchen use – especially good in recipes with chicken or fish.

Try sprinkling tomato pizza with a little thyme, or add a small amount to a bread mixture before baking.

Thyme leaves dry well and retain their flavour – dried leaves are more potent than fresh, so reduce the amount you use.

CHAPTER 5

FRUIT

There is little to beat fruit picked ripe and fresh from the garden or greenhouse and brought into the kitchen to be used immediately in a fruit salad, dessert or other recipe. These days a garden of almost any size can grow some fruit – dwarf apple trees, a couple of blackcurrant bushes, or a tub of strawberries, for example. The fruits in this chapter represent all the older, familiar types, such as apples, pears, plums and currants, as well as those which may be a little more demanding, such as melons, kiwi fruit and figs. These – especially if you choose the right variety – may not be as tricky to grow as you think, and can make wonderful additions to the kitchen.

A good tip is to grow fruits that are your own particular favourites. Also consider anything that is expensive to buy in the shops (such as figs, apricots or red currants) but is not that hard to grow at home.

As with vegetables, you must consider factors such as what space you have, how often produce needs watering, and, for some fruits, how warm or sheltered your garden or greenhouse is.

Finally, remember to experiment a little with a new variety or type of fruit, and consider your own requirements. For example, if you would like to grow enough fruit to freeze so that you have supplies all year round, heavy croppers are ideal, while if your hobby is making jam, then you might concentrate on the tastier jam fruits such as strawberries, raspberries and plums.

TIPS FOR STORING FRUIT

Detailed information for each specific fruit is given on the following pages.

- Store fruits as far away from vegetables as possible.

- Don't store apples with potatoes – the potatoes cause apples to take on a musty flavour.

- Store hard fruits in a cold, dark, frost-free place and they will keep for months.

- Quinces are usually very hard when picked and will store for months – much longer than most fruit.

FRUIT IN SEASON

The chart on the right shows the period during which each fruit can be picked, from the start of the season for early varieties to the end of the season for later varieties.

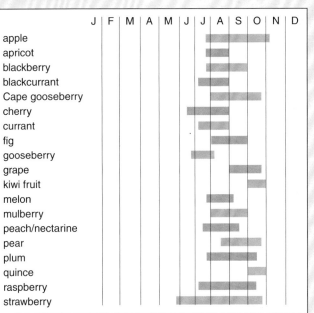

	J	F	M	A	M	J	J	A	S	O	N	D
apple								██	██	██		
apricot							██	██				
blackberry								██	██			
blackcurrant							██	██				
Cape gooseberry							██	██	██	██		
cherry						██	██					
currant							██					
fig								██	██			
gooseberry						██	██					
grape									██	██		
kiwi fruit										██	██	
melon								██	██	██		
mulberry								██	██			
peach/nectarine							██	██				
pear									██	██		
plum								██	██	██		
quince										██	██	
raspberry								██	██	██		
strawberry						██	██	██	██	██		

TIPS FOR PREPARING FRUIT

Cleaning fruit
- Stone fruits and pip fruits: rinse under cold running water to remove any pesticide/herbicide residues.
- Soft fruits and exotic fruits: wipe with a damp cloth if necessary and use minimal contact with water.

To peel or not to peel?
The skin of almost all produce is edible, either raw or cooked, but fruit is often peeled through habit. Much of the vitamin C is just under the skin, however, so do try to eat the skin too. Remove peel if skin is old and tough or damaged, or simply unpleasant (e.g. quince and kiwi fruit skins have a rough/furry texture).

For recipes in this book, assume unpeeled unless otherwise stated.

Whole, cut, sliced or diced?
- Fruits to be eaten fresh and raw can usually be left whole – the exception being large items such as melon, and fruits which have skin that can't be eaten.
- For cooking or freezing, large fruits are usually peeled and sliced or diced.
- The size of your pieces depends on the use – e.g. apple for a Waldorf salad will be diced small or even grated, but larger pieces are best for a fruit salad.
- It is best not to cut a fruit until the last possible minute before cooking/eating/freezing, as the cut sides can turn brown on contact with air.
- For cooking, slice fruit in similar-sized pieces so that they cook evenly.

TIPS FOR USING FRUIT

- Apart from a few exceptions such as quince and damsons, fruit can simply be served raw as a dessert or snack.
- Extend the fruit season by bottling your favourite fruit in sugar syrup (page 239). Good served with vanilla ice cream, crème fraîche or used in recipe dishes.
- Fruit retains most goodness, shape, flavour and aroma if cooked for as short a period as possible. Cook just to the point of tenderness.
- Fruit often works well combined with savoury flavours. Try it in a salad (e.g. pear and chicory), in a Moroccan tagine (e.g. apricot and lamb), or as a sauce served with meat (e.g. apple with pork).
- Try to use fruit that is appropriate for the dish you are making. A British crumble is good with traditional British fruits such as apples or pears. A French tart is good with fruits that grow best in a hotter climate, such as apricots or figs.

APPLE

There is little to beat going out to your own apple tree to pick and eat a ripe fruit on a warm summer's day. Apples vary a great deal in taste and acidity, crispness and keeping qualities. Dessert apples can be used in cooking, but they retain more shape and firmness than cookers, which are best used in recipes that require greater softness and acidity. Bramley's Seedling and Golden Noble are cookers that become 'fluffy' and are excellent for purées, while good varieties for retaining shape are Arthur Turner and Bountiful. Amongst the juiciest dessert apples are James Grieve and Katy. Best for crunchiness are Egremont Russet and Jonagold. Discovery, Elstar and Sunset have excellent flavour, while Granny Smith and Lord Lambourne are tangy and sharp.

STORING

Store cooking apples individually wrapped in oiled paper or newspaper in a cool but frost-free, dry, dark place at least until Christmas. Check weekly for signs of rotting. They will also keep in a rack in the larder for 2–3 weeks.

Late-season dessert varieties will keep for 2 months or more – store as for cookers. Early-season apples are best eaten within a week or two.

Apples will keep in the salad crisper of the fridge, or in a plastic bag in the fridge, for a week or more.

To freeze raw apples: peel, core and chop. Put into water with 1–2 tsp lemon juice to prevent browning. Drain and dry, then freeze in plastic bags or containers. You can also toss them with sugar before bagging for freezing.

To dry apples: see apple crisps, page 173.

NO COOKING REQUIRED

Although cooking apples are too tart to eat raw, most dessert varieties are eaten this way and are a favourite snack eaten straight from the tree. Try thin slices of apple with cheese and oatcakes or as part of a ploughman's lunch. They make a good ingredient in many salads and go well with nuts, chicken, ham and mayonnaise. See Waldorf salad (page 75).

Dessert apples add crunch and colour to fruit salads. They can be juiced either on their own or with other fruits or vegetables to make a refreshing drink.

APPLE AND CELERIAC SALAD

A refreshing change from a cabbage coleslaw or Waldorf salad. Good with ham, chicken or cheese.

Serves 4

2 red-skinned dessert apples	2 tbsp mayonnaise
juice of 1 lime	1 tbsp natural yogurt
225 g (8 oz) celeriac	salt, black pepper

- Core and very thinly slice apples, then cut into strips, put in a bowl with lime juice and toss. Grate peeled celeriac into the bowl and toss.

- Combine mayonnaise, yogurt and seasoning and stir into apple mixture. Chill to serve.

BASIC COOKING

Rinse apples under running water if necessary, then dry. Peel if recipe requires it and chop, slice or quarter as necessary. Peeled apples turn brown very quickly once the air reaches them; to prevent this, put them into a bowl of water with 1–2 tsp lemon juice as soon as they are peeled and cut.

To core: for recipes that require the apple to remain whole, twist an apple corer into the centre of the apple and continue twisting until the whole core comes out easily. For other recipes, simply quarter the apple and use a vegetable knife to remove the pip and tough membrane at the centre.

STEWED APPLES

Peel, core, chop and put in a pan with sugar as required (for cooking apples, approx. 1 tbsp sugar for every 100–150 g (3½–5 oz) apple, depending on sourness). Add 1 tbsp water, cover and simmer until tender. Some but not all varieties will keep their shape.

PURÉED APPLES

As for stewed apples, but continue cooking until very soft, then mash with a fork or masher. You can also use a blender if you want a smoother, more liquid mash. Stir in a knob of butter and taste, adding extra sugar if required. For a thicker purée, continue cooking over very low heat without a lid until it reaches the desired consistency.

FRIED APPLES

Use dessert apples or cookers that will retain shape. Peel or leave unpeeled, depending on recipe. Core and slice, then put slices in a frying pan with vegetable oil or butter, or a mixture of both. Fry over medium-high heat until golden and tender, turning once or twice.

CARAMELIZED APPLES

As for fried apples, but use butter instead of oil. When the apples begin to turn golden, add sugar (2 tsp for every dessert apple; 3 tsp for every cooking apple). Cook for a further few minutes until they are tender and there is a little syrupy sauce in the pan.

BAKED APPLES

Cookers are normally used, but you can also bake dessert apples. Core, place in a baking dish, fill with sugar and dot on a little butter. Add a little water to the dish and bake at 200°C/gas mark 6 for 30–40 minutes, or until puffed up, golden and cooked through.

Apples originated in the Middle East over 4,000 years ago and have been cultivated in the UK since Roman times.

APPLE CRUMBLE

This version of the traditional crumble has the basic butter-crumb topping. As an alternative you can stir in some ground almonds to replace a quarter of the flour, or see suggested variations for sweet crumbles, page 250.

Serves 4

900 g (2 lb) cooking apples
150 g (5 oz) sugar
175 g (6 oz) flour
salt
100 g (3½ oz) butter

- Peel, core and chop apples, then arrange in a baking dish with two-thirds of the sugar. Smooth out the top.
- Sift flour and salt into a mixing bowl and rub in the butter, using your fingertips, until the mixture resembles breadcrumbs. Stir in remaining sugar.
- Sprinkle the crumble mixture over the apples to cover completely.
- Bake at 200°C/gas mark 6 for 30 minutes, or until the top is golden and the apples tender.

APPLE FRITTERS

Children love to make the batter for this recipe and dip the apples in. Serve sprinkled with brown sugar or some maple syrup.

Serves 4

125 g (4 oz) flour
½ tsp salt
50 ml (2 fl. oz) milk
50 ml (2 fl. oz) apple juice
1 tbsp icing sugar
4 dessert apples
vegetable oil

- Sift flour and salt into a bowl. Make a well in the centre and stir in milk and apple juice, then sugar, until you have a smooth, thick batter.
- Peel and core apples whole, then cut each into five rings.
- In a large pan heat 5 cm (2 in.) oil to 180°C, or until a cube of bread dropped in turns golden in 30 seconds.
- Dip apple rings into batter, then put in the hot oil and fry until golden. Remove with tongs and drain on kitchen paper.

EVE'S PUDDING

A traditional apple sponge pudding. Serve with cream or custard (page 250).

Serves 4

450 g (1 lb) cooking apples	**75 g (3 oz) butter**	**125 g (4 oz) self-raising flour**
75 g (3 oz) soft light brown sugar	**75 g (3 oz) caster sugar**	**50 ml (2 fl. oz) milk**
½ lemon	**1 large egg**	

- Peel, core and slice apples into a greased 900 ml (1½ pint) ovenproof dish and sprinkle on brown sugar, grated lemon zest, lemon juice and 1 tbsp water.
- Cream butter and caster sugar until fluffy and light. Gradually mix in beaten egg, adding a little flour if the mixture begins to curdle.
- Lightly fold in flour, then mix in enough milk to give a dropping consistency.
- Spoon the mixture over the apples. Bake at 180°C/gas mark 4 for 30–35 minutes, or until the sponge is risen and golden.

APPLE SAUCE

A truly useful and versatile sauce – try it with pancakes, add it to cakes, spoon it over ice cream, or have it for breakfast with yogurt. You can even use it with roast pork and chops. The cinnamon is optional – you could also use nutmeg or mixed spice.

Serves 4–8

5 cooking apples   **3 tbsp sugar**
   (about 600 g/1 lb 6 oz) **pinch cinnamon**
juice of ½ lemon   **25 g (1 oz) butter**

- Peel, core and slice apples and put into a saucepan, then stir in lemon juice, sugar and cinnamon. Add 1 tbsp water, put lid on and bring to a simmer over low heat, stirring occasionally. The apples should break up and become pulpy – help this process with a potato masher or a whisk.
- Stir in butter until melted and continue cooking and stirring until you have a smooth sauce. Check for sweetness, adding more sugar if necessary. Serve hot or cold.

APPLE CRISPS

Try these instead of salted potato crisps as a snack, or use them to garnish apple fool or any soft-textured apple dessert.

Serves 4–6

100 g (3½ oz) caster sugar
juice of ½ lemon
4 dessert apples

- Put sugar in a pan with lemon juice and 100 ml (3½ fl. oz) water and stir over low heat until sugar is dissolved. Turn up heat, bring to the boil and cook for 4–5 minutes until reduced and syrupy.
- Core and slice apples and add to pan, coating thoroughly with the syrup. (You may need to do this in two batches.) Remove slices with a slotted spoon and arrange in one layer on a baking tray lined with baking parchment.
- Bake at 110°C/gas mark ¼ for 3–4 hours until dried. Put on a wire rack to cool. Best eaten the same day but will keep in an airtight tin for several days.

APPLE RECIPES

APPLE PIE

An old-fashioned double-crust pie to be served with custard (page 250) or thick cream. If you prefer, use plain shortcrust pastry (page 251).

Serves 4–6

50 g (2 oz) sultanas   **2 tsp flour**
600 g (1 lb 6 oz) sweet **100 g (3½ oz) caster**
   shortcrust pastry   **sugar**
   (page 251)   **½ tsp cinnamon**
800 g (1¾ lb) cooking   **2 tbsp milk**
   apples   **1 tbsp icing sugar**

- Soak sultanas in a little water for at least an hour to plump them up, then drain.
- Roll out two-thirds of the pastry on a floured surface and line a greased 23 cm (9 in.) pie tin. Roll out remaining pastry to make a lid.
- Peel, core and slice apples and combine with flour, caster sugar, cinnamon and sultanas. Put mixture into the lined tin. Brush the edge of the pastry base with some of the milk, then lay the lid on top. Press the edges into the base and trim.
- Make a hole in the centre of the lid and brush the lid with milk. Dust with icing sugar and bake at 190°C/gas mark 5 for 30 minutes, or until the pastry is golden and the apples tender.

BAKED STUFFED APPLES

There is nothing like the aroma of apples stuffed with dried fruits and syrup as they cook and puff up to perfection. This is an easy, old-fashioned pudding well worth reviving. Serve with custard (page 250).

Serves 4

4 cooking apples
4 tbsp mincemeat
2 tbsp golden syrup

- Core apples and cut a thin slice off the base so they stand upright. Make a shallow horizontal cut round each apple two-thirds of the way up.
- Put apples in a baking dish and stuff with mincemeat. Drizzle syrup over them and add 100 ml (3½ fl. oz) water to the dish.
- Bake at 190°C/gas mark 5 for 45 minutes, basting once or twice, until puffed up and cooked through. Serve with juices poured over.

Alternative fillings: sultanas, cinnamon and brown sugar; chopped dried apricots, hazelnuts and sugar. You can also use honey instead of golden syrup.

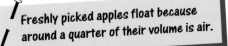
Freshly picked apples float because around a quarter of their volume is air.

TARTE TATIN

The classic French 'upside-down' tart produces a caramelized apple topping which is lovely served with cream or ice cream. Use a good juicy, tasty apple such as Cox or Granny Smith if possible. You can use puff pastry instead of shortcrust.

Serves 4

**800 g (1¾ lb) dessert apples
juice of ½ lemon
75 g (3 oz) butter
150 g (5 oz) caster sugar
300 g (11 oz) sweet shortcrust pastry
     (page 251)**

- Peel, quarter and core apples, then toss in lemon juice.
- Put apples in a frying pan with butter and sugar and cook over medium heat, stirring occasionally, until lightly golden and you have a caramel syrup – about 10 minutes.
- Arrange in a greased 23 cm (9 in.) shallow round tin with all the syrupy juices.
- Roll out pastry on a floured surface and lay over the apples, tucking the edges inside the tin.
- Bake at 200°C/gas mark 6 for 25 minutes, or until golden, then leave to cool for 10 minutes. Place serving plate on top and invert.

APPLE CHARLOTTE

Buttery white bread makes a change from pastry in this easy classic dessert. Serve with cream or custard (page 250).

Serves 4–6

150 g (5 oz) butter	**1 lemon**
½ loaf white bread	**½ tsp cinnamon**
900 g (2 lb) cooking apples	**1 tbsp caster sugar**
100 g (3½ oz) sugar	

- Thoroughly grease a baking dish with some of the butter. Remove crusts from bread and cut into slices.
- Peel, core and slice apples and simmer with sugar, grated lemon zest, cinnamon and 1 tbsp water until breaking up. Leave to cool.
- Melt remaining butter and dip bread slices in it. Line the baking dish with some of the sliced bread, cutting to fit as necessary.
- Fill with the cooled purée, then put more bread on top. Cover loosely with greased baking parchment or foil and bake at 180°C/gas mark 4 for 30 minutes. Turn out on to a plate and sprinkle with caster sugar.

STEAMED APPLE PUDDING

An old-fashioned, simple recipe. Good winter comfort food.

Serves 4

**350 g (12 oz) shredded suet
700 g (1 lb 9 oz) cooking apples
75 g (3 oz) sugar
½ lemon
4 cloves**

- Using a fork, combine suet with enough cold water to make a stiff dough. Roll out three-quarters of the dough on a floured surface to 0.5 cm (¼ in.) thick and use to line a 1 litre (1¾ pint) greased pudding basin. Roll out the remaining dough to make a lid.
- Peel, core and slice apples and layer them in the basin with sugar, grated lemon zest and cloves.
- Lay lid on top and press the edges into the base. Cover with greaseproof paper, then with a cloth, and secure with string. Stand basin on a heatproof saucer or wooden rack in a large saucepan, quarter fill the pan with boiling water and steam for 3 hours. Leave to cool slightly, then remove cloth and paper to serve.

APPLE TART

This dessert is not too time-consuming or difficult to prepare, but it tastes impressive. Good served with ice cream.

Serves 4–6

**375 g (13 oz) ready-rolled puff pastry
200 g (7 oz) thick apple purée (page 171)
5 dessert apples
juice of 1 lemon
25 g (1 oz) butter
50 g (2 oz) caster sugar
3 tbsp apricot jam**

- Roll pastry into a 30 cm x 23 cm (12 in. x 9 in.) rectangle and make a cut 2 cm (¾ in.) from the edge all the way round, but don't cut right through. Place on a baking sheet.
- Spread apple purée over pastry inside the cut. Peel, core and thinly slice apples, then toss with lemon juice, melted butter and caster sugar. Arrange slices on the purée in neat overlapping rows inside the cut.
- Bake at 190°C/gas mark 5 for 25 minutes, or until the pastry is crisp and the apples golden and tender. Warm the jam in a saucepan with 1 tbsp of water, then brush over the warm tart.

ORIGINAL SWISS MUESLI

When muesli was invented as a health-giving dish in Switzerland by Dr Maximilian Bircher-Benner over 100 years ago, it was a soft cereal and fruit dish, soaked overnight, to which fresh apple was added. Here is a similar version. For variety, stir in some blueberries or top with yogurt before serving.

Serves 4

6 tbsp rolled oats
75 ml (2½ fl. oz) apple juice
1 tbsp lemon juice
3 dessert apples

2 tbsp chopped hazelnuts
4 tbsp natural yogurt
1 tbsp runny honey

- Put oats in a bowl with 5 tbsp water, the apple juice and lemon juice. Cover and leave to soak overnight.
- In the morning, stir in grated apples, nuts, yogurt and honey. Serve as it is or with apple juice or milk poured over.

APPLE AND BLUEBERRY FOOL

You can make your own custard, but ready-made custard from a supermarket works well in this recipe. Try serving with ratafia biscuits (available from supermarkets).

Serves 4

350 g (12 oz) apple sauce (page 173)
100 g (3 ½ oz) blueberries
200 ml (7 fl. oz) whipping cream
200 ml (7 fl. oz) thick custard (page 250)

- Cool the apple sauce. Crush most of the blueberries, retaining a few.
- Whip cream to soft peak stage and fold into custard.
- Fold in the apple sauce and then the crushed blueberries. Spoon into four glass serving dishes and top with remaining blueberries. Cover and chill for 30 minutes.

APPLE, WALNUT AND CRANBERRY STUFFING

An excellent stuffing for roast goose, pork or turkey, and a change from the traditional chestnut or sausage meat stuffings. Ideal for vegetarians – serve with nut or lentil roast, use to stuff cabbage leaves before braising or to stuff marrow.

Serves 8

2 apples
1 onion
1½ tbsp vegetable oil
150 g (5 oz) breadcrumbs
1 egg
75 g (3 oz) walnut pieces
50 g (2 oz) dried cranberries
3 tbsp fresh chopped parsley
1 tbsp fresh thyme leaves
1 tbsp fresh chopped sage
100 ml (3½ fl. oz) vegetable stock
salt, black pepper

- Peel, core and finely chop apples. Sweat finely chopped onion in oil in a pan over low heat to soften but not colour. Add apple and cook for a minute, then stir in breadcrumbs for a further minute.
- Add beaten egg and remaining ingredients, combining everything well. Spoon mixture into a shallow ovenproof dish and bake at 180°C/ gas mark 4 for 30 minutes, or until golden.

APPLE AND PARSNIP SOUP

A good, sweet soup which makes a lunch in itself. For a hearty meal, grate a little cheese over the top and serve with crusty bread.

Serves 4

3 dessert apples
1 onion
4 parsnips
25 g (1 oz) butter
2 cloves garlic
1 litre (1¾ pints) vegetable stock

salt, black pepper
100 ml (3½ fl. oz) cream
2 tbsp fresh chopped parsley

- Peel and core apples. Sweat chopped onion, apples and parsnips in butter over low heat for 10 minutes until softened and just beginning to colour.
- Add chopped garlic and stir for a minute, then pour in stock. Season, bring to a simmer and cook, covered, for 20 minutes.
- Allow to cool, then blend in a blender. Reheat, stir in cream, check seasoning and serve sprinkled with parsley.

APRICOT

These golden, orange or red-tinged stone fruits have a unique flavour – very sweet and slightly nutty, with a refreshing touch of acidity. The texture is slightly creamy with a little bite. Apricots have a wide range of uses in the kitchen – in baking, desserts, ice creams, compote and trifles. They also go very well with lamb (in Moroccan cuisine, for example) and pork. Try adding some around roasted pork for the last few minutes of cooking time, or use them in stuffing for a roast.

STORING

Apricots are ripe when they come away readily from the tree. Handle carefully when picking, as the fruits bruise easily. Store in the kitchen or larder for a day or two to eat fresh. Or keep in the fridge – bring them out several hours before eating to develop their flavour.

To freeze: halve, stone and freeze in bags; they will keep for 8–12 months. They can also be frozen whole with stones and will keep for several months, though the fruits may develop an almond flavour.

For semi-dried apricots: arrange halves cut side up on a baking tray and dry on the lowest oven temperature for 3–4 hours until they are slightly pliable but with no visible moisture. Cool and put in an airtight container. Check weekly. They will last longer if kept in the fridge.

You can also pack halves in containers and top with a syrup (page 239) – they will keep for over a year.

NO COOKING REQUIRED

Fresh apricots are delicious as they are – or chop them and add to fruit salads.

BASIC COOKING

Apricots shouldn't need cleaning, but, if necessary, rinse under cold running water and pat dry on kitchen paper. If a recipe requires peeled apricots, drop them in boiling water for 20 seconds, then remove them with a slotted spoon and cool under cold water. Use a knife to pull away their skin – it should slip off.

To halve apricots, make a cut around the lengthwise seam through to the stone and twist the two halves to separate. Dip peeled, halved or sliced apricots into water with 1–2 tsp lemon juice to keep them from browning.

ROAST APRICOTS

Put stoned apricot halves cut side up in a roasting tin, brush with melted butter and sprinkle with a little caster sugar. Bake at 190°C/gas mark 5 for 20 minutes, or until tender and golden.

GRILLED APRICOTS

Thread whole or halved fresh apricots on skewers, brush with butter and grill until tender, turning once. These make a good dessert.

POACHED APRICOTS

Put apricots (peeled or unpeeled, whole or halved) in a pan with enough water to just cover and the juice of ½ lemon – a dash of orange juice can be added. Simmer until tender – about 8–10 minutes. Add whole cloves or a cinnamon stick for extra flavour. Once the apricots are poached, the liquid can be reduced (simmer for a further 10 minutes, or until reduced by half) to make a sauce.

APRICOT COMPOTE

Halve and stone apricots and put in a pan with 50 g (2 oz) sugar and 100 ml (3½ fl. oz) water for every 400 g (14 oz) apricots. Simmer gently for 10–15 minutes until the apricots are soft and broken up. Use hot or cold – it is ideal for stirring into rice pudding, or serving with custard or yogurt, in ice cream or spooned over a sponge cake or a plain cheesecake.

APRICOT RECIPES

APRICOT TART

Few desserts are easier to make, or taste better, than this uncomplicated tart which allows the flavour of the apricots to come through. The almonds ensure that the pastry doesn't get too wet with apricot juice.

Serves 4–6

900 g (2 lb) fresh apricots
350 g (12 oz) ready-rolled
  puff pastry
50 g (2 oz) ground almonds

15 g (½ oz) butter
2 tbsp soft light
  brown sugar
1 egg yolk

- Halve and stone apricots. Roll out pastry on a floured surface into a thin rectangle and trim edges. Make a cut 2 cm (¾ in.) from the edge all the way round, but don't cut all the way through. Place on a baking tray and sprinkle ground almonds on the pastry inside the cut.

- Tightly pack apricots inside the cut edge to cover the pastry completely. Brush with melted butter and sprinkle sugar evenly over. Brush pastry edge with beaten egg yolk.

- Bake at 200°C/gas mark 6 for 25 minutes. Allow to cool a little before serving.

APRICOT TRIFLE

There is little to beat a real fruit trifle, well chilled, at the end of a summer meal. If you have any apricot brandy, use it instead of the sherry and the trifle will be even nicer. If serving children, replace sherry with fruit juice or extra poaching liquid. Ready-made custard from a supermarket is fine.

Serves 4–6

400 g (14 oz) fresh apricots
16 sponge fingers
100 ml (3½ fl. oz) medium-sweet sherry
5 tbsp apricot jam
500 ml (17 fl. oz) thick custard (page 250)
400 ml (14 fl. oz) whipping cream
40 g (1½ oz) flaked toasted almonds

- Halve and stone apricots, then poach until tender. Reserve poaching liquid.

- Arrange sponge fingers in a glass bowl. Spoon sherry and apricot poaching liquid over until fingers are thoroughly coated. Spoon apricots over.

- Spread warmed jam over apricots. Spoon custard over and smooth out.

- Whip cream until just holding peaks (don't over-whip), then spoon on to the trifle. Smooth the top and decorate with almonds. Chill for several hours.

EASY LAMB TAGINE WITH APRICOTS

The national dish of Morocco, a tagine is a wonderfully rich, deep casserole with spicy and sweet flavours. Serve with couscous, bulghar wheat or rice. You can buy ready-toasted flaked almonds and ready-blended tagine spices in supermarkets.

Serves 4

600 g (1 lb 6 oz) lean cubed lamb
2 tbsp olive oil
1 onion
2 cloves garlic
600 ml (1 pint) lamb stock
1 orange
1 tsp honey
½ tsp each ground ginger, turmeric,
  cinnamon and paprika
salt, black pepper
150 g (5 oz) semi-dried apricots
100 g (3½ oz) green beans
3 tbsp fresh chopped mint
25 g (1 oz) ground almonds
25 g (1 oz) flaked toasted almonds

- Brown lamb in half the oil in a flameproof casserole over medium-high heat until browned on each side; remove from pan with a slotted spatula.

- Turn heat to low and fry chopped onion in remaining oil over medium-low heat until soft and just tinged gold. Stir in chopped garlic and return lamb to casserole.

- Add stock, orange juice and grated zest, honey, spices and seasoning. Bring to a simmer, put lid on and cook gently for 1 hour.

- Add apricots, halved green beans and half the mint. Cook for 30 minutes, or until lamb is tender. Stir in ground almonds and sprinkle on remaining mint and toasted almonds.

BLACKBERRY

A lovely native fruit for mid- to late summer. Blackberries from the garden are larger and less inclined to damage from pests and pollution than the hedgerow kind (page 232). Ideal both raw and cooked, blackberries stand alone in many recipes or are useful additions to some classics. Add a few handfuls to the apples in a pie for extra colour and flavour, include in summer pudding (page 182) or use in Eton Mess (page 220) instead of strawberries.

STORING

Once picked, blackberries are best eaten the same day but they will keep for 2 days in a lidded container in the fridge. They freeze well: open-freeze on trays then put into containers; or freeze them poached or as a coulis or butter.

NO COOKING REQUIRED

Wash berries, pat dry on kitchen paper, then eat as they are as a snack, or serve with sugar and cream, rice pudding or ice cream.

NO-COOK PURÉE

Blend berries in a blender. If you prefer a seedless purée, press it through a sieve to remove the seeds. Sweeten with icing sugar to taste, stirring in well.

BLACKBERRY HEAVEN

A perfect dessert for novice cooks, as it can't fail and is very quick and easy.

Serves 4

350 g (12 oz) blackberries   150 ml (¼ pint) cream
1 tbsp icing sugar   ½ tsp vanilla extract
250 g (9 oz) Mascarpone

- Purée all but 12 of the berries and stir in icing sugar to taste.
- Beat Mascarpone with cream and vanilla until smooth and light.
- Stir in purée until thoroughly combined. Divide between four glass dishes and decorate with whole blackberries.

There are many traditional names for blackberries, including brambleberries, brumblekites and lawers.

BLACKBERRY ICE CREAM

Indulgent 'real' ice cream is much more delicious than most shop-bought varieties and not that hard to make. If you have an ice cream maker it will make the freezing process simpler.

Makes 1 litre (1¾ pints)

350 g (12 oz) blackberries
1 tbsp icing sugar
5 egg yolks
150 g (5 oz) caster sugar
750 ml (1¼ pints) cream
1 tsp vanilla extract

- Purée blackberries and stir in icing sugar to taste.
- Whisk egg yolks with caster sugar until pale. Heat cream and vanilla in a pan until just below simmering, then add to eggs, whisk again and pour back into pan.
- Cook over low heat, stirring frequently, until the mixture thickens a little. Don't let it get too hot or the eggs will start to scramble. Pour into a freezer container and leave to cool – it will thicken a little more.
- Lightly stir in blackberry purée (you want streaks of colour). Put lid on and freeze. Remove from freezer several times during the freezing process and beat to remove ice crystals.

BASIC COOKING

Put blackberries in a colander or sieve and rinse under cold running water. Check each berry and discard damaged or discoloured ones.

SIMMERED BLACKBERRIES

Simmer blackberries with 15 g (½ oz) sugar and 25 ml (1 fl. oz) water for every 100 g (3½ oz) fruit for about 5 minutes until soft.

BLACKBERRY COULIS

Simmer blackberries, then add the juice of 1 lemon for every 400 g (14 oz) simmered fruit. Cool, then blend in a blender until smooth. Press through a sieve to remove seeds. This will keep in an airtight container in the fridge for up to 3 days.

BLACKBERRY BUTTER

Simmer blackberries with lemon juice (as coulis) and 25 g (1 oz) butter for every 100 g (3½ oz) poached fruit until soft. Use as a sauce for pancakes or drizzle over cake.

BLACKBERRY RECIPES

BLACKBERRY COBBLER

A fruit cobbler is similar to a crumble or pie, but with a light scone topping. Lovely with custard (page 250).

BLACKBERRY AND ALMOND CRUMBLE CAKE

A lovely moist cake with a fruity, crumbly topping – one of the best.

Makes 8 slices

225 g (8 oz) self-raising flour
100 g (3½ oz) cold butter
100 g (3½ oz) demerara sugar
½ tsp cinnamon
25 g (1 oz) blanched almonds
150 g (5 oz) butter at room temperature
150 g (5 oz) caster sugar
3 eggs
50 g (2 oz) ground almonds
250 g (9 oz) blackberries

- Put 100 g (3½ oz) of the flour in a mixing bowl and rub in cold butter, using your fingertips, until the mixture resembles breadcrumbs. Stir in demerara sugar, cinnamon and chopped blanched almonds.

- In another bowl beat warm butter with caster sugar until smooth. Gradually stir in beaten eggs, remaining flour and ground almonds.

- Line a greased 20 cm (8 in.) cake tin with lightly greased baking parchment. Spread batter evenly over the base and arrange blackberries over.

- Sprinkle crumble mixture on top and cook at 180°C/gas mark 4 for an hour. Allow to cool in the tin a little, then turn out and serve warm or cold.

Serves 4

600 g (1 lb 6 oz) blackberries
100 g (3½ oz) caster sugar
juice of ½ lemon
15 g (½ oz) butter
1 egg
75 ml (2½ fl. oz) milk
50 g (2 oz) melted butter
125 g (4 oz) plain flour
½ tsp salt
1 tsp baking powder

- Combine blackberrries, half the sugar and the lemon juice in a pie dish and dot with butter.

- Beat egg with remaining sugar until pale, then add milk and melted butter. Sift flour with salt and baking powder in a mixing bowl. Make a well in the flour and gradually stir in the wet mixture until you have a smooth batter.

- Pour mixture over blackberries and bake at 180°C/gas mark 4 for 30 minutes, or until risen and golden.

> Berries that are hybrids of blackberries and other berries – such as tayberries and loganberries – can be used instead of blackberries in any of these recipes, but loganberries are not so good to eat raw.

BLACKCURRANT

The small purple-black fruits smothering the blackcurrant bush are a familiar sight in many kitchen gardens during summer. Unlike white or red currants, the birds seem to leave them alone – they are probably too sour.

Blackcurrants make excellent preserves – see blackcurrant jam, page 236 – because they are so rich in pectin and acidic flavour, and they bring a beautiful colour and fragrance to a wide variety of other recipes, including pies, puddings, desserts and ice cream. The currants make a perfect dessert sauce and can be added to sauces to accompany meats, game and poultry.

STORING

Store blackcurrants in a lidded container in the fridge for a few days. Pick when the weather is dry to avoid them quickly becoming mouldy. Entire strigs (clusters) will keep longer than individual currants.

To freeze: remove currants from strigs and rinse if necessary. Dry thoroughly and either freeze in containers, or, for easy pouring, open-freeze then put in containers. The currants will keep for a year or more.

Blackcurrant purée (below) and coulis (page 181) also freeze well.

NO COOKING REQUIRED

Because blackcurrants are sour when raw, they are usually cooked, but if you choose the largest, ripest berries on the branches they will be sweeter and a few can be added to fruit salads without cooking.

PURÉED BLACKCURRANTS

Blend raw currants in a blender with approx. 75 g (3 oz) icing sugar for every 225 g (8 oz) currants to make a purée. This is very good stirred into yogurt for breakfast, or with creamed rice or in a fool. For a smoother result, press purée through a sieve.

RAW BLACKCURRANT JUICE

The raw fruits may be pressed through a sieve and the resultant juice added to drinks or recipes. Or, with the addition of icing sugar, you can use it to make ice lollies.

BLACKCURRANT SMOOTHIE

Put 100 g (3½ oz) fresh or partially thawed frozen blackcurrants in a blender with 1 small banana, 200 ml (7 fl. oz) apple juice and icing sugar to taste. Blend until smooth.

BLACKCURRANT AND BISCUIT FOOL

The biscuits give this easy dessert a lovely crunch and texture.

Serves 4

300 ml (½ pint) whipping cream
150 g (5 oz) cream cheese
2 tbsp icing sugar
4 digestive biscuits
200 ml (7 fl. oz) blackcurrant coulis

- Whip cream to soft peak stage, then beat in cream cheese and icing sugar.
- Put biscuits in a plastic bag and crush with a rolling pin. Stir into mixture, then stir coulis through lightly. Spoon into individual glasses. Chill for 15 minutes.

QUICK AND EASY BLACKCURRANT ICE CREAM

Not the classic way of making ice cream, but it tastes lovely.

Serves 6

275 ml (9 fl. oz) whipping cream
300 g (11 oz) blackcurrant purée
juice of ½ lemon

- Whip cream and stir in purée and lemon juice.
- Spoon into a 500 g (1¼ lb) loaf tin or strong container. Wrap in cling film and freeze for several hours, or until firm.
- Leave at room temperature for 15 minutes before slicing to serve.

BLACKCURRANT AND PISTACHIO TRIFLE

A trifle with a little kick to it in the form of blackcurrant liqueur – crème de cassis. Make sure the sponge cake you use is fresh. Decorate with any spare blackcurrants.

Serves 4–6

250 g (9 oz) plain sponge cake
2 tbsp blackcurrant jam (page 236)
250 ml (8 fl. oz) blackcurrant coulis
2 tbsp crème de cassis
75 g (3 oz) pistachio nuts
500 ml (17 fl. oz) custard (page 250)
300 ml (½ pint) whipping cream

- Slice cake, spread jam on slices and arrange in a trifle bowl.
- Combine coulis with cassis, then pour three-quarters of the mixture over the sponge and sprinkle on half the nuts.
- Stir remaining coulis mixture lightly into the custard to give a streaked effect and spoon evenly into the bowl.
- Whip cream to soft peak stage and spread evenly over the top, then sprinkle on remaining nuts. Chill for 30 minutes.

BASIC COOKING

Remove blackcurrants from their strigs and, using your thumb and first finger, pinch off the 'tops and tails' – the dead flower and the short stalk – of each currant. If you are in a hurry and not worried about appearance, you can leave the tops in place for some recipes – e.g. pies – as they are edible. Put in a colander or sieve, rinse, then use as required.

SIMMERED BLACKCURRANTS

Simmer currants over medium-low heat with 1 tbsp water and 1 tbsp sugar for every 125 g (4 oz) fruit. When the juices escape from the fruits and they begin to burst, remove from heat. Don't over-cook or they will lose their fresh flavour.

BLACKCURRANT JUICE

Simmer currants as above, then press through a sieve to remove all the juice.

BLACKCURRANT CORDIAL

Make juice as above, then add 450 g (1 lb) caster sugar for every 600 ml (1 pint) warm juice and stir over very low heat to dissolve. Cool and bottle – it will keep for several weeks in the fridge.

BLACKCURRANT COULIS

Simmer currants (a cinnamon stick or a few cloves can be added) and allow to cool, then put in a blender with the juice of 1 lemon for every 500 g (1¼ lb) fruit and blend until smooth. Taste and add more sugar as necessary.

BLACKCURRANT CHEESECAKE TOPPING

Simmer 375 g (13 oz) currants. Combine 2 tsp arrowroot with 2 tbsp cold water, then add to simmered currants and stir over medium heat until sauce thickens and turns glossy. Cool, then spoon over a plain cheesecake.

Blackcurrant leaves are sometimes used to make a herbal tea: pour boiling water over washed leaves in a teapot, brew for 5 minutes, strain and drink. It is said to be good for the lungs and liver.

BLACKCURRANT RECIPES

SUMMER PUDDING

Everyone loves this easy dessert, without which British summers just wouldn't be the same. You can vary the proportions of fruit and use strawberries instead of red currants. But remember, the more blackcurrants you use, the more sugar you may need. Decorate with any extra fruit and serve with cream.

Serves 4–6

225 g (8 oz) blackcurrants   **100 g (3½ oz) red currants**   **approx. ⅓ loaf white bread**
225 g (8 oz) raspberries   **150 g (5 oz) sugar**

- Lightly simmer all fruits in 3 tbsp water with sugar until juices run but shape is retained.
- Cut crusts off bread and slice. Line a 900 ml (1½ pint) lightly greased pudding basin with two-thirds of the bread slices, filling in all gaps with extra pieces.
- Spoon fruit and juices into the bowl and cover with remaining bread.
- Put a saucer with a weight on top of the bowl, stand the bowl on a large dish and refrigerate overnight. Turn out on to a plate.

BLACKCURRANT TART

The lovely creamy custard and the tangy blackcurrants make this a tart you are almost bound to want to cook again. Serve with cream or blackcurrant coulis – or both.

Serves 6

350 g (12 oz) sweet shortcrust pastry
  (page 251)
100 g (3½ oz) butter
100 g (3½ oz) caster sugar
3 eggs
100 g (3½ oz) ground almonds
200 g (7 oz) blackcurrants

- Roll out pastry and line a 23 cm (9 in.) flan tin. Bake blind.
- Cream butter and sugar in a mixing bowl until light and fluffy. Beat in eggs a little at a time. Fold in ground almonds and spoon filling into pastry case.
- Sprinkle blackcurrants on top and bake at 190°C/gas mark 5 for 45 minutes, or until golden and just firm.

BLACKCURRANT BAKED ALASKA

A dessert that all the family will enjoy. Make sure the blackcurrant mixture is completely cold before you put the ice cream on top or it will melt. You can buy ready-made flan cases in supermarkets.

Serves 6

400 g (14 oz) blackcurrants
200 g (7 oz) caster sugar
2 tsp arrowroot
1 ready-made sponge flan case
3 egg whites
750 ml (1¼ pints) vanilla ice cream

- Simmer blackcurrants with half the sugar until the juices run and the sugar is dissolved. Combine arrowroot with 1 tbsp cold water, then stir into the pan until the sauce is slightly thickened. Cool.
- Put flan case on a baking sheet and pour the blackcurrant mixture in.
- Whisk egg whites in a clean, dry, non-greasy bowl to stiff peak stage. Stir in 1 tbsp of the caster sugar, then whisk in remaining sugar until the mixture is glossy.
- Place ice cream on top of the flan filling. Quickly spoon meringue mixture over the top and sides, making sure that all the ice cream is covered.
- Bake at 230°C/gas mark 8 for 3 minutes, or until the meringue is golden. Serve immediately.

BLACKCURRANT CAKE

You can eat this cake hot or cold. It is especially good served hot with cream or with a thin custard.

Makes 6–8 slices

100 g (3½ oz) butter
175 g (6 oz) caster sugar
1 egg
½ tsp vanilla extract
200 g (7 oz) self-raising flour
¼ tsp salt
75 ml (2½ fl. oz) milk
200 g (7 oz) blackcurrants
1 tbsp demerara sugar

- Cream butter and caster sugar in a bowl until light and fluffy. Beat in egg a little at a time.
- Stir in vanilla and fold in flour and salt. Add milk and combine thoroughly, then stir in blackcurrants.
- Spoon mixture into a greased 20 cm (8 in.) baking tin lined with lightly greased baking parchment.
- Sprinkle the top with demerara sugar and bake at 180°C/gas mark 4 for 45 minutes, or until golden – a skewer inserted in the centre should come out clean. Cool a little, then turn out on to a wire rack.

BLACKCURRANT YOGURT LOLLIES

Lovely creamy, fruity, cool lollies that all the family – adults as well as children – will enjoy on a hot summer day.

Makes 12

400 g (14 oz) blackcurrants
175 g (6 oz) caster sugar
500 ml (17 fl. oz) Greek yogurt

- Simmer blackcurrants with sugar in 100 ml (3½ fl. oz) water to bursting point. Cool. Purée in a blender and press through a sieve.
- Mix purée with yogurt. Taste and add some icing sugar if necessary.
- Pour into twelve ice-lolly moulds and freeze for about 4 hours.

The French liqueur *cassis* is made from blackcurrants. A dash of *cassis* can be used to enhance blackcurrant purées and sauces.

CAPE GOOSEBERRY

Sometimes known as Physalis or Chinese lantern because of the papery calyx in which each fruit is encased, Cape gooseberry is a pretty ornamental plant with small, oval, smooth-skinned orange fruits filled with yellow seeds which are delicious, either raw or cooked. They are usually no bigger than a grape and have a sweet but slightly acidic flavour. The fruit originated in Peru but was cultivated in the African Cape of Good Hope region in the nineteenth century, hence its common name.

You are unlikely to have more than a kilo or so to use in the kitchen but, small as they are, they make a welcome addition to several dishes. Add some to an apple or pear pie or crumble for a stronger flavour, or chop and stir into a plain sponge cake before baking. They make a good cake decoration or garnish for other foods and because of their high pectin content are a good addition to jams and jellies.

They can be served poached with ice cream or made into a sauce for roast meat and poultry.

STORING

Once ripe, leave fruits in their calyxes and store in a plastic bag in the fridge – they should keep for several weeks. Unripe fruits at the end of the season can be left in a warm dry place to ripen. You can remove the calyx and freeze the fruits whole – they will be fine for desserts, sauces, preserving and baking.

NO COOKING REQUIRED

Pull back the calyxes and eat as they are. Add to fruit salads or purée with a little icing sugar to make a tasty sauce for ice cream.

TOFFEE CAPE GOOSEBERRIES

Similar to toffee apples. The sweetness of the caramel coating is counterbalanced by the acidity of the fruit to make a perfect mouthful.

Serves 8

200 g (7 oz) Cape gooseberries
250 g (9 oz) golden caster sugar

- Fold back calyx from each gooseberry to form a 'handle'.
- Line a baking tray with non-stick baking parchment.
- Melt sugar in a heavy-based pan over low heat until it is dissolved and you have a caramel sauce. Pour into a heated bowl.
- Dip each fruit in the caramel to coat thoroughly, then put on the baking tray until the caramel is set – about an hour.

CHOCOLATE CAPE GOOSEBERRIES

A very good sweet course instead of a dessert – or put some in a basket to give to a friend.

Serves 8

200 g (7 oz) Cape gooseberries
150 g (5 oz) dark chocolate

- Fold back calyx from each gooseberry to form a 'handle'.
- Line a baking tray with non-stick baking parchment.
- Break chocolate into pieces in a heatproof basin and set over a pan of boiling water – don't allow the base of the bowl to touch the water. Stir until chocolate is melted.
- Dip each fruit in the chocolate to coat, then put on the baking tray until the chocolate is set – about 30 minutes.

The Cape gooseberry is a member of the nightshade family Solanaceae and is related to tomatoes and aubergines.

QUICK CAPE GOOSEBERRY DESSERT

An easy recipe for those who have no time or don't want a fussy pudding. Amaretti can be bought in supermarkets

Serves 4

20 Cape gooseberries + 4 for decorating
400 ml (14 fl. oz) thick Greek yogurt
2 tbsp runny honey
2 tbsp toasted flaked almonds
4 amaretti biscuits

- Remove calyxes from all but four of the Cape gooseberries, lightly crush and stir into the yogurt.
- Fold in warmed honey, the almonds and lightly crushed amaretti biscuits.
- Spoon mixture into four dessert glasses and chill. Top each with one of the reserved gooseberries.

BASIC COOKING

Calyxes may be left on or removed as required. Cape gooseberries are unlikely to need washing.

POACHED CAPE GOOSEBERRIES

Remove calyxes. Put fruit in a pan with enough water to barely cover and 2 tsp sugar for every 100 g (3½ oz) fruits. Simmer gently for 5 minutes.

CAPE GOOSEBERRY COMPOTE

Follow poaching recipe, but add 1 tbsp sugar for every 100 g (3½ oz) fruit and simmer until fruits break up. Serve with duck, roast meats or grills, or in recipes.

CAPE GOOSEBERRY RECIPES

CAPE GOOSEBERRY UPSIDE-DOWN SPONGE

Try Cape gooseberries instead of peaches or apricots for a delicious, moist sponge cake. Serve with cream.

Serves 6–8

300 g (11 oz)	3 eggs
Cape gooseberries	1 tbsp milk
1 tbsp demerara sugar	1 orange
200 g (7 oz) caster sugar	125 g (4 oz) plain flour
200 g (7 oz) butter	1 tsp baking powder
175 g (6 oz) ground almonds	¼ tsp salt
1 tsp vanilla extract	

- Remove calyxes and arrange half the gooseberries in a greased 20 cm (8 in.) cake tin lined with lightly greased baking parchment. Sprinkle with demerara sugar.
- Cream caster sugar and butter until light and fluffy, then stir in ground almonds and vanilla.
- Gradually beat in eggs, then milk. Add grated orange zest and orange juice. Sift flour with baking powder and salt and stir into mixture. Stir in remaining gooseberries.
- Spoon mixture into cake tin, smooth top and bake at 170°C/gas mark 3½ for 1 hour or until golden and risen. Leave to cool a little, then turn out upside down on to a plate and serve warm.

FRUIT KEBABS

A colourful, easy and healthy dessert – try them on the barbecue.

Serves 4

15 g (½ oz) butter
100 ml (3½ fl. oz) orange juice
1 mango
2 slices pineapple
1 banana
16 Cape gooseberries
1 tbsp soft brown sugar

- Melt butter in a pan and stir in orange juice.
- Chop mango, pineapple and banana into bite-sized pieces and toss in orange juice and butter mixture. Remove calyxes from Cape gooseberries.
- Thread fruit on to four kebab sticks and grill for 3–4 minutes, turning once.
- Heat orange juice and butter mixture with sugar in a pan until bubbling and sugar is melted. Drizzle a spoonful over each kebab to serve.

CHERRY

Sweet cherries can be yellow, red or black. Yellow cherries have a juicy, tangy, firm flesh, while plump red cherries have a juicy, sweet, soft flesh. Black cherries have a deep-flavoured, succulent flesh. Cherries can be poached and used in tarts or pies and are the essential ingredient in Black Forest gateau and the traditional French pudding *clafoutis*. Cherries in the Snow (an old North American recipe) is another classic. Simmered cherries are layered with cubes of sponge cake and cream cheese whipped with sugar. Cherries are often combined with kirsch, a cherry liqueur. Black and deep red cherries tend to keep their colour better than yellow ones when cooked or frozen.

Dark red, juicy Morello cherries have a sour flavour and need to be sweetened before eating. They are used to make both black cherry jam and kirsch, and can be used in Black Forest gateau instead of sweet black cherries. Sweetened Morello cherries can be used to fill flans, pies and tarts, or used to make a sauce. Serve with yogurt, rice pudding or ice cream. They can also be preserved in jars.

STORING

Cherries will keep in a plastic bag with airholes in the fridge for 2–3 days – a week or two for Morellos. To freeze: open-freeze or bag and freeze, stoned or left whole.

To dry: stone cherries and put on baking trays in the oven at the lowest setting (less than 110°C/gas mark ¼) for 8 hours, or until leathery but still slightly sticky.

NO COOKING REQUIRED

Fresh sweet cherries are delicious as they are – some say it is a shame to cook them as they are so juicy and tasty. Stone them and use them in many types of cold dessert, such as trifle or fruit salad.

BASIC COOKING

Remove cherry stalks before cooking for most recipes. It is preferable to stone cherries before cooking, as the hard little stones can break teeth or cause choking. Use a cherry stoner – a blunt spike pushes the stone through the flesh, ensuring the shape and juices are retained. A cherry stoner can also be used for stoning olives. Don't try to stone cherries using a sharp knife – it is too easy to cut yourself.

SIMMERED CHERRIES

Simmer stoned cherries with 1 tbsp sugar and 2 tbsp water for every 200 g (7 oz) cherries for 5 minutes.

Cherries were used during the Middle Ages for their medicinal properties – and in recent years it has been found that cherry juice can help relieve sore muscles.

CHERRY COMPOTE

Put stoned cherries in a pan with 2½ tbsp sugar and 1 tbsp water for every 450 g (1 lb) cherries. Simmer for 10 minutes until cherries are broken up and you have a thick sauce. You can add ½ tsp spices such as ground cinnamon during cooking, and/or add a dash of kirsch near the end of simmering time.

CHERRY RECIPES

CHERRY PIE

A deep shortcrust pie tightly packed with sweet cherries is one of the wonders of summer. This recipe is easy to make.

Serves 6

700 g (1 lb 9 oz) stoned sweet cherries	2 tsp cornflour	2 tbsp ground almonds
50 g (2 oz) caster sugar	2 tbsp kirsch (optional)	1 tbsp milk
juice of ½ lemon	650 g (1 lb 7 oz) shortcrust pastry (page 251)	3 tsp caster sugar

- Simmer cherries with sugar, lemon juice and 100 ml (3½ fl. oz) water for 5 minutes. Dissolve cornflour in a little cold water, then stir into cherry mixture and cook for 2–3 minutes to thicken. Stir in kirsch, if using. Leave to cool.

- Roll out pastry on a floured surface and use half to line a greased 23 cm (9 in.) pie dish. Sprinkle ground almonds over the base, then spoon in the cherry mixture. Roll out remaining pastry to make a lid.

- Brush edge of pastry base with water and lay lid on top. Press the edges into the base and trim. Make a small hole in the centre of the lid and brush top with milk. Sprinkle caster sugar over and bake at 180°C/gas mark 4 for 40 minutes until golden.

CHERRY CLAFOUTIS

The classic batter-based cherry dessert from the Limousin region of central France – traditionally baked when the summer cherry harvest came in. For special occasions, you can drizzle kirsch over the fruit before adding the batter. Try with ice cream or cream.

Serves 4–6

500 g (1¼ lb) stoned sweet black cherries	¼ tsp salt
100 g (3½ oz) caster sugar	3 eggs
100 g (3½ oz) plain flour	300 ml (½ pint) milk
	1 tbsp icing sugar

- Put cherries and half the sugar in a greased shallow ovenproof dish.
- Combine flour, salt and remaining sugar, then beat in eggs and milk.
- Pour mixture over cherries and bake at 180°C/gas mark 4 for 30–40 minutes, or until lightly risen and golden. Dust with sifted icing sugar. Serve warm.

CHERRY COULIS

A smooth pouring sauce which is ideal with ice cream or a dessert cake, or with cherry omelette or strudel (page 189). If you have no sour cherries, just use all sweet cherries and an extra dash of lemon juice. If serving children, leave out the kirsch.

Serves 4

300 g (11 oz) stoned sweet cherries	50 g (2 oz) caster sugar
100 g (3½ oz) stoned sour cherries	juice of ½ lemon
	1 tbsp kirsch (optional)

- Simmer cherries with sugar, lemon juice and 4 tbsp water for 5 minutes. Stir in kirsch.
- Cool a little, then blend in a blender until smooth. Strain through a sieve and add extra water to thin as necessary. Chill to serve.

BLACK FOREST GATEAU

The favourite dessert of the 1970s has made a recent comeback and there is nothing to beat a home-made version. Great for a birthday party or celebration, it's a little time-consuming but not difficult to make.

Serves 8

225 g (8 oz) butter at room temperature
225 g (8 oz) caster sugar
4 eggs
225 g (8 oz) self-raising flour
1 tsp baking powder
3 tbsp cocoa powder

FOR THE FILLING
3 tbsp caster sugar
400 g (14 oz) stoned black cherries
1 tsp arrowroot
3 tbsp kirsch
450 ml (¾ pint) double cream

FOR THE DECORATION
100 g (3½ oz) plain chocolate
8 fresh black cherries

- Cream butter and sugar until light and fluffy, then add beaten eggs a little at a time. Stir in flour sifted with baking powder.
- Blend cocoa powder with 4 tbsp boiling water and beat into mixture.
- Divide mixture between two deep, greased 20 cm (8 in.) cake tins lined with lightly greased baking parchment. Bake at 180°C/gas mark 4 for 20–25 minutes until risen and the tops of the cakes spring back when pressed with your finger. Leave to cool a little, then turn out on to a wire rack to cool completely.
- To make the filling, heat caster sugar in 3 tbsp water until dissolved, then boil for 3 minutes. Add halved cherries, lower heat and cook for 2 minutes until juices run and cherries are softened but not broken down.
- Mix arrowroot with a little cold water, then add to pan, stirring until the syrup thickens. Stir in half the kirsch. Leave to cool.
- Slice each cake in half horizontally and sprinkle cut sides with remaining kirsch.
- Whip cream to soft peak stage and spread one fifth over one sponge round. Top with one third of the cherries and a little syrup. Place another sponge round on top, then more cream, cherries and syrup. Repeat once more, then top with the remaining sponge round.
- Use a palette knife to spread remaining cream around sides and top of cake. Press grated chocolate into sides and sprinkle over top. Decorate with fresh cherries.

FRESH CHERRY AND COCONUT CAKE

Most recipes for cherry cakes and buns use glacé cherries, but this one makes use of fresh ones and is all the nicer for that.

Serves 6

75 g (3 oz) caster sugar
75 g (3 oz) butter at room temperature
1 egg
150 g (5 oz) self-raising flour
4 tbsp milk
8 tbsp desiccated coconut
350 g (12 oz) stoned sweet cherries

- Cream caster sugar and butter until light and fluffy, then beat in egg a little at a time. Fold in flour until well combined, then stir in milk and 6 tbsp of the coconut.
- Spoon mixture into a greased 20 cm (8 in.) cake tin lined with lightly greased baking parchment. Scatter cherries evenly over the top and press lightly into the mixture.
- Bake at 180°C/gas mark 4 for 30–35 minutes until a skewer inserted in the centre comes out clean. Cool a little, then turn out on to a wire rack to cool completely. Sprinkle on remaining coconut to serve.

SWEET CHERRY SOUFFLÉ OMELETTE

Few people ever try a sweet omelette – but it makes a superb snack or dessert and is even better stuffed with tasty fruit.

Serves 2

175 g (6 oz) stoned sweet cherries
3 tbsp caster sugar
5 eggs
25 g (1 oz) butter
2 tsp vegetable oil
2 tsp icing sugar

- Simmer cherries with half the caster sugar and 1 tbsp water for 4 minutes.
- Separate eggs and whisk whites in a clean, dry, non-greasy bowl to stiff peak stage.
- Beat egg yolks together with remaining sugar, then fold in whites.
- Heat half the butter and oil in a 20 cm (8 in.) frying pan over high heat and add half the egg mixture. Cook until the underside is golden and the centre still moist. Spoon half the cherry mixture on top and fold over to serve.
- Repeat with the remaining mixture. Dust with sifted icing sugar.

CHERRY STRUDEL

Filo pastry isn't traditional for a strudel; however, it is similar to strudel pastry, and the ready-made filo considerably cuts down the time it takes to make this splendid dessert.

Serves 6

450 g (1 lb) cherry compote (page 186)
100 g (3½ oz) walnuts
50 g (2 oz) caster sugar
1 lemon
1 tsp cinnamon
6 tbsp butter
75 g (3 oz) white breadcrumbs
12 sheets filo pastry
2 tbsp icing sugar

- If the cherry compote is runny, put it into a sieve and drain thoroughly.
- Mix together finely chopped walnuts, caster sugar, grated lemon zest and cinnamon.
- Melt butter and add half to breadcrumbs, stirring to combine.
- Cut filo sheets in half. Grease a baking tray, then use remaining butter to brush each filo sheet. Stack four sheets together, top with one sixth of both the breadcrumbs and then the walnut mixture, and arrange one sixth of the cherry mixture in the centre. Roll up and tuck in edges. Brush top with butter. Repeat for remaining strudels.
- Bake at 220°C/gas mark 7 for 10 minutes. Reduce heat to 180°C/gas mark 4 and cook for a further 10 minutes, or until golden brown. Cool a little, then dust with sifted icing sugar.

CHERRY SAUCE FOR DUCK

This sauce is great with roast duck, venison or game birds. If you make it without having roasted a duck, use butter instead of the duck fat and omit the roasting juices. An alternative version uses sour cherries plus 1 tbsp red currant jelly (page 238) or bramble jelly.

Serves 4

2 tbsp duck fat
roasting juices from pan
½ tbsp cornflour
125 ml (4 fl. oz) chicken stock
75 ml (2½ fl. oz) port
½ tsp Chinese five-spice powder
salt, black pepper
350 g (12 oz) stoned sweet black cherries

- Heat fat in saucepan with roasting juices, stir in flour and blend, then cook for a minute over medium heat. Stir in stock, port and five-spice, and cook for 5 minutes. Season.
- Stir in cherries and cook for another 3 minutes.

CURRANT, RED AND WHITE

Red currants and white currants are members of the *Ribes* family and are closely related to blackcurrants. In season in midsummer, the little fruits are refreshing in flavour and their attractive jewel-like appearance makes them a beautiful garnish. They are also good made into a variety of recipes, including hot and cold desserts and cakes.

They are rich in pectin, so currant juice added to preserves helps them to achieve a good set.

STORING

Currants are best kept on their strigs (clusters) until needed. Put them in a lidded container and store in the fridge for up to a week.

Currants freeze well: remove from strigs and rinse if necessary. Dry thoroughly and either freeze in containers or open-freeze on trays then put into containers. They will keep for a year or more.

NO COOKING REQUIRED

Red currants and white currants are edible raw, although they are not as sweet as they look (white are sweeter than red). Add a few to fruit salads, use to decorate desserts and cakes, or arrange strigs on a cheeseboard as an alternative to grapes.

RED CURRANT COULIS

Put red currants in a blender with 1 tbsp sugar and the juice of ¼ lemon for every 100 g (3½ oz) currants. Blend until smooth. Add water to thin if necessary, then blend again. Chill to serve.

RED CURRANTS IN SYRUP

Gently combine 500 g (1¼ lb) red currants and 100 g (3½ oz) sugar in a bowl. Cover and leave in the fridge overnight, by which time the sugar will have dissolved, producing a pretty red syrup.

RED CURRANT ICING

There is no need to use artificial food colouring to make beautiful pink icing for cakes. Blend 125 g (4 oz) red currants in a blender, adding 300 g (11 oz) sugar in two or three batches, until you have a smooth, deep pink icing.

WHITE CURRANT VINAIGRETTE

To serve 4: combine the juice of ½ orange with 1 tbsp white wine vinegar, 1 tsp Dijon mustard, 4 tbsp hazelnut oil, salt and black pepper. Stir in 125 g (4 oz) white currants. Leave to stand for at least an hour. Drizzle over grilled meats and salads.

BASIC COOKING

Pick currants from bushes in complete strigs rather than individually, as they are very soft and easily damaged. To remove the fruit from the strig for most purposes, use a wide-tined fork and gently move it down the strig – the berries should come off. For perfect specimens, use small sharp scissors to cut off individual berries or pick off very carefully by hand.

SIMMERED CURRANTS

Simmer currants with 1 tbsp caster sugar and 1 tbsp water for every 150 g (5 oz) currants over low heat for 3–4 minutes, or until sugar is dissolved.

RED CURRANT JUICE

To make about 300 ml (½ pint) juice, simmer 500 g (1¼ lb) currants. Strain through a mesh or fine sieve into a bowl and press fruits well to get all the juice out. Discard the sieve contents and chill the juice before serving.

CURRANT RECIPES

RED CURRANT MUFFINS

The tangy currants make a perfect foil for the sweetness of the muffin mixture.

Makes 12

175 g (6 oz) plain flour   6 tbsp milk
2 tsp baking powder   ½ lemon
2 eggs   200 g (7 oz) red currants
150 g (5 oz) caster sugar   1 tbsp icing sugar
8 tbsp sunflower oil

- Sift together flour and baking powder into a bowl.
- In a separate bowl, cream eggs and sugar until smooth. Stir in oil, milk, grated lemon zest and juice, then stir the bowl contents into the flour.
- Add red currants, then divide mixture between paper cases in a 12-hole muffin tin. Bake at 180°C/gas mark 4 for 15–20 minutes, or until risen and golden. Cool on a wire rack and dust with sifted icing sugar.

RED CURRANT, ORANGE AND PORT SAUCE

This sauce is very good with game birds, venison or lamb, but can also be used with desserts such as ice cream or fruit kebabs. Ready-made red currant jelly from a supermarket is fine.

Serves 4

2 tbsp red currant jelly   3 tbsp port
   (page 238)   juice of 1 orange
100 g (3½ oz) red currants   cinnamon stick

- Put all ingredients in a pan and bring to a simmer over low heat until jelly is melted. Cook for 5 minutes. Remove cinnamon stick to serve.

RED CURRANT MERINGUE TART

A truly lovely and unusual summer dessert with a sweet, rich pastry and a sticky, meringue-like filling. Good with berry coulis and/or cream.

Serves 4

200 g (7 oz) plain flour
1 tsp baking powder
125 g (4 oz) butter at room temperature
200 g (7 oz) caster sugar
2 eggs
2 tsp cornflour
300 g (11 oz) red currants

- Sift flour and baking powder into a bowl. In a separate bowl cream butter and half the sugar until smooth, then stir in beaten egg yolks (reserve whites). Now combine wet mixture with flour to form a dough.
- Wrap pastry in cling film and put in the fridge for 30 minutes, then roll it out and line a deep, greased 20 cm (8 in.) tart tin. Bake blind.
- Beat egg whites in a clean, dry, non-greasy bowl to stiff peak stage. Gradually stir in remaining sugar and cornflour and beat again until glossy. Fold in all but 50 g (2 oz) of the red currants and pour mixture into the pastry case.
- Bake at 170°C/gas mark 3½ for 10–15 minutes, or until top is golden and centre moist. Cool a little, then turn out and decorate with remaining red currants.

RED AND WHITE CURRANT JELLIES

A straightforward dessert suitable for a dinner party or a children's teatime treat.

Serves 4

3 tsp gelatine
600 ml (1 pint) cold red currant juice
75 g (3 oz) sugar
250 ml (8 fl. oz) whipping cream
75 g (3 oz) white currants

- Stir gelatine into 200 ml (7 fl. oz) of the red currant juice and stand for 3 minutes.
- Dissolve sugar in remaining juice in a pan, then heat until nearly boiling. Stir juice into the gelatine mixture and refrigerate until set: at least 1 hour.
- Whip cream to soft peak stage. Spoon one eighth of the set jelly into an individual dessert glass, followed by one eighth of the whipped cream. Repeat the layer, then repeat with three more glasses. Top each dessert with the white currants.

FIG

Humans have been eating figs for thousands of years – they are referred to in the Old Testament. If you are lucky enough to have a productive fig tree growing in a sheltered spot in the garden, or in a greenhouse, you will know that figs picked when they are perfectly ripe (when they give a little when pressed and have a slight bloom on their skin) are one of the wonders of the fruit world. Similar in shape to a small, squat pear, their flavour and texture is unique and their moistness means they are a valuable ingredient in baking. Cooked, they make a sublime dessert – for example, baked with honey and served with Greek yogurt or sour cream.

STORING

Freshly picked figs will keep in a lidded container in the fridge for a few days. Freeze whole, uncooked figs for up to 3 months, or steam over boiling water for 2 minutes and open-freeze – they will keep for a year.

To dry figs: halve and dry as for tomatoes (page 154).

NO COOKING REQUIRED

A ripe fig is perfect eaten just as it is, off the tree. Figs are a classic accompaniment to Parma or Serrano ham or *breseaola* – Italian cured beef. They are also good stuffed with cream cheese as a canapé or snack. Try slicing one into a sandwich with ham and Mozzarella or goat's cheese.

BASIC COOKING

Handle figs carefully, as when ripe they bruise quite easily. Figs can be poached or baked whole, but if the recipe requires cut figs, halve with a sharp knife, lengthwise. The stalk can be left on.

POACHED FIGS

Put figs in a pan and cover with water. Bring to the boil, reduce heat and simmer, uncovered, over moderate heat for 15–20 minutes.

BAKED FIGS

Put halved figs on a large sheet of foil. Add 1 tsp sugar and a small knob of butter for each one. Bring edges of foil up and fold to make a sealed parcel. Put the parcel on a baking tray and cook at 180°C/gas mark 4 for 15–20 minutes. Or you can put the foil parcel at the side of a hot barbecue for a similar time.

GRILLED FIGS

Halve figs and brush cut sides with butter, adding a sprinkling of demerara sugar. Grill under high heat for 3 minutes.

PURÉED FIGS

Poach figs with 1 tbsp water or orange juice and 1 tsp sugar for each fig over low heat for 5 minutes. Blend in a blender until smooth.

FIG ROLLS

Easy to make and tastier than shop-bought fig rolls.

Makes 12 biscuits

150 g (5 oz) plain flour	¼ tsp salt
75 g (3 oz) butter	175 g (6 oz) fig purée
25 g (1 oz) caster sugar	

- Rub flour and butter together with your fingers until it resembles breadcrumbs. Stir in sugar and salt. Add 2 tbsp cold water, or enough to make a firm dough.
- Knead dough on a floured surface for 1–2 minutes, then roll it out into a wide rectangle about 0.5 cm (¼ in.) thick.
- Spread cold fig purée along one side of the strip of pastry leaving 0.5 cm (¼ in.) round the edge. Brush edge with water. Fold other half of pastry over, press top down lightly and press edges firmly together.
- Cut into 12 slices, put on a lightly greased baking tray and cook at 190°C/gas mark 5 for 20–25 minutes or until golden. Allow to cool.

FIG RECIPES

FIG BREAD PUDDING

Bread-pudding lovers will enjoy this hearty version. For a more luxurious pudding, use Italian *panettone* – a very light, fruity, bread-like cake. You can use white grape juice instead of the wine.

Serves 4

225 g (8 oz) good-quality white bread	2 eggs
500 ml (17 fl. oz) milk	100 g (3½ oz) sugar
5 figs	½ tsp ground cinnamon
75 ml (2½ fl. oz) medium-dry white wine	2 tbsp butter at room temperature

- Cut bread into bite-sized cubes and put in a bowl with milk. Soak for 15 minutes, stirring once or twice.
- Simmer chopped figs in wine for 5 minutes, uncovered, then drain.
- Beat eggs with sugar until pale, then stir in bread cubes, figs and cinnamon.
- Spoon mixture into a buttered baking dish and bake at 180°C/gas mark 4 for 45 minutes, or until a knife inserted in the centre comes out clean. Top with a sprinkle of cinnamon.

BAKED STUFFED FIGS

A nice idea for warm canapés. An alternative stuffing could be slivers of Parma ham or pineapple.

Serves 6

6 figs	2 tsp fresh chopped rosemary
75 g (3 oz) Brie	black pepper

- Using a small, sharp-pointed knife, cut open one side of each fig. Stuff each with one sixth of the Brie and a pinch of rosemary and pepper.
- Place cut side up in a baking dish and cook at 180°C/gas mark 4 for 6–7 minutes, or until figs are hot and cheese is melted.

Fig purée can be used to replace fat in cake and baking recipes. A useful rule of thumb is to replace half the fat in your traditional recipe and then reduce the quantity of sugar by a third as the fig is sweet.

FIG AND ALMOND TART

Many classic fig tart recipes include frangipane or marzipan. Here frangipane is made as part of the recipe. Ensure the ground almonds are as fresh as possible – it is easy to grind your own.

Serves 4–6

75 g (3 oz) butter at room temperature	350 g (12 oz) sweet shortcrust pastry (page 251)
75 g (3 oz) caster sugar	1 egg yolk
1 egg	12 figs
75 g (3 oz) ground almonds	2 tbsp icing sugar

- Beat together butter and sugar until creamy, then beat in the egg. Stir in almonds to make a smooth mixture (frangipane).
- Roll out pastry into a round and place on a pizza baking tray if you have one (or use an ordinary baking tray). Spread frangipane on the dough, leaving a 2 cm (¾ in.) rim around the edge.
- Fold pastry edge in to form a rough tart, pinching a little to make sure they stick. Brush the pastry rim with beaten egg yolk and bake at 200°C/gas mark 6 for 5 minutes.
- Quarter figs and arrange, cut side up, in circles on the frangipane. Sprinkle with sifted icing sugar, then bake for a further 8–10 minutes, or until the pastry is golden.

GOOSEBERRY

It is a pity that gooseberries – first grown in the UK in the time of Henry VIII – aren't grown in more gardens, as these small fruits are not only versatile but also delicious. Firm, early green gooseberries are high in pectin and ideal for preserves and chutneys, and they are excellent in pies and desserts. They can be used as a substitute for rhubarb in most recipes – in both cases a large amount of sugar will be required. The tart fruit makes a great sauce that will cut through the richness of mackerel, pork, goose and other fatty meats.

You can also grow larger later-season 'dessert' gooseberries – often white, yellow or pale pinky-red. These are sweeter and can be eaten raw when fully ripe – the surface gives when pressed.

STORING

Green gooseberries will keep for 2 weeks or more if stored straight from the bush in the fridge in plastic bags with airholes. To freeze: top and tail, wash, then pat dry and bag for freezing. Or open-freeze then bag, or freeze as a purée.

NO COOKING REQUIRED

Ripe, plump, yellow or red dessert gooseberries (which are hairless) can be eaten raw. Add to fruit salad or eat as a snack, dipped in a little sugar.

BASIC COOKING

Top and tail by pinching off the small stalks and the dead flower from the top. Rinse under cold running water. The fine hairs that cover some gooseberries won't be noticed once cooked.

SIMMERED GOOSEBERRIES

Simmer gently in a pan with 2 tbsp water for every 100 g (3½ oz) fruit and 10 g (¼ oz) sugar for sweet dessert varieties, or 25 g (1 oz) sugar for the same quantity of very sour fruit. (Add the minimum at first if you are not sure.) Cook for 5–6 minutes until gooseberries begin to burst open and are tender. Sweet white wine (e.g. Muscatel) or elderflower wine can be used instead of water.

PURÉED GOOSEBERRIES

Simmer the fruits, then blend or mash thoroughly. For a smoother sauce, push the purée through a sieve and discard the skins that remain in the sieve. Taste and add more sugar as necessary. A dash of elderflower cordial can also be added.

GOOSEBERRY SPONGE PUDDING

A no-fuss dessert that children will love – try it with custard (page 250).

Serves 4

75 g (3 oz) brown sugar	125 g (4 oz) caster sugar
500 g (1¼ lb) gooseberries	2 eggs
125 g (4 oz) butter	125 g (4 oz) flour

- Grease a 20 cm (8 in.) baking tin and line with greased baking parchment. Sprinkle brown sugar evenly over the base, then arrange gooseberries on top.

- Cream butter and sugar until light and fluffy. Gradually stir in beaten eggs, then fold in flour. Spoon mixture over gooseberries and bake at 180°C/gas mark 4 for 45 minutes, or until risen and golden. Allow to cool a little, then turn out so that the gooseberries are on top of the sponge.

GOOSEBERRY RECIPES

GOOSEBERRY AND ELDERFLOWER JELLY DESSERT

An easy jelly for any occasion. For dinner parties you could use a sweet wine such as a Muscatel or elderflower wine instead of cordial.

Serves 4

7 tbsp elderflower cordial
275 g (10 oz) dessert gooseberries

10 g (¼ oz) sachet powdered gelatine elderflowers

- Dilute cordial with 600 ml (1 pint) cold water. Simmer gooseberries in 200 ml (7 fl. oz) of the cordial for 3–4 minutes until tender but still whole.
- Heat 4 tbsp of the remaining cordial and sprinkle the gelatine over. Set aside for 10 minutes, or until dissolved.
- Strain gooseberries, reserving juice, and put into four dessert glasses. Combine cooking juice with dissolved gelatine and stir in remaining cordial. Pour into the glasses. Chill for 3–4 hours, or until set. Garnish with elderflowers if you have any, and drizzle over a little cordial to serve.

GOOSEBERRY FOOL

A perennial favourite fruit fool, as the tartness of gooseberries is well balanced by the cream and custard (shop-bought is fine). Try simmering the gooseberries using sweet wine rather than water. Serve with ice cream wafer fans.

Serves 4

2 tsp arrowroot
450 g (1 lb) simmered gooseberries
150 ml (¼ pint) whipping cream
200 ml (7 fl. oz) thick custard (page 250)

- Stir arrowroot into 1 tbsp cold water, then add to warm gooseberries. Bring to a simmer and cook for a minute, or until liquid thickens. Leave to cool.
- Whip cream to stiff peak stage. Fold together berries, cream and custard so that you still see streaks of gooseberry. Spoon into individual dishes and smooth top. Chill well before serving.

GOOSEBERRY MERINGUE PIE

A cross between lemon meringue pie and gooseberry pie. You will be asked for the recipe by all who try it! You can use sweet shortcrust pastry (page 251) instead of standard. For gooseberry pie, replace the meringue with a lid of pastry and bake as usual.

Serves 4–6

375 g (13 oz) shortcrust pastry (page 251)
275 g (10 oz) golden caster sugar
2 tbsp elderflower cordial
600 g (1 lb 6 oz) gooseberries
½ tbsp cornflour
50 g (2 oz) butter
3 egg whites

- Line a greased 23 cm (9 in.) round, straight-sided tart tin with rolled-out pastry and bake blind.
- Put 100 g (3½ oz) of the sugar in a pan with the cordial and 4 tbsp water and simmer until sugar is dissolved. Add gooseberries and simmer for a further 3–4 minutes until they are just tender but still whole. Stir in cornflour and butter. Allow to cool.
- Whisk egg whites in a clean, dry, non-greasy bowl with 1 tbsp of the remaining sugar to soft peak stage, then add remaining sugar in two batches and whisk until stiff and glossy.
- Spoon gooseberry mixture into pastry case, smooth out and spoon meringue over. Bake at 150°C/gas mark 2 for 40 minutes, or until golden.

BAKED GOOSEBERRY CUSTARD

A creamy hot custard with a layer of gooseberries. Good served with buttery biscuits.

Serves 4

600 g (1 lb 6 oz) gooseberries
175 g (6 oz) caster sugar
400 ml (14 fl. oz) double cream

175 ml (6 fl. oz) full-fat milk
6 egg yolks
½ tsp ground nutmeg

- Toss gooseberries with half the sugar and tip into a baking dish.
- Combine cream and milk in a saucepan. Bring to the boil, then remove from the heat.
- Beat egg yolks and remaining sugar until smooth. Pour in cream mixture. Stir in half of the nutmeg.
- Pour custard over gooseberries and sprinkle on remaining nutmeg.
- Place dish in a roasting tin and add hot water to come halfway up the sides of the dish. Bake at 160°C/gas mark 3 for 50 minutes, or until just set.

GRAPE

If you are lucky enough to have your own grapes you will probably eat most of them raw or press them for juice. But they appear in a surprising number of cooked sweet recipes – in cakes, tea loaves and pies, for example – and can give a delightful lift to savoury dishes, especially delicate white fish and white meats.

The leaves from the grapevine can also be eaten – stuffed vine leaves are popular in Mediterranean and Middle Eastern countries.

STORING

Freshly picked grapes will store for a week or more in the fridge in a plastic bag with airholes. They will also freeze: open-freeze then bag for use in fruit salads and any cooked dishes.

You can dry your own grapes using the method for tomatoes (page 154) to produce **sultanas** (if white grapes are used) or **raisins** (if red grapes are used).

Vine leaves can be frozen: blanch in salted water, drain, dry and freeze in plastic bags.

NO COOKING REQUIRED

Grapes are delicious raw. Add to sweet or savoury salads, or use in coleslaw instead of apple or apricot. Add slices to a chicken or cheese sandwich, or serve a small bunch with a ploughman's lunch or on a cheeseboard.

RED FRUIT SALAD

To serve 4, halve 200 g (7 oz) red grapes and combine with 1 chopped red-skinned dessert apple, 4 quartered stoned red plums, 100 ml (3½ fl. oz) red grape juice and 15 g (½ oz) caster sugar. Stir. Cover and refrigerate for an hour, stirring once or twice.

GRAPE AND GOAT'S CHEESE SALAD

To serve 1, arrange 25 g (1 oz) crisp salad leaves on a plate with a sliced celery stalk and drizzle on a little French dressing (page 250). Put a slice of goat's cheese in the centre and drizzle 1 tsp balsamic vinegar over. Top with a few walnut pieces and several halved grapes. The cheese can be grilled before adding to the plate.

CHICKEN AND GRAPE SALAD

To serve 1, toss 100 g (3½ oz) cooked chicken with 6 halved grapes, some watercress leaves and a dressing made by combining 1 tbsp mayonnaise with 1 tbsp natural yogurt and seasoning.

GRAPE AND LIME SMOOTHIE

A sweet yet refreshing smoothie.

Serves 2

400 g (14 oz) red grapes
100 ml (3½ fl. oz) purple grape juice
juice of 1 lime
1 tsp fresh finely chopped ginger
3 ice cubes

- Combine all ingredients in a blender and blend until smooth.

> Grapes have been cultivated for over 8,000 years, mainly for wine production.

GRAPE AND CHICKEN LIVER SALAD

A lovely warm salad for a late summer light lunch or starter. Serve with crusty bread.

Serves 4

4 rashers bacon
4 tbsp olive oil
6 chicken livers
salt, black pepper
100 g (3½ oz) watercress
175 g (6 oz) white grapes
1 tbsp white wine vinegar

- Cut bacon into thin slices then fry in 1 tbsp of the oil over medium-high heat until crisp.
- Remove tough connective tissue from livers and cut into bite-sized pieces; season. Push bacon to sides of pan and add 1 tbsp of the oil and the livers. Fry for 2–3 minutes until golden on the outside and just cooked inside.
- Arrange watercress, bacon and liver on four plates and top with halved grapes.
- Add vinegar to frying pan. Sizzle for a few seconds. Pour in remaining oil, season and stir. Drizzle dressing over salads.

TOFFEE GRAPES

A sweet snack for the children, and they also make a good end to a supper party, served in little *petits fours* cases.

Serves 6–8

225 g (8 oz) caster sugar
pinch cream of tartar

300 g (11 oz) seedless grapes
on their stalks

- Dissolve sugar and cream of tartar in 150 ml (¼ pint) water in a pan then bring to the boil and cook over high heat for several minutes or until you have a thick caramel. (Check with a drop on a spoon – if it hardens when dropped into cold water it is ready.)
- Dip each grape into the syrup using tongs to hold the stalk. Put on a lightly greased baking tray to cool and harden. Eat within 24 hours.

BASIC COOKING

If grapes contain pips these should be removed – halve grapes and use a very small spoon to scoop pips out. There is no need to skin grapes for most recipes – it is the skin that contains much of the goodness and flavour.
Freshly picked vine leaves should be blanched for 3 minutes before stuffing.

POACHED GRAPES Simmer grapes with enough water to cover for 3–4 minutes until just tender. Drain.

GRAPE RECIPES

SOLE VERONIQUE

A classic French dish of delicate white fish in a wine and grape sauce. If you don't want to use sole, try plaice or any tasty white fish fillets.

Serves 4

4 sole fillets	250 ml (8 fl oz) dry white wine
4 shallots	200 g (7 oz) white grapes
6 button mushrooms	25 g (1 oz) butter
2 tbsp fresh	1 tbsp flour
chopped parsley	150 ml (¼ pint) milk
1 bay leaf	juice of ½ lemon
salt, black pepper	50 ml (2 fl oz) cream

- Put fish in a shallow ovenproof dish with finely chopped shallots, thinly sliced mushrooms, herbs, seasoning, wine and 150 ml (¼ pint) water. Cover and bake at 180°C/gas mark 4 for 15 minutes.
- Simmer grapes in 3 tbsp water or wine for 2 minutes, then peel, halve and remove pips if necessary.
- Strain liquid from fish and keep fish warm. Boil liquid rapidly until reduced by half.
- In another pan, melt butter, stir in flour and cook for a minute over medium heat. Gradually stir in fish liquid and then the milk until you have a smooth sauce (you may not need all the milk).
- Stir in three-quarters of the grapes, the lemon juice and the cream. Pour over the fish and garnish with remaining grapes.

STUFFED VINE LEAVES (DOLMADES)

Don't waste the grapevine leaves – stuff the best ones in the Greek way. They go well with tzatziki (page 80).

Serves 4 (makes 20 small rolls)

20 large vine leaves	2 tbsp sultanas
1 onion	2 tbsp pine nuts
100 ml (3½ fl oz) olive oil	salt, black pepper
1 clove garlic	300 ml (½ pint) vegetable
125 g (4 oz) white rice	stock
1 tbsp each fresh chopped	juice of 1 lemon
dill, mint and parsley	

- Blanch vine leaves for 3 minutes, then drain.
- Fry finely chopped onion in 2 tbsp of the oil over medium heat until softened and tinged gold. Add chopped garlic for last minute.
- Add rice, herbs, sultanas, pine nuts and a further tbsp oil. Season and stir-fry for 2 minutes. Add 100 ml (3½ fl oz) stock, bring to a simmer and cook, covered, for 7 minutes.
- Lay leaves on a board, shiny side down, and place 1 tbsp rice mixture in the centre near the base. Roll up loosely (the rice will expand as it cooks), then turn in the sides to make a neat parcel. Repeat with all the leaves, then put them into a greased heatproof casserole so that they fit in one layer.
- Pour lemon juice, remaining stock and oil over the dolmades. Simmer gently, covered, for an hour until rice and leaves are tender and most of the stock is absorbed. Serve warm or cold.

KIWI FRUIT

With their rough brown skin, kiwi fruit don't look very promising. But cut one open and you find bright green juicy flesh filled with edible jewel-black seeds – no wonder the kiwi has become so popular in recent years. The flavour is unusual too – a little like a strawberry crossed with a pineapple – sweet but also refreshingly acidic.

Kiwi fruit make an excellent meat tenderizer – finely chop in a marinade, adding oil and seasoning. A word of warning: the fruit will cause milk to curdle and prevent gelatine from setting, so is no use for milky desserts, ice cream or jellies. They are excellent in fruit salads and trifles, for topping a cake or dessert such as pavlova (page 218) and are great for juicing and smoothies.

STORING

Ripe kiwi fruit will keep for up to a week in the fridge – store unripe ones in the kitchen where they will ripen up perfectly. To freeze: peel and slice fruits and put in containers. On thawing they will lose a little of their colour and texture.

NO COOKING REQUIRED

Kiwi fruit are probably best eaten raw – cooking tends to lessen their flavour and changes their colour. The skin is tough and inedible – peel the fruit then chop or slice as required. To eat as a snack, take off the top of the fruit (like a boiled egg) and scoop out the flesh with a small spoon.

GREEN FRUIT SALAD

A very pretty fruit salad – good at the end of a rich meal or for a late summer buffet.

Serves 4

150 ml (¼ pint) apple juice
1 tbsp runny honey
juice of ¼ lemon
½ tsp ground ginger
4 kiwi fruit
100 g (3½ oz) green grapes
1 green-skinned dessert apple
1 dessert pear
a few fresh mint leaves

- Warm apple juice in a pan with honey, lemon juice and ginger. Cool until just warm.
- Peel kiwi fruit, halve grapes, core and slice unpeeled apple, and peel, core and slice pear.
- Combine all fruit in a serving bowl with the juice. The juice should just cover the fruit. Chill in the fridge for at least an hour, stirring once or twice. Serve garnished with mint leaves.

AVOCADO, KIWI FRUIT AND PRAWN SALAD

A tasty starter or a light lunch. Make sure both avocados and kiwi fruit are perfectly ripe or the salad will be disappointing. Serve with thin slices of brown bread.

Serves 4

3 tbsp olive oil
juice of 1 lime
salt, black pepper
2 avocados
225 g (8 oz) cooked peeled prawns
25 g (1 oz) watercress
2 kiwi fruit

- Combine olive oil, lime juice and seasoning. Toss peeled and sliced avocados with the prawns in half the dressing.
- Arrange on serving plates with a little watercress. Peel kiwi fruit and slice thinly into rounds. Scatter over plates and drizzle with remaining dressing.

KIWI FRUIT SMOOTHIE

You can use kiwi fruit straight from the freezer for this pretty speckled smoothie – in which case, omit the ice cubes.

Serves 2

4 kiwi fruit
1 pear
1 tbsp honey
juice of ½ lemon
200 ml (7 fl. oz) apple juice
4 ice cubes

- Put peeled, chopped kiwi fruit and peeled, cored and chopped pear in a blender with the remaining ingredients. Blend until smooth.

KIWI FRUIT RECIPES

EASY BAKED KIWI FRUIT CHEESECAKE

Originally cheesecakes were always cooked in the oven – these days the uncooked type is more popular, but a baked cheesecake is a delight. You can drizzle over some puréed raw kiwi fruit or serve with thin cream.

Serves 6

8 digestive biscuits
50 g (2 oz) butter
600 g (1 lb 6 oz) cream cheese
2 tbsp cornflour
175 g (6 oz) caster sugar
1 tsp vanilla extract
3 eggs
150 ml (¼ pint) sour cream
6 kiwi fruit

- Put biscuits in a plastic bag and crush with a rolling pin. Combine crumbs with melted butter and press into the base of a greased 20 cm (8 in.) loose-bottomed tin.
- Beat together remaining ingredients except the kiwi slices until thoroughly combined and light. Pour half the mixture into the tin.
- Arrange four of the peeled, thinly sliced kiwi fruit in the tin, then gently pour on the remaining mixture. Bake at 180°C/gas mark 4 for 40 minutes until set. Leave to cool for 10 minutes, then turn out.
- Arrange remaining sliced kiwi fruit on top and serve at room temperature or chilled.

KIWI PUFF TARTS

The very short cooking time in this recipe means that the kiwi fruit keep most of their colour. The touch of caramel on top is delicious.

Serves 4

300 g (11 oz) ready-rolled puff pastry
1 egg
5 kiwi fruit
2 tbsp butter
1½ tbsp soft brown sugar

- Roll pastry out on a floured surface into a thin square and cut into four small squares. Make a cut 1 cm (½ in.) from the edge all the way round each one, but don't cut right through. Brush edge with beaten egg.
- Place on a greased baking tray and cook at 200°C/gas mark 6 for 15 minutes, or until golden.
- Press centre of pastry down a little with the back of a tablespoon. Arrange peeled, sliced kiwi fruit on top of each tart inside the rim, sprinkle melted butter and sugar over the fruit and flash under a hot grill for a minute, or until sugar has melted. Serve hot or cold.

Kiwi fruit are widely grown in New Zealand and are named after the famous bird from that country.

MELON

Originating in Asia at least 1,000 years BC, melons are members of the cucumber family. In the UK they are most often eaten as a cold starter or dessert, or as a between-meal snack.

There are three types of melon that you can grow: **Winter** (Casaba), which includes the greeny-yellow-fleshed Honeydew; **Netted** (Musk), which can have green, orange or pink flesh; and **Cantaloupe**, which includes Ogen, Charantais and Galia, which have green or orange flesh. Orange flesh tends to be tastiest and sweetest, and has the highest nutritional value.

Melons have a higher water content than most other fruit – around 93 per cent – so they can be used to quench thirst and make a welcome drink, juiced or added to a smoothie.

STORING

Melons will keep in the fridge for a week or two when ripe. Cut melons should be well wrapped in cling film to prevent their aroma affecting other foods.

Freeze melon in chunks or balls – open-freeze on trays, then bag. It will lose some texture when thawed so is best used for fruit salads or drinks.

NO COOKING REQUIRED

Melon is usually eaten raw. When ripe a melon will give slightly when pressed at the base. You should also be able to smell a faint aroma. It is best served at room temperature to allow the flavours and aromas to come through, so remove it from the fridge about an hour before serving.

To serve melon, cut into wedges and slice out the seed section, then use a large knife to cut the flesh away from the skin so that the flesh remains in one segment. Now cut slices lengthwise about 1 cm (½ in.) apart all the way through, then do the same crosswise so that your melon is in bite-sized cubes. Leave sitting on the skin to serve – but don't eat the skin.

If you want to remove small round balls of the flesh, which look nice for a starter or dessert, you can buy a melon baller.

MELON HALVES

Small round melons can be halved and served simply, with seeds scooped out.

Sprinkle on ground or fresh chopped ginger, or a little sugar if necessary – sweet ripe melons shouldn't need it. Melon halves can also be served filled with other fruit as a dessert.

SIMPLE MELON COCKTAIL

Serve chunks or balls of melon dredged with sugar (sweet wine or brandy or other alcohol can be added). The cocktail looks pretty if you use two melons with different coloured flesh.

MELON AND PARMA HAM

A classic Italian starter or part of an antipasti platter. Serve slices, chunks or balls of melon draped with slices of Parma ham – about 2 slices per serving.

MELON AND MANGO SALAD

You can replace the mango with orange or peach segments, or with berry fruits such as strawberries or raspberries.

Serves 4

100 g (3½ oz) sugar
½ lemon
3 tsp fresh chopped ginger
1 melon
1 mango

- Put sugar in a pan with 175 ml (6 fl. oz) water, grated lemon zest, lemon juice and ginger over medium-low heat until sugar is dissolved. Simmer for 5 minutes. Strain and cool.

- Put melon balls and slices of peeled mango in a serving bowl and pour syrup over. Stir and refrigerate for 2 hours before serving.

MELON AND GINGER ICE CREAM

Stem ginger (ginger preserved in syrup) is a really useful ingredient and a jar will last for years even after it has been opened.

Serves 6

1 orange-fleshed melon
   (approx. 500 g /1¼ lb)
juice of 1 lemon
175 g (6 oz) soft light brown sugar
300 ml (½ pint) whipping cream
50 g (2 oz) stem ginger

- Cut melon into chunks and blend in a blender with lemon juice.
- Stir in sugar and leave to stand at room temperature for an hour, stirring occasionally, until sugar is dissolved.
- Whisk cream to soft peak stage, then combine it with the melon purée and the finely chopped ginger. Spoon into a container and put in the freezer. Remove when half-frozen, beat well to remove ice crystals, then freeze again until solid.

MELON AND LIME SORBET

You can also use this sorbet mixture to fill ice-lolly moulds.

Serves 4

1 orange-fleshed melon
   (approx. 500 g /1¼ lb)
juice of 2 limes
150 g (5 oz) icing sugar

- Cut melon into chunks and blend in a blender with lime juice, adding icing sugar a little at a time until it is all absorbed. Chill.
- Spoon into a container and put in the freezer. Remove when half-frozen, beat thoroughly, then freeze again until solid.

Melon seeds can be eaten as a snack, or sprinkled on cereal or yogurt. Clean and dry them, then cook as for pumpkin seeds (page 145).

SPICY CHICKEN WITH MELON SALSA

Melon salsa makes a nice change from mango salsa with grilled chicken or fish. Jamaican jerk seasoning is available from supermarkets.

Serves 4

2 tsp Jamaican jerk seasoning	1 red onion
4 tbsp olive oil	3 tbsp fresh
juice of 2 limes	chopped coriander
4 skinless chicken breast fillets	salt, black pepper
½ melon	

- Make a paste with the jerk seasoning, 3 tbsp of the oil and the lime juice. Spread half of it on the chicken breasts and bake at 190°C/gas mark 5 until cooked through. Cut into bite-sized pieces.
- Stir remaining oil into the other half of the paste to thin. Combine with chopped melon, finely chopped onion, coriander and seasoning. Serve chicken with the salsa.

CHILLED MELON SOUP

Serve in small bowls as a starter. It is good garnished with pan-crisped crumbled Parma ham. You can omit the alcohol or use white wine instead of sherry.

Serves 2–4

1 melon	1 tbsp olive oil
juice of ½ lemon	salt, black pepper
2 tbsp dry sherry	

- Chop melon and blend in a blender until smooth.
- Combine with lemon juice, sherry, olive oil and seasoning. Chill for an hour.
- Drizzle with more olive oil to serve.

BASIC COOKING

Melon is usually eaten raw in the UK, although some varieties are cooked as a vegetable in Asia. You can pan-fry slices for 1–2 minutes in a little oil and serve as a garnish or side vegetable, or make it into a hot vegetable soup for winter.

MULBERRY

The purple-red fruits of the black mulberry tree are very good to eat. Large and juicy, they have a good balance of sweetness and tartness that makes them the best flavoured species of mulberry. Some people think they taste similar to apples, others to grapefruit. The white mulberry, the leaves of which are prized as food for silkworms, also bears fruit, but the berries aren't so good for cooking or eating. Mulberries on a single tree ripen over a period of time rather than all at once. They also crush easily if picked with the fingers. For this reason, they are best shaken from the tree on to a large sheet of plastic.

Mulberries can be used in almost any recipe given in this book for other berries and go very well with pears and apples. They make good wine and preserves.

STORING

Mulberries are best used immediately but will keep for a few days in a lidded container in the fridge. Raw mulberries don't freeze well, but you can freeze mulberry sauce (below).

NO COOKING REQUIRED

Mulberries are wonderful eaten fresh with cream and a little sugar. They are ideal for adding to fruit salads, ice cream, sorbet, smoothies and almost any recipe where raw berries are used.

MULBERRY SAUCE

To serve 4, put 250 g (9 oz) mulberries in a blender with 50 g (2 oz) sugar and blend until smooth. Press through a sieve if you prefer a smoother sauce. This will keep in the fridge for a week. Use for ice cream or for drizzling over sponge cake, or as a base for a sauce to go with savouries.

MULBERRY AND BANANA SMOOTHIE

To serve 2, put 200 g (7 oz) mulberry sauce, 1 banana and 200 ml (7 fl. oz) raspberry yogurt in a blender and blend until smooth. If too thick, thin with a little water and blend again. Chill before serving, or blend with 2–3 ice cubes.

BASIC COOKING

Mulberries may need washing. Remove stems before using.

SIMMERED MULBERRIES

Good served with cream or ice cream.

Serves 4

**500 g (1¼ lb) mulberries
2½ tbsp caster sugar**

- Put mulberries and sugar in a pan with 1 tbsp water. Heat gently to dissolve sugar, then simmer for 3–4 minutes until fruit is tender.

Mulberries were introduced into Britain during the 17th century as food for silkworms – but the trees were the wrong type and became appreciated instead for their beauty and their fruit.

MULBERRY RECIPES

MULBERRY CRUMB-TOPPED CRUMBLE

A tasty crumble with an unusual topping. Serve with thick cream or ice cream.

Serves 4

1 kg (2¼ lb) mulberries
125 ml (4 fl. oz) fresh apple juice
2 tbsp arrowroot
1½ tbsp fresh chopped mint
2 tsp vanilla extract
75 g (3 oz) sugar
75 g (3 oz) butter
125 g (4 oz) breadcrumbs
75 g (3 oz) chopped mixed nuts
½ tsp salt
1 tsp ground cinnamon

- Combine mulberries, apple juice, arrowroot, mint, vanilla and half the sugar in an ovenproof dish.
- Melt butter and stir into breadcrumbs, combining thoroughly. Add nuts, remaining sugar, salt and cinnamon, then smooth evenly on top of the fruit mixture.
- Bake at 180°C/gas mark 4 for 35 minutes, or until fruit is bubbling and topping is golden.

DOUBLE-CRUST MULBERRY PIE

You can use sweet shortcrust pastry (page 251) for this, and for a change try adding some sliced apples or pears to the filling.

Serves 6

500 g (1¼ lb) shortcrust pastry (page 251)
900 g (2 lb) mulberries
125 g (4 oz) sugar
1 tbsp flour
2 tbsp butter
1 tbsp milk

- Roll out two-thirds of the pastry on a floured surface and line a greased 23 cm (9 in.) pie tin. Roll out remaining pastry to make a lid.
- Combine mulberries with sugar and flour. Put mixture into the lined tin and brush pastry edges with water.
- Dot filling with butter, then cover with the pastry lid. Press edge into the base and trim. Cut slits in the lid and brush with milk.
- Bake at 200°C/gas mark 6 for 15 minutes, then at 180°C/gas mark 4 for a further 25 minutes, or until pastry is golden and fruit bubbling. Cool a little before serving.

MULBERRY CRUNCH CREAMS

A nice and easy dessert for any occasion. Amaretti biscuits are available from supermarkets – or use ginger biscuits or digestives. Use a skewer to stir the desserts gently once or twice before serving to give them a swirly effect.

Serves 4

300 ml (½ pint) mulberry sauce (page 202)
1 tsp arrowroot
250 ml (8 fl. oz) whipping cream
250 ml (8 fl. oz) Greek yogurt
6 amaretti biscuits

- Put mulberry sauce in a pan. Combine arrowroot with 1 tbsp cold water then add to pan, stir and bring to a simmer for 1 minute. Set aside to cool.
- Whip cream and beat in yogurt. Crumble biscuits. Put a layer of cream in the base of each of four dessert glasses and cover with a little of the sauce, then sprinkle with some of the biscuit crumbs. Repeat layers. Chill to serve.

SPICED MULBERRY SAUCE

Try this hot, tangy sauce with game, beef or duck. Cassis is blackcurrant liqueur. If you prefer, you could use kirsch instead.

Serves 4

400 g (14 oz) mulberries
½ orange
juice of ½ lemon
½ tsp ground cinnamon
½ tsp ground ginger
50 g (2 oz) caster sugar
1 tbsp cassis
15 g (½ oz) butter

- Simmer mulberries, grated orange zest, lemon juice, spices and sugar with 2 tbsp water in a covered pan for 5 minutes, or until sugar is dissolved.
- Uncover and simmer for a further 5 minutes to reduce the liquid.
- Stir in cassis, then add butter and stir until melted.

PEACH AND NECTARINE

Neither peaches nor nectarines (which are even more delicate) are easy to grow anywhere but in the warmest areas of the country – so if you do have some in your garden or greenhouse they will undoubtedly be precious to you. The gardener's first choice is to eat them raw, but they can be used in a number of simple recipes. All the recipes here can be used for either peaches or nectarines.

STORING

Store peaches or nectarines in the fridge in a lidded container for a week or two. Bring to room temperature before eating. To freeze: stone, slice and open-freeze, or bag and freeze. They will keep for several months and, although some texture will be lost, will be useful for cooked dishes.

Peaches and nectarines can be dried: put them in the oven on the lowest setting for 4–5 hours. They can also be bottled (see Bottling Fruit, page 239).

NO COOKING REQUIRED

A ripe peach or nectarine is one of the best fruits to eat raw – juicy, sweet and refreshing. Serve with some goat's cheese or a handful of fresh nuts. A raw peach or nectarine purée (made by peeling the fruit and blending the flesh in a blender) is good drizzled over other fruits or ice cream, or added to cocktails.

PEACH MELBA

Everyone's favourite fruit and ice cream dessert. It is named after Dame Nellie Melba, the Australian opera singer for whom it was invented at London's Savoy Hotel in 1893.

Serves 4

4 peaches
4 scoops vanilla ice cream
200 ml (7 fl. oz) raspberry coulis (page 216)
handful flaked almonds

- Arrange peeled, sliced peaches in four dessert glasses. Top each with a scoop of ice cream and pour coulis over. Scatter nuts over.

BELLINI

This famous peach and Prosecco cocktail was invented in 1934 at Harry's Bar, Venice – which is still going strong today. You can use any sparkling wine or champagne.

Serves 4

2 peaches   ½ bottle chilled Prosecco

- Peel and stone peaches and blend in a blender until smooth. Transfer to a lidded container and chill for several hours.

- Spoon a quarter of the purée into each of four champagne glasses. Slowly add wine to each glass, stirring to combine. Serve immediately.

BASIC COOKING

Some peach recipes require the skin to be removed. To skin, either make a cross with a knife in the base of the fruit, then immerse it in boiling water for 30 seconds, after which the skin will come off easily; or simply peel with a very sharp knife.

POACHED PEACHES OR NECTARINES

Halve and stone the fruit and put in a pan with enough water to cover. Add 1 tbsp sugar for every 100 ml (3½ fl. oz) water and heat gently to dissolve. Simmer for 5 minutes.

BAKED PEACHES OR NECTARINES

Halve and stone the fruit and put in a lightly greased baking dish. Dot with butter and drizzle honey or soft brown sugar over. Bake at 180°C/gas mark 4 for 20 minutes, or until tender, basting halfway through.

PEACH AND NECTARINE RECIPES

CARAMELIZED PEACHES WITH MACAROONS

Macaroons are rich in almonds so they go well with peaches. Try adding a dash of Amaretto to the pan.

Serves 4

50 g (2 oz) butter
2 tbsp runny honey
3 peaches
100 g (3½ oz) strawberries

4 macaroons
200 ml (7 fl. oz) vanilla
   ice cream

- Melt butter in a frying pan and add honey. Stir to form a light caramel sauce.
- Add sliced peaches and cook over medium-high heat for 2–3 minutes, turning once, until golden.
- Serve warm peaches and sliced strawberries with the pan juices drizzled over and the macaroons and ice cream on the side.

ZABAGLIONE WITH PEACHES

A classic light Italian dessert.

Serves 4

4 peaches
100 g (3½ oz) caster sugar

100 ml (3½ fl. oz) Marsala
4 egg yolks

- Put peeled, chopped peaches in a pan with 25 g (1 oz) of the sugar and 50 ml (2 fl. oz) of the Marsala. Cook over medium-high heat for 3 minutes. Spoon into dessert glasses and cool.
- Put egg yolks and remaining sugar into a heatproof bowl. Whisk for 5 minutes until thick and pale yellow.
- Set bowl over a pan of simmering water and whisk continuously for a further 5–10 minutes, adding remaining Marsala in a thin dribble. When the mixture has increased in volume and looks foamy, remove from heat, continue beating for 30 seconds, then spoon on to peaches and serve immediately.

PEACH COBBLER

A proper old-fashioned cobbler is a savoury or sweet casserole topped with individual scones – and here is a good example. Excellent with custard (page 250) or thin cream.

Serves 4

6 peaches
juice of ½ lemon
50 g (2 oz) soft light
   brown sugar

75 g (3 oz) butter
150 g (5 oz) self-raising flour
50 g (2 oz) caster sugar
150 ml (¼ pint) milk

- Put peeled, sliced peaches in a fairly deep ovenproof dish. Stir in lemon juice and soft light brown sugar.
- Rub butter and flour together to resemble breadcrumbs, then stir in two-thirds of the caster sugar and enough milk to make a soft dough.
- Roll out to 1 cm (½ in.) thick on a floured surface then cut into small rounds (use a small glass or egg cup).
- Lay the rounds evenly on the peaches. Brush with remaining milk and sprinkle with remaining caster sugar. Bake at 200°C/gas mark 6 for about 25 minutes, or until golden.

PEACH SLICES

An easy way to make pretty individual peach tarts. You can sprinkle on some blueberries before baking.

Serves 4–6

350 g (12 oz) ready-rolled puff pastry
100 g (3½ oz) ground almonds
65 g (2½ oz) caster sugar
1 egg
4 peaches
1 egg yolk
3 tbsp peach jam

- Roll out pastry thinly and cut into four or six equal pieces. Place on a lightly greased baking tray.
- Beat together ground almonds, 50 g (2 oz) of the caster sugar and the egg. Spread mixture over the pastry slices, leaving a 1 cm (½ in.) rim round the edges.
- Arrange thinly sliced peaches on the almond mixture. Brush pastry edges with beaten egg yolk, sprinkle peaches with remaining caster sugar and bake at 220°C/gas mark 7 for 8–10 minutes until pastry is risen and golden.
- Glaze fruit with the melted jam.

PEAR

Depending on the variety of your tree, you can have fresh pears from early August through to Christmas for use both in recipes and as a snack that everyone loves.

While 'cooking' pear trees are available to plant, it is better to choose all dessert varieties – firm dessert pears cook just as well, and their flavour and texture are often better than that of the cookers.

Popular varieties of pear include Conference – a firm mid-season variety ideal for cooking; Doyenne du Comice – the juiciest and tastiest of all pears for late picking and storage; Concorde – a late-pick cross between Conference and Comice and a good all-rounder; and Williams' Bon Chretien – a mid-season pear with good flavour but which doesn't keep.

STORING

Bring pears into the house from the tree when barely ripe and let them finish ripening inside. Early varieties are ready in August but won't store well. Perfect, slightly under-ripe, late-season pears will keep for several months – certainly until Christmas – if stored carefully. Store in stout boxes and make sure they are not touching each other. Keep in layers between newspaper in a cool but frost-free, dry, dark place. Check weekly for signs of rotting. Bring pears into the kitchen for a few days to finish ripening before eating.

Pears will freeze, but they lose a lot of texture when thawed. They are best frozen in syrup: peel, core and quarter or slice the pears, dipping them into lemon juice as you do so to prevent browning. Poach 2 kg (4½ lb) pears in a syrup of 450 g (1 lb) sugar to every 1 litre (1¾ pints) water for 10 minutes, put into containers, then freeze. You can also make a purée of lightly poached peeled pears using a blender, then freeze in bags for use in cakes, desserts etc. If you have a glut, make chutney as for apple chutney (page 240).

NO COOKING REQUIRED

A ripe, juicy pear is a feast on its own – just quarter, core and eat. Pears marry well with strong cheeses such as Stilton, farmhouse Cheddar and Roquefort, and are ideal for inclusion in a ploughman's lunch. They also go well with nuts, particularly walnuts, almonds and pecans. You can juice them, or use them puréed in smoothies or drizzled over cake.

PEAR AND BANANA SMOOTHIE

A quick smoothie all the family will enjoy. You can use pear juice instead of apple juice. Serve chilled.

Serves 2

1 ripe juicy pear
1 banana
1 tbsp runny honey
125 ml (4 fl. oz) natural yogurt
250 ml (8 fl. oz) apple juice

- Peel, core and chop pear, peel and chop banana. Put all ingredients in a blender and blend until smooth.

PEAR, STILTON AND WALNUT SALAD

Use Stilton, St-Agur or Roquefort cheese for this tasty lunch or starter salad. Serve with a little crusty bread.

Serves 4

3 pears	**75 g (3 oz) walnut halves**
50 g (2 oz) watercress	**4 tbsp French dressing**
25 g (1 oz) rocket	**(page 250)**
200 g (7 oz) Stilton	

- Core pears and cut each into eight slices. Arrange on serving plates with watercress and rocket.
- Crumble cheese over the top, sprinkle on nuts, then drizzle dressing over.

BASIC COOKING

If you peel pears the cut surfaces will go brown – rub with a cut lemon.

POACHED PEARS

Peel, core and halve, quarter or slice pears (as recipe requires) and put them in a pan with enough water to cover and 1–2 tsp lemon juice and ½ tbsp caster sugar for each pear. (You can omit the sugar if the pears are very sweet or if the recipe contains added sugar.) Simmer over low heat until pears are tender when pierced with a sharp knife – this will take 5–20 minutes. They will store in a lidded container in the fridge, covered in their cooking liquid, for a day or two.

BAKED PEARS

Halve pears, brush cut sides with lemon juice and scoop out cores. Lay pear halves in an oiled baking dish, dot with butter and sprinkle with a little caster sugar. Bake at 190°C/gas mark 5 for 20 minutes, or until tender.

FRIED PEARS

Slice or quarter pears, add to a frying pan with 10 g (¼ oz) butter and 2 tsp sugar for every pear. Stir until pear slices are soft and golden and there is a little caramel sauce.

PEAR RECIPES

PEAR AND BLUEBERRY CRUMBLE

Some people think pears make an even better crumble than apples. You can omit blueberries, or combine apples and pears. Serve with custard (page 250), cream or ice cream.

Serves 4–6

6 pears
1 lemon
50 g (2 oz) caster sugar
100 g (3½ oz) blueberries
2 tsp arrowroot
150 g (5 oz) cold butter
175 g (6 oz) plain flour
100 g (3½ oz) demerara sugar
75 g (3 oz) chopped mixed nuts
50 g (2 oz) porridge oats

- Poach peeled, cored and sliced pears with grated lemon zest, lemon juice, sugar and 100 ml (3½ fl. oz) water until tender – about 5 minutes.
- Transfer pears using a slotted spoon to a shallow ovenproof dish and scatter blueberries around. Combine arrowroot with 1 tbsp cold water, stir into pear juices and heat until thickened. Pour around pears.
- Rub butter into flour with your fingertips until it resembles fine breadcrumbs. Stir in sugar, chopped nuts and oats. Sprinkle crumble mixture evenly over the pears.
- Bake at 180°C/gas mark 4 for 25–30 minutes until topping is golden.

Unlike many other fruits, it is very rare for pears to cause an allergic reaction.

PEARS IN RED WINE

This is a simple dessert which always works if you have good-quality pears. To make sure the pears are covered, use a pan just big enough to fit them in side by side. You can, of course, slice the pears, in which case halve the remaining ingredients and cooking time – but it won't look as good!

Serves 4

600 ml (1 pint) red wine	**1 stick cinnamon**
225 g (8 oz) caster sugar	**4 large pears**

- Put wine in saucepan with sugar and cinnamon. Warm to dissolve sugar.
- Peel pears but keep stalks on. Drop each pear into the wine when it is peeled. They should stand upright, close together and completely covered by wine.
- Simmer for 20–30 minutes, or until pears are tender and a rich red colour. Remove them from the pan.
- Bring wine to the boil and cook until reduced by at least half to a thick syrup. Cool to room temperature. Serve the pears with some of the syrup spooned over.

PEARS BELLE HÉLÈNE

A classic French dish. For adults, add a drizzle of Poire William liqueur to the finished dessert. Ready-made chocolate sauce is available from supermarkets.

Serves 4

50 g (2 oz) sugar
juice of ½ lemon
1 tsp vanilla extract

4 pears
4 scoops vanilla ice cream
100 ml (3½ fl. oz) dark chocolate sauce

100 ml (3½ fl. oz) cream
2 tbsp walnut pieces

- Put sugar, lemon juice and vanilla in a pan with 300 ml (½ pint) water and bring to a simmer. Cook until sugar is dissolved.

- Peel, core and quarter pears, add to the syrup (they should be completely covered in the liquid) and simmer for 5–10 minutes until soft – the riper they are, the shorter the cooking time. Cool.

- Put a scoop of ice cream in each of four dessert glasses, top with pears and 1 tbsp of the cooking liquid, then chocolate sauce. Lightly whip cream and spoon over top. Sprinkle on nuts.

STICKY PEAR SPONGE CAKE

A tasty treat for a dessert. Serve with some sour or clotted cream.

Serves 8

150 g (5 oz) caster sugar	½ tsp salt
100 g (3½ oz) butter	1 tsp vanilla extract
3 eggs	5 pears
3 tbsp milk	2 tbsp maple syrup
150 g (5 oz) plain flour	juice of ½ lemon
1 tsp baking powder	

- Cream sugar and butter until light and fluffy. Gradually beat in eggs. Stir in milk. Sift in flour, baking powder and salt. Add vanilla extract.

- Peel and finely chop three of the pears and stir into the mixture.

- Pour mixture into a greased cake tin lined with lightly greased baking parchment. Peel and slice remaining pears and arrange on top of the mixture.

- Bake at 180°C/gas mark 4 for 40 minutes, or until the cake has risen and is lightly golden. Combine maple syrup and lemon juice. Make a few holes in the top of the cake with a skewer and drizzle the syrup over. Return the cake to the oven for a further 5 minutes.

- Cool in the tin for 10 minutes, then turn out on to a plate. Serve warm or cold.

PEAR AND GINGER TRAYBAKE

A great little cake for lunchboxes or parties.

Makes 16 small squares

175 g (6 oz) golden caster sugar	175 g (6 oz) self-raising flour
100 g (3½ oz) softened butter	1 tsp baking powder
2 eggs	½ tsp salt
1 tbsp stem ginger + syrup	3 pears

- Cream sugar and butter until light and fluffy. Gradually beat in eggs. Stir in finely chopped ginger and syrup. Sift in flour, baking powder and salt.

- Stir peeled, cored and chopped pears into the mixture and pour it into a greased 20 cm (8 in.) square shallow baking tin lined with lightly greased baking parchment. Bake at 190°C/gas mark 5 for 30 minutes, or until golden and firm to the touch.

- Cool in the tin for 10 minutes, then turn out on to a wire rack until cold. Cut into squares.

Pears go well with dark chocolate, walnuts, almonds, apples, blue cheese, cinnamon and ginger.

PEAR AND CHOCOLATE TART

Pears and chocolate are a winning combination and this tart will prove a favourite.

Serves 6

350 g (12 oz) shortcrust pastry (page 251)	125 ml (4 fl. oz) golden syrup
6 pears	2 eggs
3 tbsp caster sugar	½ tsp vanilla extract
75 g (3 oz) dark chocolate	100 g (3½ oz) walnut pieces
75 g (3 oz) butter	

- Roll out pastry and line a greased 23 cm (9 in.) tart tin. Bake blind.

- Poach peeled, cored and quartered pears with caster sugar (see page 207), then remove from the pan and reserve the poaching liquid.

- Melt chocolate and butter in a bowl over a pan of simmering water. Add syrup and stir for a minute. Whisk eggs into mixture. Stir in poaching liquid, vanilla extract and walnuts.

- Arrange pear quarters (rounded sides uppermost) in the pastry case and pour sauce over. Bake for 25–30 minutes, or until filling is set. Cool in the tin.

PEAR AND CHOCOLATE BROWNIES

Moist, juicy pears help lift basic chocolate brownies and make them truly delicious. Try this as a dessert with sour cream.

Makes 20 squares

200 g (7 oz) dark chocolate
250 g (9 oz) butter
250 g (9 oz) caster sugar
3 eggs
175 g (6 oz) self-raising flour
3 tbsp cocoa powder
2 pears
100 g (3½ oz) chopped mixed nuts

- Melt chocolate and butter in a bowl over a pan of simmering water.

- Cream sugar and eggs together until light and fluffy. Gradually pour in melted chocolate mixture and combine.

- Fold in flour and cocoa powder, then stir in peeled, cored and chopped pears and the nuts.

- Pour mixture into a greased shallow 30 cm x 20 cm (12 in. x 8 in.) tin lined with lightly greased baking parchment. Bake at 180°C/gas mark 4 for 30–35 minutes until the brownies are just set. Remove from the oven and allow to cool in the tin. Cut into squares.

PLUM

Plums, gages and damsons are delicious and useful mid- to late-summer stone fruits. Depending on the variety, they make great desserts, cakes, pies, ice cream or drinks and can be used for chutneys and preserves (see Chapter 8).

Dessert plums, which range from yellow through red to purple and include well-known varieties such as Victoria or Early Laxton, are best for eating raw, but they can also be used for cooking. The most usual culinary type is Czar, but this can also be eaten as a dessert plum if really ripe.

Gages, often called greengages, are smaller, round fruits with a yellow-green skin and flesh. Sweet and delicious, they can be used in similar ways to the plum.

Purple-skinned and fleshed damsons are too sour to eat raw but they have intense flavour and, being rich in pectin, make excellent jams, jellies and chutneys. They can also be cooked in a similar way to plums in desserts and cakes, but will need additional sweetening.

STORING

Ripe plums will keep for a few days in the house. Plums freeze quite well – halve, stone and bag, or freeze in syrup with lemon juice to prevent browning (see method for pears, page 206). Damsons can be frozen whole and used later for jams etc. Plums can be halved and dried (see method for apricots, page 176).

NO COOKING REQUIRED

Dessert plums and gages are lovely fruits to eat straight from the tree.

DAMSON GIN

An easy liqueur to make. Wash the damsons and prick with a needle or point of a sharp knife. Put in a sterilized jar with 150 g (5 oz) caster sugar and 1 litre (1¾ pints) gin for every 500 g (1¼ lb) damsons. Seal and leave for 3 months. Strain liquid off damsons if you prefer, or leave as is. Drink within a year.

BASIC COOKING

Plums and gages should be stoned before cooking. When they are ripe this is easy. Halve or, if whole plums are needed, make a slit in one side and remove stone by hand. Damsons are easier cooked whole – the stones can be removed from the pan quite easily. If they need to be stoned before use, halve and stone as for plums.

SIMMERED PLUMS

Stone and simmer whole or halved plums over medium-low heat with 2 tbsp water and ½ tbsp sugar for every 100 g (3½ oz) dessert plums/gages or 1 tbsp sugar for culinary plums. A vanilla pod can be added. Cook for 5–10 minutes, or until tender. Try with yogurt or breakfast cereal.

SIMMERED DAMSONS

Simmer damsons whole without stoning with 1½ tbsp sugar and 2 tbsp water for every 100 g (3½ oz) fruit. Cook for 10 minutes until broken up and mushy – the stones will be easy to remove with a slotted spoon.

PURÉED PLUMS

Cook as for simmering, but quarter plums and cook until completely broken up. Add 10 g (¼ oz) butter for every 3 plums used and stir well until butter is melted. Can be stirred through whipped cream or spooned over ice cream.

PURÉED DAMSONS

Simmer as for damsons, remove stones and stir in 10 g (¼ oz) butter for every 6 damsons.

ROAST PLUMS

Toss halved, stoned plums in 10 g (¼ oz) melted butter with ½ tbsp sugar for every 100 g (3½ oz) plums. Put in a baking dish and cook at 190°C/gas mark 5 for 20 minutes, or until tender. Try eating them on buttered toast.

PLUM RECIPES

PLUM DUFF

A plum duff is an old-fashioned steamed fruit pudding, similar to a Christmas pudding. Good with cream or custard.

Serves 6

125 g (4 oz) self-raising flour
125 g (4 oz) breadcrumbs
125 g (4 oz) suet
100 g (3½ oz) soft light brown sugar
100 g (3½ oz) currants
125 g (4 oz) sultanas
1 tsp mixed spice
275 g (10 oz) plums
1 dessert apple
1 orange
2 tbsp rum
2 eggs
200 ml (7 fl. oz) milk

- Combine flour, breadcrumbs, suet, sugar, currants, sultanas and spice in a large bowl. Add the stoned, chopped plums and peeled, chopped apple.

- Add grated orange zest and orange juice, rum and beaten eggs. Mix thoroughly. Stir in enough milk to give a good dropping consistency.

- Spoon mixture into a 1 litre (1¾ pint) greased pudding basin and cover with a folded sheet of greaseproof paper. Secure with string.

- Sit the pudding basin on a heatproof saucer or rack in a large lidded pan. Half-fill the pan with boiling water and put the lid on. Steam for 3 hours, adding extra water several times as necessary. Cool for 10 minutes before opening the cover, then turn out on to a plate to serve.

PLUM PIE

We've been eating and enjoying plum pies for hundreds of years. Try this one and you will understand why.

Serves 6

1 kg (2¼ lb) plums
150 g (5 oz) caster sugar
½ tsp ground cloves
1 tbsp cornflour
500 g (1¼ lb) shortcrust pastry (page 251)
1 egg

- Simmer stoned and quartered plums, 125 g (4 oz) of the sugar and the cloves in a pan with 2 tbsp water until sugar is dissolved and plums are barely tender – test with a sharp knife after 5 minutes.
- Mix cornflour with 1 tbsp of the cooled pan juices, stir into the fruit and simmer for a minute to thicken.
- Roll out two-thirds of the pastry on a floured surface and line a greased 23 cm (9 in.) deep pie dish; let the pastry hang over the edges a little. Spoon the plum mixture in and brush the pastry edge with a little water.
- Roll out the remaining pastry to make a lid. Lay it on and press the edges into the base, trim off any surplus and make a hole in the centre of the lid with a knife.
- Brush with beaten egg and sprinkle with remaining sugar. Bake at 200°C/gas mark 6 for 25–30 minutes, or until golden. Cool for 10 minutes before serving.

PLUM BREAD AND BUTTER PUDDING

A delightful family pudding. Serve with vanilla ice cream.

Serves 4

800 g (1¾ lb) plums
6 thin slices white bread
50 g (2 oz) butter
2 eggs
125 ml (4 fl. oz) cream
25 g (1 oz) caster sugar
½ tsp ground cinnamon
1 tbsp demerara sugar

- Simmer stoned, sliced plums in 2 tbsp water until just tender – about 10 minutes – and spoon into a baking dish.
- Remove crusts from bread, and butter generously. Cut each slice into four triangles and arrange on top of the plums, pressing down lightly.
- Beat eggs, cream, caster sugar and cinnamon together, and pour over the plums and bread. Sprinkle demerara sugar on top. Bake at 180°C/gas mark 4 for 20 minutes, or until golden.

PLUM CAKE

A simple cake that goes well with morning coffee.

Serves 10

150 g (5 oz) butter
150 g (5 oz) caster sugar
3 eggs
75 g (3 oz) plain flour
1 tsp baking powder
100 g (3½ oz) ground almonds
50 g (2 oz) walnut pieces
500 g (1¼ lb) plums

- Cream butter and sugar until light and fluffy, then gradually beat in eggs. Sift flour and baking powder into the mixture. Stir in almonds and walnut pieces.
- Spoon mixture into a greased 23 cm (9 in.) cake tin lined with lightly greased baking parchment and scatter stoned, quartered plums on top. Bake at 180°C/gas mark 4 for 40–45 minutes, or until golden and a skewer inserted in the centre comes out clean. Cool in the tin for 15 minutes, then turn out on to a wire rack to cool completely.

PLUM SAUCE

This slightly spicy sauce goes well with pork or duck. It looks best if red- or purple-fleshed plums are used.

Serves 4

3 shallots
1 tbsp oil
1 tsp fresh chopped ginger
½ tsp ground cumin
½ tsp ground coriander
6 plums
2 tbsp red wine vinegar
4 tbsp soft light brown sugar
1 tsp Worcestershire sauce

- Sweat finely chopped shallots in oil over low heat for 7 minutes. Add spices. Stir for a further minute.
- Add stoned chopped plums and remaining ingredients, bring to a simmer and cook for 6–8 minutes until you have a rough sauce.

GREENGAGE AND CUSTARD TART

You can use sweet shortcrust pastry (page 251) for this and quartered plums instead of greengages.

Serves 6

350 g (12 oz) shortcrust pastry (page 251)
1 kg (2¼ lb) greengages
3 eggs
100 g (3½ oz) icing sugar
300 ml (½ pint) cream
1 tbsp demerara sugar

- Roll out pastry into a round and line a greased 23 cm (9 in.) tart tin. Bake blind, then arrange stoned, halved greengages inside.
- Beat together eggs, icing sugar and cream, and pour over fruit. Sprinkle with demerara sugar and bake at 200°C/gas mark 6 for 30–40 minutes.

GREENGAGE AND BANANA FLAMBÉ

An easy flambé for a quick but impressive dessert. Serve with cream or ice cream.

Serves 4

12 greengages	**2 tbsp caster sugar**
2 bananas	**2 tbsp brandy**
65 g (2½ oz) butter	

- Sauté stoned, halved greengages (cut side down) and sliced bananas in butter in a large frying pan over medium-high heat for 2 minutes. Sprinkle caster sugar over and stir gently until caramelized – about 2 minutes.
- Turn up heat to high, pour on brandy and light with a match. Cook for a further 1–2 minutes after the flames have died down.

DAMSON ICE CREAM

An attractive ice cream with a great tangy taste.

Serves 4

500 g (1¼ lb) damsons	**125 g (4 oz) icing sugar**
125 g (4 oz) caster sugar	**300 ml (½ pint)**
4 egg yolks	**double cream**

- Simmer whole damsons with caster sugar and 250 ml (8 fl. oz) water until tender and broken up – about 10 minutes. Press through a sieve and discard sieve contents. Chill for an hour.
- In a bowl set over a pan of simmering water, but not touching the water, whisk egg yolks with icing sugar for 10 minutes. Remove bowl from pan and continue beating until the volume has increased and the mixture is light.
- Whisk cream to soft peak stage. Combine damsons, egg mixture and cream, spoon into a container and put in the freezer.
- When half frozen, remove from freezer and beat again to remove ice crystals. Freeze until solid. Leave at room temperature for 15 minutes before serving.

DAMSON SWIRL DESSERT

Easy and pretty.

Serves 4

250 g (9 oz) Mascarpone	**100 ml (3½ fl. oz) milk**
2 tbsp icing sugar	**300 g (11 oz) damson purée**
1 tsp vanilla extract	**3 digestive biscuits**

- Beat Mascarpone with icing sugar and vanilla. Beat in milk.
- Spoon half the mixture into four dessert glasses, then top with half the damson purée. Repeat the layers, then use a skewer to swirl the mixture a little.
- Crush biscuits and top each dessert with some of the crumbs. Chill for 30 minutes.

DAMSON MUFFINS

The sweet, soft texture of muffins is lifted by the sharp acidity of damsons.

Makes 12

275 g (10 oz) plain flour
2 tsp baking powder
½ tsp bicarbonate of soda
200 g (7 oz) caster sugar
1 egg
50 ml (2 fl. oz) milk
100 ml (3½ fl. oz) vegetable oil
250 ml (8 fl. oz) natural yogurt
350 g (12 oz) damsons

- Sift flour, baking powder and bicarbonate of soda into a large mixing bowl and stir in the sugar.
- Beat together egg and milk, then stir in oil and yogurt. Combine wet and dry ingredients. Stir in stoned, chopped damsons.
- Spoon mixture into paper cases in a 12-hole muffin tin and bake at 180°C/gas mark 4 for 15 minutes, or until muffins spring back when pressed. Cool on a wire rack.

DAMSON AND BANANA SMOOTHIE

This has a great colour and a deep, satisfying taste.

Serves 2

150 g (5 oz) damsons
40 g (1½ oz) sugar
1 large banana

- Simmer damsons with sugar and 150 ml (¼ pint) water. Remove stones.
- Put damsons into a blender with roughly chopped banana and blend until smooth. Add a little more water if necessary. Chill to serve.

QUINCE

People with a quince tree growing in the garden often wonder what to do with the fruit. Quinces look a little like pears or apples with yellow skin (often covered in a woolly 'fur'), but they are rock-hard. Raw, their flesh looks gritty and pale. However, once properly cooked, they turn a delicate pink colour, becoming a really excellent fruit with a beautiful flavour and distinctive aroma – some say of roses, others of pineapple. Use them in recipes to replace all or part of apples or pears (remembering that they need longer cooking); chunks of poached quince added to an apple pie or crumble will lift the flavour. Add them to Moroccan tagines, or use them as a side dish for meats or as a salad ingredient. Quinces also make very good jelly (page 238) and the paste (Membrillo, sometimes called quince 'cheese') made from them is world-famous.

STORING

Quinces should be picked before a frost and stored in a cool dry place. If they are not yet ripe when picked they will be greenish rather than golden yellow and it can take up to 8 weeks for them to ripen fully. If you bring some into the house and leave them in a bowl, they will ripen more quickly – you will soon smell their aroma. They will remain hard even when ripe. Quinces should be stored separately from other foods, or kept well wrapped, as their aroma can taint other produce. Freeze as a purée or in their poaching syrup.

NO COOKING REQUIRED

Quinces are extremely hard when raw and need to be cooked.

BASIC COOKING

These hard fruits are not the easiest things to peel, but most recipes require this. The best way is to halve them with a cleaver (taking care that the blade doesn't slip off the fruit) and then peel and core them with a small serrated knife.

POACHED QUINCE

Peel, core and slice quinces into a pan with enough water to cover and 1 tbsp caster sugar for every 125 ml (4 fl. oz) water. Simmer for 30–45 minutes, or until tender. Flavourings, such as grated lemon zest or spices, can be added – remove before serving.

ROAST QUINCE

Halve quinces and put in a baking dish. Sprinkle with soft brown sugar and dot with butter, then roast at 190°C/gas mark 5 for 45 minutes, or until tender. Alternatively, you can poach peeled, quartered quinces for 20 minutes, then drain and roast, dotted with butter, for 30 minutes.

PURÉED QUINCE

Drain poached quinces from most of their cooking juice and blend in a blender. Check taste and add more sugar as necessary.

For over 4,000 years quince trees have grown in Asia and the Mediterranean area. The first mention of them in the UK was in the 13th century.

MEMBRILLO (QUINCE PASTE)

A great way of using up a glut of quinces. The paste is useful for making canapés with cheese or olives, or for serving with cold meats. Try in sandwiches or spread on toast.

Makes 900 g (2 lb)

500 g (1¼ lb) quince purée
½ tsp ground cinnamon
1 tsp salt
400 g (14 oz) caster sugar

- Put quince purée in a pan over low heat with cinnamon and salt and gradually add sugar, stirring until it is dissolved.
- Cook, stirring until the mixture thickens into a paste and has turned a reddish-brown colour.
- Pour into a lightly greased shallow dish, then leave to cool and set. It will keep in the fridge for several weeks. It can also be poured into a wide-necked sterilized jar to set and will keep as for jam – see Tips, page 235.

SPICED QUINCE

Serve in a little of their juice to accompany hot dishes, or strain off liquid when using them for salads. Spiced quince also makes a perfect sauce to serve with duck, goose, game or even turkey. Will store in the fridge in a lidded container for a week or two.

Serves 8

4 quinces	**black pepper**
½ cinnamon stick	**200 g (7 oz) caster sugar**
1 tsp whole cloves	**1 lemon**
1 bay leaf	**2 tbsp cider vinegar**
2 cm (¾ in.) piece peeled ginger	

- Put peeled, sliced quinces in a pan with remaining ingredients and enough water to just cover.
- Heat gently until sugar is dissolved, then simmer, covered, for 30–45 minutes, or until tender. Drain (the juice can be reserved for a jelly).
- For a sauce, blend quince slices in a blender, adding in some of the spices from the pan, to make a coarse purée. Serve at room temperature or reheat with a little of the cooking liquid.

QUINCE RECIPES

WARM SPICY QUINCE AND DUCK SALAD

Another tasty salad – it works very well with cold leftover duck.

Serves 4

4 duck breast fillets
1 tbsp olive oil
salt, black pepper
50 g (2 oz) lamb's lettuce
50 g (2 oz) red cabbage
2 spiced quinces
+ 2 tbsp cooking liquid
4 tbsp French dressing (page 250)
50 g (2 oz) walnut pieces

- Remove skin from duck breasts and slice flesh. Season and stir-fry in oil over medium-high heat for 3–4 minutes until cooked but still a bit pink in the middle.
- Arrange lamb's lettuce and shredded cabbage on four plates and top with the warm duck and spiced quince slices.
- Combine dressing with the 2 tbsp quince cooking liquid.
- Sprinkle walnut pieces over salad, then drizzle dressing over.

QUINCE SALSA

Use this with any grilled meat or poultry, or spoon a little into a blue cheese sandwich.

Serves 4

1 fresh red chilli	**juice of ½ lemon**
2 tbsp olive oil	**½ tsp caster sugar**
2 poached quinces	**salt, black pepper**
1 tsp Dijon mustard	**1 tbsp fresh chopped coriander**

- Stir-fry finely chopped chilli in a little of the oil over medium heat for a minute. Combine warm chopped quinces and chilli in a bowl.
- Mix together remaining oil, mustard, lemon juice, sugar and seasoning, and toss with the quince. Leave to stand for 30 minutes, then stir in the coriander.

RASPBERRY

With early-, mid- and late-season varieties of raspberries growing in the garden, you will never be short of a snack or dessert all through summer and into the autumn.

The deep red berries are suitable for a wide range of recipes and their fine aroma and slightly tart sweetness make them an excellent addition to pies, cakes and desserts, as well as an ideal choice for a home-made ice cream or sorbet.

You can also grow yellow, orange, white and even black varieties, all of which can be used in these recipes.

STORING

Once picked, raspberries will last for a day in a lidded container in the fridge – perhaps another day if they are slightly under-ripe. Bring to room temperature to serve.

Raspberries freeze very well: open-freeze then put in a lidded container. They can also be made into an excellent jam (page 237).

NO COOKING REQUIRED

Handle raspberries as little as possible as they damage easily. If stalks remain on the fruit, pull them away gently, removing the central core. Do not wash unless absolutely necessary – if so, rinse quickly and pat dry, as they rapidly spoil if wet. A plate of raw raspberries – with cream and a little caster sugar – makes a perfect dessert. Serve with a slice of chocolate cake or cheesecake, or with a scoop of ice cream, add to fruit salads or use for a pretty purple-red coulis (below).

RASPBERRY COULIS

Use this easy sauce over ice cream or with cake.

Serves 6–8

**400 g (14 oz) raspberries   juice of 1 lemon
50 g (2 oz) icing sugar**

- Put all ingredients in a blender and blend until smooth. Add water if the mixture is a little thick. Press through a sieve for a smoother finish.

RASPBERRY SMOOTHIE

A nicely coloured and nutritious smoothie. If you use frozen raspberries, leave out the ice cubes.

Serves 2

**300 g (11 oz) fresh or   1 tbsp icing sugar
  frozen raspberries   juice of ½ lemon
1 small banana   3 ice cubes
125 ml (4 fl. oz) natural yogurt**

- Blend all ingredients in a blender. Thin with a little water if necessary and blend again.

KNICKERBOCKER GLORY

This old-fashioned favourite can be made with strawberries instead of raspberries. Ready-made jelly and custard from a supermarket are fine.

Serves 4

**300 ml (½ pint) raspberry jelly (page 219)
300 g (11 oz) raspberries
300 ml (½ pint) vanilla ice cream
300 ml (½ pint) custard (page 250)
100 ml (3½ fl. oz) whipping cream
4 tbsp raspberry coulis**

- Layer jelly, raspberries, ice cream and custard in four tall sundae glasses, then repeat layers.
- Top with whipped cream and coulis. Serve immediately.

Raspberries have been cultivated throughout the Western world for centuries and are related to blackberries and boysenberries. The loganberry is a cross between a blackberry and a raspberry.

RASPBERRY, BANANA AND CHOCOLATE TRIFLE

Perfect for children – and adults who enjoy a nursery dessert occasionally. Try grating chocolate over the top.

Serves 4

200 g (7 oz) chocolate sponge
250 g (9 oz) raspberries + 4 for garnish
8 tbsp raspberry coulis
2 bananas
300 ml (½ pint) thick custard (page 250)
200 ml (7 fl. oz) whipping cream

- Cut up the sponge and divide it between four dessert glasses (sundae glasses are ideal). Add a few raspberries to each and 1 tbsp of coulis. Thinly slice in some banana, then add the rest of the raspberries and coulis.

- Spoon in the custard. Top with whipped cream and garnish each dessert with a raspberry. Chill to serve.

RASPBERRY LIQUEUR

An easy recipe for a delicious 'framboise'.

Makes approx. 1 x 75 cl bottle

900 g (2 lb) raspberries (approx.)
225 g (8 oz) sugar
½ lemon
50 cl vodka (approx.)

- Fill a 1 litre (1¾ pint) jar three-quarters full of crushed raspberries. Add sugar and strips of lemon zest, then pour in the vodka to fill the jar. Seal and leave in a dark, dry place for a month to steep, shaking occasionally.
- Strain through a muslin and then a coffee filter. Put the strained liquid in a clean jar and keep for a month before drinking.

RASPBERRY CRANACHAN

A traditional Scottish recipe often served on Burns Night.

Serves 4

65 g (2½ oz) rolled oats
3 tbsp honey
4 tbsp whisky
300 ml (½ pint) whipping cream
350 g (12 oz) raspberries

- Toast oats in a non-stick frying pan, turning occasionally, until golden. Cool.
- Fold oats, honey and whisky into whipped cream and layer in four dessert glasses with raspberries, finishing with some berries on top. Chill to serve.

RASPBERRY PAVLOVA

Raspberries contrast well with the snowy meringue. You can also use kiwi fruits, strawberries or any fruit with plenty of juice and a little acidity. Golden caster sugar gives a lovely texture, flavour and appearance to the meringue, but plain white is fine.

Serves 6

4 egg whites
225 g (8 oz) golden caster sugar
1 tsp cornflour
1 tsp vinegar
1 tsp vanilla extract
300 ml (½ pint) whipping cream
1 lemon
500 g (1¼ lb) raspberries
4 tbsp raspberry coulis
1 tbsp icing sugar

- Whisk egg whites to soft peak stage. Add caster sugar gradually, whisking thoroughly between each addition. When all sugar is in, continue whisking until meringue is glossy and forms stiff peaks.
- Whisk in cornflour and vinegar. Spoon mixture on to a baking sheet covered with baking parchment and smooth into a circle with a palette knife.
- Bake at 180°C/gas mark 4 for 5 minutes, then turn the oven down to 120°C/gas mark ½ and cook for 1½ hours. Turn the oven off and leave the meringue to cool inside.
- Peel off baking parchment and put the pavlova on a serving dish.
- Stir vanilla into cream and whip to soft peak stage, stir in grated lemon zest, then spoon on to the pavlova.
- Arrange raspberries on top of cream, then drizzle coulis and icing sugar over to serve.

BASIC COOKING

Raspberries are rarely cooked when they are to be eaten alone, but they make excellent additions to recipes.

RASPBERRY GRANITA

An Italian sorbet, a granita has a nice almost slushy texture and makes a great end to a meal.

Serves 4

750 g (1 lb 10 oz) raspberries
150 g (5 oz) granulated sugar
juice and zest of 1 lemon

- Heat all ingredients in a pan over low heat until sugar is dissolved. Turn up heat a little and simmer for 10 minutes. Cool and push through a sieve.
- Pour into a lidded container and partially freeze, then put the mixture into a bowl and beat well to remove ice crystals. Return to the freezer and freeze until solid. Allow to stand at room temperature for 10 minutes before serving.

RASPBERRY RECIPES

EASY BERRY GRATIN

A light adult dessert with a foamy egg and sugar topping – quick to prepare. If you haven't made your own liqueur, you can buy it in miniatures labelled framboise. Or substitute Marsala instead.

Serves 4

400 g (14 oz) raspberries
100 g (3½ oz) blueberries
2 tbsp raspberry liqueur
3 tbsp caster sugar
3 egg yolks
2 tsp cornflour
½ tsp vanilla extract

- Toss fruit with liqueur and 1 tbsp of the sugar. Tip into a shallow ovenproof dish and even out.
- In a bowl set over a pan of simmering water, but not touching the water, beat the remaining sugar with the egg yolks, cornflour and vanilla until the mixture is light, pale and foamy and makes a light trail when you lift the whisk. Remove from heat and spoon over fruit. Bake at 200°C/gas mark 6 for 10 minutes.

RASPBERRY CAKE

A moist and lovely cake. Try serving with some crème fraîche for afternoon tea.

Serves 10

225 g (8 oz) butter at room temperature
225 g (8 oz) caster sugar
4 eggs
225 g (8 oz) self-raising flour
½ tsp baking powder
½ tsp salt
25 g (1 oz) ground almonds
275 g (10 oz) raspberries
100 ml (3½ fl. oz) raspberry coulis

- Cream butter and sugar until light and fluffy. Gradually beat in eggs, sift in flour, baking powder and salt, and combine thoroughly. Stir in ground almonds.
- Fold in three-quarters of the raspberries and the coulis. Spoon the mixture into a greased 20 cm (8 in.) square cake tin lined with lightly greased baking parchment. Arrange remaining raspberries on top.
- Bake at 180°C/gas mark 4 for about 50 minutes, or until a skewer inserted into the centre comes out clean. Cool in the tin for 15 minutes, then put on a wire rack to cool completely.

RASPBERRY FLAPJACKS

Flapjacks are delicious but very sweet – the raspberries give them a perfect fruity finish.

Makes 8

125 g (4 oz) butter
100 g (3½ oz) demerara sugar
2 tbsp golden syrup
250 g (9 oz) rolled oats
250 g (9 oz) raspberries

- Melt butter with sugar and syrup over medium heat. Mix in oats. Lightly crush raspberries with a fork.
- Press half the flapjack mixture into a greased 20 cm (8 in.) square shallow baking tin. Arrange raspberries over the top.
- Finish with remaining flapjack mixture, smoothing it down evenly. Bake at 180°C/gas mark 4 for 25 minutes, or until golden. Cool a little, then mark into eight oblongs. Leave to cool completely, then remove from tin and cut through markings.

RASPBERRY JELLY

Raspberries make a particularly good dessert jelly as it comes out such a lovely crimson colour. This jelly has whole raspberries in it for added juiciness and interest.

Serves 6

500 g (1¼ lb) raspberries
150 g (5 oz) caster sugar
5 leaves gelatine

- Simmer three-quarters of the raspberries in a pan with the sugar and 400 ml (14 fl. oz) water over low heat until sugar is dissolved. Cool a little, then press through a sieve into a clean pan. Keep warm.
- Soak gelatine in a bowl of cold water until soft. Squeeze out excess water, then stir gelatine into raspberry mixture until completely dissolved. Stir in remaining raspberries and pour jelly into a 1 litre (1¾ pint) terrine-shaped jelly mould.
- Chill overnight to set completely, then turn out on to a plate. Cut into slices to serve.

Each raspberry is made up of numerous smaller fruits called 'drupelets' which are clustered around a central core or 'receptacle'.

STRAWBERRY

The nation's favourite summer fruit – and strawberries eaten straight from the garden taste so much better than shop-bought ones, particularly if you are growing a variety such as the flavoursome Elsanta or Tenira, or the small and juicy Bounty. Make the most of these fruits – the season is relatively short if you grow just one variety, but if you grow early, mid and late varieties you can be eating strawberries for several months. Wild (alpine) strawberries extend the season into autumn – they are tiny but have a good flavour. While strawberries are usually used raw in recipes (cooking can lead to loss of flavour and colour), they make an excellent jam (page 237).

STORING

Once picked (preferably in the morning and when the fruits are dry) strawberries will last for a day (with their stalks intact) in a lidded container in the fridge – perhaps another day if they are slightly under-ripe. Bring to room temperature to serve.

Whole strawberries don't freeze as well as other berries, but if slightly under-ripe berries are open-frozen or packed in containers they can be used for cooked recipes. Freeze as a purée or coulis. If you have a glut, make jam (page 237) or strawberry liqueur (follow recipe for raspberry liqueur, page 218).

NO COOKING REQUIRED

Straight from the garden and held by their stalks, strawberries make an instant good and thirst-quenching snack. Discard the central core ('hull') and serve with sugar and cream for a perfect dessert. If the fruits are truly ripe, the hulls should pull out easily but they can also be cut out with a sharp knife. If strawberries need washing, rinse them quickly and pat them dry. Try them drizzled with a little balsamic vinegar, sprinkled with black pepper or dipped in melted chocolate. They are also good sliced into summer fruit salad, used to top a pavlova (page 218), as a filling for sponge cake instead of jam, made into ice cream, or blended in a smoothie (follow the recipe for raspberry smoothie, page 216).

RAW STRAWBERRY PURÉE

Blend strawberries in a blender with 2 tsp icing sugar and 1 tsp lemon juice for every 100 g (3½ oz) fruit.

STRAWBERRY COULIS

Thin down raw strawberry purée with water to make a pouring sauce and blend again.

STRAWBERRY MILKSHAKE

A home-made strawberry milkshake is much nicer than one made from a packet and takes only a little longer to prepare.

Serves 2

> 250 g (9 oz) strawberries
> 300 ml (½ pint) milk
> 2 scoops vanilla ice cream

● Blend all ingredients in a blender until smooth.

ETON MESS

A perennially popular, quick and easy summer dessert. You can buy meringues ready-made from the supermarket. For adults you can add a dash of framboise or strawberry liqueur to the coulis.

Serves 4

> 250 ml (8 fl. oz) whipping cream
> 1 tbsp icing sugar
> 2–3 individual meringues
> 400 g (14 oz) strawberries
> 150 ml (¼ pint) strawberry coulis

● Whip cream with the sugar to soft peak stage – don't over-whip. Fold in lightly crushed meringues, sliced strawberries and coulis. Spoon into dessert glasses.

STRAWBERRY CHEESECAKE

A more-ish, no-cook, biscuit-based cheesecake with strawberries used in three ways.

Serves 8

250 g (9 oz) digestive biscuits	275 ml (9 fl. oz) double cream
100 g (3½ oz) butter	400 g (14 oz) strawberries
600 g (1 lb 6 oz) cream cheese	juice of ½ lemon
115 g (4 oz) icing sugar	

- Crush biscuits and combine with melted butter. Press into the base of a greased 23 cm (9 in.) flan tin. Chill for an hour.
- Beat together cheese and all but 1 tbsp of the icing sugar until smooth. Add cream and beat again until combined.
- Finely chop one third of the strawberries and stir in.
- Spoon mixture on to base, smooth over top and leave to set for 3–4 hours. Purée all but 3 of the remaining strawberries in a blender with remaining icing sugar, the lemon juice and 1 tsp water.
- Slice the 3 strawberries and arrange them in the centre of the cheesecake, then pour purée over.

STRAWBERRIES IN WINE

If you ever get bored with strawberries and cream, try this version. You can use champagne or white wine instead of red.

Serves 4

500 g (1¼ lb) strawberries	½ bottle fruity medium-dry red wine
75 g (3 oz) caster sugar	
juice of ½ lemon	

- Put strawberries in a bowl with sugar and lemon juice and pour wine over. Stir, cover and leave at room temperature for an hour or so. Chill for a further hour.
- Serve strawberries with a little of the wine juice poured over.

STRAWBERRY AND RUM COCKTAIL

An easy, pretty cocktail to whip up if you have any white rum – you could use vodka instead.

Serves 4

100 ml (3½ fl. oz) white rum	juice of 1 lime
50 ml (2 fl. oz) rose hip syrup (page 229)	400 g (14 oz) strawberries
	4 ice cubes

- Blend all ingredients in a blender. Serve in cocktail glasses.

RED FRUIT SALAD

A pretty summer dessert with plenty of flavour. Serve with a spoonful of whipped cream.

Serves 4

250 g (9 oz) strawberries
100 g (3½ oz) raspberries
50 g (2 oz) caster sugar
juice of ½ lemon
1 red-skinned apple
200 g (7 oz) watermelon
100 g (3½ oz) red currants

- Put half the strawberries and all the raspberries in a bowl and sprinkle on the sugar and lemon juice. Cover and leave overnight. Next day the fruit will have made its own juicy sauce.
- Cut apple into thin bite-sized slices, de-seed and cut watermelon into bite-sized cubes and add to salad with red currants. Stir well. Slice remaining strawberries and add to the salad.

STRAWBERRY ICE CREAM

Serve with the red fruit salad or try drizzled with strawberry coulis.

Serves 8

500 g (1¼ lb) strawberries
500 ml (17 fl. oz) whipping cream
125 g (4 oz) icing sugar

- Blend strawberries in a blender until smooth.
- Whip cream, adding sugar a little at a time, until thick and at soft peak stage.
- Fold strawberry purée into cream. Spoon into a lidded container and freeze until partially solid, then remove from freezer and beat to remove ice crystals.
- Freeze until solid. Leave at room temperature for 15 minutes before serving.

STRAWBERRY SHORTCAKES

This is one teatime treat or dessert that is very hard to resist – you are bound to want two. You can use clotted cream instead of the whipping cream.

Serves 8

100 g (3½ oz) cold butter	100 ml (3½ fl. oz) milk	juice of ½ lemon	1 tbsp icing sugar
350 g (12 oz) self-raising flour	1 egg	250 ml (8 fl. oz) whipping	250 g (9 oz) strawberries
100 g (3½ oz) caster sugar	1 tsp vanilla extract	cream	3 tbsp strawberry jam

- Rub butter into flour until it resembles breadcrumbs and stir in caster sugar. Stir in all but 1 tbsp of the warmed milk, the beaten egg, half the vanilla and the lemon juice, and use your hands to make a dough.
- Roll out lightly on a floured surface to about 2 cm (¾ in.) thick. Cut out 8 rounds. Glaze just the tops with milk, transfer to a lightly floured baking tray and bake at 220°C/gas mark 7 for 10–12 minutes until risen and golden – if they sound hollow when you tap the base, they are cooked. Cool on a wire rack.
- Whip cream to stiff peak stage with the remaining vanilla and the icing sugar. Cut each shortcake in half and spread jam over each half. Top with the vanilla cream and finish with the sliced strawberries.

STRAWBERRY REFRIGERATOR CAKE

Easy to put together – just leave it in the fridge to set, then enjoy.

Serves 4–6

150 ml (¼ pint) orange
  juice
2 tbsp strawberry liqueur
2 tbsp icing sugar
400 g (14 oz) strawberries
2 tbsp golden syrup

2 egg yolks
100 g (3½ oz) butter
  at room temperature
24 sponge fingers
200 ml (7 fl. oz)
  whipping cream

- Combine orange juice, liqueur and sugar. Slice 300 g (11 oz) of the strawberries, put in a bowl and pour orange juice mixture over. Cover and leave to marinate for an hour.
- Heat syrup gently until runny, then whisk thoroughly with egg yolks until the mixture is pale and creamy.
- Beat butter until pale and soft, then gradually beat in syrup mixture.
- Remove sliced berries from marinade and drain. Dip 8 sponge fingers in the marinade, then arrange side by side (touching) on a sheet of baking parchment.
- Using a spatula, cover the sponge fingers evenly with half the butter and syrup mixture. Arrange half the strawberry slices on top. Repeat the layers, then top with the remaining 8 dipped sponge fingers. Cover and chill to set.
- Before serving, spread whipped cream over the top and decorate with strawberry halves.

Strawberries go surprisingly well with oranges. Add orange juice to your strawberries and cream, or try them with a dash of Grand Marnier (orange liqueur).

STRAWBERRY PROFITEROLES

If you like the standard chocolate profiteroles you will love these. You will need a piping bag.

Serves 6

125 g (4 oz) butter
150 g (5 oz) plain flour
4 eggs
300 g (11 oz) strawberries
300 ml (½ pint) whipping cream
2 tbsp icing sugar
1 tsp vanilla extract
75 g (3 oz) plain chocolate

- Melt butter in a pan with 300 ml (½ pint) water. Increase heat and bring to a fast boil. Remove pan from heat and quickly beat in flour until mixture forms a ball. Cool a little.
- Gradually beat eggs into dough to give a soft dropping consistency. Put mixture into a piping bag with a large plain nozzle and pipe 12 rounds on to a lightly oiled baking tray.
- Bake at 220°C/gas mark 7 for 10 minutes, then reduce temperature to 190°C/gas mark 5 and cook for a further 15 minutes, or until the mixture is risen and golden. Make a hole in the base of each profiterole, then put them on their sides and cook for a further 5 minutes. Cool on a wire rack.
- Mash 200 g (7 oz) of the strawberries. Whip cream to soft peak stage with the icing sugar and vanilla, and combine with the mashed berries.
- Spoon or pipe cream mixture into the profiteroles (if using a spoon, carefully slit open each one to make the job easier).
- In a bowl set over a pan of simmering water, but not touching the water, melt the chocolate then drizzle it over the profiteroles. Serve with the remaining strawberries, sliced, on the side.

BASIC COOKING

Some varieties of strawberry have a tasteless, fairly tough white inner section around the hull – halve the berries then cut this away before cooking.

POACHED STRAWBERRIES

Put strawberries in water to just cover, with 2 tsp sugar for every 100 ml (3½ fl. oz) water and 1 tbsp lemon juice. Heat gently until soft.

PURÉED STRAWBERRIES

Purée poached strawberries in a blender, check sugar and add more if necessary. You can add more lemon juice to bring out the flavour.

FRIED STRAWBERRIES

You can fry whole or sliced strawberries over medium heat in 10 g (¼ oz) butter and 1 tsp caster sugar for every 100 g (3½ oz) strawberries. Cook for 3 minutes, stirring until sugar is dissolved. Serve with cream or spoon on to toast. Add a dash of balsamic vinegar, black pepper or lemon juice to bring out the flavour.

CHAPTER 6

ORNAMENTALS

Many of the plants we grow in our gardens for their looks are also edible, or at least have edible parts. However, while many plants can be consumed safely, not all taste good. The flowers, plants, shrubs and trees listed in this chapter are some of the most useful in the kitchen and the most pleasant to eat or drink.

Others have different uses – for example, pot marigold can be used instead of the very expensive saffron to colour dishes. And many flowers make beautiful garnishes for salads, desserts and cakes. But the rule is never to garnish a dish with a flower that is not edible, even if you are confident it won't be eaten.

In addition to the listed plants, you may find recipes using the following ornamentals: chrysanthemum, cornflower, fuchsia, gladiolus, hibiscus, hollyhock, jasmine, lilac, and leaves of rose-, lemon- and peppermint-scented geranium (pelargonium).

USING ORNAMENTALS

CHOOSE THE RIGHT FLOWER Edible flowers as a garnish make any dish look special, but be sure that their flavour compliments the dish. For example, use sweet rose, viola or lavender for a cake or dessert, and spicy nasturtium or marigold petals for a salad or savoury.

PICK EARLY Pick flowers in the morning when the water content is high and they are at their freshest.

SELECT FLOWERS CAREFULLY Avoid flowers that have been sprayed with insecticides or fungicides – see warning box. Check all flowers, leaves etc. for signs of disease or bugs. Use only those that are disease- and pest-free.

DECORATING CAKES/DESSERTS Sweet flowers or petals can be crystallized for decoration (see crystallized rose petals, page 229).

DECORATING DRINKS Freeze small flowers in water in an ice-cube tray – one flower per cube – and add the cube to summer drinks such as Pimm's or punches.

FLAVOURING SUGAR Flower petals and scented leaves can be used to add flavour and aroma to sugar in a similar way to a vanilla pod or a cinnamon stick.

DON'T OVERDO IT Use ornamental flowers, leaves etc. sparingly, especially if you are not used to eating them.

WARNING

The culinary uses of the ornamentals in this chapter have been established over the centuries in Britain – these uses have stood the test of time. However, before using one of the recipes you must make sure that the plant in your garden is indeed the ornamental referred to in the text. Only use an ornamental as a food or garnish if you are *absolutely* confident of its identity.

Do not use ornamentals which have been sprayed with a pesticide. If you are asthmatic or prone to allergies, flowers should be tried in small amounts so that you can judge their effect.

STORING

FLOWERS Use soon after picking. To keep for 1–2 days, cut whole stems and immerse in a jug of cold water, as for cut flowers. Store flower heads and petals in a plastic bag in the fridge for a day. Most flowers do not freeze well.

LEAVES Shrub and tree leaves will keep for several days in a bag in the fridge, or you can cut small branches and steep them in water until the leaves are needed. Most leaves will also freeze well in plastic bags.

PREPARATION

See notes for individual plants. Flower petals with a whiteish base where they join the stem can often be bitter and should be discarded. All flowers for kitchen use are best used dry – those coated with dust, dirt etc. can be washed gently in cold water and patted dry on kitchen paper.

Leaves are generally more robust and can be washed without spoiling.

CRAB APPLE *(Malus sylvestris)*

Crab apples – the small, sharp fruits of the crab apple tree – are the ancestors of all our cultivated apples. The wild tree is an attractive plant, but the several hybrids found in our gardens also produce fruit that can be eaten.

Harvest in September or later – some say a light frost improves the flavour. Eaten raw, most – but not all – are quite acidic and are probably better used in cooking and for wines, jellies and preserves. They are rich in pectin which helps low-pectin fruits to set when making jam, so peel, core and chop a few just-ripe crab apples and toss them in with the jam fruit before boiling.

You can also make a pleasant tea from the leaves: steep 2 tbsp fresh leaves in 300 ml (½ pint) boiling water for 6–7 minutes, then strain.

For crab apple jelly, use the recipe for apple jelly, page 238.

CRAB APPLE WINE

This makes a mildly sweet wine. Pectin enzyme (to help clear the liquid and improve flavour), nutrient and yeast are all available in amounts to make 1 gallon.

Makes approx. 4.5 litres (8 pints)

3 kg (6¾ lb) crab apples	pectin enzyme
1.5 kg (3½ lb) sugar	yeast nutrient
450 g (1 lb) raisins	sauternes yeast

- Crush crab apples (using a rolling pin is ideal), put in a bowl and pour 4.5 litres (8 pints) boiling water over. Stir and mash each day for 10 days.
- Press mashed apples through a strainer. Mix liquid with remaining ingredients. Cover and stand for 2 weeks. Strain into a jar with a fermentation lock.
- When bubbles are no longer passing through the lock, siphon the wine off the sediment into bottles and store for at least 6 months – a year is better.

ELDER *(Sambucus)*

Elder is a striking ornamental tree often found in garden hedgerows. Both flowers and berries can be used in the kitchen. In June, the lovely, frothy white flower heads can be used to make champagne or fritters. Dried, the flowers make a pleasant-tasting tea: steep 1 tbsp flowers in 300 ml (½ pint) boiling water for 3–4 minutes, then strain.

In September the striking, deep purple berries make one of the best country wines, or a good cordial. The little berries are ready when they are deep purple and can be stripped from the heads with a fork. They can be cooked in a variety of recipes such as pies, jams, jellies or sauces.

Note: The berries should not be eaten raw as they can be toxic, as can the rest of the plant.

ELDERBERRY WINE

If left for at least a year, elderberry wine can turn out as good, deep and rich as a French claret.

Makes 4.5 litres (8 pints)

1.5 kg (3½ lb) elderberries (de-stalked weight)	wine yeast
	yeast nutrient
1 tsp citric acid	1.5 kg (3½ lb) sugar

- Put berries into a fermenting bucket and crush. Add 4.5 litres (8 pints) boiling water. Cool, then add citric acid, yeast and nutrient.
- Leave for 3 days, stirring once a day. Strain and combine with sugar. Pour into a jar with a fermentation lock. When bubbles are no longer passing through the lock, siphon the wine off the sediment, bottle and keep for a year.

ELDERFLOWER CHAMPAGNE

A delicious, light summer drink which you don't have to wait months to enjoy. It is said you should pick the flowers on a dry day. If they don't ferment, add yeast.

Makes approx. 4.5 litres (8 pints)

8 heads elderflowers in full bloom
2 lemons
650 g (1 lb 6 oz) caster sugar
2 tbsp white wine vinegar

- Put flower heads in a large bowl with 4.5 litres (8 pints) water. Peel rind off lemons and add that to the bowl with lemon juice and remaining ingredients. Stir and leave for a day. Check for signs of fermentation, then leave for a further day.
- Strain, decant into strong champagne bottles and cork. Allow to mature in a cool, dark place for 2 weeks, by which time it should be drinkable but will keep for a few months.

HAWTHORN (*Crataegus*)

Your hawthorn hedge is a good source of food. An old nickname for the plant is 'bread and cheese' because in spring the young, deeply serrated leaves taste nutty and are good in salads. Later in the season they become too chewy but can then be turned into a tea, using the method for crab apple leaves (page 225).

The white flowers which appear in late May make a good flavoured brandy – put enough hawthorn flowers to fill a 1 litre (1¾ pint) pot into a sterile jar and top up with 1 litre (1¾ pints) brandy. Put on the lid and leave for a year before straining and bottling. You can also make wine – see right.

The red berries, which appear from September to November, taste a little like apples and make good wine and jelly.

HAWTHORN BLOSSOM WINE

An alternative to elderflower champagne (page 225).

Makes approx. 4.5 litres (8 pints)

1 litre (1¾ pints) hawthorn blossom (de-stalked)	1.5 kg (3½ lb) caster sugar
1 lemon	wine yeast

- Put blossom in a bowl and pour on 4.5 litres (8 pints) boiling water. Add lemon juice and strips of zest. Cover with muslin and leave for a week. Stir daily.
- Strain into a pan containing the sugar and stir over low heat to dissolve, then cool. Add yeast. Pour into a sterile jar with a fermentation lock.
- Leave for at least 3 months to ferment in a warm place. Siphon the wine off the sediment into a clean jar and cork. Leave for 6 months before bottling.

HEATHER (*Calluna*)

You can use both the flowers and the shoot tips of heather to make tea, which is said to have a range of health benefits: steep 1 tbsp finely chopped heather (flowers and/or leaves) in 300 ml (½ pint) boiling water. Stand for 6–8 minutes, then strain.

The oldest known use of the little plant is to make a heather ale – records show that this light beer has been brewed in Scotland, where heather grows wild on the moorlands, for at least 4,000 years and has recently been enjoying a revival. It is a mixture of malted barley, bog myrtle, heather shoot tips and flowers. It has a peaty, spicy aroma.

You can dry the leaves and flowers by spreading them on a tray in a dry, warm place or in a low oven until lightly crisp. Store in an airtight container.

LAVENDER (*Lavandula*)

Lavender is often thought of as an aromatic herb for pillows or pot-pourri – but the uniquely fragrant flowers (and leaves) of this small, evergreen shrub are very useful in the kitchen. They can be added to desserts, biscuits, cakes, conserves, salads and dressings; they are a good garnish and also make a soothing tea.

Lavender goes very well with other herbs, especially oregano, rosemary, thyme, sage, fennel and savory, and with coriander seed. It has a sweet, flowery flavour with a hint of lemon.

The flowers are best picked when they just reach full colour. To use fresh, put stems in water as you would cut flowers and use within the next day or two. They dry well – some colour is lost but the flavour remains just as potent. Simply cut stalks and hang them upside down in small bunches in a warm, dry place for a week or so. The flower heads can then be cut off and stored in an airtight, opaque jar.

Some uses for lavender:

- Sprinkle a few fresh leaves or small flower heads into a salad to go with lamb.
- Sprinkle chopped flowers into the flour when making bread, cakes or biscuits.
- Add a few flower stalks to sugar in the canister to flavour it for use in desserts and cakes.
- Steep stalks for an hour in milk for custard or in cream for ice cream; remove before use.
- Add 1 tsp per 50 ml (2 fl. oz) to cream when whipping it.
- Add the leaves to meat and poultry dishes instead of rosemary.
- Use fresh flowers to garnish a chocolate cake.
- Beat chopped lavender flowers with the ingredients for a plain or lemon cheesecake, or stir into home-made vanilla ice cream before freezing.
- Add some stalks to gooseberries (with which it goes very well), rhubarb or blackcurrants. Lavender reduces the tartness of acidic fruits.

LAVENDER SHORTCAKE

Rich biscuits to accompany afternoon tea or to serve with berry fruits and lavender whipped cream.

Serves 10

100 g (3½ oz) butter	zest of 1 lemon
65 g (2½ oz) caster sugar	1 tbsp fresh chopped lavender flowers
100 g (3½ oz) plain flour	
50 g (2 oz) cornflour	

- Beat together butter and 50 g (2 oz) of the sugar until soft and creamy. Mix in flour, zest and lavender.
- Press the mixture into a 20 cm (8 in.) round, loose-bottomed tin and sprinkle with remaining sugar. Bake at 160°C/gas mark 3 for 30 minutes, or until golden.
- Mark into 10 wedges. Leave to cool in the tin, then cut through marks with a sharp knife.

MALLOW *(Malva)*

All varieties of mallow have edible, pleasant-tasting leaves, but it is the common musk mallow (*M. moschata*) that is probably best for kitchen use. The pink, mauve or white flowers of this hardy, shrub-like perennial sit on top of long, woody stems of soft, deeply cut, maple-like leaves which are very useful to bulk out a green salad. Unlike many weed or ornamental leaves, they have a mild flavour so can be scattered in with abandon if you have no lettuce. They are best eaten raw, as when cooked they turn slightly slimy due to their high soluble-fibre content.

The flowers or buds can also be added to salads or used as a garnish.

MARIGOLD *(Calendula, Tagetes)*

The bright orange or sometimes yellow single flowers of the pot marigold (*Calendula*) have been a cottage-garden favourite for hundreds of years, not only for their cheerful appearance but because of their culinary and medicinal uses. If dead-headed frequently they will produce flowers for many months. Pick flowers just as they open in summer for fresh use and for drying (arrange on a tray and leave in a warm, dry, airy place).

The flowers have a range of flavours but are always quite strong – spicy, bitter, tangy or peppery.

Petals can be sprinkled on soups, or stirred into pasta, salads and rice. For marigold tea follow the recipe for elder tea. Ground marigold petals are known as 'poor man's saffron', because they can be added to any dish requiring saffron to give a similar yellow-gold colour and some flavour.

Remove the white base from the petals, as this can be bitter. *Calendula* leaves can also be eaten.

French marigold (*Tagetes*) is another annual marigold, the flowers of which can also be eaten and have a hint of tarragon in their flavour. Use as for pot marigold.

NASTURTIUM *(Tropaeolum)*

One of the most popular garden plants for eating, these pretty, low-growing or trailing annuals have both tasty flowers (with shades of spice and pepper) and leaves that in flavour somewhat resemble watercress, to which they are related. The seed pods are also edible and can be pickled and used instead of expensive capers in salads and savoury dishes. They can also be dried and ground to use as a pepper substitute.

Some uses for nasturtiums:
- Add whole flowers or leaves to salads or toss into cooked pasta.
- Chop and use flowers or leaves to liven up meat dishes and vinaigrettes.

- Using a pestle and mortar or a blender, pound leaves or flowers with softened butter and lemon juice. Form into small patties and use as a herb butter with fish, meat or vegetables.
- Beat chopped leaves into crushed cooked potatoes (1 tbsp for each 250 g/9 oz potato) with butter, lemon juice, chopped chives, garlic and salt. Form into patties and fry.

PICKLED NASTURTIUM SEEDS

Put green, unripe seed pods in a bowl and cover with a brine made from 1 tbsp salt to every 250 ml (8 fl. oz) water. Leave for a day, then drain and rinse. Pack into a sterilized jar and cover with pickling vinegar that has just boiled. Seal and store for 3–4 weeks.

PINK *(Dianthus)*

The flowers of pinks and carnations can be eaten raw or cooked, and taste similar to cloves. The crimson-flowered carnation (*D. caryophyllus*) is sometimes called the 'nutmeg clove' or 'clove pink'. Pick flowers when first open and remove the bitter white base.

Some uses for pinks and carnations:
- Chop and add to a ham sandwich.
- Try alpine pinks (*D. alpinus*) as garnish for cakes, trifles, mousses and salads.
- Add a few to a fruit pie – such as apple or pear – to bring out their flavour.
- Crystallize small flowers (use the recipe for crystallized rose petals, page 229).

ROSE *(Rosa)*

Both the flowers and hips of roses are good kitchen ingredients – the flower petals can be used for decoration, drinks, and to add flavour and aroma in sweet recipes such as ice cream, cheesecake, Turkish delight, cupcakes and jellies, and in savoury recipes such as stuffings and spice pastes. They have a warm, distinctive yet gentle flavour. The hips are a great source of vitamin C and can be made into rose hip syrup.

Petals

Petals from almost any type of rose can be used – *R. rugosa* has large single flowers with the best flavoured petals of all. It is followed by old roses such as damasks and gallicas. New hybrids and shrubs can be used, but remember only fragrant roses have flavoursome petals. Some modern types can also leave an aftertaste, so try a petal before picking a lot for kitchen use.

HARVESTING PETALS For maximum volume while retaining essential fragrance, harvest when the petals are a day or two away from falling from the bush. Pull them very lightly from the plant with a basket held underneath to catch the petals.

STORING PETALS Petals are best used the same day – preferably within an hour or so of picking. They can, however, be dried: spread them out on a tray and dry in a warm, airy place. Store in an airtight jar and use in cooked recipes.

PREPARING PETALS Ensure before use that you remove the white bases from the petals, as this part is sour. Try not to wash them (pick the day after rain and don't use windfalls to avoid having to wash), as they are delicate and easily bruised.

Hips

Some hips have much more flesh than others and some roses were actually cultivated for their large, fleshy hips. All hips can be eaten, but the large species and old shrub roses produce large hips in quantity and are better to use than the hips which appear on floribundas or hybrid teas when not dead-headed. *R. villosa* – a shrub with single pink flowers – has one of the best fruits for culinary use. Other good types are *R. canina* (dog rose) and *R. rugosa*.

Note: Just below the outer layer of skin and flesh of the hip is a layer of 'hairs' which surrounds the seeds and which shouldn't be eaten – see Preparing Hips.

HARVESTING HIPS It is best to wait until the fruit is just going soft before picking them (usually after a frost) and then they are quite palatable raw – sometimes they can be sweet and delicious. If you want hips, you mustn't cut off the dead flower heads.

STORING HIPS Hips are best used soon after picking or their vitamin C content will diminish; otherwise put in a covered container or large plastic bag and store in the fridge for a few days. They can be frozen: open-freeze or bag and freeze. They can also be dried, but much of their goodness will be lost.

PREPARING HIPS Wash if necessary and dry on kitchen paper. Further preparation depends on the recipe. To remove seeds and hairs, slit open the hips with a paring knife (wear thin rubber gloves), scrape out the seeds with the hairs and discard. Wash again.

Some uses for roses:

- Use petals raw in salads and to garnish cakes and desserts.
- Stir petals into rice to serve with, for example, Moroccan- and Turkish-based dishes.
- Add some petals to strawberry or rhubarb jam.
- Boil hips in a muslin bag to extract vitamin C-rich juice. This can be drunk or used with crab apples to make jelly (see apple jelly, page 238).
- Make rose shortcake, using the lavender shortcake recipe (page 226) and substituting chopped rose petals for lavender.
- Stir dried petals into a jar of sugar and use in baking and desserts.
- Make a calming, fragrant tea: steep ¼ cup of fresh rose petals in 300 ml (½ pint) boiling water for 5 minutes, strain and add a little honey if liked.
- Make rosewater: fill a heatproof bowl with petals and pour boiling water over. Stir, cover and leave for 30 minutes. Strain and bottle. This will keep in the fridge for up to 2 weeks. Add to fresh fruit, such as sliced strawberries; ice cream, mousses or sponges; or stir into natural yogurt, whipped cream or sweetened Mascarpone.

ROSE HIP SYRUP

This recipe is based on one issued by the UK Ministry of Food during the Second World War, when children were given a spoonful of rose hip syrup at home every day. Try to pick the hips as late in the season as possible so that they will be nice and soft. Apart from using it as a medicine, try pouring a little over ice cream, stirring into yogurt, adding to fruit when poaching, or dilute with water as a drink.

Makes 1.5 litres (2½ pints)

1 kg (2¼ lb) soft rose hips
500 g (1¼ lb) caster sugar

- Blend topped and tailed hips in a blender or mince in an old-fashioned mincer. Add to a pan with 1.75 litres (3 pints) boiling water and bring back to the boil.
- Remove from heat and leave for 15 minutes. Pour through a jelly bag and allow the majority of the liquid to drip through into a bowl.
- Return pulp to the pan and add a further 900 ml (1½ pints) boiling water. Boil, stand and strain as before.
- Discard pulp and pour liquid into a clean saucepan. Boil until reduced to 1 litre (1¾ pints).
- Add sugar, dissolve over low heat, then boil rapidly for a further 5 minutes. Pour into hot, sterilized bottles and seal immediately.

ROSE HIP WINE

Make sure the hips are nice and soft. The wine – which is not too sweet – will be ready to drink about 6 months after bottling.

Makes approx. 4.5 litres (8 pints)

1 kg (2¼ lb) rose hips
pectin enzyme
1 kg (2¼ lb) caster sugar
juice of 1 lemon
wine yeast
yeast nutrient

- Mince hips or chop lightly using a food processor. Put in a bowl and pour 4.5 litres (8 pints) boiling water over. Cool to tepid and add pectin enzyme. Stir and stand for a day, covered.
- Add sugar, stirring well to dissolve it, then add lemon juice, yeast and nutrient and stir again.
- Keep in a warm place, covered, for 5 days, stirring daily, or until fermentation slows down.
- Using fine muslin, strain into a jar with a fermentation lock. When bubbles are no longer passing through the lock, siphon the wine off the sediment and bottle.

ROSE PETAL JELLY

Try stirring this into yogurt or eating on scones.

Makes approx. 4 x 200 g (7 oz) jars

approx. 450 g (1 lb) rose petals
450 g (1 lb) caster sugar
juice of 1 lemon

- Put half the petals in a preserving pan and cover with 600 ml (1 pint) boiling water. Cover and leave to stand for 2 hours. Strain into a clean pan, discarding the used petals.
- Stir sugar into pan over low heat until dissolved. Add lemon juice and most of the remaining petals (reserve a handful). Boil until setting point is reached (page 235).
- Add last petals and simmer gently for a minute, then pour into sterilized jars and seal.

CRYSTALLIZED ROSE PETALS

Use to decorate cakes or chilled desserts. Make sure the petals are fresh, dry and unblemished.

Makes enough to decorate 2 large cakes

2 egg whites   **2 tbsp icing sugar**
40 rose petals

- Beat egg whites lightly. With a 1 cm (½ in.) clean, unused paint brush, paint egg white over all surfaces of each petal and put separately on a wire rack.
- Sieve icing sugar evenly over the petals and leave them to dry. Use as soon as you can.

ROSE HARISSA

Spicy harissa paste is widely used in Moroccan cooking – the type that contains rose petals is the most prized of all. Use 1–2 tsp to flavour casseroles, tagines, soups, stews and sauces during cooking.

Makes approx. 150 g (5 oz)

100 g (3½ oz) red chillies	**½ cup rose petals**
8 cloves garlic	**1 tbsp ground cumin**
salt, black pepper	**1 tbsp ground coriander seed**
3 tbsp olive oil	**1 tsp smoked paprika**

- Chop de-seeded chillies and peeled garlic and put in a mortar with ½ tsp salt. Pound with a pestle to crush, then add half the oil and the rose petals and pound again until petals are well crushed.
- Add pepper and other spices and continue pounding until you have a thick paste. Put in a jar and drizzle remaining oil over the top to prolong shelf life. Will keep in the fridge for a few weeks.

ROWAN (*Sorbus*)

The large bunches of bright orange mountain ash berries in early autumn are a familiar sight in gardens, parks and in the wild. They are one of the easiest types of berry to harvest and will stay on the tree for months if the birds don't get them. The berries – rich in vitamin C – can be used half and half with crab apples to make a tart, beautifully coloured jelly good for serving with game (use recipe for apple jelly, page 238). They also make a good wine, and various countries have their own recipes for beer, mead, spirits etc.

Note: Take care with raw berries. They are very acidic and the seeds within can be toxic – remove before eating. Cooking destroys the toxins.

ROWAN WINE

Some people think this wine tastes like a fine, dry Spanish sherry. It has a lovely colour.

Makes 4.5 litres (8 pints)

2 kg (4½ lb) rowan berries
1.2 kg (2½ lb) caster sugar
1 lemon
pectin enzyme
yeast nutrient
wine yeast

- Crush fruit. Dissolve sugar in 4.5 litres (8 pints) water in a pan, add fruit and bring to the boil. Cool to tepid. Add lemon juice and grated zest, pectin enzyme and nutrient. Stand for 24 hours.

- Add wine yeast and leave to ferment for a week, stirring daily. Strain into a jar with a fermentation lock, topping up with water as necessary. Put on the fermentation lock and leave for 3 months.

- Siphon the wine off the sediment into a clean jar, then leave to ferment for a further month. Siphon wine off sediment again, put into bottles and leave for a year.

SUNFLOWER (*Helianthus annuus*)

The different varieties of sunflower, short to tall, yellow to deep red, make a wonderful display in the garden and their seeds offer a valuable food. The larger types of flower (e.g. *H. giganteus*) will produce more and larger seeds per head.

Sunflower seeds are ready to be harvested when the back of the flower turns brown.

Remove the black husks before eating – the kernel is a creamy colour and delicious eaten raw or lightly toasted until golden in a dry pan or in the oven.

Eat as a snack, add to salads and stir-fries, or pound and use to replace peanut butter. Store the seeds in their husks in an opaque, airtight tin in a cool, dark place to retain most nutrition and remove husks only when you need them.

VIOLA (*Viola*)

The viola family (including the violet and the larger cultivated pansies) are the only edible flowers you will find in the garden during a normal winter and very early spring. The tiny, delicate mauve flowers of the native *V. odorata* have a mild, pleasant flavour and make a superb garnish for desserts and cakes, used as they are or crystallized (use method for crystallized rose petals, page 229). The

flower heads can be stirred into sponge cake mixtures before cooking or used to flavour ice creams and sorbets, rice puddings, creams and custards.

Scatter the larger petals of pansy into salads or use them as garnish. The leaves of the plant are also edible as a salad ingredient or can be used (with the flowers) to make a tea: steep 1 tbsp in 300 ml (½ pint) boiling water for 4–5 minutes, strain and serve with sugar or honey added.

WALNUT (*Juglans regia*)

If your ornamental walnut tree is the common walnut (*J. regia*) rather than the black walnut (*J. nigra*), then you may in time get regular crops of walnuts in autumn. Crack open the tough shells and use the nuts in any walnut recipe or as a snack.

If the tree is laden with unripe, soft green nuts in June, harvest some to make your own pickled walnuts. It's easy but takes some time. For every

1 kg (2¼ lb) shelled nuts make a brine with 175 g (6 oz) salt in 600 ml (1 pint) hot water. Prick walnuts all over and put in a bowl, cover with brine and leave for 5 days, stirring daily. Drain, then repeat the process with new brine. Drain again and pat dry. Place in a single layer on a tray and leave in a warm, sunny place to dry and turn black (a greenhouse or conservatory is ideal). Pack into sterilized jars, pour pickling vinegar over, seal and store for 2 months before eating.

CHAPTER 7

WEEDS

No one would choose to have weeds growing in the garden. In the ornamental garden they spoil the effect of our flowers and shrubs, in the kitchen garden they take nutrients, light and moisture away from the vegetables and fruit. However, the good news is that many of our common weeds can be used as vegetables or herbs. So instead of always digging them up for the compost heap, see if any are suitable for taking into the kitchen.

Most of the weeds described in this chapter can be used raw in salads or cooked like a green vegetable. Most of them have a strong taste so are best used mixed with other greens. They may also be good for soups, sauces etc.

Only those weeds which are commonly found in gardens throughout Britain are listed here, although living-off-the-land recipe books include many others. Here you can find a wide range of edible weeds growing in hedgerows, fields and woods etc. Examples include hairy bittercress, burdock, cow parsley, Good King Henry, goosegrass (cleavers), Jack-by-the-hedge (hedge garlic/garlic mustard) and sowthistle.

USING WEEDS

WEED WITH TWO BUCKETS When you go into the garden to weed, have two buckets – one for inedible weeds and the other for those you are going to take into the house.

WEED IN THE COOL On a hot day, try to weed for the kitchen at the start or end of the day and/or take the edible weeds into the house and cool shade as soon as you can – they will quickly wilt otherwise.

WEED WITH CARE Weeds for kitchen use need gentler handling than you might give to other weeds. Some, particularly smaller annual weeds, are quite delicate and spoil easily.

WARNING

The culinary uses of the weeds in this chapter have been established over the centuries in Britain – these uses have stood the test of time. However, before using one of the recipes you must make sure that the plant in your garden is indeed the weed referred to in the text. Only use weeds as a food or garnish if you are *absolutely* confident of their identity.

Do not use weeds which have been sprayed with a weedkiller or pesticide.

STORING

Weeds are best eaten within 2–3 hours of harvesting – but at least on the same day.

Otherwise, the more robust leaves, berries and flowers can be stored in a plastic bag in the fridge for a day or two. Roots will last longer – up to a week. Some leaves, such as nettle and dandelion, can be blanched and frozen for use like cooked spinach.

PREPARATION

If leaves/berries/flowers are clean, leave them as they are. Wash dirt-covered weeds in a sink of cold water. Swish them about for a minute, then remove and, if necessary (e.g. for eating raw or before frying), pat them dry gently on kitchen paper or in a clean tea-towel.

Roots should be scrubbed, trimmed and peeled as necessary, then chopped as your recipe requires.

BRAMBLE *(Rubus fruticosus)*

The prickly, hard to eradicate stems of the common bramble can be a problem in the garden, but they provide delicious berries in autumn. The young leaves can be used raw, cooked or as a tea. The leaves taste like the fruits, and can even be added to fruit salad.

The pretty flowers become fruit by late August and the berries can be used just like the cultivated type, raw or in pies, smoothies, jam and wine. Check them over carefully for maggots. The berries are also good steeped in a variety of spirits to make a tasty drink for the winter months ahead.

BLACKBERRY WHISKY

A simple recipe for a blackberry-flavoured spirit.

Makes 1 litre (1¾ pints)

750 g (1 lb 10 oz) blackberries	whisky of choice 200 g (7 oz) caster sugar

- Put clean, dry blackberries in a 1 litre (1¾ pint) jar. Top up with whisky. Add sugar. Seal. Leave for 3 months, shaking now and then. Strain and re-bottle.

CHICKWEED *(Stellaria media)*

One of the nicest-tasting weeds of spring, named because it was used to feed birds. The little leaves of the annual plant look like a cross between thyme and marjoram, and taste like lettuce, so can be used in reasonable quantity in a salad. Try a mixed salad of chickweed, dandelion and daisy petals. Cooked, chickweed makes a good substitute for spinach, or can be mixed with spinach to make it go further. Try braising it for a few minutes with chopped spring onions, lemon juice, butter and seasoning. The stalks are tender and edible too – harvest them with scissors.

CLOVER *(Trifolium pratense)*

Red clover is well known as fodder for cattle, but for centuries humans have also eaten it and it was a staple vegetable for the Amerinds in America. It is associated with grassland, and in the garden it is a common weed affecting lawns everywhere. Both the pretty leaves and the red flowers are edible raw or cooked.

The flowers make a good garnish, wine or sweet tea. The leaves can be chopped or dried and added to cake mixtures – they give a vanilla flavour. If you want to try clover wine, use the recipe for hawthorn blossom wine (page 226).

The flower seeds are tiny, but you can collect and sprout them like other seeds (page 134) and use them in salads and sandwiches.

DAISY *(Bellis perennis)*

The scourge of the fine lawn from spring through to late autumn, daisies make rather good eating. The flower petals give a pleasantly sour flavour when added to salads. Tight buds can also be pickled in vinegar (use the method for pickled nasturtium seeds, page 227) as a substitute for capers.

Daisy leaves are also edible but can become tough as they age, so pick the smallest, youngest ones. Stir into salads or sprinkle on to savouries like a herb garnish.

DANDELION *(Taraxacum officinale)*

One of our most prolific weeds, its serrated green leaves appearing almost all year round, dandelion is also thoroughly useful. It has been used as a food for at least 1,000 years and the leaves, flowers and roots can all be consumed in a variety of ways. This unwanted plant is one of the tastier weeds in the garden, albeit with a fairly strong flavour.

Young leaves are good in a green or French bacon salad (see below), or as a cooked vegetable similar to spinach, either as it is or in a variety of dishes such as vegetarian lasagne, soup, stir-fry, curry or casserole, or baked Greek-style in filo pastry with cheese (page 140). The bright yellow flower tastes a little of honey if picked young. Flowers can be made into tea, beer or a wine which some say is the best herbal wine of all. Dandelion is often combined with burdock in drinks such as cordial and beer. Individual petals can be used to garnish a salad or dessert, or stirred through plain boiled rice before serving. Lastly the root – somewhat like turnip – can be used as a vegetable or ground to make a coffee substitute.

Both leaves and flowers become bitter as they age, but it is said that steeping them in water overnight makes older specimens edible.

Choose the smaller leaves from the centre of the plant and pick them by hand. For milder, paler leaves, cover the plant with a pot or bucket to blanch for a week before picking, or earth up plants like potatoes. For a regular supply of young leaves, remove flowers and don't allow them to seed. Store in a plastic bag in the fridge.

For dandelion tea: steep 1 tbsp flower buds in 300 ml (½ pint) boiling water for 5–6 minutes, then strain.

To make dandelion coffee: harvest roots in autumn. Scrub well, then leave to dry in a warm, airy place for a few days. Chop and roast until golden, either in the oven at 180°C/gas mark 4 or under a medium grill, turning frequently. Grind. Use 1–2 tsp for every 300 ml (½ pint) water and steep in boiling water as for ground coffee beans. Strain before drinking. Add sugar/milk to taste.

To make a dandelion salad: wash young leaves and pat dry. Tear larger ones. Put them in a salad bowl and sprinkle on a dressing made with three parts olive oil, one part lemon juice, seasoning and a well-crushed clove of garlic. Shake together thoroughly before use. To turn this into the French *pissenlit au lard* – dandelion and bacon salad – dry-fry cubes of fatty bacon until golden and toss with the dandelion salad, using any melted fat in the pan to drizzle over.

Stir-fried dandelion root: to serve 2, thoroughly scrub 200 g (7 oz) trimmed dandelion roots and slice into thin rounds. Stir-fry over high heat in 2 tbsp sesame seed oil for 3 minutes. Turn heat down, then add 2 tbsp vegetable stock and 2 tsp soy sauce. Simmer until tender: approx. 5 minutes.

DANDELION FLOWER WINE

A beautiful golden wine which has been likened in flavour to the Greek drink retsina.

Makes 4.5 litres (8 pints)

1 litre (1¾ pints) dandelion flower heads	wine yeast
1 kg (2¼ lb) caster sugar	wine nutrient
	2 oranges

- Pour 2.3 litres (4 pints) boiling water over the flower heads in a bucket. Stir and leave to stand for 3 days. Strain through fine muslin into a jar which has a fermentation lock.

- Over low heat, dissolve sugar with 1 litre (1¾ pints) water. Cool to tepid, add yeast, nutrient, orange juice and grated zest, and stir. Pour into jar with dandelion liquid and fill jar up with water as necessary.

- Put on fermentation lock and leave to ferment for several weeks. When bubbles are no longer passing through the lock, siphon wine off sediment into a clean jar and leave for at least 3 months before bottling and drinking.

DANDELION AND BURDOCK CORDIAL

Dilute this with 4 parts water, lemonade or soda water. For an aniseed flavour, include 1–2 whole star anise, or add chopped fennel or dill to the boiling water.

Makes approx. 750 ml (1¼ pints)

2 tsp finely chopped burdock root	2 cm (¾ in.) piece fresh chopped ginger
2 tsp finely chopped dandelion root	juice of 1 lemon
	300 g (11 oz) caster sugar

- Put roots, ginger and lemon juice in a pan with 600 ml (1 pint) water. Bring to the boil and cook for 20 minutes.

- Strain through fine muslin into a clean pan and, over low heat, stir in sugar until dissolved. Cool.

DEAD-NETTLE *(Lamium album)*

The annual nettle with non-stinging leaves and pretty erect stems of white flowers makes a good alternative to the perennial nettle as a green vegetable. Pick leaves (preferably young and tender ones) and steam or boil as for spinach. The plant has been used this way in France for centuries. The leaves can also be added to stews and sauces as a herb, and raw leaves can be used sparingly in salads.

Use the flower heads to make a tea: 1 tbsp chopped flower heads to 300 ml (½ pint) boiling water. Steep for 5 minutes, then strain.

DOCK *(Rumex obtusifolius)*

The leaves of dock are bitter but edible and can be used as a green vegetable. Only the young, small leaves should be eaten, as they are less bitter and have a slightly lemony hint. To reduce bitterness, bring them to the boil in a pan of water, then discard the water and cook as greens in a fresh pan.

You can also make a tea from the leaves: steep ½ tbsp very young leaves in boiling water for 2 minutes. Drain, then steep again in 300 ml (½ pint) fresh boiling water for 3 minutes and strain.

GROUND ELDER
(Aegopodium podagraria)

The scourge of gardeners, ground elder is said to have been introduced to the UK by the Romans as an edible garden plant and was later used as ground cover. It was also said to cure gout, hence its nickname 'goutweed'. Opinion is divided over the leaves, which can be used as a herb to provide flavour and aroma, eaten raw in mixed green salads, or (stems intact) cooked as spinach, added to soups, stews etc. Some people find them deliciously tangy – in Russia and Scandinavia they are used as a side vegetable – but others are less sure.

The leaves are best harvested in spring when they are young, before the tiny white flowers appear, after which taste and texture deteriorate. Harvest shoots as they push through the ground, steam for a minute only and serve with melted butter and lemon juice as an early asparagus-like taste.

The strong flavour of the more mature leaves lends itself well to the addition of herbs and spices. Add a pinch of crushed cumin seeds to the leaves and stir-fry them, or add them to a basic onion and potato soup with a pinch of coriander.

NETTLE *(Urtica dioica)*

The wild stinging nettle has been used as a vegetable for at least 2,000 years, and it has also been cultivated, being used as a 'poor man's kale' in spring. The leaves should be harvested only from when the first shoots appear around March, through to June; after that they become tough and bitter and can be toxic.

It may not need saying that you should not eat nettles raw – they will sting your mouth just as much as they will sting your hands if you do not wear gloves to pick them. The sting disappears on cooking and on thorough drying. A simple use is to harvest the young shoots and leaves and cook as for spinach, with the addition of plenty of butter and seasoning (and perhaps some garlic or chopped spring onions), as the flavour is quite mild. Or add them to pasta or any dish in which you would normally use spinach.

Nettles make a particularly good soup (see right) and nettle beer is an old favourite. Leaves can be dried: hang up bunches of stems in a warm, airy place until crisp and use to make tea.

To make nettle beer: add 4.5 litres (8 pints) water to a bucket of shoot tops or young shoots in a large pan and boil for 20 minutes. Strain, put in a clean pan and dissolve 500 g (1¼ lb) caster sugar over low heat, then stir in 15 g (½ oz) cream of tartar. Cool to tepid and add 7 g (¼ oz) yeast for beer. Cover and leave for 3–4 days. Siphon beer off sediment into a jar with a fermentation lock. Leave for another few days, then bottle. This is drinkable straight away.

NETTLE SOUP

A lovely spring soup with a pretty mid-green colour.

Serves 4

1 onion	½ tsp ground nutmeg
1 tbsp olive oil	2 potatoes
25 g (1 oz) butter	1 litre (1¾ pints)
2 cloves garlic	vegetable stock
1 bucketful young nettle	200 ml (7 fl. oz) cream
leaves/shoots	salt, black pepper

- Sweat finely chopped onion in oil and butter over low heat to soften but not colour, adding chopped garlic for the last minute.

- Stir in nettles and nutmeg and cook for a minute. Add peeled, chopped potatoes and stock, bring to a simmer and cook for 30 minutes. Cool a little, then blend in a blender until smooth.

- Return to the pan to reheat and stir in cream and seasoning.

PLANTAIN *(Plantago major)*

The young leaves of this common garden weed can be eaten, although they are not to everyone's taste as they are quite bitter and fibrous. They are best if the stalk portion is removed. They can be used raw, but are better blanched then added to other dishes – e.g. soups or stews – in small amounts.

CHAPTER 8

PRESERVES AND PICKLES

Home-made preserves and pickles are not just great tasting, they are also a good way to use up any gluts from the kitchen garden. They will fill your store cupboard for much of the year and can also make welcome gifts for friends and family at Christmas. Preserving garden produce in the kitchen is not as popular as it was as recently as fifty years ago, but the art is not difficult and the results are much better than shop-bought.

Always use vegetables and fruit that are in good condition and not past their prime. When making jams it is important to use 'just-ripe' fruit – over-ripe fruit will have a low pectin content which makes it more difficult to get it to set (see 'Boiling to setting point' below).

STERILIZING JARS

In order for preserves to last (for example, jams should keep for a year) they need to be potted into sterile jars.

To sterilize jars:
- Wash in soapy water, rinse well and dry on kitchen paper.
- Place jars on a baking tray in a cool oven – 140°C/gas mark 1 – for 20 minutes.

To sterilize lids:
- Wash and rinse. Put into boiling water for 10 minutes, then dry on kitchen paper.

The jars need to be sterilized just before you are going to use them so that they are still warm when filled. Avoid touching sterilized jars (especially inside the rims) with dirty hands or cloths etc.

BOILING TO SETTING POINT

Jams and jellies will not set unless the mixture reaches 'setting point', which occurs when the fruit and sugar mixture has boiled for a certain length of time. If the mixture is potted before setting point is reached, the jam or jelly will be runny – a 'light set'. For some fruits (e.g. cherry) this may be preferred. A light set helps keep good flavour and colour but the jam will not keep as long as with a firmer set.

To test for set: put 1 tsp of the hot jam from the preserving pan on to a cold saucer (keep a few in the freezer while you make the jam), then put it in the fridge for 2 minutes. Remove from the fridge and push one side of the mixture with your finger – if it crinkles up, you have a set. If it isn't ready, bring the pan back to the boil, boil for a further few minutes, then test again. Repeat until set is reached. Note: take the pan off the heat every time you test for set.

It can take from just a few minutes up to 30 minutes to reach setting point, depending on the pectin content and ripeness of the fruit, the temperature at which the jam was boiled, and the amount and type of sugar in the recipe. Fruits such as damsons, plums, blackcurrants, gooseberries and apples are high in pectin, while berries are low. Adding lemon juice to the recipe increases pectin content, or you can buy sugar with added pectin, or sachets of pectin to add.

TIPS

- While preserving sugar dissolves more quickly than other sugars, you don't have to use it. Ordinary caster or granulated will do, but scrape any remnants in the pan and ensure it is all dissolved.
- Don't have the pan more than half full. When boiling starts, volume increases and the jam can spit and burn.
- Foamy white 'scum' may appear on top of the jam when boiling. Much of this will disappear by the time setting point is reached and any that remains can be removed with a flattish, long-handled, sterilized metal spoon, or by stirring in a knob of butter.

- You can pot as soon as setting point has been reached, but for preserves containing whole fruits or pieces of fruit, wait 15–20 minutes and stir with a sterilized spoon so that the fruit doesn't sink to the bottom of the jar.
- Fill jars right to the top to avoid air pockets and spoilage. Place greaseproof or wax circles on top immediately.
- Put on lids and stick on labels when the jam is cold.
- Store in a cool, dark, dry place. Jams should keep for up to a year, pickles and chutneys for 6 months.

JAM RECIPES

APRICOT JAM

You can also use this recipe for peach jam.

Makes approx. 5 x 400 g (14 oz) jars

**1.3 kg (3 lb) apricots
juice of 1 lemon
1.3 kg (3 lb) preserving sugar**

- Put halved, stoned apricots in a preserving pan with 300 ml (½ pint) water and the lemon juice. Simmer until tender and breaking up – about 20 minutes.
- Add sugar and stir over very low heat until dissolved. Bring to a rapid boil and boil for 15 minutes, or until set is reached. Pot.

BLACKCURRANT JAM

Blackcurrants make a really good jam with great taste and colour – and because they are so high in pectin, the jam is easy to set.

Makes approx. 5 x 400 g (14 oz) jars

**1.2 kg (2½ lb) blackcurrants
1.5 kg (3½ lb) preserving sugar**

- Put de-stalked blackcurrants in a preserving pan with 750 ml (1¼ pints) water and simmer, stirring occasionally, for 10 minutes until fruits are all burst and pan contents slightly reduced.
- Add sugar and stir until dissolved. Bring to a rapid boil and boil for 10 minutes, or until set is reached. Pot.

CHERRY JAM

You can make this with any cherries, but black cherries are great, as are Morello.

Makes approx. 5 x 400 g (14 oz) jars

**1.8 kg (4 lb) cherries
juice of 2 lemons
1.2 kg (2½ lb) preserving sugar
with added pectin**

- Put stoned cherries in a preserving pan with lemon juice. Over very low heat, bring to a simmer and cook for 20 minutes, stirring occasionally and gently, until cherries are very soft.
- Add sugar and stir until dissolved. Bring to a rapid boil and boil for 15 minutes, or until set is reached. Pot.

DAMSON JAM

One of the best jams for colour and intense flavour. It also sets easily as long as the damsons aren't over-ripe.

Makes approx. 6 x 400 g (14 oz) jars

**2 kg (4½ lb) damsons
1.5 kg (3½ lb) preserving sugar**

- Put de-stalked damsons in a preserving pan with 200 ml (7 fl. oz) water. Bring to a simmer and cook for 15 minutes, or until the fruits are soft. Press them against the sides of the pan with a large wooden spoon to help release the stones.
- Add sugar and stir over very low heat until dissolved. Bring to a rapid boil and boil without stirring for 10 minutes, or until set is reached.
- Remove any scum and as many stones as you can see, using a sterilized spoon. Leave to cool for 15 minutes, then stir to distribute fruit. Pot.

GOOSEBERRY JAM

Even people who think they don't like gooseberries will enjoy this jam.

Makes approx. 6 x 400 g (14 oz) jars

1.5 kg (3½ lb) gooseberries
1.5 kg (3½ lb) preserving sugar

- Simmer topped, tailed gooseberries in a preserving pan with 500 ml (17 fl. oz) water until tender, then mash.
- Add sugar and dissolve over low heat, stirring occasionally.
- Bring to a rapid boil and boil for 10 minutes, or until set is reached. Pot.

PLUM JAM

You can use this recipe for greengages too.

Makes approx. 6 x 400 g (14 oz) jars

1.5 kg (3½ lb) plums
1.5 kg (3½ lb) preserving sugar

- Halve and stone plums. Crack a third of the stones and remove kernels.
- Put plums, kernels and 500 ml (17 fl. oz) water in a preserving pan, bring to a simmer and cook for 30 minutes until plums are tender. Remove kernels.
- Add sugar and dissolve over low heat, stirring occasionally.
- Bring to a rapid boil and boil for 12 minutes, or until set is reached. Cool for 15 minutes, then stir with a sterilized spoon to distribute the fruit. Pot.

RASPBERRY JAM

You can also use this recipe for similar berries, such as blackberries, mulberries and loganberries.

Makes approx. 5 x 400 g (14 oz) jars

1.3 kg (3 lb) raspberries
juice of 1 lemon
1.3 kg (3 lb) preserving sugar
  with added pectin

- Put raspberries in a preserving pan with lemon juice and bring to a simmer over very low heat, stirring occasionally.
- When raspberries are broken up, add sugar and stir over low heat until dissolved. Bring to a rapid boil and boil for 15 minutes, or until set is reached. Pot.

The world's first known book of recipes, *Of Culinary Matters*, written by the Roman gastronome Marcus Gavius Apicius in the first century AD, included recipes for fruit preserves. The making of jam and jellies probably began in Middle Eastern countries, where sugar cane grew wild.

RHUBARB AND GINGER JAM

The ginger in this recipe gives the rhubarb a real kick and a good lift.

Makes approx. 6 x 400 g (14 oz) jars

2 kg (4½ lb) rhubarb
2 kg (4½ lb) preserving sugar
5 cm (2 in.) piece fresh ginger
juice of 1 lemon

- Layer chopped rhubarb in a bowl with sugar, cover and leave overnight, by which time much of the sugar should have dissolved.
- Put rhubarb mixture into a preserving pan. Put peeled, lightly crushed ginger in a small muslin bag and add to the pan with the lemon juice. Heat gently until all sugar is dissolved.
- Bring to a rapid boil and boil for 15 minutes, or until set is reached. Remove muslin bag. Pot.

WHOLE STRAWBERRY PRESERVE

This isn't a 'jam' as such, as it is quite runny and contains whole berries – but it has a fresh, not too sweet taste and a lovely pale colour. Well worth making. It is essential that you don't use over-ripe berries.

Makes approx. 6 x 400 g (14 oz) jars

2 kg (4½ lb) strawberries
1.5 kg (3½ lb) preserving sugar
  with added pectin
juice of 1 lemon

- Hull strawberries and combine in a bowl with the sugar. Cover and leave overnight, by which time much of the sugar should have dissolved.
- Put strawberry mixture into a preserving pan and heat very gently, without stirring, until all sugar is dissolved.
- Add lemon juice, bring to the boil and boil for 8 minutes, or until set is reached. Cool for 15 minutes, then stir with a sterilized spoon to distribute the fruit. Pot.

JELLY RECIPES

APPLE JELLY

You need to use cooking apples rather than dessert apples to make a successful jelly. This is good with pork and ham. The same recipe can be used to make crab apple jelly.

Makes approx. 5 x 400 g (14 oz) jars

2.4 kg (5 lb) cooking apples
juice of 2 lemons
approx. 1.3 kg (3 lb) sugar

- Roughly chop apples (no need to peel or core) and put in a pan with enough water to cover. Bring to a simmer and cook for 20 minutes, stirring occasionally, until apples are soft and broken up.
- Strain using a muslin (jelly) bag into a large bowl – this will take several hours. Don't press the fruit through to try to speed up the process, as this would cause the juice to become cloudy.
- Put measured juice into a preserving pan with lemon juice and 450 g (1 lb) sugar for every 500 ml (17 fl. oz) juice. Stir over low heat until sugar is dissolved, then bring to a rapid boil and boil for 12 minutes, or until set is reached. Pot.

QUINCE JELLY

A pretty jelly, ideal served with meats, goose, duck or poultry.

Makes approx. 5 x 400 g (14 oz) jars

2 kg (4½ lb) quinces
approx. 1.4 kg (3¼ lb) sugar
juice of 2 lemons

- Peel and quarter quinces (no need to remove pips or cores). As you work, put quince pieces in a pan with 2 litres (3½ pints) barely simmering water so that they don't discolour.
- Top up water if quince pieces aren't completely covered. Bring to the boil, put lid on pan and simmer for 45–60 minutes, or until tender and the water has turned into a pinky-red juice.
- Cover and leave quinces in the liquid overnight. Strain using a muslin (jelly) bag into a large bowl – this will take several hours. Don't press the fruit through to try to speed up the process, as this would cause the juice to become cloudy.
- Put measured juice into a preserving pan with 350 g (12 oz) sugar for every 500 ml (17 fl. oz) juice. Add lemon juice and heat gently until sugar is dissolved, then bring to a rapid boil and boil for 10 minutes, or until set is reached. Pot.

MINT JELLY

This is an excellent alternative to standard mint sauce and keeps for over a year. You can omit the food colouring, although it does appear in most versions of this recipe.

Makes approx. 6 x 150 g (5 oz) jars

1.3 kg (3 lb) cooking apples
750 ml (1¼ pints) white wine vinegar
approx. 750 g (1 lb 10 oz) sugar
20 long stalks fresh mint
few drops green food colouring

- Chop apples (no need to peel or core) and put in a pan with 750 ml (1¼ pints) water. Bring to a simmer and cook for 20 minutes, stirring occasionally, until apples are soft and broken up. Add vinegar, bring to the boil and boil for 5 minutes.
- Strain using a muslin (jelly) bag into a large bowl – this will take 2–3 hours. Don't press the fruit through to try to speed up the process, as this would cause the juice to become cloudy.
- Put measured juice into a preserving pan with 450 g (1 lb) sugar for every 500 ml (17 fl. oz) juice.
- Tie three-quarters of the mint stalks together with string and add to the pan. Heat gently until sugar is dissolved, stirring occasionally. Bring to a rapid boil and boil for 12 minutes, or until set is reached.
- Remove bunch of mint, stir in food colouring and cool for 15 minutes. Remove leaves from remaining mint stalks, finely chop and stir into jelly. Pot.

RED CURRANT JELLY

The classic jelly for roast lamb, this is good with duck, goose and game too. It can also be melted for glazing fruit tarts.

Makes approx. 6 x 150 g (5 oz) jars

1 kg (2¼ lb) red currants on the stalk
approx. 800 g (1¾ lb) sugar

- Put red currants on their stalks into a pan with enough water to cover. Bring to the boil and boil until fruit is soft and broken up. Strain using a muslin (jelly) bag into a large bowl – this will take several hours. Don't press the fruit through to try to speed up the process, as this would cause the juice to become cloudy.
- Put measured juice into a preserving pan with 200 g (7 oz) sugar for every 250 ml (8 fl. oz) juice. Heat gently until sugar is dissolved. Bring to a rapid boil and boil for 5 minutes, or until set is reached. Pot.

BOTTLING FRUIT

Apricots, cherries, gooseberries, peaches, pears, plums and quinces are all suitable for bottling. Place whole or halved fruits in jars and pour over sugar syrup (below), leaving 2.5 cm (1 in.) between fruit and lid. Seal and sterilize jars *after* they have been filled. Note: jars should also be sterilized before filling (see page 235).

To make sugar syrup: for every 1 kg (2¼ lb) fruit dissolve 250 g (9 oz) sugar in 500 ml (17 fl. oz) water. Heat gently, stirring, until the sugar is dissolved, then bring to the boil, still stirring. Allow to cool before using.

This syrup can also be used when packing stone fruits in containers for freezing. Allow a 2 cm (¾ in.) gap between fruit and lid for expansion.

To sterilize in boiling water: after filling, put on screw-top lids but don't completely tighten them. Put jars (not touching) in a deep pan with a wooden rack in the base. Add enough warm water to come up to the bottom of the lids. Gradually heat the water until small bubbles rise from the base of the pan – a bare simmer. Simmer for 30 minutes, then remove the bottles using tongs. Tighten lids to seal.

To sterilize in the oven: after filling, put on screw-top lids but don't completely tighten them. Put jars (not touching) on a thick layer of newspaper on a baking tray. Put in the oven at 140°C/gas mark 1 for 45 minutes. Remove from the oven and tighten lids to seal.

CHUTNEY RECIPES

APPLE CHUTNEY

You can also use this recipe for pear chutney. Try this with cheese or cold pork, or in a ham sandwich.

Makes approx. 5 x 400 g (14 oz) jars

1.5 kg (3½ lb) apples
750 g (1 lb 10 oz) onions
1 litre (1¾ pints) malt vinegar
500 g (1¼ lb) sultanas
1 kg (2¼ lb) soft light brown sugar
2 tsp fresh chopped ginger
1 tsp ground cinnamon
¼ tsp ground cloves
1 tsp mustard powder
2 tsp salt

● Put peeled, cored and chopped apples and peeled, chopped onions into a pan with vinegar. Simmer for an hour, then add remaining ingredients and stir over very low heat until sugar is dissolved.
● Bring back to a simmer and cook for 30 minutes, stirring occasionally. Pot.

TOMATO CHUTNEY

A great all-round chutney, ideal for using up a glut of ripe tomatoes.

Makes approx. 5 x 400 g (14 oz) jars

2.4 kg (5 lb) tomatoes
450 g (1 lb) red onions
300 ml (½ pint) malt vinegar
1 tbsp salt
2 tsp paprika
¼ tsp cayenne pepper
350 g (12 oz) sugar

● Put peeled, chopped tomatoes and finely chopped onions in a preserving pan with half the vinegar and simmer for 20 minutes until tender.
● Add salt, paprika, cayenne and remaining vinegar. Cook gently for 45 minutes, or until mixture begins to thicken.
● Add sugar and stir over very low heat until dissolved.
● Bring back to a simmer and cook for 45 minutes, or until mixture becomes thick. Pot.

Apricots, beetroots, courgettes, figs, marrows, peaches, pears, squashes and pumpkins are also good ingredients for chutney.

GREEN TOMATO CHUTNEY

If you have any tomatoes that won't ripen, this is a great way of using them up. It is quick, easy and has an excellent taste.

Makes approx. 5 x 400 g (14 oz) jars

1.5 kg (3½ lb) green tomatoes
2 cooking apples
450 g (1 lb) onions
2 cloves garlic
2 tbsp pickling spices
500 ml (17 fl. oz) white malt vinegar
1 tbsp salt
400 g (14 oz) sugar

● Chop tomatoes, peel and chop apples, onions and garlic. Put pickling spices in a small muslin bag.
● Put all ingredients except sugar into a preserving pan. Simmer gently for an hour until everything is tender and thoroughly combined.
● Add sugar and stir over very low heat until dissolved.
● Bring back to a simmer and cook for 45 minutes, or until mixture is thick. Remove muslin bag. Pot.

PLUM CHUTNEY

A delicious, rich chutney, good served with cold meats or cheese.

Makes approx. 5 x 400 g (14 oz) jars

1.5 kg (3½ lb) plums
750 g (1 lb 10 oz) onions
4 cloves garlic
150 g (5 oz) raisins
1 litre (1¾ pints) red wine vinegar
750 g (1 lb 10 oz) soft dark brown sugar
1 orange
2 sticks cinnamon
1 tsp fresh chopped rosemary
1 tsp salt

● Halve and stone plums and put into a preserving pan with finely chopped onions and garlic, raisins and vinegar. Bring to a simmer and cook for 30 minutes.
● Add sugar and stir over low heat to dissolve. Add orange juice and grated zest, cinnamon, rosemary and salt. Stir well. Simmer very gently for an hour or more, until the chutney is thick and jam-like.
● Remove cinnamon sticks. Pot.

SWEET PEPPER CHUTNEY

Pretty red chutney with a little kick to it. Omit the chillies if you prefer a milder taste.

Makes 6 x 150 g (5 oz) jars

6 sweet red peppers	2 tsp black pepper
400 g (14 oz) red onions	1 tsp mustard powder
3 fresh red chillies	300 ml (½ pint) red
400 g (14 oz) tomatoes	wine vinegar
½ tbsp sweet paprika	200 g (7 oz) sugar
½ tbsp salt	

- Put chopped peppers, finely chopped onions and chillies and peeled, chopped tomatoes in a preserving pan with all remaining ingredients except sugar. Simmer for 45 minutes, or until soft.
- Add sugar, stir over gentle heat to dissolve and cook for a further 30 minutes, or until most of the moisture has evaporated. Pot.

MARROW CHUTNEY

You can also use this recipe for courgette chutney.

Makes approx. 6 x 400 g (14 oz) jars

1.5 kg (3½ lb) marrow	2 tsp ground ginger
500 g (1¼ lb) onions	1 tsp dried chilli powder
500 g (1¼ lb) tomatoes	1 tsp mustard powder
100 g (3½ oz) sultanas	1 tbsp salt
600 ml (1 pint) white	2 tsp black pepper
vinegar	600 g (1 lb 6 oz) soft
2 tsp ground allspice	light brown sugar

- Put peeled, de-seeded and diced marrow into a preserving pan with peeled, chopped onions and tomatoes, sultanas and vinegar. Bring to a simmer and cook for 30 minutes, or until everything is soft.
- Add spices and seasonings and continue simmering for 15 minutes, then add sugar, turn heat to low and stir until dissolved. Increase heat a little and simmer for 20 minutes, or until mixture is thick and most of the liquid has evaporated. Pot.

RHUBARB CHUTNEY

Let this mature for a few months in the pots. It will then be ready for you to enjoy with ham, cheese, chicken or pork.

Makes approx. 6 x 400 g (14 oz) jars

1.5 kg (3½ lb) rhubarb
500 g (1¼ lb) onions
2 cooking apples
5 cloves garlic
1 tbsp fresh chopped ginger
1.5 litres (2½ pints) white vinegar
900 g (2 lb) soft light brown sugar
500 g (1¼ lb) sultanas
1 tbsp salt
1 tsp turmeric
½ tsp ground cinnamon

- Put chopped rhubarb and peeled, chopped onions, apples, garlic and ginger in a preserving pan with vinegar. Bring to a simmer and cook for 30 minutes.
- Add remaining ingredients and stir over very low heat until sugar is dissolved. Increase heat a little and simmer for an hour, or until thick, stirring occasionally. Pot.

SWEET CORN RELISH

A tasty relish which should keep for up to 3 months.

Makes approx. 6 x 150 g (5 oz) jars

1 kg (2¼ lb) sweet corn kernels
400 g (14 oz) onions
1 green pepper
1 red pepper
3 mild red chillies
1 tsp each salt and black pepper
500 ml (17 fl. oz) cider vinegar
225 g (8 oz) sugar
1 tsp cornflour
2 tsp mustard powder
1 tsp turmeric

- Boil sweetcorn for 3 minutes, then drain.
- Put finely chopped onions, pepper and chillies in a preserving pan with seasoning and pour all but 2 tbsp of the vinegar over.
- Simmer for 20 minutes, then add sweet corn. Add sugar and stir until dissolved.
- Combine cornflour, mustard and turmeric with remaining vinegar and stir into the pan. Simmer for a further 5 minutes. Pot.

PICKLE RECIPES

PICCALILLI

A spicy and sour pickle that goes very well with ham, cold roast meats and cheese.

Makes approx. 4 x 400 g (14 oz) jars

  1 cauliflower head
  1 cucumber
  500 g (1¼ lb) small onions
  250 g (9 oz) runner beans
  100 g (3½ oz) salt
  1 litre (1¾ pints) pickling vinegar
  25 g (1 oz) pickling spice
  8 whole hot dried chillies
  2 tbsp turmeric
  2 tsp ground ginger
  50 g (2 oz) sugar
  25 g (1 oz) plain flour
  1 tbsp mustard powder

- Divide cauliflower into small florets, peel and chop cucumber and onions, slice beans. Put vegetables in a bowl and add salt and 1 litre (1¾ pints) water. Leave overnight, then rinse and drain well.
- Put pickling spices and chillies in a small muslin bag. Put in a pan with all but 2 tbsp of the vinegar, the turmeric, ginger and sugar. Bring to the boil.
- Combine flour and mustard with remaining vinegar to make a paste. Add to the pan and stir well. Add all the vegetables and bring back to the boil. Simmer for 5 minutes. Cool, then remove muslin bag. Pot.

PICKLED BEETROOT

Good in a cheese sandwich or as part of a ploughman's lunch. To prevent staining your fingers when rubbing off skins, wear disposable gloves.

Makes approx. 5 x 400 g (14 oz) jars

  1 kg (2¼ lb) beetroot
  750 ml (1¼ pints) red wine vinegar
  100 g (3½ oz) granulated sugar
  1 tbsp coriander seeds
  1 tbsp peppercorns
  8 cloves
  1 tsp salt

- Put whole unpeeled beetroots in a pan with enough water to cover and boil for 45 minutes, or until tender. Drain, cool and rub off skins with fingers. Slice or quarter beetroots – very small beetroots can be left whole. Pack into jars.
- Heat vinegar, sugar, spices and salt until sugar is dissolved. Pour over the beetroots and seal. Leave for at least 2 weeks before eating.

PICKLED CABBAGE

A good side dish for cold roast pork, lamb, duck or goose. If you store this for more than a few months, the red cabbage will lose its colour.

Makes approx. 4 x 400 g (14 oz) jars

  1 red cabbage (approx. 1 kg/2¼ lb)
  100 g (3½ oz) salt
  1 litre (1¾ pints) malt vinegar
  1 tbsp whole allspice
  1 tbsp peppercorns
  4 whole cloves
  3 bay leaves
  2 dried chillies
  ½ tsp ground cinnamon

- Put thinly sliced cabbage in a bowl. Dissolve salt in 1 litre (1¾ pints) water and pour over the cabbage to cover completely. Leave overnight, then drain, rinse well and drain thoroughly again.
- Bring vinegar to the boil with remaining ingredients. Remove from the heat and leave to cool for 2 hours. Strain.
- Pack cabbage into jars, cover with vinegar and seal. Leave for at least 2 weeks before eating.

PICKLED ONIONS

You can use pickling (Silverskin) onions or shallots for this recipe. If you want to save time, use 2 tbsp ready-blended pickling spices, or ready-made pickling vinegar from the supermarket.

Makes approx. 5 x 400 g (14 oz) jars

  2 kg (4½ lb) small onions
  100 g (3½ oz) salt
  1 litre (1¾ pints) white malt vinegar
  1 tbsp whole allspice
  ½ tbsp whole cloves
  ½ tbsp black peppercorns
  ½ cinnamon stick
  1 hot dried chilli

- Put peeled onions in a bowl. Dissolve the salt in 1 litre (1¾ pints) water and pour over the onions to cover completely. Stir, cover and leave for 24 hours. Drain, rinse well and drain again, then pack into jars.
- Put vinegar and spices into a pan, bring to a simmer and cook, covered, for 10 minutes.
- Strain, pour over onions to cover completely and seal. Leave for at least 2 weeks before eating.

CHAPTER 9

COOK'S MISCELLANY

CONVERSION CHART

Length

0.5 cm	=	¼ in.
1 cm	=	½ in.
2 cm	=	¾ in.
2.5 cm	=	1 in.
10 cm	=	4 in.
23 cm	=	9 in.
25 cm	=	10 in.
30 cm	=	12 in.

Weight

10 g	=	¼ oz
15 g	=	½ oz
20 g	=	¾ oz
25 g	=	1 oz
40 g	=	1½ oz
50 g	=	2 oz
65 g	=	2½ oz
75 g	=	3 oz
100 g	=	3½ oz
125 g	=	4 oz
130 g	=	4½ oz
150 g	=	5 oz
165 g	=	5½ oz
175 g	=	6 oz
200 g	=	7 oz
225 g	=	8 oz
250 g	=	9 oz
275 g	=	10 oz
300 g	=	11 oz
350 g	=	12 oz
375 g	=	13 oz
400 g	=	14 oz
425 g	=	15 oz
450 g	=	1 lb
500 g	=	1¼ lb
675 g	=	1½ lb
750 g	=	1 lb 10 oz
800 g	=	1¾ lb
900 g	=	2 lb
1 kg	=	2¼ lb
1.2 kg	=	2½ lb
1.3 kg	=	3 lb
1.8 kg	=	4 lb

Volume

50 ml	=	2 fl. oz
75 ml	=	2½ fl. oz
100 ml	=	3½ fl. oz
125 ml	=	4 fl. oz
150 ml	=	¼ pint
175 ml	=	6 fl. oz
200 ml	=	7 fl. oz
250 ml	=	8 fl. oz
300 ml	=	½ pint
350 ml	=	12 fl. oz
400 ml	=	14 fl. oz
450 ml	=	¾ pint
475 ml	=	16 fl. oz
500 ml	=	17 fl. oz
550 ml	=	18 fl. oz
600 ml	=	1 pint
750 ml	=	1¼ pints
900 ml	=	1½ pints
1 litre	=	1¾ pints
1.2 litres	=	2 pints
1.5 litres	=	2½ pints
1.75 litres	=	3 pints
2 litres	=	3½ pints
2.3 litres	=	4 pints
3 litres	=	5 pints
3.4 litres	=	6 pints
4.5 litres	=	8 pints
6.8 litres	=	12 pints
8 litres	=	14 pints
9.1 litres	=	16 pints

Spoon measures

1 tsp liquid	=	5 ml
1 tbsp liquid	=	15 ml

Oven temperatures

110°C	=	225°F	=	gas mark ¼
120°C	=	250°F	=	gas mark ½
140°C	=	275°F	=	gas mark 1
150°C	=	300°F	=	gas mark 2
170°C	=	325°F	=	gas mark 3½
180°C	=	350°F	=	gas mark 4
190°C	=	375°F	=	gas mark 5
200°C	=	400°F	=	gas mark 6
220°C	=	425°F	=	gas mark 7
230°C	=	450°F	=	gas mark 8
240°C	=	475°F	=	gas mark 9

Cool oven	120–140°C
Warm oven	150–170°C
Hot oven	180–200°C
Very hot oven	210°C and above

US CONVERSIONS

Solid measures

1 cup flour	=	115 g
1 cup rice	=	225 g
1 cup butter	=	225 g
1 cup dried fruit	=	225 g
1 cup brown sugar	=	180 g
1 cup granulated sugar	=	225 g
1 stick butter	=	115 g

Liquid measures

1 cup	=	250 ml
1 pint	=	475 ml
1 quart	=	950 ml

Spoons

US tablespoons differ in size from British spoons. Note that the recipes in this book use British tablespoons.

EQUIPMENT

While even the keenest kitchen-garden cook does not really need a large array of fancy utensils, pots and pans, a few good-quality basic items will make cooking much easier and the results more consistently good.

CHOPPING, PEELING AND PREPARING

Different cutting and chopping jobs require different tools. Stainless-steel knives are the most useful and long-lasting and are easy to sharpen.

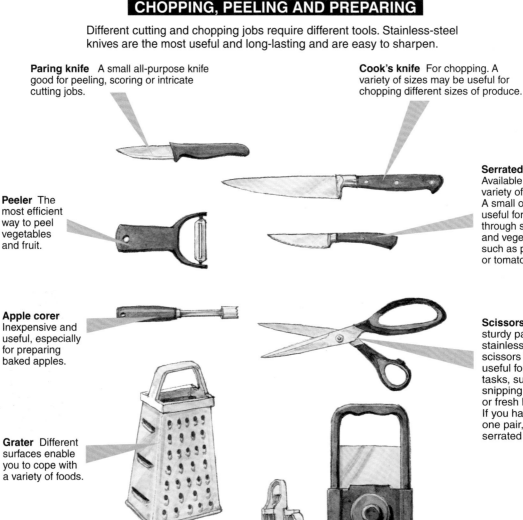

Paring knife A small all-purpose knife good for peeling, scoring or intricate cutting jobs.

Cook's knife For chopping. A variety of sizes may be useful for chopping different sizes of produce.

Serrated knife Available in a variety of sizes. A small one is useful for slicing through soft fruit and vegetables, such as peaches or tomatoes.

Peeler The most efficient way to peel vegetables and fruit.

Apple corer Inexpensive and useful, especially for preparing baked apples.

Scissors A sturdy pair of stainless-steel scissors will be useful for many tasks, such as snipping bacon or fresh herbs. If you have just one pair, non-serrated is best.

Grater Different surfaces enable you to cope with a variety of foods.

Zester The most efficient way to grate zest from citrus fruit, leaving the bitter white pith behind.

Bean slicer Inexpensive and useful for de-stringing and slicing a glut of beans.

Mandolin Good for uniform slices, chips or julienne strips of vegetable or fruit in large quantities. A top-quality safety shield is essential as cut fingers are a common hazard.

SPOONS AND SPATULAS

Keep a range of spoons in a jar on the work surface – you'll use them all the time.

Teaspoons An efficient way to measure tiny quantities of liquid and ideal for measuring herbs, spices and seasoning. A set of cook's spoons, which come in standard measures, is useful.

Wooden spoons Durable, ideal for stirring in non-stick pans, and slow to transfer heat from pan to hand.

Tablespoons An efficient way to measure small quantities of liquid and ideal for measuring sugar, flour and spices. A set of cook's spoons, which come in standard measures, is useful.

Straining spoons For removing vegetables or fruit from a pan while leaving liquid or fat behind.

Spatulas Rubber types are good for removing mixture from bowls and smoothing when baking; metal types are good for removing fried food. Avoid those that are not heatproof.

Ladle For serving soup – 2 full ladles is an average portion.

Masher Choose one that is heavy and well balanced, with round edges to work easily in a saucepan.

Preserving spoons For skimming the scum from jams and stocks. The long handle prevents you burning yourself when stirring large amounts of hot food.

COOKING VESSELS

Saucepans Choose good-quality steel pans with non-metal handles. A heavy base helps prevent burning while a copper layer in the base helps fast boiling. Ensure the pans will fit your hob.

Frying pan A non-stick interior is useful but will need replacing regularly. Choose a lightweight pan with a heatproof handle.

Deep-fat fryer basket Choose one to fit inside your largest pan.

Preserving pan For cooking large quantities of jams and preserves. Choose one that is made of aluminium and is light, large and wide with a bucket handle and at least one lip for pouring.

Casserole Choose one that is suitable for use on the hob as well as in the oven. Look for a tight-fitting lid with a large stout handle.

Roasting tin For roasting a joint of meat and/or a selection of vegetables. High sides prevent spillage. A detachable wire rack is useful for roasting meat.

Soufflé dish Deeper than a gratin dish and with straight sides to help a soufflé to rise. Also useful for recipes such as fruit crumbles and sponge puddings.

Shallow ovenproof dish A china or glass dish – sometimes called a gratin dish – useful for baking recipes such as cauliflower cheese and lasagne.

Steamer Sits over a saucepan, allowing one vegetable to boil while another steams using only one pan and hob.

Roasting tray A tray with 1–2 cm (½–¾ in.) tall sides suitable for a wide range of baking or roasting when no liquid is involved. Ideal when food should be well browned.

STORING AND PROTECTING

Lidded plastic boxes/tubs
For storing dry foods, dried fruit and vegetables, frozen foods and liquids.

Freezer and food bags Strong plastic bags in a range of sizes and strengths. Ziplock tops prevent contents spilling.

Opaque jars
For storing herbs and spices away from light.

Jars, bottles, lids and labels A range of sizes is useful for making and storing preserves, oils and dressings.

MISCELLANEOUS

Colander For draining boiled vegetables. A metal one can substitute as a steamer.

Rolling pin Almost essential for rolling out pastry. A simple cylinder without handles is the best shape, as you can use its full width to roll larger amounts.

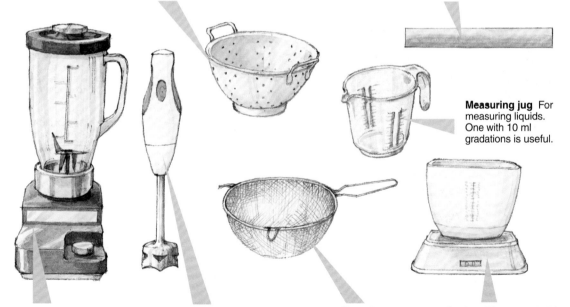

Measuring jug For measuring liquids. One with 10 ml gradations is useful.

Blender A goblet-type **electric blender** is useful for soups, sauces, purées, smoothies, crumbs and much more. Choose one with a large goblet and several different speeds. Some also have a small herb chopper/crumb goblet attachment.

A **hand blender** – a motorized blade which can be put into a soup/sauce etc., rather than transferring the sauce to a goblet, is useful.
(A multi-purpose **food processor**, which will handle such jobs as cake- and dough-mixing, pastry-making, slicing and chopping, may be a good investment.)

Sieve For straining stocks, sauces and jellies; also useful for draining small quantities of vegetables. Choose one with a good lip so that it will rest on top of a saucepan.

Scales Choose an 'add and weigh' scale so you can set the dial/display back to zero each time you add a food. Those with a range from 5 g ($1/8$ oz) to 5 kg (11 lb) and which also weigh liquids are ideal.

GLOSSARY

Al dente Food that is cooked but still slightly firm to bite into – typically used when referring to pasta that is correctly cooked.

Bake blind To part-bake an unfilled pastry case before it is filled and returned to the oven to finish cooking. The tin is lined with uncooked pastry, then a layer of baking parchment or similar is put inside and the parchment is filled with ceramic baking beans, dried pulses or similar and baked at, usually, 190°C/gas mark 5 for 10 minutes. The beans and parchment are then removed from the case, which is returned to the oven for a further 3 minutes. It should be a pale golden colour and can then be filled and returned to the oven to finish cooking as described by your recipe.

Baste To spoon a liquid, such as oil, sauce or stock, over an item during cooking – e.g. to spoon fat from the pan over roasting vegetables.

Béchamel See white sauce, page 251. A basic white sauce recipe to which other flavourings such as cheese, parsley or onions are added.

Bhaji A spicy Indian version of a vegetable fritter, ball-shaped and deep-fried in oil.

Blanch To plunge prepared vegetables into a pan of boiling water for a short period (usually 1–3 minutes, depending on size and type). This method is used to prepare vegetables before freezing (blanching breaks down enzymes and so prolongs storage life) or to part-cook before another cooking method is used (e.g. blanching green beans before stir-frying).

Coulis A smooth, cold fruit sauce made by puréeing raw soft fruits with sugar (and sometimes water and/or other ingredients) in a blender, or by cooking harder fruits and then cooling and blending. Used to accompany cake, ice cream etc.

Cream To beat together butter (or other fat) and sugar for baking. When the mixture is pale, light and creamy it is ready for other ingredients to be added.

Crudités

Thin but firm batons – 5 cm (2 in.) or so in length – of raw vegetables such as carrot, celery, cucumber, spring onion or sweet pepper, usually used as a vehicle for a savoury dip and eaten with the fingers.

Drizzle To add a small amount of liquid, such as dressing or oil, to an item during or after cooking, pouring it slowly and evenly over the complete dish.

Dropping consistency

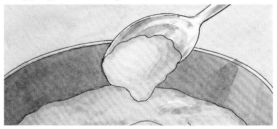

The ideal thickness of a raw cake or pudding batter mixture when it is ready to be put into the baking tin. If a spoonful of mixture is lifted from the bowl, the mixture should easily drop off the spoon within a few seconds, rather than staying in the spoon (too solid) or pouring off (too liquid).

Dry-fry To cook in a frying pan which is either dry or lightly brushed with oil. The method is used to cut down on fat when cooking a high-fat food (e.g. bacon), to achieve a chargrilled effect (e.g. steak) or to toast (e.g. pine nuts).

Falafel A Middle Eastern snack food – mashed chick peas and seasoning formed into small balls and deep-fried.

Finely chopped Chopped as small as is practical to ensure thorough cooking, avoid lumps (e.g. in a sauce) and/or to release maximum flavour.

Flash 'To flash under the grill' means to put food in a heatproof container under a pre-heated, very hot grill for a short period – from ½–2 minutes is typical – to brown the item, e.g. the top of a flat omelette, or a cheese sauce topping.

Fold A gentle method of mixing ingredients together – e.g. for a cake, dessert or ice cream. An ingredient is folded in to retain its own characteristics (e.g. a **coulis** folded into an ice cream for ripple effect) or to avoid beating all the air out of the mixture.

Gremolata An Italian chopped herb mixture of parsley, garlic and lemon juice or grated lemon **zest**, usually sprinkled on a savoury dish before serving.

Hull The central core of a fruit (usually a strawberry). 'To hull' the fruit is to remove this core. When a strawberry is ripe, it should be possible to remove the hull simply by pulling the stalk.

Italian seasoning A mixture of dried Italian herbs such as oregano, thyme, basil, parsley, sage and bay. Can be bought ready-made.

Jelly bag A fine-meshed bag made from muslin or nylon, often conical-shaped, used to strain the liquid from the solids when making jam, jelly and wine.

Julienne Thin strips of vegetables – e.g. carrot or celery – cut like matchsticks, which need only a very short cooking time or can be used raw as garnish.

Liquidize To use an electric processor or hand blender to make a smooth vegetable purée, soup or fruit/vegetable drink, for example, from a recipe which otherwise would contain lumps.

Mexican seasoning A spicy blend of dried hot chillies, peppers, salt and black pepper. Can be bought ready-made.

Parboil To part-cook vegetables in boiling water before their cooking is completed by another method. For example, potatoes are often parboiled for 5–7 minutes before being roasted. The parboiled vegetables should be well drained before further cooking. To roast parboiled vegetables, put them back in the pan in which they were parboiled (without water) and shake over the hot hob for a minute to dry them out thoroughly. This increases the crisp outer coating.

Passata Peeled and sieved tomatoes used as a sauce, especially in Italian recipes – see page 153.

Pesto From the Italian word *pestare*, meaning to pound or crush, pesto is a rough, thick sauce traditionally made with crushed fresh basil leaves pounded with garlic, cheese, nuts and oil, but other types of pesto can also be made. See page 161.

Provençale A term used to describe a Provence-style preparation containing garlic, tomatoes and olive oil alongside other ingredients.

Refresh To rinse cooked vegetables under cold running water (in a sieve or colander) to cool them down quickly after being cooked. This helps to stop the cooking process, retain colour and reduce heat. Vegetables should be thoroughly drained after refreshing and, if necessary, dried with a clean tea-towel or kitchen paper.

Roux A combination of fat and flour used to thicken savoury and sweet sauces, casseroles, soups etc. For making a sauce, the fat is usually melted in a pan, flour is stirred in over heat to make a paste, then the liquid gradually added. For thickening stews etc., flour and solid fat may be beaten together in a bowl, then added in marble-sized nuggets towards the end of cooking time and stirred in well until the liquid thickens.

Salsa The Spanish word for 'sauce'. The term is now commonly used to describe a traditional Mexican sauce or dip, often made from raw ingredients and usually including chopped tomatoes and chillies. See pages 56, 58 and 151.

Smoke point The temperature at which an oil or fat when heated begins to produce smoke. A fat with a high smoke point is preferable for high-temperature frying as the food will taste fresher and there is less risk of burning and kitchen smells.

Soft peak stage
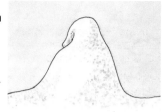
Egg whites or cream beaten or whisked until firm enough to stand up in soft peaks with slightly floppy tops. Used for setting mousses, soufflés, omelettes.

Sterilized jar A jar cleansed of any bacteria that could be growing on the glass. Using unsterilized jars to preserve garden produce can lead to infected food which can spoil quickly. See page 235 for how to sterilize.

Stiff peak stage
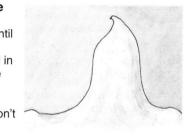
Egg whites or cream beaten until glossy and firm enough to stand in stiff peaks in the bowl and, if the bowl is turned upside down, won't fall out. Used to make meringue.

Stir-fry To cook thinly sliced vegetables or other foods in a small amount of oil in a frying pan or wok over very high heat whilst constantly stirring. The vegetables should be of even size and should be golden and cooked through – but retain some bite – in about 2–4 minutes, depending on vegetables and thickness of pieces.

Sweat To cook chopped vegetables, such as onion, leeks or celery, in a pan in a little oil or butter over a very low heat, stirring now and then, so that they soften but do not take on any colour This can take 10–20 minutes.

Tabbouleh A Lebanese salad of bulghar wheat with chopped parsley, tomato, mint and spring onions.

Tagine A lidded cooking pot widely used in Morocco and Tunisia to slow-cook a variety of meat or vegetable casseroles. The finished dish then takes the name of the cooking vessel.

Tempura batter A light, crisp Japanese batter traditionally made from just flour, salt and ice-cold water, used to coat vegetables, fish etc. before deep-frying.

Zest The outermost layer of the peel of citrus fruit, without the bitter white pith. Used as a flavouring.

TOOLBOX RECIPES

The following basic recipes make frequent appearances throughout this book. While most are available ready-made from supermarkets, you may prefer to make them up at home.

CREAM CHEESE ICING

An easy icing (frosting) for carrot cake or other sponges, or for muffins or fairy cakes. Unlike many icings, this type is not available ready-made – and it is more delicious than most shop-bought toppings.

Makes 400 g (14 oz) – enough to ice an average cake

250 g (9 oz) cream cheese
25 g (1 oz) butter at room temperature
150 g (5 oz) icing sugar
1 tsp vanilla extract
juice of 1 lemon

- Beat together cream cheese and butter. Sift in icing sugar, add vanilla and lemon juice, and combine thoroughly.
- Spread over cooled cake.

CRUMBLE TOPPING – PLAIN

This topping can be used instead of pastry or mashed/sliced potato for meat, poultry, fish and vegetable pies and bakes.

Serves 4

175 g (6 oz) wholewheat flour
½ tsp salt and black pepper
75 g (3 oz) butter
50 g (2 oz) grated Parmesan or Cheddar

- Combine flour and seasoning, then rub in butter using fingertips until the mixture resembles breadcrumbs. Stir in cheese.

Variations:
- Add ½ tsp ground paprika.
- Add 1 tbsp fresh chopped parsley.
- Add 1 tsp dried herbs.

CRUMBLE TOPPING – SWEET

For a basic dessert crumble topping, see Apple Crumble, page 171.

Variations:
- Add 50 g (2 oz) chopped mixed nuts.
- Add 25 g (1 oz) rolled oats.
- Add 50 g (2 oz) fruit and nut muesli.
- Add 25 g (1 oz) desiccated coconut.
- Add 50 g (2 oz) crushed amaretti or gingernut biscuits.
- Use soft dark brown sugar instead of white.

CUSTARD

Making custard is not difficult – it just needs a very low heat when thickening to avoid 'cooking' the eggs. Perfect for trifles or with fruit pies, crumbles and sponges. Full-cream is the best milk to use. For an even richer custard, use half cream, half milk.

Serves 4/makes 500 ml (17 fl. oz)

500 ml (17 fl. oz) milk
4 egg yolks
65 g (2½ oz) caster sugar
1 tsp vanilla extract
20 g (¾ oz) cornflour

- Heat milk in a pan until on the point of coming to the boil. Remove pan from heat immediately.
- Beat egg yolks, sugar, vanilla and cornflour in a heatproof bowl. Pour hot milk slowly over the egg mixture, beating well.
- Return mixture to the saucepan and stir over very low heat for several minutes until the mixture thickens. Leave to cool a little before serving.

FRENCH DRESSING

You can vary this basic dressing by adding crushed garlic or chopped herbs such as parsley, or by using lemon juice or red wine vinegar instead of white. If you add garlic or herbs, it won't keep so long.

Makes 8 tbsp

6 tbsp olive oil
2 tbsp white wine vinegar
1 tsp caster sugar
½ tsp Dijon mustard
salt, black pepper

- Combine all ingredients in a screw-top jar and shake thoroughly. The dressing will keep in the fridge for several weeks.

HONEY AND MUSTARD DRESSING

Excellent with any salad containing apple, beetroot or cheese, or to dress a crisp green salad to accompany ham, pork or chicken.

Makes 8 tbsp

6 tbsp light olive oil
1½ tbsp cider vinegar
1 tsp wholegrain Dijon mustard
2 tsp runny honey
salt, black pepper

- Combine all ingredients in a screw-top jar and shake thoroughly. The dressing will keep in the fridge for several weeks.

PIZZA BASE

It is not difficult to make your own pizza dough – and the result tastes a lot better than many of the ready-made bases that you can buy.

Makes one 30 cm (12 in.) base

10 g (¼ oz) dried yeast   1 tsp salt
2 tsp caster sugar   2 tbsp olive oil
375 g (13 oz) plain flour

- Mix yeast and sugar with 3 tbsp lukewarm water and leave in a warm place for 10 minutes.
- Sift flour into a mixing bowl and add salt. Make a well in the centre and pour in the yeast mixture, 200 ml (7 fl. oz) lukewarm water and the oil.
- Mix into a stiff dough, then knead on a floured surface until smooth and elastic.
- Put in a warm bowl, cover with a clean cloth and leave in a warm place for 45 minutes, or until doubled in size.
- Knead for a further 4 minutes, then roll out into a circle. Add toppings of choice and put on a pizza baking tray. Bake at 190°C/gas mark 5 for 20–25 minutes until the topping is cooked and the edges are golden.

SHORTCRUST PASTRY – PLAIN

Pastry is easy to make. All-butter shortcrust is delicious and crumbly, but you can also make it using half butter, half lard or margarine. You can freeze any pastry leftover from your recipe.

Makes approx. 500 g (1¼ lb)

300 g (11 oz) plain flour   150 g (5 oz) butter
½ tsp salt

- Combine flour and salt in a mixing bowl. Cut butter into small knobs, add to bowl and, using your fingertips, rub in butter until the mixture resembles breadcrumbs.
- Stir in just enough water – about 50 ml (2 fl. oz) – to make a firm dough that leaves the sides of the bowl clean. Put it in a plastic bag and leave it in the fridge for 30 minutes before using.

SHORTCRUST PASTRY – SWEET

This pastry can be used instead of plain shortcrust for dessert recipes. The amount of sugar can be altered to suit your own taste – you may prefer less.

Makes approx. 500 g (1¼ lb)

225 g (8 oz) plain flour
½ tsp salt
100 g (3½ oz) butter
100 g (3½ oz) caster sugar
2 egg yolks

- Combine flour and salt in a mixing bowl. Cut butter into small knobs, add to bowl and, using your fingertips, rub in butter until the mixture resembles breadcrumbs.
- Stir in sugar. Mix with the beaten egg yolks and a little water to make a firm dough that leaves the sides of the bowl clean. Put it in a plastic bag and leave it in the fridge for 30 minutes before using.

VEGETABLE STOCK

An easy stock which will keep in the fridge for 1–2 days or can be frozen.

Makes approx. 1 litre (1¾ pints)

2 onions   1 bouquet garni
2 carrots   1 tbsp black
2 leeks   peppercorns
3 stalks celery   1 tsp salt

- Peel and chop all vegetables and put into a large pan with the remaining ingredients. Add enough water to cover.
- Bring to a simmer and cook for 1½ hours. Strain.

WHITE SAUCE

A basic white sauce recipe to which you can add other flavourings such as cheese, parsley or onions. Use white pepper if you don't want black flecks in the sauce. For a sweet white sauce, omit the seasoning and stir in 1 tbsp caster sugar (or to taste) once the sauce is thick and smooth.

Makes 400 ml (14 fl. oz)

25 g (1 oz) butter   350 ml (12 fl. oz) milk
1 tbsp flour   salt, pepper

- Melt butter in a pan over low heat. Add flour and stir with a wooden spoon to combine. Turn heat up a little and continue stirring for 2 minutes to remove the floury taste.
- Turn heat to medium. Add 50 ml (2 fl. oz) of the warmed milk and stir thoroughly to make a smooth paste. Gradually add remaining milk, stirring until you have a smooth white sauce. Season.

CHAPTER 10

RECIPE AND PRODUCE INDEX

ACKNOWLEDGEMENTS

Grateful acknowledgement is made for the help received from Tony Allen, Gill Jackson, Angelina Gibbs, Jane Turnbull, Brenda and Robert Updegraff, and from Phil Lord, Maddy Price and Susanna Wadeson (Transworld). The authors are also grateful for the artworks produced by Christine Wilson and the photographs received from Graham Precey and Charles Montgomery (Food and Drink Photos and Tips Images) and home economist, Wendy Sweetser.

All photographs © Food and Drink Photos and Tips Images.